Muwatalli's Prayer

to the Assembly of Gods Through the Storm-God of Lightning

(*CTH* 381)

by

Itamar Singer

American Schools of Oriental Research

Muwatalli's Prayer to the Assembly of Gods Through the Storm-God of Lightning (*CTH* 381)

Muwatalli's Prayer to the Assembly of Gods Through the Storm-God of Lightning (*CTH* 381)

by
Itamar Singer

Muwatalli's Prayer to the Assembly of Gods Through the Storm-God of Lightning (*CTH* 381)

by

Itamar Singer

SCHOLARS PRESS • ATLANTA, GEORGIA

Muwatalli's Prayer to the Assembly of Gods Through the Storm-God of Lightning (*CTH* 381)

by

Itamar Singer

The royal seal of Muwatalli II on the cover is from T. Beran, *Die hethitische Glyptik von Boğazköy.* Boğazköy-Ḫattuša V. Berlin: Gebr. Mann Verlag, 1967, Abb. 250a. Used with permission.

Library of Congress Cataloging in Publication Data
Singer, Itamar.
Muwatalli's prayer to the assembly of gods through the storm-god of lightning (CTH 381) / by Itamar Singer.
p. cm.
Includes bibliographical references.
ISBN 0-7885-0281-6 (alk. paper)
1. Prayers. 2. Muwatalli II, King of the Hittites. 3. Hittites—Religion. 4. Gods, Hittite. I. Muwatalli II, King of the Hittites. Prayer to be spoken in an emergency. II. Title.
BL2370.H5S56 1996
299'.199—dc20 96-9169
CIP

Printed in the United States of America
on acid-free paper

To my mother Trude Singer (Herling)
and to the memory of my father Zoltán Singer

Table of Contents

Acknowledgements			ix
Introduction			1
Part One	THE TEXT		
	Ch. I	Transliteration and Translation	7
	Ch. II	Commentary	47
	Ch. III	Glossaries	73
Part Two	THE SCRIBES		
	Ch. IV	Writing Features	121
	Ch. V	Redactional History	135
Part Three	THE PRAYER		
	Ch. VI	Structure	145
	Ch. VII	Purpose of the Prayer	147
	Ch. VIII	Prayers to the Assembly of Gods	149
	Ch. IX	The Ritual Offerings	155
Part Four	THE AUTHOR		
	Ch. X	*CTH* 382: Muwatalli's Prayer to the Storm-god	161
	Ch. XI	A List of Local Gods: KBo 9.98 +	165
Part Five	GEOGRAPHY and THEOLOGY		
	Ch. XII	The Long List of Gods	171
	Ch. XIII	Sun Deities	179
	Ch. XIV	Šeri and Ḫurri, the Divine Bulls	183
	Ch. XV	The Storm-god of Lightning (*piḫaššašši*)	185
Epilogue	From Ḫattuša to Tarḫuntašša		191
Plates			195

Table of Contents

Acknowledgements

The great Muwatalli Prayer was one of the first Hittite texts to arouse my interest during my postgraduate studies at Tel Aviv University. Its long list of cult centers was one of the focal points of my M.A. thesis on "Geographical Aspects of the Proto-Hattian Problem" submitted to Prof. Aharon Kempinski in 1973. (The main results of this thesis were published in my article "Hittites and Hattians in Anatolia at the Beginning of the Second Millennium B.C.", *Journal of Indo-European Studies* 9, 1981, pp. 119-134.)

In 1973 I was invited to Marburg to continue my Hittite studies with Prof. Heinrich Otten. In weekly tutorials we read parts of the prayer, and I was able to improve substantially my rudimentary understanding of the text and my methods of philological investigation. My interest in Hittite historical-geography gradually led me to other topics, especially to the cult administration system of AGRIG towns. Since these overseers figure prominently in the KI.LAM festival, I eventually chose this text as the topic of my doctoral dissertation. *CTH* 381 remained on the shelf for many years, though I occasionally returned to it in articles and teaching.

In the spring of 1994 I read the text with some of my postgraduate students in the Department of Archaeology and Ancient Near Eastern Cultures of Tel Aviv University (Arie Cohen, Shani Bar, Henrietta Bruner and Rosa Contini) and decided to venture a full philological treatment in my ensuing sabbatical year in the United States. I first collated the two main tablets and obtained excellent photographs, for which I am most grateful to the staff of the Vorderasiatisches Museum in Berlin. Prof. H. Otten kindly provided me with his copies of two unpublished fragments (1785/u; 1111/z).

My stay at the Oriental Institute in Chicago in the autumn of 1994 as a guest of the Chicago Hittite Dictionary project was indispensable for the successful completion of the manuscript. The wealth of information stored in the files of the *CHD* and, even more importantly, the dialogue with leading experts in Hittitology provided optimal working conditions and inspiration. Prof. Harry A. Hoffner, Jr. read through the transliteration, the translation, and the commentary, providing most valuable comments and advice. His unsurpassable lexicographic experience and philological insight helped solve several difficult textual cruxes. Prof. Hans G. Güterbock, whose library I was able to use during my stay in Chicago, discussed with me various issues regarding the form and meaning of the prayer. Rosa Contini (Tel Aviv) and Steve Thurston (Chicago) assisted me in the preparation of the glossaries.

The Oriental Institute is one of the few places where one can as soon as the need arises consult with leading experts in neighboring disciplines of ancient Near Eastern studies. I am grateful to many colleagues for their advice and assistance, especially to Profs. Robert D. Biggs, Edward F. Wente, and Dennis G. Pardee who patiently answered my questions on Mesopotamian, Egyptian and Ugaritic prayers, respectively.

Prof. H. Craig Melchert of the University of North Carolina and Prof. Gary M. Beckman of the University of Michigan painstakingly read and commented upon the manuscript, providing valuable advice on philological and linguistic issues. Dr. Cem Karasu of the Ankara University kindly checked for me at the Ankara Museum possible joins to KBo 9.98+ (see Ch. XI).

I gratefully acknowledge the help and advice of all the persons with whom I discussed the text, but I assume final responsibility for all assertions which are not specifically attributed to other scholars.

Last but not least, I wish to thank Dr. Billie Jean Collins, Director of Publications, and Prof. Victor H. Matthews, General Book Editor, for accepting the manuscript for publication by the American Schools of Oriental Research.

Tel-Aviv, Oct. 1995

Acknowledgments

Introduction

The two main exemplars of *CTH* 381 were among the first tablets found in Winckler's excavations at Boğazköy.[1] Their good state of preservation and their theological and geographical interest immediately attracted the attention of scholars. As early as 1910, F. M. Th. Böhl copied and transliterated the tablets in Berlin, as exemplars *A* (VAT 7456) and *B* (VAT 7512), a designation kept in all subsequent studies. Six years later he ventured a first publication, which included a transliteration annotated with textual variants and with some preliminary comments.[2] It is to the credit of Böhl that at this preliminary stage of Hittitology he was able to produce not only a relatively accurate transliteration, but also some valuable philological[3] and geographical[4] comments.[5]

The tablets were published in autograph by O. Weber in 1923, as KUB 6. 45 (*A*) and 46 (*B*). The quality of these handcopies, which have served ever since as the basis for all transliterations and studies, leaves much to be desired, despite some corrections later appended to that volume (p. iii, *Verbesserungen*).

A year later M. Witzel included the Muwatalli Prayer in his anthology of Hittite texts.[6] A comparison with Böhl's first attempt demonstrates how rapidly the study of Hittite advanced after Hrozný's first achievements. Witzel was already able to benefit from the pioneering studies of Forrer, Sommer, and Friedrich[7] and presented the first translation of the text. Despite A. Götze's justified criticism of the book,[8] one has to admit that Witzel at least managed to understand the text in broad terms.

After these pioneering studies no comprehensive treatments of the text were attempted until the fifties, although selected passages were translated and commented upon in various studies on Hittite religion.[9]

The first modern translation of the text was provided by A. Goetze in *ANET*.[10] It excludes the long list of cult centers and the offering lists. The former gap was filled in J. Garstang & O. R. Gurney's book on

[1] For the find places and the outer appearance of the tablets, see Ch. IV.1.

[2] "Ausgewählte Keilschrifttexte aus Boghaz-köi, No IV", *Theologisch Tijdschrift* 50 (1916), 303-326.

[3] E.g., he proposed an etymological relation between *weštaraš* (unique phonetic spelling for ^{LÚ}SIPA) and Latin *pastor*. Obviously, there is no want of less successful attempts, e.g., the comparison of *tiyauwaš* with IE *Diaus*, "god". Böhl informed Weber about this important "discovery", and the latter published it in the *Umschau* of 25. 3. 1916.

[4] Ḫalab = Cl. Aleppo; Ḫupišna = NA Ḫubušna; Tegarama = OT Togarma.

[5] It is of interest to note that due to the misreading of *tarkummai* as *Tarqu ku-i*, Böhl fortuitously hit on the Hittite/Luwian name of the Storm-god, which he then correctly compared to the *Tarkondemos* seal and to the name *Tarquinius* (p. 319 f.)!

[6] *Hethitische Keilschrift-Urkunden = Keilschriftliche Studien*, IV (1924), 86-98.

[7] ibid., p. XI.

[8] *OLZ* 1925, 234 -239.

[9] E.g., E. Tenner, "Zwei hethitische Sonnenlieder", in F. Sommer – H. Ehelolf, *Kleinasiatische Forschungen* (Weimar 1930), 391; A. Götze, *Kleinasien* (München 1933; 1957), *passim*; G. Furlani, *La religione degli hittiti* (Bologna 1936), *passim.*

[10] "Hittite Prayers" in J. B. Pritchard, *Ancient Near Eastern Texts* (Princeton 1950), 397-399.

Hittite geography.[11] A full transliteration, French translation, and commentary are included in R. Lebrun's monograph on Hittite hymns and prayers.[12] To the best of my knowledge, none of these scholars examined the tablets for collations. Several recent anthologies of Hittite prayers do not include any of Muwatalli's prayers.[13]

Although the text was unearthed nearly a century ago, a complete and accurate transliteration was until now unavailable. Collation of the two main tablets in the Vorderasiatisches Museum in Berlin has demonstrated how imperative a reliable transliteration is for any in-depth study based on this text.[14]

CTH 381 presents a variety of interests for the scholarly world. To start with, it is one of the longest and best preserved Hittite texts. The two main duplicates restore each other's lacunae almost entirely. Out of 289 lines only three are almost entirely lost in both texts, although their contents may be inferred with considerable confidence (iii 76 – iv 2). Thus, *CTH* 381 provides a large, practically complete text, a rare and valuable asset for various thematic studies, including investigations on script and language in the poorly documented age of Muwatalli II.

There are presently four known duplicates of the text. Two small fragments, *C* and *D*, are of little value, but the two main exemplars, *A* and *B*, provide an excellent opportunity to compare their ductus, orthography, and language. If my conclusion that the two duplicates are contemporary is valid, the marked differences between them are most valuable for a synchronic study of scribal skills and habits, a complementary approach to the more common diachronic studies (Ch. IV).

The comparison between the main exemplars, both of which exhibit corrections and additions, enables a plausible reconstruction of the redactional history of the text. Ph. H. J. Houwink ten Cate produced a textual criticism in 1968,[15] and his main results have been found to be valid. Collation enabled a close examination of the editorial activity performed on both tablets, including "proofreading" performed by some additional person(s) (Ch. V).

The structure of the text emerges with great clarity and is compared to other prayer(s) of Muwatalli and other Hittite kings (Chs. VI-VIII).[16] Of particular interest are the three intercessories to gods who are implored to mediate between the suppliant and the Assembly of Gods. Another important asset of this text is the inclusion of an elaborate description of the ritual offerings to the gods, rarely found (or preserved) in other Hittite prayers (Ch. IX).

Muwatalli's prayer contains the largest number of gods listed within a single Hittite text, altogether some 140 deities belonging to 83 different localities, in addition to deified mountains and rivers. This vast "collection" of theonyms provides a rich source for the study of the Hittite pantheon, its composition and characteristics (Ch. XII). Divinities playing a central role in this text are studied in more detail (Chs. XIII-XV), notably the Storm-god of Lightning (*piḫaššašši*), Muwatalli's personal god and later to be the patron god of Tarḫuntašša.

CTH 381 has always served as one of the main sources for Hittite geography. Besides the usual comments on individual entries and names, this study raises more general questions, such as the order of

---

11 *The Geography of the Hittite Empire* (London 1959), 116-119.

12 *Hymnes et prières hittites* (Louvain-la-neuve 1980), 256-293; see the reviews by G. Kellerman, *Numen* 30 (1983), 274 f.; M. Marazzi, *Studi e materiali di Storia delle Religioni* 49 (1983), 327.

13 C. Kühne, "Hittite Texts", in W. Beyerlin (ed.), *Near Eastern Religious Texts Relating to the Old Testament* (Philadelphia 1978), 165-174; L. Christmann-Franck in *Prières de l'Ancien Orient* (Paris 1989), 39-57; A. Ünal in *Texte aus der Umwelt des Alten Testaments, II/6, Lieder und Gebete II* (Gütersloh 1991), 791-817.

14 In 25 cases (marked "coll." in the footnotes to the transliteration) O. Weber's handcopy misdraws or omits signs (the latter especially on the edges of text *B*). In one case the paragraph-dividers are inaccurately drawn, resulting in a confusion of the text (B i 38 f.). The autograph also fails to show the marked difference in the hand-writing of the "Postscript" in *A* iv 59-61 (see Ch. IV. 2 and Ch. V).

15 "Muwatallis' 'Prayer to be Spoken in an Emergency,' an Essay in Textual Criticism," *JNES* 27 (1968), 204-208.

16 Important observations on the structure of the text were made by H. G. Güterbock in articles on Hittite prayers, especially: "The Composition of Hittite Prayers to the Sun", *JAOS* 78 (1958), 245; "Some Aspects of Hittite Prayers" in T. T. Segerstedt (ed.), *The Frontiers of Human Knowledge* (Uppsala 1978), 136.

listing, the limits of the covered area, and their possible theological and geo-political significance (Ch. XII).

As one of the few texts of Muwatalli discovered in Ḫattuša, it is of great value as a possible source for indirect evidence on his eventful reign. The combined evidence of *CTH* 381, *CTH* 382, Muwatalli's prayer on the cult of Kummanni (Ch. X), and a fragmentary third prayer (Ch. XI), may provide better insight into the theological climate of one of the major changes in Hittite history, the transfer of the capital from Ḫattuša to Tarḫuntašša (Epilogue).

Last but not least, parts of this text, in particular the long intercessory to the Storm-god of Lightning, are of great literary and intellectual value. Their interest transcends the confines of Hittite studies and contributes to the comparative study of ancient Near Eastern and Biblical literature and theology.

Aside from the list below, the abbreviations conform to those of the Chicago Hittite Dictionary (*CHD*) of the Oriental Institute of the University of Chicago, edited by H. A. Hoffner and H. G. Güterbock.

H. G. Güterbock, "Some Aspects of Hittite Prayers"
in T. T. Segerstedt (ed.), *The Frontiers of Human Knowledge* (Uppsala 1978), 125-139.

V. Haas, *Gesch. der heth. Rel.*
Geschichte der hethitischen Religion. *Handbuch der Orientalistik.* Abt. 1, Bd. 15 (Leiden 1994).

Ph. H.J. Houwink ten Cate, "The Sun God of Heaven"
"The Sun God of Heaven, the Assembly of Gods and the Hittite King",
in: D. van der Plas (ed.), *Effigies Dei: Essays on the History of Religions* (Leiden 1987), 13-34.

Ph. H.J. Houwink ten Cate, "The Hittite Storm God"
"The Hittite Storm God: his Role and his Rule According to Hittite Cuneiform Sources",
in: D. J.W. Meijer (ed.), *Natural Phenomena. Their Meaning, Depiction and Description in the Ancient Near East* (Amsterdam 1992), 83-148.

E. Laroche, *Dieux*
"Recherches sur les noms des dieux hittites", *Revue Hittite et Asianique* VII/46 (Paris 1947).

E. Laroche, Prière
"La prière hittite: vocabulaire et typologie",
École pratique des Hautes Études, V^e section, Sciences Religieuses; Annuaire, 72 (Paris 1964), 3-29.

R. Lebrun, *Hymnes et prières*
Hymnes et prières hittites. Centre d'Histoire des Religions (Louvain-la-neuve 1980).

R. Lebrun, "Observations sur la prière hittite" in: H. Limet & J. Ries (eds.),
L'Expérience de la prière dans les grandes religions (Louvain-la-neuve 1980), 31-57.

Part One

THE TEXT

Chapter I: Transliteration [17]

A. KUB 6. 45 + 1111/z + unnumbered frgm. + KUB 30. 14

B. KUB 6. 46 = A

C. KUB 12. 35 = A II 13-23

D. 1785/u = A III 55-61

Obv. I

1 ⌊*UM-MA*⌋ ta-ba-ar-na ^{M}NIR.GÁL LUGAL.GAL LUGAL KUR ^{URU}Ḫa-at-ti
(1)]Ḫa-at-ti

2 [DUMU] ^{M}Mur-ši-i-li LUGAL.GAL LUGAL KUR ^{URU}Ḫa-at-ti UR.SAG ma-a-an **UN-[ši]**
(2) m]a-a-an **an-tu-uḫ-ši**

3 [me-m]i-aš ku-iš-ki na-ak-ki-ia-aš-zi nu-za *A-NA* DINGIR^{MEŠ} ar-ku-wa-ar[18]
(3) DINGIR$^{ME.}$]^{EŠ} [19] ar-ku-wa-ar

4 [D]Ù-zi šu-uḫ-ḫi-kán še-er ^{d}UTU-i me-na-aḫ-ḫa-an-da 2 ^{GIŠ}BANŠUR AD.KID
(4) me-na-aḫ-ḫa-a]n-da 2 ^{GIŠ}BANŠUR AD.KID

5 [k]a![20]-ri-ia-an-da da-a-i 1 ^{GIŠ}BANŠUR *A-NA* ^{d}UTU ^{URU}TÚL-na *Ù* DINGIR^{MEŠ} LÚ^{MEŠ}
(5) da-a-]i 1 ^{GIŠ}BANŠUR (6) [

6 [1 ^{GIŠ}BA]NŠUR da-a-i nu-uš-ša-an 35 NINDA.GUR$_4$.RA tar-na-aš *ŠA* ZÌ.DA D[U]R$_5$
da-a]-⌈i⌉ nu-uš-ša-an 35[21] NINDA.GUR$_4$.R[A] (7) [

7 [^{DUG}DÍLIM.G]AL[22] SIG LÀL ŠÀ.BA Ì.DÙG.GA NINDA.Ì.E.DÉ.A ^{DUG}ÚTUL šu-u-wa-an me-[m]a-al-ma
Ì.DÙG.]GA NINDA.Ì.E.DÉ.A ^{DUG}ÚTUL (8) [

8 ^{DUG}DÍLIM. GAL[23] šu-u-wa-an 30 ^{DUG}*KU-KU-UB* GEŠTIN nu GIM-an ki-i S[IxSÁ?-z]i
]30 ^{DUG}*KU-KU-UB* GEŠTIN (9) [

9 nu-kán LUGAL-uš šu-uḫ-ḫi ša-ra-a pa-iz-zi na-aš *A-NA* ^{d}UTU *[Š]A-⌈ME-E⌉*[24] ***[UŠ-KE]-EN***
-u]š šu-uḫ-ḫi ša-ra-a pa-**a**-iz-zi (10) [ ]-**i** [25]

---

[17] Transliteration follows *HZL*, except for SAL (=MUNUS) and Ḫat (=GIDRU). All variants are highlighted in bold face; variant word-order is underlined; erased sections are crossed over. Exclamation mark signifies "sic" (misspellings are not corrected).

[18] Here joins 1111/z col. I, which provides the ends of lines 3-9. H. Otten & Ch. Rüster, *ZA* 64, 242 f.

[19] The traces of the long horizontal wedge before *arkuwar* most probably belong to ME.EŠ (rather than *-aš*), which is consistently written by this scribe with the late form (see Ch. IV.2).

[20] The extant traces are less clear than drawn in the autograph. There is sufficient space for a possible [*ka*]-⌈*a*⌉- , but this would provide an aberrant spelling. A simple [*k*]*a-* cannot be entirely excluded.

[21] Coll.: The second digit is written on the line of the column divider, but collation indicates 35, as in *A*.

[22] Coll.: see Commentary.

[23] Coll.: DÍLIM (LIŠ) omitted in the autograph.

[24] Collation provides clear preference for this restoration, rather than ^{d}UTU [^{UR}]^{U}T[ÚL-*na*. See also Houwink ten Cate, "The Sun God of Heaven...", *Effigies Dei* (1987), 20.

[25] *A* has a clear]-*EN* written on the column divider (in 1111/z), whereas *B* has a clear]-*i* ; see Commentary.

10 nu ki-iš-ša-an me-ma-i ^{d}UTU *ŠA-ME-E Ù* ^{d}UTU ^{URU}TÚL-na GAŠAN-*IA* [SA]L.LUGAL
(11) ^{U}]^{RU}TÚL-na GAŠAN-*IA* (12) [

11 GAŠAN-*IA* SAL.LUGAL *Š*[*A* KU]R ^{URU}Ḫa-at-ti ^{d}U LUGAL *ŠA-ME-E* EN-*IA* ^{d}Ḫé-pát
]^{d}U LUGAL *ŠA-ME-E* EN-*IA* (13) [

12 SAL.LUGAL GAŠAN-*IA* ^{d}U [^{UR}]^{U}·[^{GI}]^{Š}Ḫat-ti LUGAL *ŠA-ME-E* BAD KUR $^{URU.GIŠ}$**Ḫat-ti** EN-*IA*
-t]i LUGAL *ŠA-ME-E* BAD KUR ^{URU}**KÙ.BABBAR-ti** EN-*IA*

13 ^{d}U ^{URU}Zi-ip-la-an[-da] EN-*IA* ŠA ^{d}U a-aš-ši-ia-an-za DUMU-aš
(14)[-*I*]*A* ŠA ^{d}U a-aš-< ! >-ia-an-za DUMU-aš

14 EN KUR $^{URU.GIŠ}$Ḫat-ti ^{DINGIR}Š[e-r]i-**uš**$^{!}$ [26] ~~GUD *ŠA*~~ ^{GUD}**Ḫur-ri** ~~KUR ^{URU}Ḫa-at-ti ku-iš~~
(15) [$^{DINGIR.GU}$]^{D}[27] [Še]-r[i-iš] **GUD *ŠA*** ^{URU}**Ḫa-at-tu-ši KUR-e ku-iš**

15 ~~pé-ra-an ti-ia-an-za~~ DINGIR.LÚ^{MEŠ} DINGIR.SAL^{MEŠ} ḫu-u-ma-an-te-eš ḪUR.SAG^{MEŠ}
(16)[**pé-ra-an ti-ia-a**]**n-⸢za⸣** DINGIR.LÚ$^{ME.EŠ}$ DINGIR.SAL$^{ME.EŠ}$ ḫu-u-ma-an-te-eš ḪUR.SAG$^{ME.EŠ}$

16 ÍD^{MEŠ} *ŠA* KUR $^{URU.GIŠ}$**Ḫat-ti** ḫu-u-ma-an-te-eš EN^{MEŠ} DINGIR$^{ME.EŠ}$ ÍD$^{ME.EŠ}$
(17) [*ŠA* KUR ^{UR}]^{U} **⸢Ḫa⸣-at**[28] **-ti** ḫu-u-ma-an-te-eš$_{17}$ EN$^{ME.EŠ}$DINGIR$^{ME.EŠ}$

17 EN$^{ME.EŠ}$ ^{d}UTU ^{URU}TÚL-na GAŠAN-*IA Ù* DINGIR^{MEŠ} ḫu-u-ma-an-**du-uš** *ŠA* KUR ^{URU}**KÙ.BABBAR-ti**
EN$^{ME.EŠ}$ ^{d}UTU ^{URU}TÚL-na (18) GAŠAN-*IA Ù* DINGIR$^{ME.EŠ}$ ḫu-u-ma-an-**te-eš$_{17}$** *ŠA* KUR ^{URU}**Ḫa-at-ti**

18 EN$^{ME.EŠ}$ ^{LÚ}SANGA-az ku-e-da-aš *ŠA* KUR ^{URU}Ḫa-at-ti-mu-kán
EN$^{ME.EŠ}$ ^{LÚ}SANGA-az (19) ku-e-da-aš *ŠA* KUR ^{URU}Ḫa-at-ti-mu-kán

19 EN-*UT-TA* **ḫu-u-ma-an-da-az** ku-i-e-eš me-mi-iš-tén
EN-*UT-TA* **da-< pí->az**[29] (20) ku-i-e-eš *eras.* me-mi-**uš**$^{!}$- tén

---

20 ki-nu-na-mu DINGIR^{MEŠ} am-me-el *ŠA* ^{LÚ}SANGA-*KU-NU* ÌR-*KU-NU* me-mi-an
(21)ki-nu[30]-na-mu DINGIR$^{ME.EŠ}$ am-me-el *ŠA* ^{LÚ}SANGA-*KU-NU* ÌR-*KU-NU* me-mi-an

21 ar-ku-wa-ar iš-ta-ma-aš-tén ḫu-u-da-ak-ma-az **šu**[31]**-me-el**-pát *ŠA*[32] **EN-*LÍ* DINGIR^{MEŠ}**
ar-ku-wa-ar-**ra** (22) iš-ta-ma-aš-tén ḫu-u-da-ak-ma-az **am-me-el**-pát *ŠA* DINGIR$^{ME.EŠ}$ ***BE-LU***

22 *ŠA* É$^{ME.EŠ}$ DINGIR-*LIM-KU-NU* ~~šu-me-el~~ (?) *ŠA* ALAM-*KU-NU* ar-ku-wa-ar
ŠA É$^{ME.EŠ}$ (23) DINGIR-*LIM-KU-NU* **šu-me-el** *ŠA* ALAM-*KU-NU* ar-ku-wa-ar

---

[26] The following phrase has been erased in *A*, but the remaining traces with the help of *B* and the parallel expression in i 33 enable the reconstruction of the original text. Upon the erasure the scribe wrote ^{GUD}*Ḫur-ri*. See Commentary.

[27] Cf. *B* i 34: $^{DINGIR.GUD}$*Še-ri-iš* (= *A* i 33 ^{d}*Še-ri-iš*).

[28] Coll.: clear *-at-* (not *-du-* as in the autograph).

[29] Omission of the internal *-pí-* of *da-pí-aš* (cf. iii 35) is more likely than an omission of most of *ḫuma*(*n*)*daz* See Commentary.

[30] Written over erasure.

[31] *A* probably corrected *am-* into *šu-*, and then erased *šumel* in the next line. See Commentary.

[32] Written over erasure. See Commentary for the redactional history of this and the following line.

23 i-ia-mi DINGIR^{MEŠ} *ŠA* KUR $^{\text{URU.GIŠ}}$**Ḫat-ti** GIM-an i-ia-an-te-eš
i-ia-mi (24) DINGIR$^{\text{ME.EŠ}}$ *ŠA* KUR $^{\text{URU.}}$**Ḫa-at-ti** GIM-an i-ia-an-te-eš$_{17}$

24 **GIM-an**-na-at i-da-la-wa-aḫ-ḫa-an- te-eš
ma-aḫ-ḫa-na-at (25) i-da-la-**a-u**-wa-aḫ-ḫa-an- te-eš$_{17}$ (*erasure*)

---

25 EGIR-*ŠU*-ma-za *ŠA* ZI-*IA* *A-WA-TE*^{MEŠ} ar-ku-wa-ar i-ia-mi nu-mu DINGIR^{MEŠ}
(26) EGIR-**an<<-na>>-da**-ma-za[33] *ŠA* ZI-*IA* *A-WA-TE*$^{\text{ME.EŠ}}$ ar-ku-wa-ar i-ia-mi (27) nu-mu DINGIR$^{\text{ME.EŠ}}$

26 EN^{MEŠ} GEŠTUG-an pa-ra-a e-ep-tén nu-mu ke-e ar-**ku**-wa-ar-ri$^{\text{ḪI.A}}$
EN$^{\text{ME.EŠ}}$ GEŠTUG-an pa-ra-a e-ep-tén nu-mu ke-e *eras.*[34] ar-**u**$^{!}$-wa-ar-ri$^{\text{ḪI.A}}$[35]

27 iš-ta-ma-aš-tén nu-za *A-WA-TE*^{MEŠ} ku-e *A-NA* DINGIR^{MEŠ} EN^{MEŠ} ar-ku-wa-ar
(28) iš-ta-< ! >-aš-tén nu-za *A-WA-TE*$^{\text{ME.EŠ}}$ ku-e *A-NA* DINGIR$^{\text{ME.EŠ}}$ EN$^{\text{ME.EŠ}}$ ar-ku-wa-ar

28 **DÙ-mi** nu ki-i *A-WA-T*⌜*E*⌝^{MEŠ} DINGIR^{MEŠ} EN^{MEŠ} **da-at-ti-in** iš-ta-ma-aš-ti-ni-ia-at
i-ia-mi (29)nu ki-i *A-WA-TE*$^{\text{ME.EŠ}}$DINGIR$^{\text{ME.EŠ}}$EN$^{\text{ME.EŠ}}$ **ta-at-ti-ni** **uš**$^{!}$-ta-ma-aš-ti-< ! >ia-at

29 ku-e-ma-mu *A-WA-TE*^{MEŠ} *Ú-UL* iš-ta-ma-aš-te-ni am-mu-uk-ma-za-at
(30) ku-e-ma-mu *A-WA-TE*$^{\text{ME.EŠ}}$ *Ú-UL* iš-ta-ma-aš-te-ni am-mu-uk-ma-za-at

30 *A-NA* DINGIR^{MEŠ} ar-ku-wa-ar i-ia-mi-pát na-at-mu-kán **UN-az**
(31)*A-NA* DINGIR$^{\text{ME.EŠ}}$ ar-ku-wa-ar i-ia-mi-pát na-at-mu-kán **an-tu-uḫ-ša-aš**

31 KAxU-az ša-ra-a ú-iz-zi-pát na-at DINGIR^{MEŠ} EN^{MEŠ}
(32) KAxU-az ša-ra-a ú-iz-zi-pát na-at DINGIR$^{\text{ME.EŠ}}$ EN$^{\text{ME.EŠ}}$

32 iš-ta-ma-aš-šu-wa-an-zi pa-ra-a tar-ni-iš- tén
iš-ta-ma-aš-šu-wa-an-[z]i (33) pa-ra-a tar-ni-iš- tén[36]

---

33 ^{DINGIR}Še-ri-iš-ma EN-*IA* GUD *ŠA* ^{d}U *ŠA* KUR ^{URU}**KÙ.BABBAR-ti** pé-ra-an ti-an-za
(34) $^{\textbf{DINGIR.GUD}}$Še-ri-iš-ma ⌜EN-*IA*⌝ GUD *ŠA* ^{d}U *ŠA* KUR ^{URU}**Ḫa-at-ti** pé-ra-an ti-an-za

34 nu-mu ke-e-da-aš *A-NA* *A-WA-TE*^{MEŠ} ar-ku-wa-ar ti-ia-u-wa-aš
(35) nu-mu ke-e-d[a-aš] *A-NA* *A-WA-TE*$^{\text{ME.EŠ}}$[37] ar-ku-wa-ar ti-ia-u-wa-aš

35 *A-NA* DINGIR$^{\text{ME.EŠ}}$ tar-kum-ma-i nu-mu DINGIR$^{\text{ME.EŠ}}$ EN^{MEŠ} ke-**e** *A-WA-TE*^{MEŠ}
(36)*A-NA* DINGIR$^{\text{ME.EŠ}}$ [tar-k]um-ma-i nu-mu DINGIR$^{\text{ME.EŠ}}$ EN$^{\text{ME.EŠ}}$ ki-**i** *A-WA-TE*$^{\text{ME.EŠ}}$

36 ar-ku-wa-ar DINGIR^{MEŠ} EN^{MEŠ} ne-pí-ša-aš **KI-aš-ša** iš-ta-ma-aš-ša-**an**-du
ar-ku-wa-ar (37) **ti-[ia-u-wa-]aš** DINGIR$^{\text{ME.EŠ}}$ EN$^{\text{ME.EŠ}}$ ne-pí-ša-aš **da-ga-zi-pa-aš-ša<<-aš-ša>>**
(38) **[ḫu-u-ma]-an-te-eš**$_{17}$ iš-ta-ma-aš-ša-du[38]

---

33 Cf. *B* iii 65, iv 50.

34 Two superimposed *Winkelhaken*s erased.

35 Coll.: *-u-* written over erasure; last sign (on the column divider) is a clear ḪI.A (not *ia* as in autograph).

36 Written over an erased *-kán* or *-du*.

37 Written over erasure.

38 Coll.: The drawing of the division lines in the autograph is inaccurate and the resulting text confused. See

---

37 ^{d}UTU *ŠA-ME-E* ^{d}UTU ^{URU}TÚL-na ^{d}U ^{URU}TÚL-na ^{d}**Mi**-iz-zu-ul-la-aš
(ii 2) [39] ^{d}UTU [*ŠA-ME-E*] (3) [ ]⌜^{d}⌝U ^{URU}[ ] ⌜^{d}⌝**Me**-ez-zu-ul-la-aš

38 ^{d}Ḫu-ul-la-aš $^{\text{DINGIR.SAL}}$Zi-in-du-ḫi-ia-aš DINGIR.LÚ^{MEŠ} DINGIR.SAL^{MEŠ} ḪUR.SAG$^{\text{ME.EŠ}}$
^{d}Ḫu-ul-la-aš $^{\text{DINGIR.SAL}}$Zi-in-< ! >ḫi-ia-aš[40] / (4) [ ] ⌜ḪUR.S⌝[AG$^{\text{ME.EŠ}}$

39 ÍD^{MEŠ} ŠA URU A-ri-in-na ^{d}U e[41]-ḫi-el-li-bi ^{d}U šu-ḫur-ri-bi
ÍD^{ME}]^{Š} ŠA URU A-ri-in-na (5) [-b]i ^{d}U š[u-ḫ]ur$^{?}$-ri-bi[42]

---

40 ^{d}U ḪI.ḪI ^{d}Ḫé-bat ^{URU}Ša-mu-ḫa DINGIR.LÚ^{MEŠ} DINGIR.SAL^{MEŠ} ḪUR.SAG^{MEŠ} ÍD^{MEŠ} *ŠA* ^{URU}**Ša-mu-ḫa**
(6) [*erasu*]*re* ^{d}Ḫé-bat ^{URU}Ša-mu-ḫa[43] *eras.* (7) [ ]DINGIR.SAL$^{\text{ME.EŠ}}$ ḪUR.SAG$^{\text{ME.EŠ}}$ ÍD$^{\text{ME.EŠ}}$ *ŠA* ^{URU}**Ti-wa**

---

41 ^{d}U pí-ḫa-aš-ša-aš-ši-**iš** ^{d}UTU ^{URU}TÚL-na ^{d}Ḫé-bat SAL.LUGAL ***ŠA-ME-E***
(8) [^{d}U pí-ḫ]a-aš-ša-aš-ši ^{d}UTU ^{URU}TÚL-na ^{d}Ḫé-bat SAL.LUGAL **AN-*I***

42 ^{d}U DU$_6$ DINGIR^{MEŠ} *ŠA* É.GAL ḫu-uḫ-ḫa-aš
^{d}U DU$_6$ DINGIR$^{\text{ME.EŠ}}$ *ŠA* É.GAL ḫu-uḫ-ḫa-aš

---

43 ^{d}U ^{URU}Ḫa-la-ab ^{d}Ḫé-bat ^{URU}Ḫa-la-ab ^{d}IŠTAR.LÍL ^{URU}Ša-mu-ḫa
(9) ^{d}[U] ^{URU}Ḫa-la-ab ^{d}Ḫé-bat ^{URU}Ḫa-la-ab ^{URU}Ša-mu-ḫa ^{d}IŠTAR.LÍL

44 ^{d}*BE-E-*⌊*LA*⌋*-AT*[44] *A-IA-**AK**-KI* ^{d}A-pa-a-ra-aš *ŠA* ^{URU}Ša-mu-ḫa DINGIR.LÚ^{MEŠ}
(10) ^{d}*BE-E-LA-AT* *A-IA-KI* ^{d}A-pa-a-ra-aš *ŠA* ^{URU}Ša-mu-ḫa[45] DINGIR.LÚ$^{\text{ME.EŠ}}$

45 DINGIR.⌊SAL^{MEŠ} ḪUR.SAG⌋^{MEŠ} ÍD^{MEŠ} *ŠA* ^{URU}Ša-mu-ḫa
DINGIR.SAL$^{\text{ME.EŠ}}$ ḪUR.SAG$^{\text{ME.EŠ}}$ ÍD$^{\text{ME.EŠ}}$ *ŠA* ^{URU}Ša-mu-ḫa

---

46 [ ]^{d}Ḫé-bat ^{d}U ^{URU}Ša-aḫ-pí-na DINGIR.LÚ^{MEŠ} DINGIR.SAL^{MEŠ}
(11) ⌜^{d}⌝[U] NIR.GÁL ^{d}Ḫé-bat ^{d}U ^{URU}Ša-aḫ-pí-na DINGIR.LÚ$^{\text{ME.EŠ}}$ DINGIR.SAL$^{\text{ME.EŠ}}$

47 [Í]D^{MEŠ} *ŠA* ^{URU}Ka-**da**-pa
(12) ⌜ḪUR⌝.SAG$^{\text{ME.EŠ}}$ ÍD$^{\text{ME.EŠ}}$ *ŠA* ^{URU}Ka-**ta**-pa[46]

Commentary.

[39] In *B* the long list of deities actually begins in ii 3 ff., but, as in I 39, the scribe added the Sun-god of Heaven to the end of line 2 (after an X-like marker). The signs are written in small characters and are very eroded. See Comm.

[40] Coll.: $^{\text{DINGIR.SAL}}$Zi-in-<du->ḫi-ia-aš is written on the edge (omitted in the autograph). It is followed by a superfluous division line (only in *B*).

[41] Coll., already indicated by Otten apud Güterbock, *SBo I*, p. 20 n. 57.

[42] Coll.: The damaged second sign has a vertical wedge which precludes *-ḫur-*, unless it was written (as quite often in *B*) over an erased sign. The third sign is clearly a *-ri-* (and not *-ta-* as drawn in the autograph).

[43] Šamuḫa is written over a long erasure which continues almost to the edge of the tablet.

[44] In both texts *-at* is inserted above the line. See Commentary and Ch. V.2.2.

[45] *ŠA* ^{URU}*Ša-mu-ḫa* is inserted above the line in small characters.

[46] Coll.: *-ta-* written over erasure (not *-da-* as drawn in the autograph).

---

48 [-i]a-aš SAL.LUGAL ^{URU}K[a-**da**-pa] DINGIR.LÚ^{MEŠ} DINGIR.SAL$^{ME.EŠ}$ Ḫ[UR.SAG ^{MEŠ}]
(13) ^{d}[U] šar-ti-ia-aš SAL.LUGAL ^{URU}Ka-**a-ta**-pa DINGIR.LÚ$^{ME.EŠ}$ DINGIR.SAL$^{ME.EŠ}$ ḪUR.SAG $^{ME.EŠ}$

49 [^{UR}]^{U} Ka-**da**-pa ^{d}U t[e-e]t-[ḫi-i]š-na-aš ^{d}U$^{ḪI.A}$ ḫ[u-]
ÍD$^{ME.EŠ}$ (14) *ŠA* ^{URU}Ka-**a-ta**-pa ^{d}U te-et-ḫi-iš-na-aš ^{d}U$^{ḪI.A}$ ḫu-u-ma-an-te-eš

---

50 ^{d}U ^{URU}**KÙ.BABBAR-⸢ti⸣** šar-ku-uš AMAR-uš ^{d}U KARAŠ ^{d}UTU $^{URU.GIŠ}$**Ḫat-t[i]**
(15) ^{d}U ^{URU}**Ḫa-at-ti** šar-ku-uš AMAR-uš ^{d}U KARAŠ ^{d}UTU ^{URU}**Ḫa-at-ti**

51 ^{d}LAMMA ^{URU}**KÙ.BABBAR-ti** ^{d}U ^{URU}Ḫa-la-ab ^{d}Ḫé-bat ^{URU}Ḫa-la-ab ^{URU}**K[Ù.BABBAR-t]i**
(16) ^{d}⸤LAMMA ^{URU}**Ḫ⸥a-at-ti** ^{d}U ^{URU}Ḫa-la-ab ^{d}Ḫé-bat ^{URU}Ḫa-la-ab (17) ^{URU}**Ḫ[a-at-t]i**

52 ^{d}A-a-aš ^{d}Dam-ki-in-na-aš ^{d}ZA.BA$_{4}$.BA$_{4}$ ^{d}DAG-**iš** ^{d}Al-la-tum
^{d}A-a-aš ^{d}Dam-ki-in-na-aš ^{d}ZA.BA$_{4}$.BA$_{4}$ ^{d}DAG-**ti-iš** (18) ^{d}A[l-la]-tum[47]

53 ^{d}IŠTAR ^{URU}Ni-nu-wa DINGIR^{MEŠ} lu-la-ḫi-ia-aš ^{DINGIR}Ku-pa-pa-aš
^{d}IŠTAR ^{URU}Ni-nu-wa DINGIR$^{ME.EŠ}$ lu-la-ḫi-ia-aš $^{DINGIR.SAL}$Ku-pa-**a**-pa-aš

---

54 ^{d}IŠTAR ^{URU}Ḫa-ad-**da**-ri-na ^{d}Pí-ir-wa-aš ^{d}Aš-ga-ši-pa-aš $^{ḪUR.SAG}$Piš-ku-ru-nu-wa
(19) ^{d}IŠTA[R ^{URU}Ḫ]a-at-**ta**-ri-na ^{d}Pí-ir-wa-aš ^{d}Aš-ga-ši-pa-aš $^{ḪUR.SAG}$Piš-ku-ru-nu-wa

55 DINGIR.LÚ^{MEŠ} DINGIR.SAL^{MEŠ} ḪUR.SAG^{MEŠ} ÍD^{MEŠ} *ŠA* ^{URU}⸤**KÙ.BABBAR⸥-ti** ^{d}Kar-zi-iš[48]
(20) DINGIR.LÚ^{M}[^{EŠ}] DINGIR.SAL$^{ME.EŠ}$ *ŠA* ^{URU}**Ḫa-at-ti** ḪUR.SAG$^{ME.EŠ}$ ÍD$^{ME.EŠ}$ ^{d}Kar-zi-iš

56 ^{d}Ḫa-pa-an-**da**-li-ia-aš $^{ḪUR.SAG}$Ta-at-⸢ta⸣ $^{ḪUR.SAG}$⸢Šum-mi⸣-ia-ra
(21) ^{d}Ḫa-p[a]-an-**ta**-li-ia-aš $^{ḪUR.SAG}$Ta-at-ta $^{ḪUR.SAG}$Šum-mi-ia-ra

---

57 ^{d}U ^{URU}Zi-ip-la-an-da $^{ḪUR.SAG}$**Da**-ḫa DINGIR.LÚ^{MEŠ} DINGIR.SAL^{MEŠ} ḪUR.SAG$^{ME.EŠ}$
(22)^{d}U ^{UR}[^{U}Z]i-ip-**pa**-la-an-da $^{ḪUR.SAG}$**Ta**-ḫa DINGIR.LÚ$^{ME.EŠ}$ DINGIR.SAL$^{ME.EŠ}$(23) ḪUR.S[AG$^{ME.EŠ}$]

58 ÍD ^{MEŠ} *ŠA* ^{URU} Zi-ip-la-an-**da**
ÍD $^{ME.EŠ}$ *ŠA* ^{URU} Zi-ip-**pa**-la-an-**ta**

---

59 [^{d} Z]i-it-ḫa-ri-ia-aš ^{d}U KARAŠ DUMU ^{d}U ^{d}LAMMA ^{KUŠ}kur-ša-aš ^{d}~~LÍL~~
(24) ^{d}[-]ḫa-ri-ia-aš ^{d}U KARAŠ DUMU ^{d}U ^{d}LAMMA ^{KUŠ}kur-ša-aš ^{d}LÍL

60 ^{d}~~Zi-it-ḫa-ri-ia-aš~~ ḪUR.SAG^{MEŠ} ÍD^{MEŠ} *ŠA* ^{URU}Zi-it-ḫa-ra
(25)[*eras*]*ure*[49] ^{d}Zi-it-ḫa-ri-ia-aš ḪUR.SAG$^{ME.EŠ}$[50] ÍD$^{ME.EŠ}$*ŠA* ^{URU}Zi-it-ḫa-ra

---

47 Written over erasure.

48 Coll.: traces of *-zi-* clearly visible.

49 The whole line was squeezed in after the division line below it was already drawn.

50 ḪUR.SAG^{MEŠ} inserted above the line.

61 [ ]x[51] ^{d}UTU ^{URU}TÚL-na DINGIR.LÚ^{MEŠ} DINGIR.SAL^{MEŠ} ḪUR.SAG$^{ME.EŠ}$ ÍD$^{ME.EŠ}$ *ŠA* ^{URU} U-ra-u-na
(26)$^{⌈d⌉}$[^{d}]UTU ^{URU}TÚL-na DINGIR.LÚ$^{ME.EŠ}$ DINGIR.SAL$^{ME.EŠ}$ ḪUR.SAG$^{ME.EŠ}$ ÍD$^{ME.EŠ}$ *ŠA* ^{URU} U-ra-u-na

---

62 [^{d}U ^{UR}]^{U}Kum-ma-an-ni ^{d}Ḫé-bat ^{URU}Kum-ma-an-ni ^{d}U ši-na-ap-ši
(27) -m]a-an-ni ^{d}Ḫé-bat **KI.MIN** ^{d}U ši-na-ap-ši

63 [^{d}Ḫ]é-bat ^{GIŠ} ši-na-ap-ši ^{d}U $^{ḪUR.SAG}$ Ma-nu-zi-ia ^{d}NIN.GAL
^{d}Ḫé-bat **LUGAL**[52] **KI.MIN** (28) [ ]$^{ḪUR.SAG.URU}$Ma-nu-zi-ia ^{d}NIN.GAL

64 [^{d}Pí-š]a-nu-ḫi-iš $^{ḪUR.SAG}$Gal-li-iš-ta-pa-aš DINGIR.LÚ^{MEŠ} DINGIR.SAL^{MEŠ}
^{d}Pí-ša-nu-ḫi-iš (29) $^{ḪUR.SAG}$Gal-[li-i]š-ta-pa-aš DINGIR.LÚ$^{ME.EŠ}$ DINGIR.SAL$^{ME.EŠ}$

65 [ḪUR.SAG^{MEŠ} Í] D^{MEŠ} *ŠA* ^{URU}Kum-ma-an-ni *Ù* *ŠA* KUR ^{URU}Kum-ma-an-ni
ḪUR.SA[G$^{ME.EŠ}$ Í]D$^{ME.EŠ}$ (30) *ŠA* ^{URU}Kum-ma-[a]n-⌊ni⌋ ⌊*Ù*⌋ *ŠA* KUR ^{URU}Kum-ma-an-ni

---

66 [ ]-iš DINGIR.SAL-*TUM* *ŠA* ^{d}U pí-ḫa-mi *ŠA* ^{URU}Ša-na-ḫu-it-ta
(31)^{d}U pí-ḫa-mi-iš DI[NGIR] ⌊^{d}U⌋ p[í-ḫ]a-mi *ŠA* ^{URU}Ša-na-ḫu-it-ta

67 [ ] ḪUR.SAG^{MEŠ} ÍD^{MEŠ} *ŠA* ^{URU}Ša-na-ḫu-it-ta
(32) DINGIR.LÚ$^{ME.EŠ}$ DINGIR.SAL$^{ME.EŠ}$ ḪUR.S[AG$^{ME.EŠ}$ ÍD$^{ME.EŠ}$ *ŠA*] ^{URU}Ša-na-ḫu-it-ta

---

68[53] [^{URU} **N**]**e**[- ^{d}Z]A.BA$_4$.BA$_4$ KI.MIN ^{d}Te-li-pí-nu-uš ^{d}Za-ḫa-pu-na-aš
(33) ^{d}U ^{URU}**Ni**-ri-iq-qa ^{d}Z[A.BA$_4$.BA$_4$ KI.]MIN ^{d}Te-li-pí-nu-uš (34) ^{d}Za-ḫa-pu-na-aš

69 [$^{ḪUR.SAG}$]Za-li-ia-[nu-uš *ŠA*] ^{URU} ⌊**Ga**⌋-aš-ta-ma $^{ḪUR.SAG}$Za-li-ia-nu-uš
$^{ḪUR.SAG}$Za-l[i-ia-n]u-uš *ŠA* ^{URU} **Ka**-aš-ta-ma (35) $^{ḪUR.SAG}$[54] Za-li-ia-nu-uš

70 [^{d}T]a-az-zu-w[a-ši-iš DINGIR.L]Ú[^{ME}]^{Š} DINGIR.SAL^{MEŠ} *ŠA* ^{URU} **Ga**-aš-ta-ma
eras. ^{d}T[a-az-zu-w]a-ši-iš DINGIR.LÚ$^{ME.EŠ}$ DINGIR.SAL$^{ME.EŠ}$ *ŠA* ^{URU}**Ka**-aš-ta-ma

---

71 [^{d}LAM]MA ^{URU}Ḫa-te-i[n-zu-wa $^{ḪUR.}$]^{SAG}Ḫa-a-ḫar-wa DINGIR.LÚ^{MEŠ} DINGIR.SAL^{MEŠ}
(36) ^{d}LAMMA ^{URU}Ḫa-te-in-zu-wa $^{ḪUR.}$[^{SAG}Ḫa]-a-ḫar-wa DINGIR.LÚ$^{ME.EŠ}$ DINGIR.SAL$^{ME.EŠ}$

72 [*ŠA* ^{UR}]^{U}Ne-ri-i[q- *Ù* *Š*]*A* KUR ^{URU}Ta-ku-up-ša
(37) *ŠA* ^{URU}Ne-ri-iq-qa *Ù* *Š*[*A* KU]R ^{URU}Ta-ku-up-ša

---

51 Traces of a sign ending in two superimposed *Winkelhakens*.

52 LUGAL is inserted above the line; cf. ii 78 ^{d}*Ḫebat* LUGAL-*ma-aš*

53 A fragment missing in Weber's autograph provides the beginnings of lines 68 to 78. It has been glued to VAT 7456 (KUB 6.45), but it does not have a Bo-number and there are no records in the files of the Vorderasiatisches Museum regarding the execution of the join. It already appears in the photographs made by Frau Ehelolf.

54 *B* ii 35: ḪUR.SAG is written over an erasure and it protrudes into the column divider. Perhaps the scribe first wrote DINGIR and then corrected it to ḪUR.SAG.

73 [^{d}U] ^{URU}Ša-ri-iš-š[a -i]š DINGIR.LÚ^{MEŠ} DINGIR.SAL^{MEŠ} *ŠA* ^{URU}Ša-ri-iš-ša
(38) ^{d}U ^{URU}Ša-ri-iš-ša ^{d}IŠTAR-li-⌞iš⌟ DINGIR.LÚ$^{ME.EŠ}$ DINGIR.SAL$^{ME.EŠ}$ *ŠA* ^{URU}Ša-ri-iš-ša

---

74 [^{d}U ^{UR}]^{U}Ḫur-ma *ŠA* ^{URU}[ ] ^{d}Ḫa-an-ti-da-aš-šu-uš ^{d}U ^{d}Ḫé-bat
(39) ^{d}U ^{URU}Ḫur-m[a] *ŠA* ^{URU}Ḫur[55] -ma ^{d}Ḫa-an-ti-< ! >-šu-uš ^{d}U ^{d}Ḫé-bat

75 [^{URU}Ḫ]a-la-ab **ŠA** ^{URU}[Ḫur-m]a DINGIR.LÚ^{MEŠ} DINGIR.SAL^{MEŠ} ḪUR.SAG^{MEŠ}ÍD$^{ME.EŠ}$ KI.MIN
^{URU}Ḫa-la-ab ^{URU}Ḫur[56]-ma (40) DINGIR.LÚ$^{ME.EŠ}$ [DINGI]R.SAL$^{ME.EŠ}$ ḪUR.SAG$^{ME.EŠ}$ ÍD$^{ME.EŠ}$ KI.MIN

---

76 [*ŠA* ^{UR}]^{U}La-u-wa-an-a$^{!}$[57]-[ti-i]a ^{d}Ḫa-a-ši-ga-aš-na-wa-an-za ^{d}Mu-ul-li-ia-ra-aš
(41) *ŠA* ^{URU}L[a-u-w]a-an-a$^{!}$-ti-ia ^{d}Ḫa-a-ši-ga-aš-na-wa-an-za ^{d}Mu-ul-li-ia-ra-aš

77 [DINGIR.LÚ^{ME}]^{Š} DINGIR.SAL^{MEŠ} Ḫ[UR.S]AG^{MEŠ} ÍD^{MEŠ} *ŠA* ^{URU}La-u-wa-za[58]-**an**-ti-ia
(42) DINGIR.LÚ$^{ME.EŠ}$[DINGIR.SAL]$^{ME.EŠ}$Ḫ[UR.S]AG$^{ME.EŠ}$ ÍD$^{ME.EŠ}$ *ŠA* ^{URU}La-u-wa-za-ti-ia

---

78 [ ]x-x-[- **i]k**[59] \ ^{d}U ^{URU}U-da ^{d}Ḫé-bat LUGAL-ma-aš DINGIR.LÚ^{MEŠ}
(43) ^{d}U ^{URU}[-i]a-**ri-ka** \ ^{d}U ^{URU}U-da ^{d}Ḫé-bat LUGAL-ma-aš (44) DINGIR.LÚ$^{ME.EŠ}$

79 [DINGIR.SAL^{MEŠ} ḪUR.SAG^{MEŠ} Í]D$^{ME.EŠ}$ *ŠA* ^{URU}U-da
D[INGIR.SAL^{ME}]^{Š} ḪUR.SAG$^{ME.EŠ}$ ÍD$^{ME.EŠ}$ *ŠA* ^{URU}U-da

---

obv. II

1 [DINGIR-*L*]*IM*[60] ^{URU}⌜Pár-ša⌝ ták-na-aš ^{d}[UTU-uš DINGIR.LÚ]^{MEŠ} DINGIR.SAL^{MEŠ}
(45) DINGIR-*LIM* ^{URU}Pár-š[a *er*]*asure* ták-na-aš ^{d}UTU-uš (46) DINGIR.LÚ$^{ME.EŠ}$DINGIR.SAL$^{ME.EŠ}$

2 [ḪUR.SAG^{MEŠ}] Í[D]^{M}[^{EŠ}][61] *ŠA* ^{URU} Pár-ša
ḪUR.SAG$^{ME.EŠ}$ ÍD$^{ME.EŠ}$ *ŠA* ^{URU} Pár-ša

---

3 ^{d}U ^{URU}Ḫi-iš-ša-aš-[ḫa-]pa ^{d}U ^{URU}Ku-li-wi$_{5}$-iš-na DINGIR.LÚ^{MEŠ}
(47) ^{d}U ^{URU}Ḫi-iš-ša-aš-ḫa-pa ^{d}U ^{URU}Ku-li-wi$_{5}$-iš-na DINGIR.LÚ$^{ME.EŠ}$

4 DINGIR.SAL^{MEŠ} *ŠA* É.GAL ^{d}UTU-*ŠI*
DINGIR.SAL$^{ME.EŠ}$ *ŠA* É.GAL ^{d}UTU-*ŠI*

---

55 Ḫurma is inserted above the line. The horizontals of *ḫur* here and at the end of the line are hardly visible (but not *tin* as drawn in the autograph).

56 *Ḫur-* written like above.

57 Coll.: Both texts have a clear *-a-* instead of *-za-* (but cf. next line!). See Ch. V.2.4.

58 Coll.: *-za-* written over erasure.

59 Perhaps *Pitiy]arik(a)*.

60 Here joins KUB 30. 14 ii.

61 Here joins 1111/z ii (*ZA* 64, 242 f.).

5 ^{d}U ^{URU}**Ga**-ra-aḫ-na ^{d}LAMMA ^{URU}**Ga**-ra-aḫ-na $^{\text{DINGIR.SAL}}$A-la-a-aš [62] ^{d}U ^{URU}DU$_{6}$
(48) ^{d}U ^{URU}**Ka**-ra-aḫ-na ⸢^{d}⸣[LAMM]A ^{U}[^{RU}**K**]**a**-ra-aḫ-na $^{\text{DINGIR.SAL}}$A-la-a-aš[63] ^{d}U ^{URU}DU$_{6}$

6 DINGIR.LÚ^{MEŠ} DINGIR.SAL^{MEŠ} ḪUR.SAG$^{\text{ME.EŠ}}$ ÍD$^{\text{ME.EŠ}}$ *ŠA* ^{URU}Ka-ra-aḫ-na
(49) DINGIR.LÚ$^{\text{ME.EŠ}}$ DINGIR.SAL$^{\text{ME.EŠ}}$ ḪUR.SAG⸢$^{\text{ME.EŠ}}$ ÍD$^{\text{ME.EŠ}}$⸣ *ŠA* ^{URU}Ka-ra-aḫ-na

---

7 ^{d}U ^{URU}Šu-gaz-zi-ia ^{d}Zu-ú-li-ma-aš DINGIR.LÚ$^{\text{ME.EŠ}}$ DINGIR.SAL$^{\text{ME.EŠ}}$ *ŠA* ^{URU}Šu-gaz-zi-ia[64]
(50) ^{d}U ^{URU}Šu-gaz-zi-ia ^{d}Zu-ú-li-ma-aš DINGIR.LÚ$^{\text{ME.EŠ}}$ DINGIR.SAL$^{\text{ME.EŠ}}$ *ŠA* ^{URU}Šu-gaz-zi-ia

---

8 ^{d}U ^{URU}Li-iḫ-ši-n[a ^{d}]Ta-ši-mi-iš DINGIR.LÚ^{MEŠ} DINGIR.SAL^{MEŠ}
(51) ^{d}U[65] ^{URU}Li-iḫ-ši-na ^{d}Ta-ši-mi-iš DINGIR.LÚ$^{\text{ME.EŠ}}$DINGIR.SAL$^{\text{ME.EŠ}}$

9 [ḪUR.S]AG$^{\text{ME.EŠ}}$ Í[D$^{\text{ME.EŠ}}$ *Š*]*A* ^{URU}Li-iḫ-ši-na
ḪUR.SAG$^{\text{ME.EŠ}}$ ÍD$^{\text{ME.EŠ}}$ **KI.MIN**[66]

---

10 ^{d}Te-l[i- *ŠA* ^{UR}]^{U}Dur-mi-it-ta DINGIR.LÚ^{MEŠ} DINGIR.SAL^{MEŠ}
(52) ŠA ^{URU}Dur-mi-it-ta ^{d}Te-li-pí-nu-uš DINGIR.LÚ$^{\text{ME.EŠ}}$ DINGIR.SAL$^{\text{ME.EŠ}}$

11 ḪUR.SAG^{MEŠ} [ ] ^{URU}Dur-mi-it-ta
(53) ḪUR.SAG$^{\text{ME.EŠ}}$ ÍD$^{\text{ME.EŠ}}$ *ŠA* ^{URU}Dur-mi-it-ta

---

12 ^{d}U ^{URU}Ne-[*Š*] *A* ^{URU}Ne-na-aš-ša ^{d}Lu-ši-ti-iš
(54) ^{d}U ^{URU}Ne-na-aš-ša *ŠA* ^{URU}[N]e-na< ! > ^{d}Lu-ši-ti-iš

13 ^{ÍD}Ma-ra-aš-[ ]-aš DINGIR.LÚ^{MEŠ} DINGIR.SAL^{MEŠ}
(55) ^{ÍD}Ma-ra-aš-ša-an-ti-ia-aš DINGIR.LÚ$^{\text{ME.EŠ}}$ DINGIR.SAL$^{\text{ME.EŠ}}$
C 1' ^{ME}]^{Š} [DINGIR.]SA[L

14 ḪUR.SAG$^{\text{ME.EŠ}}$ ÍD$^{\text{ME.EŠ}}$ [*Š*]*A* ^{URU}Ne-na-aš-ša
ḪUR.SAG$^{\text{ME.EŠ}}$ ÍD$^{\text{ME.EŠ}}$ **KI.MIN**
C 2']-ša

---

15 ^{d}GAZ.BA.IA ^{URU}Ḫ[u- -n]a ^{d}U ^{URU}Ḫu-u-pí-iš-na-~~aš~~[67]
(56) ^{d}GAZ.BA.IA ***ŠA*** ^{URU}Ḫu-u-pí-iš-na ^{d}U ^{URU}Ḫu-u-pí-iš-na
C 3'] ^{d}U ^{URU}Ḫu-˻u˼-[

16 ^{d}ZA.BA$_{4}$.BA$_{4}$ ^{URU}Ḫu-u-pí-⸢iš⸣-[na ^{ḪUR}]^{SAG} Šar-la-**i**-mi-iš
(57) ^{d}ZA.BA$_{4}$.BA$_{4}$ **KI.MIN** $^{\text{ḪUR.SAG}}$Šar-la-**im**-mi-iš

---

62 In both texts $^{\text{DINGIR.SAL}}$*A-la-a-aš* is written over erasure.

63 Coll.: $^{\text{DINGIR.SAL}}$A-la-a-aš (*-a-* omitted in the autograph).

64 Coll.: *-ia* on the edge (omitted in the autograph).

65 ^{d}U is in the line (inserted above the line in the autograph).

66 KI.MIN written over erasure.

67 A final *-aš* was deleted, though traces of it are still visible.

C 4'] $^{\text{ḪUR.SAG}}$ Šar-la[-

17 DINGIR.LÚ^{MEŠ} DINGIR.SAL^{MEŠ} ḪUR.SAG$^{\text{ME.EŠ}}$ Í[D^{ME}]^{EŠ} *ŠA* ^{URU}Ḫu-u-piš-na
DINGIR.LÚ$^{\text{ME.EŠ}}$ DINGIR.SAL$^{\text{ME.EŠ}}$ ḪUR.SAG$^{\text{ME.EŠ}}$ ÍD$^{\text{ME.EŠ}}$ **KI.MIN**
C 5']⌈ÍD⌉^{MEŠ} *ŠA* ^{UR}[^{U}

---

18 ^{d}U ^{URU}Tu-wa-nu-wa ^{d}Ša-aḫ-ḫa-aš-š[a-ra-a]š ŠA ^{URU}Tu-wa-nu-wa
(58) ^{d}U ^{URU}Tu-wa-nu-wa ^{d}Ša-aḫ-ḫa-aš-ša-ra-aš ŠA ^{URU}Tu-**u**-wa-nu-wa
C 6' -ḫ]a-aš-ša-ra-aš < ! > ^{URU}T[u-

19 DINGIR.LÚ^{MEŠ} DINGIR.SAL^{MEŠ} ḪUR.SAG^{MEŠ} ÍD[^{MEŠ} *ŠA*] ^{URU}Tu-wa-nu-wa
(59) DINGIR.LÚ$^{\text{ME.EŠ}}$ DINGIR.SAL$^{\text{ME.EŠ}}$ ḪUR.SAG$^{\text{ME.EŠ}}$ ÍD$^{\text{ME.EŠ}}$ *ŠA* ^{URU}Tu-**u**-wa-nu-wa
C 7' ^{ME}]^{Š} ÍD^{MEŠ} *ŠA* ^{URU}[

---

20 ^{d}U ^{URU}Il-la-ia ^{d}ZA.BA$_4$.BA$_4$ *ŠA* ^{URU}[68] I[l-l]a-ia DINGIR.LÚ^{MEŠ}
(60) ^{d}U ^{URU}Il-la-ia ^{d}ZA.BA$_4$.BA$_4$ **KI.MIN** DINGIR.LÚ$^{\text{ME.EŠ}}$
C 8' ^{d}ZA.]BA$_4$.BA$_4$ *ŠA* ^{URU}[

21 DINGIR.SAL^{MEŠ} ḪUR.SAG^{MEŠ} ÍD^{MEŠ} *ŠA* ^{URU}Il-la-ia
DINGIR.SAL$^{\text{ME.EŠ}}$ (61) ḪUR.SAG$^{\text{ME.EŠ}}$ ÍD$^{\text{ME.EŠ}}$ *ŠA* ^{URU}Il-la-ia
C 9' ^{M}]^{EŠ} ÍD^{MEŠ} *ŠA* ^{URU}[

---

22 *ŠA* ^{URU}Šu-wa-an-za-na ^{d}Šu-wa-an-zi-pa-aš DINGIR.LÚ^{MEŠ} DINGIR.SAL^{MEŠ}
(62) *ŠA* ^{URU}Šu-wa-an-za-na ^{d}Šu-wa-an-zi-pa-aš DINGIR.LÚ$^{\text{ME.EŠ}}$ DINGIR.SAL$^{\text{ME.EŠ}}$
C 10' ^{d}]Šu-wa-an-zi-pa-aš DI[NGIR.LÚ^{MEŠ}

23 ḪUR.SAG$^{\text{ME.EŠ}}$ ÍD^{MEŠ} *ŠA* ^{URU}Šu-wa-an-za-na
(63) ḪUR.SAG$^{\text{ME.EŠ}}$ ÍD$^{\text{ME.EŠ}}$ *ŠA* ^{URU}Šu-wa-an-**zi-pa**
C 11']Šu-wa-an-za-na

---

24 ^{d}ZA.BA$_4$.BA$_4$ ^{URU}Ar-zi-ia DINGIR.LÚ^{MEŠ} DINGIR.SAL^{MEŠ}
(64) ^{d}ZA.BA$_4$.BA$_4$ ^{URU}Ar-zi-ia DINGIR.LÚ$^{\text{ME.EŠ}}$ DINGIR.SAL$^{\text{ME.EŠ}}$

25 ḪUR.SAG^{MEŠ} ÍD^{MEŠ} *ŠA* ^{URU}Ar-zi-ia
(65) ḪUR.SAG$^{\text{ME.EŠ}}$ ÍD$^{\text{ME.EŠ}}$ *ŠA* ^{URU}Ar-zi-ia

---

26 ^{d}U ^{URU}Ḫur-ni-ia *ŠA* ^{URU}Ḫur-ni-ia LUGAL-uš DINGIR-***LUM***$^{!}$-uš$^{!}$(?)[69] DINGIR.LÚ^{MEŠ}
(66) ^{d}U ^{URU}Ḫur-ni-ia *ŠA* ^{URU}Ḫur-ni-ia LUGAL-uš DINGIR-***LIM***$^{!}$-uš$^{!}$(?) (67) DINGIR.LÚ$^{\text{ME.EŠ}}$

[68] Coll.: URU (not *ma*) as in the autograph.

[69] In both texts the sign(s) following DINGIR are written over erasure and are not clear. In *B* the sign which resembles IGI+URUDU must probably be dissolved into -*LIM*-uš. Perhaps *A* also first wrote DINGIR-*LIM*-uš, but then corrected it into DINGIR-*LUM*-uš (see Commentary). In any case, the deity in question is certainly not ^{d}UTU , as suggested (with question mark) in J. Garstang & O. R. Gurney, *Geography*, 118 with note 1.

27 DINGIR.SAL^{MEŠ} ḪUR.SAG^{MEŠ} ÍD^{MEŠ} *ŠA* ^{URU}Ḫur-ni-ia
DINGIR.SAL$^{\text{ME.EŠ}}$ ḪUR.SAG$^{\text{ME.EŠ}}$ ÍD$^{\text{ME.EŠ}}$ *ŠA* ^{URU}Ḫur-ni-ia

---

28 ^{d}U ^{URU}Za-ar-wi$_5$-ša ^{d}Na-wa-ti-ia-la-aš *Š[A* ^{URU}Za-ar]-wi$_5$-ša[70]
(68) ^{d}U ^{URU}Za-ar-wi$_5$-ša ^{d}Na-wa-ti-ia-la-aš *ŠA* ^{URU}Za-ar-wi$_5$-ša

29 DINGIR.LÚ^{MEŠ} DINGIR.SAL^{MEŠ} ḪUR.SAG$^{\text{ME.EŠ}}$ ÍD$^{\text{ME.EŠ}}$ *Š[A* ^{U}]^{RU}[ ]
(69) DINGIR.LÚ$^{\text{ME.EŠ}}$ DINGIR.SAL$^{\text{ME.EŠ}}$ ḪUR.SAG$^{\text{ME.EŠ}}$ ÍD$^{\text{ME.EŠ}}$ *ŠA* **<<*ŠA*>>**^{URU}Za-ar-wi$_5$-ša

---

30 DINGIR.MAḪ ^{URU}Ša-aḫ-ḫa-ni-ia ^{d}U ^{URU}Ša-⸢aḫ-ḫa⸣-[ni-ia]
(70) DINGIR.MAḪ ^{URU}Ša-aḫ-ḫa-ni-ia ^{d}U ^{URU}Ša-aḫ-ḫa-ni-ia (71) DINGIR.LÚ$^{\text{ME.EŠ}}$

31 DINGIR.SAL^{MEŠ} ḪUR.SAG^{MEŠ} ÍD^{MEŠ} *ŠA* ^{URU}Ša-a[ḫ-ḫa-ni-ia]
DINGIR.SAL$^{\text{ME.EŠ}}$ ḪUR.SAG$^{\text{ME.EŠ}}$ ÍD$^{\text{ME.EŠ}}$ **KI.MIN**

---

32 ^{d}U ^{URU}Pa-aḫ-ti-ma ^{d}U ^{URU}Ša-aḫ-ḫu-w[i$_5$-ia]
(iii 1) ^{d}U ^{URU}Pa-aḫ[-]Ša-aḫ-ḫu-wi$_5$-ia

33 ^{d}UTU ^{URU}Ma-li-ta-aš-ku-ri- [-ia]
33 ^{d}UTU ^{URU}Ma-[li- -k]u-ri-ia

---

34 ^{d}Wa-aš-ḫa-li-ia-aš *ŠA* ^{URU}Ḫar-zi-ú-na ^{d}[U ^{URU}Ḫar-zi-ú-na]
(3) ^{d}Wa-aš-ḫa-li-ia[-aš *Š]A* ^{URU}Ḫar-zi-ú-na ^{d}U **KI.MIN**

35 DINGIR.LÚ^{MEŠ} DINGIR.SAL^{MEŠ} ḪUR.SAG$^{\text{ME.EŠ}}$ ÍD^{MEŠ} *ŠA* ^{URU}[Ḫar-z]i-⸢ú⸣-⸢na⸣
(4) DINGIR.LÚ$^{\text{ME.EŠ}}$ DINGIR.SAL$^{\text{ME.EŠ}}$ ḪU[R.SA]G$^{\text{ME.EŠ}}$ ÍD$^{\text{ME.EŠ}}$ *ŠA* ^{URU}Ḫar-zi-ú-na

---

36 *ŠA* ^{URU}Šal-la-pa ^{d}Za-an-du-za EN-aš ^{d}U ^{UR}[^{U}Šal-la-pa] DINGIR.LÚ^{MEŠ}
(5) *ŠA* ^{URU}Šal-la-pa ^{d}Za-⸢an⸣-du-za EN-aš ^{d}U ^{URU}Šal-la-pa (6) DINGIR.LÚ$^{\text{ME.EŠ}}$

37 DINGIR.SAL^{MEŠ} ḪUR.SAG^{MEŠ} ÍD^{MEŠ} *ŠA* ^{URU}Šal-la-p[a]
DINGIR.SAL$^{\text{ME.EŠ}}$ ḪUR.S[A]G$^{\text{ME.EŠ}}$ ÍD$^{\text{ME.EŠ}}$ *ŠA* ^{URU}Šal-la-pa

---

38 ^{d}U ^{URU}U-uš-ša ^{d}U ^{URU}Pár-aš-ḫu-un-ta $^{\text{ḪUR.SAG}}$Ḫu-wa-la[71]-nu-wa-an-da
(7) ^{d}U ^{URU}U-uš-ša ^{d}U ^{URU}P[ár-a]š-ḫu-un-ta $^{\text{ḪUR.SAG}}$Ḫu-wa-la-nu-wa-an-da

39 ^{ÍD}Ḫu-**u**-la-ia DINGIR.LÚ^{MEŠ} DINGIR.SAL^{MEŠ} ḪUR.SAG^{MEŠ} ÍD^{MEŠ}
39 ^{ÍD}Ḫu-la-ia DINGIR.LÚ^{M}[^{EŠ} D]INGIR.SAL$^{\text{ME.EŠ}}$ ḪUR.SAG$^{\text{ME.EŠ}}$ ÍD$^{\text{ME.EŠ}}$

40 *ŠA* KUR *ŠAP-LI-* *TI*
ŠA KUR *ŠAP* < ! >

---

[70] Coll.: The last signs, written on the edge, are omitted in the autograph.

[71] Coll.: In both texts the sign is clearly a *-la-*. See Commentary. The last two signs are omitted in the autograph.

41 ^{d}IŠTAR ^{URU}Wa-šu-⌞du-wa⌟-an-da ^{d}Ḫé-bat ^{URU}Wa-šu-du-wa-an-da
(9) ^{d}IŠTAR ^{URU}Wa-šu-du-wa-an[-da] ^{d}Ḫé-bat ^{URU}Wa-šu-du-wa-an-da

42 ^{d}IŠTA[R ^{URU} I]n-nu-wi$_5$- ta
(10) ^{d}IŠTAR ^{URU}In-nu-wi$_5$- ta

---

43 ^{d}U ^{URU}A-la-az-ḫ[a-na] ^{d}Te-li-pí-nu-**uš** *ŠA* ^{URU}Ḫa-**an**-ḫa-na
(11) ^{d}U ^{URU}A-la-az-ḫa-na *ŠA* ^{URU}Ḫa-ḫa-na ^{d}Te-li-pí-nu

44 ^{d}Am-ma-ma-aš ŠA ^{URU}Ḫa-ḫa-na $^{\text{ḪUR.SAG}}$Ta-ku-úr-ga ~~*ŠA* ^{URU}Ḫa-ḫa-na~~
(12) *ŠA* ^{URU}Ḫa-ḫa-na ^{d}Am-ma-ma-aš DINGIR.LÚ^{MEŠ} DINGIR.SAL$^{\text{ME.EŠ}}$

45 DINGIR.LÚ^{MEŠ} < ! > SAL^{MEŠ} ḪUR.SAG^{MEŠ} ÍD^{MEŠ} *ŠA* ^{URU}Ḫa-ḫa-na
(13) *ŠA* ^{URU}Ḫa-ḫa-na $^{\text{ḪUR.SAG}}$Ta-ku-úr-ga ḪUR.SAG$^{\text{ME.EŠ}}$ ÍD$^{\text{ME.EŠ}}$ *ŠA* ^{URU}Ḫa-ḫa-na

---

46 *ŠA* ^{URU}Ta-˹wi˺$_5$-ni-ia ^{d}Te-li-pí-nu-uš ^{d}Ka-taḫ-ḫa-**aš**
(14) *ŠA* ^{URU}Ta-wi$_5$-ni-ia ^{d}Te-li-pí-nu-uš ^{d}Ka-taḫ-ḫa

47 DINGIR.LÚ^{MEŠ} DINGIR.SAL^{MEŠ} ḪUR.SAG$^{\text{ME.EŠ}}$ ÍD$^{\text{ME.EŠ}}$ *ŠA* ^{URU}Ta-wi$_5$-ni-ia
(15) DINGIR.LÚ$^{\text{ME.EŠ}}$ DINGIR.SAL$^{\text{ME.EŠ}}$ ḪUR.SAG$^{\text{ME.EŠ}}$ ÍD$^{\text{ME.EŠ}}$ *ŠA* ^{URU}Ta-wi$_5$-ni-ia

---

48 ^{d}UTU ^{URU}Wa-aš-ḫa-ni-ia DINGIR.LÚ^{MEŠ} DINGIR.SAL^{MEŠ} ḪUR.SAG$^{\text{ME.EŠ}}$
(16) ^{d}UTU ***ŠA*** ^{URU}Wa-aš-ḫa-ni-ia DINGIR.LÚ[$^{\text{ME.EŠ}}$] DINGIR.SAL$^{\text{ME.EŠ}}$ (17) ḪUR.SAG$^{\text{ME.EŠ}}$

49 ÍD$^{\text{ME.EŠ}}$ *ŠA* **KUR** ^{URU} Wa-aš-ḫa-ni- ia
ÍD$^{\text{ME.EŠ}}$ *ŠA* ^{URU} Wa-aš-ḫ[a]-ni-ia

---

50 EN ^{URU}La-a-an-**ta** DINGIR.LÚ^{MEŠ} DINGIR.SAL^{MEŠ} ḪUR.SAG^{MEŠ} ÍD^{MEŠ}
(18) EN ^{URU}La-a-an-**da** DINGIR.LÚ$^{\text{ME.EŠ}}$ DINGIR.SAL$^{\text{ME.EŠ}}$ ḪUR.SAG$^{\text{ME.EŠ}}$ ÍD$^{\text{ME.EŠ}}$

51 *ŠA* ^{URU}La-a-an-**ta** DINGIR.LÚ^{MEŠ} DINGIR.SAL^{MEŠ} ḪUR.SAG^{MEŠ} ÍD^{MEŠ} *ŠA* ^{URU}Ḫa-at-ti-na
(19) *ŠA* ^{URU}La-a-an-**da** DINGIR.LÚ$^{\text{ME.EŠ}}$ DINGIR.SAL$^{\text{ME.EŠ}}$ ḪUR.SAG$^{\text{ME.EŠ}}$ ÍD$^{\text{ME.EŠ}}$ *ŠA* ^{URU}Ḫa-at-ti-na

---

52 DINGIR.LÚ^{MEŠ} DINGIR.SAL^{MEŠ} ḪUR.SAG^{MEŠ} ÍD^{MEŠ} *ŠA* ^{URU}Ḫa-ar-pí-ša
(20) DINGIR.LÚ$^{\text{ME.EŠ}}$ DINGIR.SAL$^{\text{ME.EŠ}}$ ḪUR.SAG$^{\text{ME.EŠ}}$ ÍD$^{\text{ME.EŠ}}$ *ŠA* [^{UR}]^{U}Ḫa-ar-⌞pí⌟-ša

53 *ŠA* ^{URU}Ka-li-mu-na ^{d}Kar-ma-ḫi-iš DINGIR.LÚ^{MEŠ} DINGIR.SAL^{MEŠ}
(21) *ŠA* ^{URU}Ka-li-mu-na ^{d}Kar-ma-ḫi-iš DINGIR.LÚ$^{\text{ME.EŠ}}$ DINGIR.SAL^{M}[^{EŠ}]

54 ḪUR.SAG$^{\text{ME.EŠ}}$ ÍD$^{\text{ME.EŠ}}$ *ŠA* ^{URU}Ka-li-mu-na
(22) ḪUR.SAG$^{\text{ME.EŠ}}$ ÍD$^{\text{ME.EŠ}}$ *ŠA* ^{URU}Ka-li-mu-na

--- B om.

55 DINGIR.LÚ^{MEŠ} DINGIR.SAL^{MEŠ} ḪUR.SAG^{MEŠ} ÍD^{MEŠ} *ŠA* ^{URU}Ḫa-ak-pí-iš-ša
DINGIR.LÚ$^{\text{ME.EŠ}}$ DINGIR.SAL$^{\text{ME.EŠ}}$ (23) ḪUR.SAG$^{\text{ME.EŠ}}$ ÍD$^{\text{ME.EŠ}}$ *ŠA* ^{URU}Ḫa-ak-pí-iš-ša

---

56 ^{d}LAMMA.LÍL ^{d}LAMMA.LUGAL DINGIR.LÚ^{MEŠ} DINGIR.SAL^{MEŠ} *ŠA* ***A-BI A-BI*** ^{d}UTU-*ŠI*
(24) ^{d}LAMMA.LÍL ^{d}LAMMA.LUGAL DINGIR.LÚ$^{ME.EŠ}$ DINGIR.SAL$^{ME.EŠ}$ *ŠA* ***A-BI*** ^{d}UTU-*ŠI*

B om.

57 DINGIR.LÚ^{MEŠ} DINGIR.SAL^{MEŠ} *ŠA* ***A-BI*** ^{d}UTU-*ŠI*
(25) DINGIR.LÚ$^{ME.EŠ}$ DINGIR.SAL$^{ME.EŠ}$ *ŠA* ~~*A-BI*~~ ***A-BI*** ^{d}UTU-*ŠI*

B om.

58 DINGIR.LÚ^{MEŠ} DINGIR.SAL^{MEŠ} *ŠA* AMA.AMA ^{d}UTU-*ŠI*
DINGIR.LÚ$^{ME.EŠ}$ DINGIR.SAL$^{ME.EŠ}$ (26) *ŠA* AMA.AMA ^{d}UTU-*ŠI*

B om.

59 DINGIR.LÚ^{MEŠ} DINGIR.SAL^{MEŠ} *ŠA* É ^{URU}Gaz-zi-ma-ra
DINGIR.LÚ$^{ME.EŠ}$ DINGIR.SAL$^{ME.EŠ}$ *ŠA* É ^{URU}Gaz-zi-ma-ra

B om.

60 *ŠA* ^{URU}An-ku-wa ^{d}Ḫa-taḫ-ḫa-aš ^{d}U *ZU-UN-NI* ^{d}IŠTAR.LÍL (27)
erasure *ŠA* ^{URU}An-ku-wa ^{d}Ḫa-taḫ-ḫa-aš[72] ^{d}U *ZU-UN-NI* ^{d}IŠTAR.LÍL

61 DINGIR.LÚ^{MEŠ} < ! > SAL^{MEŠ} ḪUR.SAG$^{ME.EŠ}$ ÍD$^{ME.EŠ}$ *ŠA* ^{URU}An-ku-wa
(28) DINGIR.LÚ$^{ME.EŠ}$ DINGIR..SAL$^{ME.EŠ}$ ḪUR.SAG$^{ME.EŠ}$ ÍD$^{ME.EŠ}$ *ŠA* ^{URU}An-ku-wa

---

62 *ŠA* ^{URU}Ne-ni-ša-ku-wa ^{d}Pí-ir-wa-aš *ŠA* ^{URU}Du-ru-**wa**-du-ru-wa
(29) *ŠA* ^{URU}Ne-ni-ša-**an**-ku-wa ^{d}Pí-ir-wa-aš *ŠA* ^{URU}Du-ru-**ud**-du-ru-wa

63 ^{d}Pí-ir-wa-**aš** *ŠA* ^{URU}**Ik-šu-na** ^{d}**Pí-ir-wa-aš**
(30) ^{d}Pí-ir-wa *ŠA* ^{URU}**Ik-šu-nu-wa** \

B om.

64 ^{d}IŠTAR ^{URU}Šu-ul-la-ma ^{d}U ^{URU}Ḫa-at-ra-a DINGIR.LÚ^{MEŠ}
^{d}IŠTAR ^{URU}Šu-ul-la-ma (31) ^{d}U ^{URU}Ḫa-at-ra-a DINGIR.LÚ$^{ME.EŠ}$

65 DINGIR.SAL^{MEŠ} ḪUR.SAG^{MEŠ} ÍD^{MEŠ} *ŠA* KUR ^{URU}I-šu-wa [ ]
DINGIR.SAL$^{ME.EŠ}$ ḪUR.SAG$^{ME.EŠ}$ ÍD$^{ME.EŠ}$ *ŠA* KUR ^{URU}I-šu-wa

---

66 ^{d}U ^{URU}Te-ga-ra-ma DINGIR.LÚ^{MEŠ} DINGIR.SAL^{MEŠ} ḪUR.SAG$^{ME.EŠ}$
(32) ^{d}U ^{URU}Te-ga-ra-ma DINGIR.LÚ$^{ME.EŠ}$ DINGIR.SAL$^{ME.EŠ}$ ḪUR.SAG$^{ME.EŠ}$

67 ÍD$^{ME.EŠ}$ *ŠA* KUR ^{URU}Te-ga-ra-ma
ÍD$^{ME.EŠ}$ (33) *ŠA* KUR ^{URU}Te-ga-ra-ma \

B om.

68 SAL.LUGAL ^{URU}Pa-li-ia
SAL.LUGAL ^{URU}Pa-li-ia

---

[72] Coll.: ^{d}*Ḫa-taḫ-ḫa-aš* inserted above the line; it was probably first written before *ŠA* ^{URU}*An-ku-wa* and was then erased and added after Ankuwa.

69 ^{d}U ^{URU}Tu-u-pa-**az**-zi-ia DINGIR.LÚ^{MEŠ} DINGIR.SAL ^{M}[^{EŠ}]
(34) ^{d}U ^{URU}Tu-u-**up**-pa-zi-ia DINGIR.LÚ$^{ME.EŠ}$ DINGIR.SAL$^{ME.EŠ}$ ḪUR.SAG$^{ME.EŠ}$

70 ÍD$^{ME.EŠ}$ *ŠA* ^{URU}Tu-u-pa-**az**-zi-ia [ ]
ÍD$^{ME.EŠ}$ (35) *ŠA* **KUR** ^{URU}Tu-u-**up**-pa-zi-ia

---

71 *ŠA* ^{URU}Ka-ri-**u**-na ^{d}Ka-ru-na-aš [ ]
(36) *ŠA* ^{URU}Ka-ri-**ú**-na ^{d}Ka-ru-na-aš \

--- B om.

72 ^{d}U mi-ia-an-na-aš ^{d}U ^{d}Ḫé-bat ⸤^{URU}Ap⸥-z[i-
^{d}U[73] mi-ia-an-na-aš (37) ^{d}U ^{d}Ḫé-bat[74] ^{URU}Ap-zi-iš-na

73 DINGIR.LÚ^{MEŠ} DINGIR.SAL^{MEŠ} *ŠA* ^{URU}**Ap**-zi[-
DINGIR.LÚ$^{ME.EŠ}$ DINGIR.SAL$^{ME.EŠ}$ (38) *ŠA* ^{URU}**A-pa**-zi-iš-na \

--- B om.

rev. III

1 ⸢^{d}LAMMA⸣ ^{URU}Ka-la-aš-mi-it-ta
^{d}LAMMA ^{URU}Ka-la-aš-mi-it-ta

---

2 *ŠA* ^{URU}Ta-pí-iq-**qa** ^{d}Ta-mi-ši-ia-aš DINGIR.LÚ^{MEŠ} DINGIR.[SAL^{MEŠ}]
(39) *ŠA* ^{URU}Ta-pí-iq-**aš**$^{!}$ ^{d}Ta-mi-**iš**-ši-ia-aš DINGIR.LÚ$^{ME.EŠ}$ DINGIR..SAL$^{ME.EŠ}$

3 ḪUR.SAG^{MEŠ} ÍD$^{ME.EŠ}$ *ŠA* ^{URU}Ta-pí-iq-qa
(40) ḪUR.SAG$^{ME.EŠ}$ ÍD$^{ME.EŠ}$ *ŠA* ^{URU}Ta-pí-iq-qa

---

4 ^{d}U *ŠA* É ^{SAL}Ta-wa-an-na-an-na ^{d}U ḫu-la-aš-ša-aš-ši-iš [ ]
(41) ^{d}U *ŠA* É ^{SAL}Ta-wa-an-na-an-na ^{d}U ḫu-la-aš-ša-aš-ši-iš (42) DINGIR.LÚ$^{ME.EŠ}$

5 DINGIR.SAL^{MEŠ} *ŠA* LUGAL-***RI*** *Ù* *ŠA* SAL.LUGAL-***TI*** ku-i-e-eš da-ra-an[-te-eš]
DINGIR.SAL$^{ME.EŠ}$ *ŠA* LUGAL *Ù* *ŠA* SAL.LUGAL-***UT-TI*** ku-i-e-eš (43) da-ra-an-te-eš

6 ku-i-e-eš *Ú-UL* da-ra-an-te-eš ku-**e**-ta-aš *A-NA* É^{MEŠ} DINGIR^{MEŠ}
erasure ku-i-e-eš ⸤*Ú-UL*⸥ da-ra-an-te-eš (44) [k]u-**i**-ta-aš *A-NA* **É**$^{EŠ!}$[ ]

7 LUGAL SAL.LUGAL pé-ra-an EGIR-pa i-ia-an-ta-ri ku-e-**ta**-ša-a[t]
] SAL.LUGAL (45) [pé-r]a-an EGIR-pa ⸤i⸥[- -r]i ku-e-**da**-ša-at

8 *A-NA* É^{MEŠ} DINGIR^{MEŠ} pé-ra-an EGIR-pa *Ú-UL* i-ia-an-ta-ri
(46) [ ] ⸤É⸥$^{ME.EŠ}$ ⸤DINGIR⸥^{M}[^{EŠ}] ⸤*Ú-UL*⸥ i-ia-an-ta-ri

9 na-aš LÚ^{MEŠ} SANGA ši-ip-pa-an-za-kán-zi DINGIR.LÚ^{MEŠ} DINGIR.SAL^{MEŠ}
(47) [LÚ$^{ME.EŠ}$] SANGA ši-ip-pa-an-za-kán-zi DINGIR.LÚ$^{ME.EŠ}$ [DINGIR.SAL^{ME}]^{Š}

[73] Coll.: U omitted in the autograph.

[74] *-bat* inserted above the line.

10 **[A]N-aš** **GE$_6$-iš** **KI-aš** ne-pí-iš te-kán al-pu-uš **IM$^{ḪI.A}$-uš**
(48) **[ne-p]í-aš** **da-an-ku-ia-aš** **da-ga-zi-pa-aš** ne[-p]í-[i]š (49) [te-k]án al-pu-uš **ḫu-u-wa-an-te-eš**

11 [t]e-et-ḫi-ma-aš wa-an-te-wa-an-te-ma-aš tu-li-ia-aš **pé-e-da-aš**
te-et-ḫi-ma-aš (50) [wa-a]n-te-wa-an-te-ma-aš *eras.* tu-li-ia-aš[75] **pé-te**[76]

12 DIN[G]IR^{MEŠ} ku-e-da-ni pé-**di** tu-li-ia ti-iš-kán-zi
DINGIR$^{ME.EŠ}$ ku-**i**-e-da-ni (51) [p]é-**te**[79] tu-**u**-li-ia ti-iš-kán-zi

---

13 ^{d}[UT]U *ŠA-ME-E* EN-*IA* *ŠA* DUMU.LÚ.U$_{19}$.LU ^{LÚ}**SIPA-aš** ša-ra-a-kán
(52) ^{d}UTU *ŠA-ME-E* EN-*IA* *ŠA* DUMU.LÚ.U$_{19}$.LU ***-UT-TI*** $^{LÚ?}$**ú-e-eš-ta-ra-aš** (53) ša-ra-a-kán

14 ú-w[a-š]i **ne-pí-ša-aš** ^{d}UTU-uš a-ru-na-az nu-uš-ša-an ne-pí-ši
ú-wa-ši **ne-pí-aš** ^{d}UTU-uš a-ru-na-az (54) nu-uš-ša-an ne-pí-ši

15 ti-[ia]-ši ^{d}UTU *ŠA-ME-E* EN-*IA* *ŠA* DUMU.LÚ.U$_{19}$.LU-***TI*** UR.GI$_7$-**maš**$^{!}$[77]
ti-ia-ši ^{d}UTU *ŠA-ME-E* (55) EN-*IA* *ŠA*[78] DUMU.LÚ.U$_{19}$.LU-***UT-TI*** UR.GI$_7$-aš

16 ŠAḪ-aš gi-im-ra-aš-**ša** ḫu-it-**na**-aš ***DI-NAM*** **UD-ti-li**
ŠAḪ-aš gi-im-ra-aš ***DI*** **-šar** (56) ḫu-it-**ta**-aš **UD^{KAM}-li**

17 zi-ik[79] ^{d} UTU-uš ḫa-an-**ne**-iš-ki- ši
zi-ik ^{d} UTU-uš ḫa-an-**ni**-iš-ki-ši

---
[80]

18 nu ka-a-ša am-mu-uk ^{M}NIR.GÁL LUGAL-uš ^{LÚ}SANGA *ŠA* ^{d}UTU ^{URU}**TÚL-na**
(57) nu ka-a-ša am-mu-uk ^{M}NIR.GÁL LUGAL-uš ^{LÚ}SANGA (58) *ŠA*[81] ^{d}UTU ^{URU}**A-ri-in-na**

19 *Ù* DINGIR$^{ME.EŠ}$ ḫu-u-ma-an-da-aš **ne-pí-ša-aš** ^{d}UTU-i ar-ku-iš-ki-mi
Ù ***ŠA*** DINGIR$^{ME.EŠ}$ ḫu-u-ma-an-da-aš (59) **ne-pí-aš** ^{d}UTU-i ar-ku-**ú-i**-iš-ki-mi

20 nu **ne-pí-ša-aš** ^{d}UTU-uš EN-*IA* ke-e-da-ni **UD^{KAM}-ti**
nu **ne-pí-aš** ^{d}UTU-uš (60) EN-*IA* ke-e-da-ni **UD-ti**

21 DINGIR$^{ME.EŠ}$ a-ra-a-i nu DINGIR^{MEŠ} ku-i-e-eš ke-**e**-da-ni UD-ti
DINGIR$^{ME.EŠ}$ a-ra-a-i nu DINGIR$^{ME.EŠ}$[82] ku-i-e-eš (61) **ku-u-uš** ki-**i**-da-ni UD-ti

---

75 *-aš* inserted above the line.

76 Coll.: *pí-te*(*di*$_{12}$) in both lines, and not *-di* as drawn in the autograph. The *te* is identical to those in [*wa-a*]*n-te-wa-an-te-ma-aš* in l. 50.

77 Probably a graphic error for *aš* (see Commentary). In *B* *-aš* is written over erasure.

78 Inserted above the line.

79 Coll.: in the autograph the two signs have been inverted.

80 Coll.: The division lines after *B* iii 56 and 61 were added only after the entire paragraph *B* iii 52-64 (= *A* iii 13-24) was already written. In both places it is a faint line which runs through part of the column only. The new paragraph-dividers are also marked with a horizontal wedge protruding into the column-divider (slightly below the paragraph-divider itself). See Ch. V.4.4.6.

81 Added on the column divider.

82 Written over erasure.

22 ku-e-da-ni ar-ku-**u**-e-eš-ni *IŠ-TU* EME-*IA* ḫal-zi-iḫ-ḫu-un
ku-**i**-e-da-ni ar-ku-e-eš-ni \ \[83] (62) *IŠ-TU* EME-*IA* ḫal-zi-iḫ-ḫu-**u**-un

---

23 na-aš **ne-pí-ša-aš** ^{d}UTU-uš ne-pí-ša-az **KI-az** ḪUR.SAG$^{\text{ME.EŠ}}$-az
na-aš **ne-pí-aš** ^{d}UTU-uš (63) ne-pí-ša-az **ták-na-az** ḪUR.SAG$^{\text{ME.EŠ}}$-az

24 ÍD$^{\text{ME.EŠ}}$-az *IŠ-TU* É^{MEŠ} **DINGIR^{MEŠ}**-*ŠU-NU* ^{GIŠ}GU.ZA^{MEŠ}-*ŠU-NU* ḫal-za-a-i
ÍD$^{\text{ME.EŠ}}$-az (64) *IŠ-TU* É$^{\text{ME.EŠ}}$ **DINGIR$^{\textit{LIM}}$**-*ŠU-NU* ^{GIŠ} GU.ZA$^{\text{ME.EŠ}}$-*ŠU-NU* ḫal-za-a-i

---

25 **EGIR-*ŠÚ*-ma** LUGAL-uš ki-iš-ša-an me-ma-i ^{d}U pí-ḫa-aš-ša-aš-ši-iš
(65) **EGIR-an-da** LUGAL-uš ki-iš-ša-an me-ma-i ^{d}U pí-ḫa-aš-ša-aš-ši-iš

26 EN-*IA* DUMU.LÚ.U$_{19}$.LU-aš e-šu-un *A-BU-IA*-ma *A-NA* ^{d}UTU ^{URU}**TÚL-na**
(66) EN-*IA* DUMU.LÚ.U$_{19}$.LU-aš e-šu-un *A-BU-IA*-ma (67) *A-NA* ^{d}UTU ^{URU}**A-ri-in-na**

27 *Ù* *A-NA* DINGIR^{MEŠ} ḫu-u-ma-**an**-da-aš ^{LÚ}SANGA e-e[š]-ta
Ù *A-NA* DINGIR$^{\text{ME.EŠ}}$ ḫu-u-ma-da-aš (68) ^{LÚ}SANGA e-eš-ta

28 nu-mu-za *A-BU-IA* **DÙ-at** ^{d}U pí-ḫa-aš-ša-aš-ši-iš-ma-mu an-na-az
nu-mu-za *A-BU-IA* **i-ia-at** (69) ^{d}U pí-ḫa-aš-ša-aš-ši-iš-ma-mu an-na-az

29 da-a-aš nu-mu šal-la-nu-ut nu-mu *A-NA* ^{d}UTU ^{URU} **TÚL-na**
da-a-aš (70) nu-mu šal-la-nu-ut nu-mu *A-NA* ^{d}UTU ^{URU}**A-ri-in-na**

30 ***Ù*** *A-NA* DINGIR^{MEŠ} ḫu-u-ma-an-da-aš ^{LÚ}SANGA i-ia-at
(71) *A-NA* DINGIR$^{\text{ME.EŠ}}$ ḫu-u-ma-an-da-aš ^{LÚ}SANGA i-ia-at

31 *A-NA* KUR ^{URU}Ḫa-at-ti-ma-mu LUGAL-iz-na-an-ni da-a-iš
(72) *A-NA* KUR ^{URU}**Ḫa-< ! >ti**-ma-mu LUGAL-iz-na-an-ni da-a-iš

---

32 [k]i-nu-na am-mu-uk ^{M}NIR.GÁL LUGAL-uš tu-e-da-az
(iv 1)]-⸢az⸣

33 [*IŠ*-]*TU* ^{d}U pí-ḫa-aš-ša-aš-ši šal-la-nu-wa-an-za ar-ku-ú-e-eš-ki-mi
(2) -]⸢e-eš-ki⸣-mi

34 [nu *I*]*Š-TU* EME-*IA* ku-i-e-eš DINGIR^{MEŠ} ḫal-zi-iḫ-ḫu-un
(3) [

35 n[u *A-N*]*A* DINGIR^{MEŠ} ar-ku-wa-nu-un nu-mu-kán DINGIR^{MEŠ}-aš ú-wa-ia-nu-ut da-pí-aš
n]u *A-NA* DINGIR$^{\text{ME.EŠ}}$ar-ku-wa-nu-un (4) nu-mu-kán [DINGIR$^{\text{ME.EŠ}}$-aš d]a$^{?}$-[p]í$^{?}$-aš ú-wa-ia-nu-ut

36 a[m-me-e]l-ma *ŠA* ^{M}NIR.GÁL *ÌR-KA* *A-*[*W*]*A-TE*^{MEŠ} *ŠA* EME-*IA*
am-me-el-ma (5) *ŠA* ^{M}NIR.GÁL ⸢*ÌR-KA*⸣ *A-WA-TE*$^{\text{ME.EŠ}}$ *ŠA* EME-*IA*

---

[83] See n. 80.

37 [d]a-[a n]a-[a]t-kán ***A-NA*** *PA-NI* DINGIR^{MEŠ} ⸤šu⸥-un-ni nu-za *A-NA* DINGIR^{MEŠ}
da-a (6) na-at-kán *PA-NI* DINGIR$^{\text{ME.EŠ}}$ šu-un-ni nu-za *A-NA* DINGIR$^{\text{ME.EŠ}}$

38 [ku-e *A-WA-TE*^{MEŠ}] ⸤ar-ku-wa-ar⸥ ⸤i-ia-mi⸥
ku-e (7) *A-WA-TE*$^{\text{ME.EŠ}}$ ar-ku-wa-ar i-ia-mi

39 n[a-at-mu EGIR]-⸢pa le-e⸣ ⸢wa-aḫ-nu⸣-wa-an-zi
na-at-mu EGIR-pa le-e (8) wa-aḫ-nu-wa-an-zi[84]

---

40 MUŠEN-⸤**iš**?⸥ [85] ^{GIŠ}⸢tap-tap⸣-pa-an EGIR-pa e-ep-zi na-aš **TI-zi** [86]
(9) *eras.* MUŠEN-**za** *eras.* ^{GIŠ}tap-tap-pa-an EGIR-pa e-ep-zi (10) na-aš **ḫu-i-iš-zi** *eras.*

41 **ú-u[k-ma?-z]a-[ká]n**[87] ^{d}U pí-ḫa-aš-ša-aš-ši-in EN-*IA* EGIR-pa *AṢ-BAT*
am-mu-uk-ma-kán ^{d}U pí-ḫa-aš-ša-aš-ši-in EN-*IA* (11) EGIR-pa *AṢ-BAT*

42 nu[-mu TI-]nu-ut nu-za *A-NA* DINGIR^{MEŠ} ku-it ar-ku-wa-⸤ar⸥ i-ia-mi
nu-mu TI-nu-ut nu-za *A-NA* DINGIR$^{\text{ME.EŠ}}$ ku-it ar-ku-wa-ar (12) i-ia-mi

43 nu-kán *A-WA-TE*^{MEŠ} *A-NA* DINGIR^{MEŠ} an-da šu-un-ni nu[-m]u ⸤iš⸥-ta-ma-aš-ša-an-du
nu-kán *A-WA-TE*$^{\text{ME.EŠ}}$ *A-NA* DINGIR$^{\text{ME.EŠ}}$ an-da šu-un-ni (13) nu-mu iš-ta-ma-aš-ša-an-du

44 nu a-pí-ia-ia ^{d}U pí-ḫa-aš-ša-aš-ši-in šar-li-iš-ki-mi
nu a-pí-ia-ia ^{d}U pí-ḫa-aš-ša-aš-ši-in (14) šar-li-iš-ki-mi \

--- B om.

45 nu am-me-el ku-wa-pí *A-WA-TE*^{MEŠ} DINGIR^{MEŠ} iš-ta-ma-aš-ša-an-zi
nu am-me-el ku-wa-pí DINGIR$^{\text{ME.EŠ}}$ *A-<!>-TE*$^{\text{ME.EŠ}}$ (15) iš-ta-ma-aš-ša-an-zi

46 nu-mu-kán ku-iš i-da-lu-uš me-mi-aš ZI-ni an-da
nu-mu-kán ku-iš i-da-lu-uš me-mi-aš (16) ZI-ni *eras.* an-da

47 na-an-mu DINGIR^{MEŠ} EGIR-pa **SIG$_5$-aḫ-ḫa-an-zi** šar-la-an-zi
na-an-mu DINGIR$^{\text{ME.EŠ}}$ EGIR-pa **SIG$_5$-aḫ-zi** šar-la-an-zi

48 nu-za ku-e-el wa-al-li-ia-tar *Ú-UL*-za *ŠA* ^{d}U pí-ḫa-aš-ša-aš-ši
(17) nu-za ku-e-el wa-al-li-ia-tar *Ú-UL*-za *ŠA*[88] ^{d}U pí-<<**pí**>>-ḫa-aš-ša-aš-ši

49 EN-*IA* wa-al-li-ia-tar nu ma-a-an DINGIR-*LAM* na-aš-ma DUMU.LÚ.U$_{19}$.LU-*TI*
(18) EN-*IA* wa-al-li-ia-tar nu ma-a-an DINGIR-*LAM* na-aš-ma DUMU.LÚ.U$_{19}$.LU-***UT-TI***

50 a-uš-zi nu ki-iš-ša-an me-ma-i ḫa-an-da-an-wa
(19) a-uš-zi nu ki-iš-ša-an me-ma-i ḫa-an-da-an-wa

---

84 *-an-zi* written over erasure.

85 The sign following MUŠEN is damaged in *A*, but a *-za* seems to be excluded.

86 Coll.: *-zi* written over an erased *-iš*

87 Surface worn off. *-uk-* and *-za-* seem certain; between them there is space for an additional sign, possibly *-ma-*, as in *B*. Cf. iii 60, 74.

88 *ŠA* inserted above the line.

51 ^{d}U pí-ḫa-aš-ša-aš-ši-iš EN-*IA* **ne-pí-ša-aš** LUGAL-uš **UN-an**
(20) ^{d}U pí-ḫa-aš-ša-aš-ši-iš EN-*IA* **ne-pí-aš** LUGAL-uš **an-tu-uḫ-ša-an**

52 **ka**-ni-iš-ta nu-wa-ra-an \ ku-la-**a**-ni-it-ta
(21) **ga**-ni-iš-ta nu-wa-ra-an \ ku-la-ni-it-ta

53 nu-wa-ra-an-kán aš-ša-nu-ut nu-wa-ra-an-kán me-**e**-ḫu-na-aš ar-nu-ut
nu-wa-ra-an-kán (22) aš-ša-nu-ut nu-wa-ra-an-kán me-ḫu-na-aš[89] ar-nu-ut

54 nu ú-wa-an-zi zi-la-ti-ia DUMU-*IA* DUMU.DUMU-*IA* LUGAL^{MEŠ} **SAL.LUGAL^{MEŠ}**
(23)[n]u ú-wa-an-zi \ zi-la-ti-ia **am-me-el** DUMU-*IA* DUMU.DUMU-*IA* (24) LUGAL$^{\text{ME.EŠ}}$ **SAL.LUGAL$^{\text{ḪI.A}}$**

55 *ŠA* ^{URU}Ḫa-at-ti DUMU^{MEŠ} LUGAL ***BE-LU***^{MEŠ}-ia *A-NA* ^{d}U pí-ḫa-aš-ša-aš-ši
ŠA ^{URU}Ḫa-at-ti DUMU$^{\text{ME.EŠ}}$LUGAL **EN$^{\text{ME.EŠ}}$**-ia (25) *A-NA* ^{d}U pí-ḫa-aš-ša-aš-ši
D[90] 1' DUM]U^{MEŠ} LUGAL[

56 EN-*IA* na-aḫ-**šar**-ri-iš-ki-u-an ti-ia-an-zi
EN-*IA* na-aḫ-**ša**-ri-iš-ki-u-**wa**-an ti-ia-an-zi
D 2' **-ša]r**[91]-ri-iš-ki-u-a[n

57 nu ki-iš-ša-an me-ma-an-zi ḫa-an-da-an-wa a-ši DINGIR-*LIM*
(26) nu ki-iš-ša-an me-ma-an-zi ḫa-an-da-an-wa a-ši DINGIR-*LIM*
D 3' -w]a a-ši DINGIR-*LIM* š[ar-

58 šar-ku-uš UR.SAG-iš pa-ra-a ḫa-an-da-a[n-za **DINGIR -*LU*]*M*?**[92]
(27) šar-ku-uš UR.SAG-iš pa-ra-a ḫa-an-da-an-za **DINGIR -*LIM***

59 nu-ut-ta DINGIR^{MEŠ} *ŠA-ME-E* ḪUR.⌞SAG⌟⌞^{MEŠ}⌟ Í[D^{MEŠ} wa-li-**i**]**a**-an-zi
(28) nu-ut-ta[93] DINGIR$^{\text{ME.EŠ}}$ *ŠA-ME-E* ḪUR.SAG$^{\text{ME.EŠ}}$ ÍD$^{\text{ME.EŠ}}$ *erasure* wa-li-an-zi[94]
D 4' -t]a DINGIR^{MEŠ} *ŠA-ME-E* Ḫ[UR.SAG

---

60 **ú-ga-kán** *A-NA* ^{M}NIR.GÁL [*A-NA* ÌR-*K*]*A* **ZI-an-za** an-da
(29) **[am]-mu-ga-kán** *A-NA* ^{M}NIR.GÁL *A-NA* ÌR-*KA* **ZI-za** an-da
D 5' *A-N*]*A* ^{M}NIR.GÁL ⌞*A-NA*⌟ [

61 du-uš-ga-i nu ^{d}⌞U⌟ [-a]š-ši-in EN-*IA* šar-la-a-mi
(30) [du-u]š-ga-i nu ^{d}U pí-ḫa-aš-ša-aš-ši-in EN-*IA* šar-la-a-mi
D 5' n]u ⸢^{d}U pí-ḫa⸣-aš[-

---

89 Written over erasure.

90 1785/u

91 According to H. Otten's autograph, traces of two vertical wedges ("late" *šar*, as in *B* and *C*).

92 The traces of the last sign , a *Winkelhacken* followed by a horizontal, are certainly not of *LIM*. Other than *LU*]*M*, only]x-*aš* seems possible, which would hardly make sense here.

93 *-ut-ta* inserted above the line.

94 Written over erasure.

62 É^{MEŠ} DINGIR^{MEŠ}-ia-⌈at-ta⌉[95] ⌈ku-e⌉ [i-i]a-mi ša-ak-la-uš-ša-**da**
(31) [ ] DINGIR$^{\text{ME.EŠ}}$-ia-at-ta ku-e i-ia-mi ša-ak-la-uš-ša[96]

63 ku-i-e-eš [DÙ/iya-]mi nu-za-kán ^{d}U pí-ḫa-aš-ša-aš-ši-iš EN-*IA*
ku-< ! >-e-eš (32) [DÙ/iya-m]i nu-za-kán ^{d}U pí-ḫa-aš-ša-aš-ši-iš EN-*IA*

64 pa-[ra-a d]u-uš-kat-ti nu NINDA.GUR$_{4}$.RA iš-pa-an-du-uz-zi-ia
pa-ra-a du-uš-kat-ti (33) [NINDA.GUR$_{4}$.]RA$^{\text{ḪI.A}}$ iš-pa-an-du-⸤uz-zi⸥-ia

65 [ku-i]n *A-NA* ^{d}U pí-ḫa-aš-ša-aš-ši EN-*IA* pé-eš-ki-mi
ku-in (34) [^{d}]U pí-ḫa-aš-ša-aš-ši [p]é-eš-ki-mi

66 na-an-**ši** du-uš-ga-ra-u-wa-an-za pí-iš-ke-el-lu
na-an-**ta** (35) [-g]a-ra-u-wa-an-za [

67 píd-**du**-li-ia-**u-wa**-an-za-ma-**da** le-e pé-eš-ki-mi
p[ít]-**tu**[97]-li-ia-an-za-ma-**ta** (36) ⌈le⌉-e pé-⸤eš⸥-ki-m[i

68 nu-mu ^{d}U pí-ḫa-aš-ša-aš-ši-iš EN-*IA* ar-mu-wa-la-aš-ḫa-aš
]-ši-iš EN-*IA* (37) ar-mu-wa-la[-

69 i-wa-ar še-er ar-mu-**u**-wa-la-i ne-pí-ša-aš-ma-mu
-]mu-wa-la-**a**-i (38) ne-pí-ša-aš-ma-m[u

70 ^{d}UTU-aš i-wa-ar še-er wa-an-ta-a-i
-a]n-ta-a-i

---

71 nu-mu ZAG-ni GÉŠPU *eras.* kat-ta i-ia-an-ni nu-mu-kán GUD-i
(39) nu-mu ZAG-ni GÉŠ[PU -n]i nu-mu-kán GUD-i

72 **GIM-an** ḫu-it-ti-ia-u-wa-an-zi ḫar-pí-ia-aḫ-ḫu-ut
(40) **ma-aḫ-ḫa-an** ḫu-it-[-p]í-ia-aḫ-ḫu-ut

73 ^{d}U-ni-li-ma-mu a-wa-an ša-ra-a i-ia-an-ni nu ḫa-an-da-an
(41) ^{d}U-ni-li-ma-mu [ ]-an-ni (42) nu ḫa-an-da-an

74 **ú-uk** ki-iš-ša-an me-ma-al-lu *IŠ-TU* ^{d}U pí-ḫa-aš-ša-aš-ši-wa-za
am[-mu-uk] me-ma-al-lu (43) *IŠ-TU* ^{d}U pí-ḫa-a[š-

75 ka-ni-iš-⸤ša⸥-[an-za šal-l]a-⸤nu-wa-an-za⸥ ⸤**mi**- im⸥-ma-**me**-iš-ša
-š]a-an-za šal-la-nu-wa-an-za[98] (44) **me**-em-ma-**mi**-iš-š[a

---

[95] Here joins KUB 30.14 iii.

[96] *-ša* inserted above the line and *-da* omitted.

[97] Coll.: text has clear *-tu-*.

[98] *B* iv 43 adds an unidentified sign (perhaps preceded by a *Glossenkeil*) written vertically on the column-divider.

76[99] nu-wa-kán [-t]a$^{?}$
]x[ ]x$^{ME.EŠ}$ x (-)x-eš-ta

A IV

1 z]i(?) aš-ša-nu-uz-zi
(iv 45)nu-kán GIM$^{!}$-an [ ]ḫal-z[i-]x[ ]x [\\[100]

2]x-[š]i$^{?}$-ia-az-zi[101]

(B i 39)[102] **[3 NIND]A.GUR$_4$.RA** ***A-NA*** **^{d}UTU AN-*I*** **KI.MIN**

---

3 -]ši-ia
(40) [EGIR-*Š]U*-ma NINDA.GUR$_4$.RA $^{ḪI.A}$ pár-ši-ia

--- B om.

4 [EGIR-*ŠU*-ma(?)[103] t]a[r-na-aš] *A-NA* ^{d}UTU^{URU}**TÚL-na**
3 NINDA.GUR$_4$.RA *ŠA* ZÌ.DA DUR$_5$ tar-na-aš (41) [*A-NA*] ^{d}UTU ^{URU}**A-ri-in-na**[104]

5 šu-u]n-⸢ni⸣-ia-zi na-aš-kán ^{GIŠ}BANŠUR-⸢i⸣
na-aš-kán ŠÀ-*BI* LÀL Ì[105].DÙG.GA šu-un-ni-ia-zi (42) [na-a]š-kán ^{GIŠ}BANŠUR-i[106]

6 EGIR-**Š]*U*-⸢ma⸣** NINDA.Ì.E.DÉ.A me-ma-al
ŠA ^{d}UTU ^{URU}**A-ri-in-na** da-a-i (43) [EG]IR-***ŠU***-ma NINDA.Ì.E.DÉ.A me-ma-al

7]⸢šu-uḫ-ḫa⸣-i 1 ^{DUG}*KU-KU-UB* GEŠTIN ši-pa-**an**-ti
A-NA NINDA.GUR$_4$.RA$^{ḪI.A}$ še-er šu-uḫ-ḫa-i (44) [^{D}]^{UG}*KU-KU-UB* GEŠTIN **pé-ra-an** ši-**ip**-pa-ti

---

8 [EGI]R-⸢***ŠU***⸣-ma [pí-ḫa]-aš-ša-aš-ši 3 NINDA.GUR$_4$.RA BABBAR ŠÀ.**BA** 1 SA$_5$
(45) [EGIR-*Š*]***U***-ma *A-NA* ^{d}U pí-ḫa-aš-ša-aš-ši 3 NINDA.GUR$_4$.RA BABBAR ŠÀ.**PA** 1 SA$_5$

---

99 As clearly visible in the join KUB 30.14, *A* iii has only 76 lines, and not 77 as drawn in the autograph of KUB 6.46. *A* iii 76 must correspond to the second half of *B* iv 44, which unfortunately is also badly mutilated. So is the next line of *B*, which has been inserted in minuscule characters as an addition; it must somehow correspond to *A* iv 1-2, but the reconstruction of these lines remains problematical. See Commentary.

100 In the gap at the end of *B* iv 45 (with column divider) there is sufficient space for about 4 to 6 signs. After the paragraph-divider (which must correspond to the one following *A* iv 2) *B* iv 46 jumps to *A* iv 46.

101 Lebrun, *Hymnes*, 269, restores *pár-š*]*i-ia-az-zi*$^{?}$. The traces before *-ia-* may conform with a *-ši-*, but the preserved traces of the previous sign do not seem to have the vertical wedge of *pár-*.

102 The continuation is duplicated by *B* i 40 ff., but *B* i 39 inserts here an extra offering to the Sun-god of Heaven , which is probably missing in *A* (see Commentary). The gap at the beginning of *A* iv 3 is too small to accommodate this addition, unless it was appended in a more abbreviated form.

103 *B* i 40 begins directly with 3 NINDA.GUR$_4$.RA etc., but the gap in *A* requires more text.

104 *pár-ši-ia* (cf. iv 24) is omitted in *B* and, by measuring the available space, probably also in *A*.

105 Coll.: Ì missing in the autograph.

106 Followed by erasure.

9 [pá]r-ši-ia ⸢na-aš-kán⸣ ⸢ŠÀ⸣[- LÀ]L Ì.DÙG.GA šu-un-ni-ia-zi
pár-ši-ia (46) [na]-aš-kán ŠÀ-*BI* LÀL Ì.DÙG.GA šu-un-ni-ia-zi

10 na-aš-kán ^{GIŠ}BANŠUR-i ⸢*ŠA*⸣ ⸢^{d}U⸣ pí-ḫa-aš-ša-aš-ši da-a-i
na-aš-kán ^{GIŠ}BANŠUR-i (47) [*Š*]*A* ⸢^{d}⸣U pí-ḫa-aš-ša-aš-ši da-a-i

11 EGIR-*ŠU*-ma-**kán** me-ma-al NINDA.Ì.E.DÉ.A *A-NA* NINDA.GUR$_4$.RA$^{ḪI.A}$ še-er
EGIR-*ŠU*-ma NINDA.Ì.E.DÉ.A me-**em**-ma-al (48) [ ] NINDA.GUR$_4$.RA$^{ḪI.A}$ še-er

12 šu-uḫ-ḫa-i 1 ^{DUG}*KU-KU-UB* GEŠTIN pé-ra-an ši-ip-pa-**an**-ti
šu-uḫ-ḫa-i 1 ^{DUG}*KU-KU-UB* GEŠTIN pé-ra-an ši-ip-pa-ti

---

13 EGIR-***ŠU***-ma *A-NA* ^{d}Ḫé-bat 3 NINDA.GUR$_4$.RA BABBAR ŠÀ.**BA** 1 SA$_5$ pár-ši-ia
(49) [EGI]R-***ŠÚ***-ma *A-NA* ^{d}Ḫé-bat 3 NINDA.GUR$_4$.RA BABBAR ŠÀ.**PA** 1 SA$_5$ pár-ši-ia

14 na-aš-kán ŠÀ-*BI* LÀL Ì.DÙG.GA šu-un-ni-ia-zi
na-aš-kán ŠÀ-*BI* (50) [LÀ]L Ì.DÙG.GA šu-un-ni-ia-zi

15 na-aš-kán ^{GIŠ}BANŠUR ^{d}Ḫé-bat da-a-i EGIR-*ŠU*-ma NINDA.Ì.E.DÉ.A
na-aš-kán ^{GIŠ}BANŠUR-**i** ***ŠA*** ^{d}Ḫé-bat da-a-i (51) [EG]IR-*ŠU*-ma NINDA.Ì.E.DÉ.A

16 me-ma-al *A-NA* NINDA.GUR$_4$.RA$^{ḪI.A}$ še-er šu-uḫ-ḫa-i 1 ^{DUG}*KU-KU-UB* GEŠTIN
me-**em**-ma-al *A-NA* NINDA.GUR$_4$.RA$^{ḪI.A}$ še-er šu-uḫ-ḫa-i (52) 1 ^{DUG}*KU-KU-UB* GEŠTIN

17 pé-ra-an ši-ip-pa-**an**-ti
pé-ra-an ši-ip-pa-ti

---

18 EGIR-*ŠU*-ma 3 NINDA.GUR$_4$.RA BABBAR ŠÀ.**BA** 1 SA$_5$ ***A-NA*** ^{d}U *ŠA-ME-E*
(53) EGIR-*ŠU*-ma 3 NINDA.GUR$_4$.RA BABBAR ŠÀ.**PA** 1 SA$_5$ *eras.* ^{d}U *ŠA-ME-E*

19 pár-ši-ia na-aš-kán ŠÀ-*BI* LÀL Ì.DÙG.GA šu-un-ni-ia-zi
pár-ši-ia (54) ***A-NA*** ^{d}**U** ***ŠA-ME-E*** na-aš-kán ŠÀ-*BI* LÀL Ì.DÙG.GA šu-un-ni-ia-zi

20 na-aš-kán ^{GIŠ}BANŠUR ^{d}U *ŠA-ME-E* da-a-i EGIR-***ŠÚ***-ma NINDA.Ì.E.DÉ.A
(55) na-aš-kán ^{GIŠ}BANŠUR-**i** ***ŠA*** ^{d}U *ŠA-ME-E* da-a-i EGIR-***ŠU***-ma NINDA.Ì.E.DÉ.A

21 me-ma-al *A-NA* NINDA.GUR$_4$.RA$^{ḪI.A}$ še-er šu-uḫ-ḫa-i
(56) me-ma-al *A-NA* NINDA.GUR$_4$.RA$^{ḪI.A}$ še-er šu-uḫ-ḫa-i

22 1 ^{DUG} *KU-**UK**-KU-UB* GEŠTIN pé-ra-an ši-ip-pa-**an**-ti
1 ^{DUG} *KU-KU-UB* GEŠTIN pé-ra-an ši-ip-pa-ti

---

23 EGIR.-***ŠÚ***-ma 3 NINDA.GUR$_4$.RA *ŠA* ZÌ.DA DUR$_5$ tar-na-aš *A-NA* ^{d}U ^{URU}**KÙ.BABBAR-ti**
(57)EGIR.-***ŠU***-ma 3 NINDA.GUR$_4$.RA$^{ḪI.A}$ pár-ši-ia *ŠA* ZÌ.DA DUR$_5$ tar-na-aš (58) *A-NA* ^{d}U ^{URU}**Ḫa-at-ti**

24 pár-ši-ia na-aš-kán ŠÀ-*BI* LÀL Ì.DÙG.GA šu-un-ni-ia-zi
na-aš-kán ŠÀ-*BI* LÀL Ì.DÙG.GA šu-un-ni-ia-zi

25 na-aš-kán ***A-NA*** ^{GIŠ}BANŠUR *ŠA* ^{d}U ^{URU}**KÙ.BABBAR-ti** da-a-i
(59) na-aš-kán ^{GIŠ}BANŠUR-**i** *ŠA* < ! > ^{URU}**Ḫa-at-ti** da-a-i

26 EGIR-*ŠU*-ma NINDA.Ì.E.DÉ.A me-ma-al *A-NA* NINDA.GUR$_4$.RA$^{ḪI.A}$ še-er
EGIR-*ŠU*-ma NINDA.Ì.E.DÉ.A (60) me-ma-al *A-NA* NINDA.GUR$_4$.RA$^{ḪI.A}$ še-er

27 šu-uḫ-ḫa-i 1 ^{DUG}*KU-KU-UB* GEŠTIN pé-ra-an ši-ip-pa-**an**-ti
šu-uḫ-ḫa-i 1 ^{DUG}*KU-KU-UB* GEŠTIN pé-ra-an ši-ip-pa-ti

---

28 EGIR-*ŠU*-ma 3 NINDA.GUR$_4$.RA BABBAR ŠÀ.**BA** 1 SA$_5$ *A-NA* ^{d}U ^{URU}Zi-ip-la-an-**da**
(61) EGIR-*ŠU*-ma 3 < ! >.GUR$_4$.RA BABBAR ŠÀ.**PA** 1 SA$_5$ *ŠA* < ! > ^{URU}Zi-ip-**pa**-la-an-**ta**[107]

29 [**pár-š]i-ia** na-aš-kán ŠÀ-*BI* LÀL Ì.DÙG.GA šu-un-ni-ia-**an**-zi
(62) na-aš-kán ŠÀ-*BI* LÀL Ì.DÙG.GA šu-un-ni-ia-zi

30 [na-aš-ká]n ⌊***A-NA***⌋ ^{GIŠ}BANŠUR *ŠA* ^{d}U ^{URU}Zi-ip-pa-la-an-da
na-aš-kán ^{GIŠ}BANŠUR-**i** (63) *ŠA* ^{d}U < ! > Zi-ip-pa-la-an-da

31 [EGIR-*Š*]*U*-ma NINDA.Ì.E.DÉ.A me-ma-al *A-NA* NINDA.GUR$_4$.RA$^{ḪI.A}$
da-a-i EGIR-*ŠU*-ma NINDA.Ì.E.DÉ.A me-ma-al (64) *A-NA* NINDA.GUR$_4$.RA$^{ḪI.A}$

32 [ ]-i 1 ^{DUG}*KU-KU-UB* GEŠTIN ši-ip-pa-**an**-ti
še-er šu-uḫ-ḫa-i 1 ^{DUG}*KU-KU-UB* GEŠTIN **pé-ra-an** ši-ip-pa-ti

---

33 NINDA.GUR$_4$].RA BABBAR ŠÀ.**BA** 1 SA$_5$ DINGIR.LÚ^{MEŠ} ḫu-u-ma-an-da-aš
(65) EGIR-*ŠU*-ma 3 NINDA.GUR$_4$.RA BABBAR ŠÀ.**PA** 1 SA$_5$ DINGIR.LÚ$^{ME.EŠ}$ ḫu-u-ma-an-da-aš

34 [^{URU}KÙ.BABBA]R-ti pár-⌈ši-ia⌉ **KI.MIN** na-aš-kán ^{GIŠ}BANŠUR
ŠA ^{URU}KÙ.BABBAR-ti (66) pár-ši-ia na-aš-kán ^{GIŠ}BANŠUR-**i**

35 [*ŠA* ^{d}U] pí-ḫa-aš-ša-aš-ši da-a-i
ŠA ^{d}U pí-ḫa-aš-ša-aš-ši da-a-i[108]

36] 3 NINDA.GUR$_4$.RA BABBAR ŠÀ.**BA** 1 SA$_5$ *A-NA* ^{d}Še-ri[109] ^{d}Ḫur-ri
(67) EGIR-*ŠU*-ma 3 NINDA.GUR$_4$.RA BABBAR ŠÀ.**PA** 1 SA$_5$ *A-NA* ^{d}Še[110]-ri ^{d}Ḫur-ri

37 p[ár-ši-i]a KI.MIN[111] **na-aš-kán** ^{GIŠ}BANŠUR-i ⌊*ŠA* ^{d}U⌋ pí-ḫa-aš-ša-aš-ši da-a-i
pár-ši-ia KI.MIN[112] (68) *ŠA* ^{GIŠ}BANŠUR-i ^{d}U pí-ḫa-aš-ša-aš-ši da-a-i

---

38 ⌈EGIR⌉-*ŠU*-ma 3 NINDA.GUR$_4$.RA BABBAR ŠÀ.**BA** 1 SA$_5$ DINGIR.SAL$^{M[EŠ]}$
(69) EGIR-*ŠU*-ma 3 NINDA.GUR$_4$.RA BABBAR ŠÀ.**PA** 1 SA$_5$ DINGIR.SAL$^{ME.EŠ}$

---

107 Followed by long erasure.
108 Followed by traces of a long erasure.
109 Clear *-ri,* both here and in *Ḫur-ri* (as already indicated by O. Weber in his "Verbesserungen").
110 Written over erasure; apparently he first wrote GUD and then erased it. Cf. *B* i 34 and see Commentary.
111 Written over erasure.
112 Coll.: KI.MIN on the column divider (omitted in the autograph).

39 ḫu-u-ma-an-da-aš *ŠA* $^{URU\ GIŠ}$**Ḫat-ti** pár-ši-ia KI.MIN
ḫu-u-ma-an-da-aš *ŠA* ^{URU}**Ḫa-at-ti** (70) pár-ši-ia KI.MIN

40 na-aš-kán ^{GIŠ}BANŠUR-i *ŠA* ^{d}UTU ^{URU}**TÚL-na** da-a-i
na-aš-kán ^{GIŠ}BANŠUR-i *ŠA* ^{d}UTU ^{URU}**A-ri-in-na** da-a-i

---

41 EGIR-*ŠU*-ma 3 NINDA.GUR$_4$.RA BABBAR ŠÀ.**BA** 1 SA$_5$ ***A-NA*** ḪUR.SAG$^{ME.EŠ}$
(71) EGIR-*ŠU*-ma 3 NINDA.GUR$_4$.RA BABBAR ŠÀ.**PA** 1 SA$_5$ ***ŠA*** ḪUR.SAG$^{ME.EŠ}$

42 pár-ši-ia KI.MIN na-aš-kán ^{GIŠ}BANŠUR-i *ŠA* ^{d}U $^{URU!}$**pí-ḫa-aš-ša-aš-ši** da-a-i
pár-ši-ia KI.MIN (72) na-aš-kán ^{GIŠ}BANŠUR-i *ŠA* ^{d}U pí-ḫa-aš-ša-aš-ši da-a-i

---

43 EGIR-*ŠU*-ma 3 NINDA.GUR$_4$.RA BABBAR ŠÀ.**BA** 1 SA$_5$ ***A-NA*** ÌD^{MEŠ} pár-ši-ia
(73) EGIR-*ŠU*-ma 3 NINDA.GUR$_4$.RA BABBAR ŠÀ.**PA** 1 SA$_5$ ***ŠA*** ÌD$^{ME.EŠ}$ pár-ši-ia

44 KI.MIN na-aš-kán *A-NA* ^{GIŠ}BANŠUR *ŠA* ^{d}U pí-ḫa-aš-ša-aš-ši da-a-i
KI.MIN (74) ⌊na-aš-kán⌋ *A-NA* ^{GIŠ}BANŠUR-**i** *ŠA* ^{d}U pí-ḫa-aš-ša-aš-ši da-a-i

---

45 GIM-an-ma NINDA.GUR$_4$.RA$^{ḪI.A}$ pár-ši-ia-u-wa-an-zi zi-in-na-i
(ii 1) p]ár-ši-ia-u-wa-an-zi zi-in-na-i[113]

46 nu-kán ku-**e** *A-WA-TE*^{MEŠ} *A-NA* ^{d}UTU-*ŠI* ŠÀ-ta
(iv 46) nu-kán ku-**i** *A-WA-TE*$^{ME.EŠ}$ ⌈*A*⌉-*NA* ^{d}UTU-*Š*[*I*

47 na-at-za *A-NA* DINGIR^{MEŠ} ar-ku-wa-ar DÙ-zi GIM-an-ma-kán
] (47) *A-NA* DINGIR$^{ME.EŠ}$ ar-ku-wa-ar DÙ-zi [

48 ar-ku-wa-ar ti-ia-u-wa-ar kar-ap-ta-ri
] (48) ti-ia-u-wa-ar kar-ap-ta-ri \

B om.

49 nu EGIR-***ŠU*** 3 N[INDA.GUR$_4$.R]A BABBAR ŠÀ.BA 1 SA$_5$ *A-NA* DINGIR.LÚ^{MEŠ} KUR-e-aš
nu EGIR-***ŠÚ*-ma**[114] 3 [

50 ḫu-u-ma-an-da-aš pá[r-š]i-ia NINDA.Ì.E.DÉ.A me-ma-al iš-ḫu-u-wa-i
(49) ḫu-u-ma-an-da-aš pár-ši-ia NINDA.Ì.E.DÉ.A [

51 LÀL Ì.DÙG.GA la-ḫu-u-wa-i[115] **1 ^{DUG}*KU-KU-UB* GEŠTIN BAL-ti**
(50) LÀL Ì.DÙG.GA la-ḫu-u-wa-i

B om.

---

113 Here follows in text *B* the Long List of local gods.

114 nu EGIR-*ŠÚ*-ma inserted above the line.

115 Coll.: The rest of the line (omitted in *B*) was added in a smaller and shallower script, the same as the one found in lines 59-61 (also omitted in *B*).

52 **EGIR-*ŠU*-ma** 3 NINDA.GUR$_4$.RA BABBAR *A-NA* DINGIR.SAL^{MEŠ} KUR-e-aš ḫu-u-ma-an-da-aš
EGIR-an-da[116] [ ]

53 pár-ši-ia ar-ku-wa-ar-za ku-e-da-aš da-a-iš NINDA.Ì.E.DÉ.A
(51) pár-ši-ia ar-ku-wa-ar-za ku-e-da-aš ⌈da-a-iš⌉ (***rest omitted in B***)

54 me-ma-al *A-NA* NINDA.GUR$_4$.RA$^{\text{ḪI.A}}$ še-er šu-uḫ-ḫa-i LÀL Ì.DÙG.GA la-ḫu-u-wa-i

---

55 **EGIR-*ŠU*-ma** 2 NINDA.GUR$_4$.RA *A-NA* ḪUR.SAG^{MEŠ} ÍD^{MEŠ} **pár-ši-ia KI.MIN**
(52) **EGIR-an-ma**[!117] 2 NINDA.GUR$_4$.RA *A-NA* ḪUR.SAG$^{\text{ME.EŠ}}$ ÍD$^{\text{ME.EŠ}}$ **KUR pár-ši-ia-a[z-zi]**

B om.

---

56 **EGIR-*ŠU*-ma** 1 NINDA.GUR$_4$.RA [118] **ku-ut-ru-i** ^{d}UTU-i **pár-ši-ia**
(53) 1 NINDA.GUR$_4$.RA**-ma** \ **ḫu-u-wa-ia-al-li** ^{d}UTU-i **pár-ši-ia-a[z-zi]**

57 NINDA.Ì.E.DÉ.A me-ma-al *A-NA* NINDA.GUR$_4$.RA$^{\text{ḪI.A}}$ še-er
(54) ⌈NINDA⌉.Ì.E.DÉ.A me-ma-al *A-NA* NINDA.GUR$_4$.RA$^{\text{ḪI.A}}$ še-er

58 **šu-uḫ-ḫa-i** LÀL Ì.DÙG.GA pé-ra-an la-ḫu-u-wa-i
iš-ḫu-u-⌈i⌉[119] (55) LÀL Ì.DÙG.GA pé$^{!}$-ra$^{!}$-an la-**a**[120]-ḫu-u-wa-i

---

59[121] **nam-ma**[122] ***ŠA IṢ-ṢI* 2 GUNNI DÙ-an-zi**

60 **nu NINDA.GUR$_4$.RA ku-e pár-ši-ia na-aš ar-ḫa**

61 ***PA-NI* 2**[123] **^{GIŠ}BANŠUR-pát BIL-nu-zi *QA-TI***

---

[116] Part of the following sentence must have been omitted in *B*.

[117] Cf. EGIR-*an-da* in *B* iii 65, iv 50 and see Commentary.

[118] Followed by small erasure.

[119] Only the bottom horizontal of *i* is preserved before the break. An alternative spelling -*w*[*a-i*] (as in *A* iv 50) is not entirely excluded.

[120] Coll.: omitted in the autograph.

[121] The last three lines, which are missing in *B*, were added in a smaller and shallower script, the same as in the addition in line 51. See Ch. IV.2.

[122] Written over erasure; apparently he first wrote EGIR and then erased it.

[123] Coll.: clearly 2 (and not 1 as in the autograph).

Chapter I: Translation[124]

Preamble

i 1 Thus (says) *tabarna* Muwatalli, Great King, King of Ḫatti,
2 [so]n of Muršili, Great King, King of Ḫatti, the hero: If some problem
3 burdens a man('s conscience), he [mak]es a plea to the gods.

Preparations for the ritual offerings

4 He places on the roof, facing the sun, two covered wickerwork tables:
5 He places one table for the Sun-goddess of Arinna and for the male gods
6 [one ta]ble. On them (there are): 35 thick breads of (one) *tarna* of moist flour,
7 a thin [bow]l (of) honey mixed with fine oil, a full pot (of) fat-bread, a full bowl
8 (of) groats, thirty pitchers of wine. And when he p[repare]s these, the king
9 goes up to the roof and he [bo]ws before to the Sun-god of [He]aven.

Invocation of the gods of Ḫatti

10 He says as follows: Sun-god of Heaven and Sun-goddess of Arinna, my lady,
11 Queen, my lady, queen of Ḫatti, Storm-god, king of Heaven, my lord,
12 Ḫebat Queen, my lady, Storm-god of Ḫatti, king of Heaven, lord of Ḫatti,
13 my lord, Storm-god of Ziplanda, my lord, beloved son of the Storm-god,
14 lord of the Land of Ḫatti, Šeri (and) Ḫurri,[125]
15 all the male gods (and) the female gods, all the mountains
16 (and) the rivers of the Land of Ḫatti, (my) lords.
17 Divine lords – Sun-goddess of Arinna, my lady, and all the gods
18 of the Land of Ḫatti, (my) lords – whose priest I am, who have
19 conferred upon me, from (among) all (others)[126], the rulership over Ḫatti.

---

[124] The translation follows text *A*, noting significant variants of *B*.

[125] *B* has: "Šeri, the bull who is champion in Ḫattuša, the land" (cf. i 33). *A* originally had a similar phrase, then erased it and added "Ḫurri" instead. See Commentary.

[126] Or: "in every respect". See Commentary.

Agenda of the pleas to follow

20 Now, gods, listen to me, to the word (and)[127] plea of me, your priest,
21 your servant. First, I shall make a plea with regard to yourselves,[128]
22 my divine lords, about your temples, about your statues;
23 how the gods of Ḫatti are treated
24 and also how they are mistreated.

---

25 Thereafter, I shall make the matters of my (own) soul into a plea.
26 Divine lords, lend me (your) ear, and listen to these my pleas !
27 And the words which I will make into a plea to the divine lords,
28 these words, divine lords, accept and listen[129] to them !
29 And whatever words you do not (wish to) hear from me,
30 and I nevertheless persist in making them into a plea to the gods,
31 they merely emerge from my human mouth;
32 refrain[130] from listening to them, divine lords.

Invocation of Šeri, Herald of Ḫatti

33 Šeri, my lord, bull of the Storm-god, champion of Ḫatti: [131]
34 In these words of the presentation of the plea
35 introduce[132] me before the gods. Let the divine lords listen to
36 these words (and) plea,[133] the divine lords of heaven and earth ! [134]

---

[127] So according to *B*'s version (with conjunction *-a*). *A*' s version, without conjunction, could also be translated "word of plea" (lit.: "the word, the plea"). See Commentary.

[128] *B*: "First, I shall make a plea about my own lordly gods, about your temples, about your statues". *A* had a similar version and then corrected it. See Commentary.

[129] *B* has the two verbs in present-future, whereas *A* probably renders them in the imperative. See Commentary.

[130] For this rendering see Commentary.

[131] Lit.: "the one who steps in front in the Land of Ḫatti". For other interpretations see Commentary.

[132] Or: "announce me".

[133] *B* has , "these words of pre[senting] a plea." See Commentary.

[134] *B* adds "all (of them)" (*[ḫum]anteš*).

Invocation of the Gods of all the Lands[135]

37 Sun-god of Heaven, Sun-goddess of Arinna, Storm-god of Arinna, Mezzulla,

38 Ḫulla, Zinduḫiya, male gods, female gods, mountains,

39 (and) rivers of Arinna, Storm-god of Salvation, Storm-god of Life.

---

40 Storm-god *piḫaššašši* (ḪI.ḪI), Ḫebat of Šamuḫa, male gods, female gods, mountains (and) rivers of Šamuḫa (*B*: Tiwa).

---

41 Storm-god *piḫaššašši*, Sun-goddess of Arinna, Ḫebat, queen of Heaven,

42 Storm-god of the Ruin, gods of the palace of the grandfather.

---

43 Storm-god of Ḫalab, Ḫebat of Ḫalab, IŠTAR-of-the-field of Šamuḫa,

44 "Lady of the *ayakku*", Apara of Šamuḫa, male gods,

45 female gods, mountains (and) rivers of Šamuḫa.

---

46 Valiant Storm-god, Ḫebat, Storm-god of Šaḫpina, male gods, female gods,

47 mountains (and) rivers of Kadapa.

---

48 [Storm]-god of Help, Queen of Kadapa, male gods, female gods, mountains

49 (and) rivers of Kadapa, Storm-god of Thunder, all the Storm-gods.

---

50 Storm-god of Ḫatti, Prominent Calf, Storm-god of the Army, Sun-god of Ḫatti,

51 Protective-god of Ḫatti, Storm-god of Ḫalab (and) Ḫebat of Ḫalab of Ḫatti,

52 Aya, Damkina, ZABABA, Ḫalmašuit, Allatum,

53 IŠTAR of Nineveh, *lulaḫi*-gods, Kubaba.

---

54 IŠTAR of Ḫaddarina, Pirwa, Ašgašipa, Mount Piškurunuwa,

55 male gods, female gods, mountains (and) rivers of Ḫatti, Karzi,

---

135 In *B* this list follows after the ritual offerings (*B* ii 2 ff.). See Ch. VI.

56 Ḫapandaliya, Mount Tatta, Mount Šummiyara

---

57 Storm-god of Ziplanda, Mount Daḫa, male gods, female gods, mountains
58 (and) rivers of Ziplanda.

---

59 Zitḫariya, Storm-god of the Army, son of the Storm-god,
60 Protective-god of the ^{KUŠ}*kuršaš* -~~of the field, Zitḫariya~~, mountains (and) rivers of Zitḫara.

---

61 [ ], Sun-goddess of Arinna, male gods, female gods, mountains (and) rivers of Urauna.

---

62 [Storm-god of] Kummanni, Ḫebat of Kummanni, Storm-god of the *šinapši,*
63 Ḫebat of the *šinapši,* Storm-god of Mount Manuziya, NIN.GAL,
64 Pišanuḫi, Mount Gallištapa, male gods, female gods,
65 mountains (and) rivers of Kummanni and of the Land of Kummanni.

---

66 Storm-god *piḫami,* Goddess of the Storm-god *piḫami* of Šanaḫuita,
67 male gods, female gods, mountains (and) rivers of Šanaḫuita.

---

68 Storm-god of Neriqqa, ZABABA ditto, Telipinu, Zaḫapuna,
69 Mount Zaliyanu, Mount Zaliyanu of Gaštama,
70 Tazzuwaši, male gods (and) female gods of Gaštama.

---

71 Protective-god of Ḫatenzuwa, Mount Ḫaḫarwa, male gods (and) female gods
72 of Neriqqa and of the Land of Takupša.

---

73 Storm-god of Šariššа, IŠTAR-*li,* male gods (and) female gods of Šariššа.

---

74 Storm-god of Ḫurma, Ḫantidaššu of Ḫurma, Storm-god (and) Ḫebat
75 of Ḫalab of Ḫurma, male gods, female gods, mountains (and) rivers ditto.

---

76 Ḫašigašnawanza of Lawan(z)atiya$^{!}$, Mulliyara,
77 male gods, female gods, mountains (and) rivers of Lawazantiya.

---

78 Storm-god of [Pittiy]arik(?). \ Storm-god of Uda, Ḫebat-Šarruma, male gods,
79 female gods, mountains (and) rivers of Uda.

---

ii 1 Deity of Parša, Sun-goddess of the Earth, male gods, female gods,
2 mountains (and) rivers of Parša.

---

3 Storm-god of Ḫiššašḫappa, Storm-god of Kuliwišna, male gods
4 (and) female gods of the palace of His Majesty.

---

5 Storm-god of Garaḫna, Protective-god of Garaḫna, Alā, Storm-god of the Ruin,
6 male gods, female gods, mountains (and) rivers of Karaḫna.

---

7 Storm-god of Šugazziya, Zulima, male gods (and) female gods of Šugazziya.

---

8 Storm-god of Liḫšina, Tašimi, male gods, female gods,
9 mountains (and) rivers of Liḫšina.

---

10 Telipinu of Durmitta, male gods, female gods,
11 mountains (and) rivers of Durmitta.

---

12 Storm-god of Nenašša, Lušiti of Nenašša,
13 River Maraššantiya, male gods, female gods,
14 mountains (and) rivers of Nenašša.

---

15 GAZ.BA.IA of Ḫupišna, Storm-god of Ḫupišna,

16 ZABABA of Ḫupišna, Mount Šarlaimi,

17 male gods,female gods,mountains (and) rivers of Ḫupišna.

---

18 Storm-god of Tuwanuwa, Šaḫḫaššara of Tuwanuwa,

19 male gods, female gods, mountains (and) rivers of Tuwanuwa.

---

20 Storm-god of Illaya, ZABABA of Illaya, male gods,

21 female gods, mountains (and) rivers of Illaya.

---

22 Šuwanzipa of Šuwanzana, male gods, female gods,

23 mountains (and) rivers of Šuwanzana.

---

24 ZABABA of Arziya, male gods, female gods,

25 mountains (and) rivers of Arziya.

---

26 Storm-god of Ḫurniya, the "King(ly) god" of Ḫurniya, male gods,

27 female gods, mountains (and) rivers of Ḫurniya.

---

28 Storm-god of Zarwiša, Nawatiyala of Zarwiša,

29 male gods, female gods, mountains (and) rivers of Zarwiša.

---

30 Mighty Goddess of Šaḫḫaniya, Storm-god of Šaḫḫaniya, male gods,

31 female gods, mountains (and) rivers of Šaḫḫaniya.

---

32 Storm-god of Paḫtima, Storm-god of Šaḫḫuwiya

33 Sun-god(dess) of Malitaškuriya.

---

34 Wašhaliya of Ḫarziuna, Storm-god of Ḫarziuna,

35 male gods, female gods, mountains (and) rivers of Ḫarziuna.

---

36 Zanduza of Šallapa, the Lord, Storm-god of Šallapa, male gods,

37 female gods, mountains (and) rivers of Šallapa.

---

38 Storm-god of Ušša, Storm-god of Parašḫunta, Mount Ḫuwalanuwanda,

39 River Ḫulaya, male gods, female gods, mountains (and) rivers

40 of the Lower Land.

---

41 IŠTAR of Wašuduwanda, Ḫebat of Wašuduwanda,

42 IŠTAR of Innuwita.

---

43 Storm-god of Alazḫana, Telipinu of Ḫanḫana,

44 Ammama of Ḫa(n)ḫana, Mount Takurga ~~of Ḫaḫana~~,

45 male gods, female <gods>, mountains (and) rivers of Ḫaḫana.

---

46 Telipinu of Tawiniya, Kataḫḫa,

47 male gods, female gods, mountains (and) rivers of Tawiniya.

---

48 Sun-god(dess) of Wašḫaniya, male gods, female gods, mountains

49 (and) rivers of Wašḫaniya.

---

50 Lord of Lanta, male gods, female gods, mountains (and) rivers

51 of Lanta; male gods, female gods, mountains (and) rivers of Ḫattina.

---

52 Male gods, female gods, mountains (and) rivers of Ḫarpiša.

53 Karmaḫi of Kalimuna, male gods, female gods,

54 mountains (and) rivers of Kalimuna.

---

55 Male gods, female gods, mountains (and) rivers of Ḫakpiša.

---

56 Protective-god-of-the-Field, Protective-god-of-the-King, male gods (and) female gods of His Majesty's grandfather.

---

57 Male gods (and) female gods of His Majesty's father.

---

58 Male gods (and) female gods of His Majesty's grandmother.

---

59 Male gods (and) female gods of the House of Gazzimara.

---

60 Ḫataḫḫa of Ankuwa, Storm-god of the Rain, IŠTAR-of-the-field,

61 male gods, female <gods>, mountains (and) rivers of Ankuwa.

---

62 Pirwa of Nenišakuwa, Pirwa of Duruwaduruwa,

63 Pirwa of Ikšuna.

---

64 IŠTAR of Šulama, Storm-god of Ḫatrā, male gods,

65 female gods, mountains (and) rivers of the Land of Išuwa.

---

66 Storm-god of Tegarama, male gods, female gods, mountains

67 (and) rivers of the Land of Tegarama.

---

68 Queen of Paliya.

---

69 Storm-god of Tupazziya, male gods, female gods, mountains

70 (and) rivers of Tupazziya.

---

71 Karuna of Kariuna.

---

72 Storm-god of the Growth, Storm-god (and) Ḫebat of Apzišna,
73 male gods (and) female gods of Apzišna.

---

iii 1 Protective-god of Kalašmitta.

---

2 Tamišiya of Tapiqqa , male gods, female gods,
3 mountains (and) rivers of Tapiqqa.

---

4 Storm-god of the House of the *tawannanna*, Storm-god *ḫulaššaššiš*, male gods
5 (and) female gods of the king and the queen who have been invoked
6 (and) who have not been invoked, to whose temples
7 the king (and) queen attend (and)
8 to whose temples they do not attend,
9 (but) priests make offerings to them,[136] male gods (and) female gods
10 of the [sk]y (and) of the dark netherworld, sky (and) earth, clouds (and) winds,
11 thunder (and) lightning, place of assembly,
12 at which place the gods are wont to assemble.

Invocation of the Sun-god of Heaven, Supreme Judge[137]

13 Sun-god of Heaven, my lord, shepherd of mankind;
14 you, Sun-god of Heaven, arise from the sea, and you
15 take your stand in heaven. Sun-god of Heaven, my lord;
16 you Sun-god, give daily judgment over man, dog,
17 swine, and the beast of the field.

---

[136] For this rendering see Commentary.

[137] *B* originally had the entire invocation to the Sun-god of Heaven as a single paragraph; he later added two sub-divisions (which were taken up in *A*). See Ch. V.

18 Here (am) I, Muwatalli the king, priest of the Sun-goddess of Arinna
19 and of all the gods, pleading to the Sun-god of Heaven.
20 Sun-god of Heaven, my lord, halt the gods on this day !
21 And the gods[138] whom I have summoned with my tongue
22 on this day, in whatever plea,

---

23 summon them, Sun-god of Heaven, from heaven (and) earth,
24 from mountains (and) rivers, from their temples and their thrones !

Invocation of the Storm-god of Lightning (piḫaššašši), personal god of the king

25 Thereafter the king says as follows: Storm-god of Lightning,
26 my lord, I was but a mortal, (whereas) my father was a priest
27 to the Sun-goddess of Arinna and to all the gods.
28 My father begat me, but the Storm-god of of Lightning took me
29 from (my) mother and reared me; he made me priest
30 to the Sun-goddess of Arinna and to all the gods;
31 for the Ḫatti land he appointed me to kingship.

---

32 So now I, Muwatalli the king, who have been reared by you,
33 by the Storm-god of Lightning, am pleading:
34 The gods whom I have invoked with my tongue
35 and have pleaded to them, intercede for me with (these) gods, with all (of them) !
36 Take the words of my tongue, (that) of Muwatalli, your servant,
37 and transmit[139] them before the gods !
38 The words of prayer which I will present to the gods,
39 let them not turn them back to me !

---

138 *B* adds "these".

139 Lit.: "fill them before the gods".

The bird takes refuge in the cage[140] and survives; I, too, have taken refuge with the Storm-god of Lightning and he has kept me alive.[141] The plea which I make to the gods, emit (its) words to the gods, and let them listen to me ! Then, I too shall constantly praise the Storm-god of Lightning.

When the gods will hear my word, the bad thing which is in my soul, the gods will put it right and lift it from me. Whose (cause of) praise will I be ?[142] Will I not be the praise of the Storm-god of Lightning, my lord ? And when a god or a mortal will look,[143] he will say as follows: "Surely, the Storm-god of Lightning, my lord, king of Heaven, has honored the man, has promoted him, has provided for him, and has brought him to (good) times." And in the future it will come to pass that my son, my grandson, kings (and) queens of Ḫatti, princes and lords, will always show reverence towards the Storm-god of Lightning, my lord, and they will say as follows: "Truly that god is a mighty hero, a rightly guiding god !" The gods of heaven, the mountains (and) the rivers will praise you.

As for me, Muwatalli, your servant, (my) soul will rejoice inside (me), and I will exalt the Storm-god of Lightning. The temples that I will erect for you and the rites that I will [perfo]rm for you, Storm-god of Lightning, my lord, you shall rejoice (in them). The thick breads and the libations

---

140 For "cage" rather than "nest" see Commentary.

141 Also possible an imperative "save my life !" See Commentary.

142 For this rendering see Commentary.

143 For this rendering see Commentary.

65 which I constantly offer to the Storm-god of Lightning, my lord,

66 let me offer it to him[144] joyfully,

67 let me not offer it to you reluctantly !

68 Storm-god of Lightning, glow over me like

69 the moonlight, shine over me

70 like the Sun-god of Heaven !

---

71 Walk with me at my right hand,

72 team up with me as (with) a bull to draw !

73 Ascend with me in true Storm-godly fashion !

74 Truly, let me say as follows:

75 "I have been recognized, reared and favored by the Storm-god of Lightning,

76 and [ ]." [145]

Ritual offerings for the Gods of Ḫatti

iv 1 When he finishes ca[lling the gods (?)][146]

2 He [-]s [ ].

< (B i 39)[147] [Three sacri]ficial bread(s) for the Sun-god of Heaven, ditto. >

---

3 [There]after he breaks the thick breads.

---

4 [ ], three thick bread(s) of moist flour of (one) *tarna* to the Sun-goddess

5 of Arinna; he dips them in the honey (mixed with) fine oil and puts them on the

6 table of the Sun-goddess of Arinna. Thereafter he pours out fat-bread (and)

7 groats upon the thick breads. He libates in front (of them) one pitcher of wine.

---

144 *B* has "to you". See Commentary.

145 From the direct speech particle at the beginning of l. 76 it appears that the king's projected speech on the favors bestowed upon him by the Storm-god *p.* is continued in this line.

146 For the tentative restoration of this difficult line see Commentary.

147 *B* inserts here an extra offering to the Sun-god of Heaven which is apparently missing in *A*. See Commentary.

8 Thereafter, for the Storm-god of Lightning he breaks three white thick breads,
9 including one red;[148] he dips them in the honey (mixed with) fine oil
10 and puts them on the table of the Storm-god of Lightning.
11 Thereafter he pours out groats (and) fat-bread[149] upon the thick breads.
12 He libates in front (of them) one pitcher of wine.

---

13 Thereafter, for Ḫebat he breaks three white thick breads, including one red;
14 he dips them in the honey (mixed with) fine oil
15 and puts them on the table of Ḫebat. Thereafter he pours out fat-bread (and)
16 groats upon the thick breads.
17 He libates in front (of them) one pitcher of wine.

---

18 Thereafter he breaks three white thick breads, including one red, for the
19 Storm-god of Heaven; he dips them in the honey (mixed with) fine oil.
20 He puts them on the table of the Storm-god of Heaven. Thereafter he pours out
21 fat-bread (and) groats upon the thick breads.
22 He libates in front (of them) one pitcher of wine.

---

23 Thereafter he breaks three thick bread(s) of moist flour of (one) *tarna*
24 to the Storm-god of Ḫatti; he dips them in the honey (mixed with) fine oil.
25 He puts them on the table of the Storm-god of Ḫatti.
26 Thereafter he pours out fat-bread (and) groats upon the thick breads.
27 He libates in front (of them) one pitcher of wine.

---

28 Thereafter he breaks three white thick breads, including one red,
29 for the Storm-god of Ziplanda; he dips them in honey (mixed with) fine oil.
30 He puts them on the table of the Storm-god of Zippalanda.

---

[148] A common mode of expression meaning two white and one red bread.

[149] Inverted order; *B* has the regular order: "fat bread and groats".

31 Thereafter he pours out fat-bread (and) groats upon the thick breads.
32 He libates in front (of them) one pitcher of wine.

---

33 Thereafter he breaks three white thick breads, including one red,
34 for all the male gods of Ḫatti. He puts them on the table
35 of the Storm-god of Lightning.

---

36 Thereafter he breaks three white thick breads, including one red, for Šeri (and)
37 Ḫurri. Ditto. He puts them on the table of the Storm-god of Lightning.

---

38 Thereafter he breaks three white thick breads, including one red,
39 for all the female gods of Ḫatti. Ditto.
40 He puts them on the table of the Sun-goddess of Arinna.

---

41 Thereafter he breaks three white thick breads, including one red, for the
42 mountains. Ditto. He puts them on the table of the Storm-god of Lightning.

---

43 Thereafter he breaks three white thick breads, including one red,
44 for the rivers. Ditto. He puts them on the table of the Storm-god of Lightning.

Insert personal prayer here !

45 When he finishes breaking the thick breads,
46 the things which are in His Majesty's heart,
47 he makes them into a plea to the gods.
48 When the presentation of the plea is finished,

Ritual offerings for the Gods of all the Lands and the Witness Sun-god

49 thereafter he breaks three white thick breads, including one red,
50 for the male gods of all the lands. He pours out fat-bread (and) groats.

51 He pours out honey (mixed with) fine oil. He libates one pitcher of wine.[150]

---

52 Thereafter he breaks three white thick breads, including one red,

53 for the female gods of all the lands, to whom he presented a plea.[151] He pours out

54 groats upon the thick breads. He pours out honey (mixed with) fine oil.

---

55 Thereafter he breaks two thick breads for the mountains (and) rivers. Ditto.[152]

---

56 Thereafter he breaks one thick bread for the Witness[153] Sun-god.

57 he pours out fat-bread (and) groats upon the thick breads.

58 He pours out in front (of them) honey (mixed with) fine oil.[154]

==

Postscript: Burning of the ritual offerings.

59 Further, they make two pyres of wood,

60 and the breads which he breaks,

61 he burns in front of the same two tables. Complete.

---

150 This sentence only appears in *A*.

151 Rest of the paragraph omitted in *B*.

152 *B* adds '(of the) land(s)", but omits "ditto".

153 *A* has a Hittite, *B* a Luwian word.

154 The rest only in *A*.

Chapter II: Commentary [155]

i 1 An opening with *UMMA* followed by the king's name is probably to be restored also in KUB 31.123 i 1, the prayer of Arnuwanda and Ašmunikal (*CTH* 375). In other preserved preambles to prayers, including Muwatalli's prayer to the Storm-god (*CTH* 382), the addressed god(s) always precede the name of the author.

Muwatalli II's name is usually spelled logographically, NIR.GÁL, but a phonetic spelling is probably restored in the Talmi-Tešub Treaty (*CTH* 75): *M*[*u-w*]*a-t*[*al*]-*l*[*i*] (KBo 1. 6 obv. 1). Thus, the differentiation suggested by O. Carruba[156] – logographic spellings for the two kings named Muwatalli, phonetic spelling for other namesakes – cannot be accepted uncritically. The logographic spelling is already found on the seal of Muwatalli I and in the Maşat texts.[157] For the Valiant Storm-god, ᵈU NIR.GÁL, Muršili's personal god, see n. 338.

i 2 Here and in the Alakšandu Treaty Muwatalli gives only his filiation. In his other prayer (*CTH* 382) his forefathers are not mentioned at all. On the other hand, in the Talmi-Šarruma treaty he reaches back to his grandfather, Šuppiluliuma (KBo 1. 6 obv. 1 f.).

mān can be rendered here both as temporal "when" and as conditional "if"; the same applies to iii 49. Goetze applies in both places the temporal sense; Lebrun renders both with conditional "*si*". I have opted to translate "if" in the first case and "when" in the second.

UN / *antuḫša-* Throughout the text *A* uses the ideographic, *B* the phonetic spelling for "man".

i 3 *nakkiya-* is usually rendered as "to become troublesome to, bother, trouble, haunt, urge someone" (*CHD*, L-N, 371 f.), but here I would opt for a more pregnant meaning, "burden someone's conscience"; see Ch. VII. The burdened "man" is obviously the king himself, who composed the prayer (iii 25). See further Ch. X.

arkuwar: This term, literally "argument, plea,"[158] (etymologically related to Latin *arguo, argumentum*), has been thoroughly discussed by Laroche and others.[159] It is interesting to note that the most common Biblical Hebrew term for "to pray" (*hitpallēl*) and "prayer" (*tĕpillā*) has a very similar connotation: "the placing of a case, a situation, before God for consideration, for God's assessment." [160] Since this text records all the attested forms of the verb *arkuwai-* and the derived nouns, it may be useful to present an analytical list of all occurrences:

---

155 Unless specifically indicated as *B*, all references are to line numbers of text *A* (even if it is text *B* that is being discussed at that point). Besides the regular commentaries the reader is also referred to more extensive thematic commentaries in other chapters.

156 "Muwatalli I", *X. Türk Tarih Kongresi, Ankara 1986* (Türk Tarih Kurumu Basimevi, Ankara 1990), 547.

157 H. Otten, *Das hethitische Königshaus im 15. Jahrhundert v. Chr. Zum Neufund einiger Landschenkungsurkunden in Boğazköy* (Wien 1987), 28 ff., with n. 28.

158 Harry Hoffner thinks that the basic meaning of *arkuwai-* is "to reply, to answer", and hence the derived meaning "to account for, plead". In the Ullikummi Myth, Tablet 2, B ii 10-12, when IŠTAR sings, heaven and earth *arkuškanzi*, rendered by Hoffner "echoed (it) back" (*Hittite Myths*, 56).

159 E. Laroche, *Prière*, 13 ff.; R. Lebrun, *Hymnes et prières*, 426 ff.; *"Observations sur la prière hittite'*, 48 f.; D. Sürenhagen, *AoF* 8, 136 ff.

160 Sh. H. Blank, *HUCA* 21 (1948), 337-38 n. 12; M. Greenberg, *Biblical Prose Prayer* (University of California Press 1983), 22 ff. See also P. D. Miller, *They Cried to the Lord: The Form and Theology of Biblical Prayer* (Minneapolis 1994), 38 ff.

Verb simple, without *-za* (*arkuwai-* , *arkuweške-*): "to argue, plead"

iii 35 nu *A-NA* DINGIR^{MEŠ} ar-ku-ua-nu-un

iii 18 nu ka-a-ša am-mu-uk ^{M}NIR.GÁL LUGAL-uš ^{LÚ}SANGA *ŠA* ^{d}UTU ^{URU}TÚL-na
(19) *Ù* DINGIR^{MEŠ} ḫu-u-ma-an-da-aš ne-pí-ša-aš ^{d}UTU-i ar-ku-iš-ki-mi

iii 32 [k]i-nu-na am-mu-uk ^{M}NIR.GÁL LUGAL-uš tu-e-da-az
(33) [*IŠ-*]*TU* ^{d}U pí-ḫa-aš-ša-aš-ši šal-la-nu-ua-an-za ar-ku-ú-e-eš-ki-mi

-za arkuwar iya- / *dai-,* with single accusative: "to make / present a plea"

i 3 f. nu-za *A-NA* DINGIR^{MEŠ} ar-ku-ua-ar [D]Ù-zi

iii 42 nu-za *A-NA* DINGIR^{MEŠ} ku-it ar-ku-ua-ar i-ia-mi (43) nu-kán *A-UA-TE*^{MEŠ}
A-NA DINGIR^{MEŠ} an-da šu-un-ni nu-mu iš-ta-ma-aš-ša-an-du

iv 52 EGIR-*ŠU*-ma 3 NINDA.GUR$_{4}$.RA BABBAR *A-NA* DINGIR.SAL^{MEŠ} KUR-e-aš
ḫu-u-ma-an-da-aš (53) pár-ši-ia ar-ku-ua-ar-za ku-e-da-aš da-a-iš

i 21 ḫu-u-da-ak-ma-az šu-me-el-pát *ŠA* EN-*LÍ* DINGIR^{MEŠ}
(22) *ŠA* É^{MEŠ} DINGIR-*LIM-KU-NU* *ŠA* ALAM-*KU-NU* ar-ku-ua-ar (23) i-ia-mi

-za arkuwar iya- , with double accusative: "make things / wishes into a plea"

iv 46 nu-kán ku-e (B: ku-i) *A-UA-TE*^{MEŠ} *A-NA* ^{d}UTU-*ŠI* ŠÀ-ta
(47) na-at-za *A-NA* DINGIR^{MEŠ} ar-ku-ua-ar DÙ-zi

i 25 EGIR-*ŠU*-ma-za *ŠA* *ZI-IA* *A-UA-TE*^{MEŠ} ar-ku-ua-ar i-ia-mi

i 27 nu-za *A-UA-TE*^{MEŠ} ku-e *A-NA* DINGIR^{MEŠ} EN^{MEŠ} ar-ku-ua-ar
(28) DÙ-mi ... (29) ku-e-ma-mu *A-UA-TE*^{MEŠ} *Ú-UL* iš-ta-ma-aš-te-ni
am-mu-uk-ma-za-at (30) *A-NA* DINGIR^{MEŠ} ar-ku-ua-ar i-ia-mi-pát

iii 37 nu-za *A-NA* DINGIR^{MEŠ} (38) ku-e *A-UA-TE*^{MEŠ} ar-ku-ua-ar i-ia-mi

arkuwar ištamaš, "hear / listen to a plea" (without *-za*)

i 26 nu-mu ki-e ar-ku-ua-ar-ri$^{HI.A}$ (27) iš-ta-ma-aš-tén

i 20 ki-nu-na-mu DINGIR^{MEŠ} am-me-el *ŠA* ^{LÚ}SANGA-*KU-NU* ÌR-*KU-NU*
me-mi-an (21) ar-ku-ua-ar (B i 21: ar-ku-wa-ar-ra) iš-ta-ma-aš-tén

i 35 nu-mu DINGIR^{MEŠ} EN^{MEŠ} ki-e *A-UA-TE*^{MEŠ} (36) ar-ku-ua-ar
(*B* adds tiyauwaš) DINGIR^{MEŠ} EN^{MEŠ} ne-pí-ša-aš KI-aš-ša iš-ta-ma-aš-ša-an-du

arkuwar tiyawar (from *dai-*), "presentation of a plea"

i 34 nu-mu ki-e-da-aš *A-NA A-UA-TE*^{MEŠ} ar-ku-ua-ar ti-ia-u-ua-aš
(35) *A-NA* DINGIR^{MEŠ} tar-kum-ma-i

iv 47 GIM-an-ma-kán (48) ar-ku-ua-ar ti-ia-u-ua-ar kar-ap-ta-ri

arkueššar extended noun (*hapax* !)

iii 21 nu DINGIR^{MEŠ} ku-i-e-eš (B adds ku-u-uš) ki-e-da-ni UD-ti
(22) ku-e-da-ni ar-ku-u-e-eš-ni *IŠ-TU* EME-*IA* ḫal-zi-iḫ-ḫu-un

The simple verb *arkuwa(i)-* and its iterative *arkuweške-* appear without the reflexive *-za*. More frequently, however, the notion is expressed by *-za arkuwar iya-/ dai-* ,"to make / present a plea", invariably with *-za*. This includes both normal transitive sentences, with *arkuwar* as object accusative, and double accusatives with the sense "make a thing / wish into a plea." The occurrences in this text fully confirm Th. van den Hout's observations[161] on the criterion governing the presence of the particle *-za*: a relation between the subject and the *Affect*, i.e. the object accusative, in this case the "words / things / problems" (*memian; AWATE*^{MEŠ}) of the pleading person. The particle *-za* appears both when a "third party" (the invoked gods) is present in the phrase (i 27 f., 29 f., iii 37 iv 46) and when it is absent (i 25).

The verbal substantive *arkuwar* (reduced from **arkuwawar*) appears to be attested only in direct case, whereas for the oblique the extended noun *arkueššar* is used. The dat.-loc. *arkuešni* (iii 22) is, so far, only attested in this text. The full ritual performance is expressed by *arkuwar tiyawar* (from *dai-*), "presentation of the pleading", gen. *AWATE*^{MEŠ} *arkuwar tiyawaš*, "the words of the presentation of the pleading".

i 4 *šuḫḫa-* The structure on the roof of which the prayer and the offering ritual takes place is nowhere indicated. Whether it is the roof of a temple, a palace, or some other structure cannot be established,[162] and perhaps the author left the location deliberately unspecified. From other texts we learn that ritual activities with the participation of the king take place on roofs of various edifices,[163] including that of the *ḫalentuwa*-house, i.e. the main palace complex.[164]

^{d}UTU-*i menaḫḫanda*: Since the time of day is not otherwise specified, this must be an indication that the prayer takes place during (sunny) daytime. However, since bird-oracle texts sometimes use ^{d}UTU-*i* and ^{d}UTU-*un* as an indication of direction,[165] the possibility of a wind direction,

161 "Remarks on Some Double Accusative Constructions", in O. Carruba (ed.), *Per una grammatica Ittita* (*Studia Mediterranea* 7, Pavia 1992), 277-304, (especially 278 ff.).

162 V. Haas, *Nerik* (1970), 188, assumes the roof of a temple; Ph. H. J. Houwink ten Cate, "The Sun God of Heaven, the Assembly of Gods and the Hittite King", in D. van der Plas (ed.), *Effigies Dei; Essays on the History of Religions* (Leiden 1987), 20, allows for the roof of the palace or a temple.

163 See N. Boysan-Dietrich, *Das hethitische Lehmhaus aus der Sicht der Keilschriftquellen* (*TdH* 12, Heidelberg 1987), 85-105; Ph. Houwink ten Cate, "The Hittite Storm God", *Natural Phenomena* (1992), 96. In KUB 57.63, an evocation to the Sun-goddess of Arinna, the king performs the ritual on the roof of the temple of the goddess (iii 26'-32'); A. Archi, "Eine Anrufung der Sonnengöttin von Arinna", *Fs. Otten*^{2} (1988), 6, 24.

164 KUB 55. 39 obv.19'; quoted (as Bo 2372) in S. Alp, *Beiträge zur Erforschung des hethitischen Tempels* (Ankara 1983), 228. Alp maintains that the *ḫalentuwa-* is the adyton of the temple (see also A. Kammenhuber, *HW*^{2} III, 20 f.). The Hurrian-Hittite bilingual renders Hittite *ḫalentuwa-* with Hurrian *ḫikalli*, obviously a loan-word from É.GAL / *ekallu*, *"palace"*; see J. Klinger, *OLZ* 88 (1993), 506, n. 5. This further supports the view which maintains that the *ḫalentuwa-* is the palace(-complex). See, most recently, H. G. Güterbock and Th. van den Hout, *The Hittite Instruction for the Royal Bodyguard* (Chicago 1991), 59 f., with previous literature (to which add I. Singer, *StBoT* 27, 111 f.).

165 A. Archi, *SMEA* 16 (1975), 119-180; J. de Roos, "To the East or to the West? Some Comments on Wind

probably "east", cannot be excluded. When the preparations for the ritual are completed, the king goes up to the roof and prostrates himself to the Sun-god of Heaven[166] who is here conceived as the celestial star itself.[167] See further Ch. XIII.

^{GIŠ}BANŠUR AD.KID *kariyanda,* "covered wickerwork tables"; usually the texts specify "covered with a cloth" (GAD-*it* e.g.: KUB 11. 21a vi 15, KUB 56. 45 i 7). Some notion of how these portable offering tables might have looked may be derived from cultic scenes on Hittite reliefs, decorated pottery, and seals.[168]

i 5 The join piece 1111/z, identified by H. Otten and Ch. Rüster (*ZA* 62, 242) has established, against all expectations, that the second table is not for all the other gods, but rather for the "male gods" only. In fact, as seen in the ritual offerings, the two tables (note the chiastic formulation) serve the male and the female gods respectively, the former also designated as the table of the Storm-god *piḫaššašši*. For more on this division see Ch. IX.

i 6 ff. The list of ingredients specifies exact quantities only for the sacrificial breads and for the wine pitchers,[169] which are the generic sacrificial offerings (cf. iii 64). The other products – honey mixed with fine oil, fat-bread and groats – are measured by their containers: a full *(cooking-)pot* (^{DUG}ÚTUL) for the fat-bread, a *bowl* (^{DUG}LIŠ.GAL) for the groats, and some sort of *thin* [*bo*]*wl* (^{DUG}LIŠ.G]AL SIG; see below) for the honey (mixed with) fine oil. As shown by *memal,* the products are expressed in nominative case rather than as a genitive governed by the containers, literally: "groats: a bowl", etc. For the offerings see further Ch. IX.

i 7 The restoration of the beginning of the line is problematic. Otten and Rüster, *ZA* 64, 242 (followed by Lebrun) suggested [*me-m*]*a-al*$^{?}$, but collation excludes a reading *-al* for the last sign. It is most probably SIG, as recognized by Goetze, *ANET*, 397b, "[x] thin loaves (?)". The traces of the sign preceding it are best fitted for a GAL, certainly not NINDA. Indeed, one expects here the name of a container for the following honey and fine oil. A perfectly suited candidate would be ^{DUG}DÍLIM(LIŠ).GAL SIG, "thin (or delicate) bowl", a rarely attested vessel, which holds water and other liquids.[170] However, the available space can hardly accomodate both a DUG and a DÍLIM (cf. ^{DUG}DÍLIM.GAL just underneath it). A ^{DUG}GAL SIG does not seem to be attested; therefore I assume that, unless written with minuscule characters, either DUG or DÍLIM were omitted.

For the mixture of honey and oil (and other ingredients) see, e.g., H. Otten and Vl. Souček, *StBoT* 8 (1969) ii 7-13 (honey and oil burnt for the gods); KBo 9. 106 ii 45 (filling a vessel with wine, plain olive oil and honey), and especially KUB 15. 34 i 34: LÀL Ì.DÙG.GA *anda imiyanit ,* "mixed honey and fine oil".[171]

Directions in Hittite Texts", *Journal of Ancient Civilizations* 5 (1990), 87-96.

166 As noted in the transliteration, collation has provided ^{d}UTU [*Š*]*A*-⸢*ME-E*⸣ rather than ^{d}UTU [^{UR}]^{U}T[ÚL-*na* , as transliterated by Otten – Rüster, *ZA* 64, 242.

167 Cf., e.g., KBo 4.8+ ii 23 *nu nepišaš* ^{d}UTU-*un* IGI$^{\text{HI.A}}$-*it uškizzi* "she beholds the sun of heaven with her eyes"; H. A. Hoffner, *JAOS* 103 (1983), 188.

168 See A.Ünal, "Zur Beschaffenheit des hethitischen Opfertisches aus philologischer und archäologischer Sicht", in P. Calmeyer , K. Hecker , L. Jakob-Rost und C.B. F.Walker, *Beiträge zur Altorientalischen Archäologie und Altertumskunde: Fs. Barthel Hrouda* (Wiesbaden 1994), 283-291.

169 *CAD*, K, 499 defines *KUKKUBU* as a small container of metal, glass or clay serving as alabastron, libation jar, and drinking flask .

170 The files of the *CHD* have the following examples: KUB 43. 52+ ii 3 (*CTH* 390: Ritual of Ayataršа, etc.); KUB 7.29 obv. 15 (*CTH* 399: Ritual of Iyarri); KBo 29. 124, 4' (*CTH* 694: Ḫuwaššana cult); KUB 5.2 iv 56 (*CTH* 471: Ritual of Ammiḫatna); KBo 32. 13 ii 23; Hur. – Hit. biling.; see E. Neu, in B. Janowski, i. a., *Religionsgeschichtliche Beziehungen* (n, 172), 341; M.Vieyra, *RA* 59 (1965), p. 131, text P 3, l. 8' (fragmentary).

171 V. Haas & G. Wilhelm, *Hurritische und Luwische Riten aus Kizzuwatna* (1974), 184. For the Hittite reading of

i 9 The restoration of text *B* poses a problem. *UŠ-KE-EN* usually corresponds to Hittite *aruwaizzi* or *ḫin(i)kzi*, "bows before"[172], but *B* has a verb ending in]-*i* . One possibility would be the rare verb [*ḫa-li-iḫ-la*]-*i*, "kneels down, throws himself at the feet of (the Sun-god of Heaven)."[173] Another, suggested to me by Hoffner, is a supine + *da-a-*]*i*. A rare supine form of *aruweške-* is indeed attested in KUB 13.9 + 40.62 i 5,[174] but I wonder whether "he (the king) begins to bow down before the Sun-god of Heaven" provides a sensible meaning. Perhaps the best way out is to assume variant formulations in the two versions. In that case one may adopt Ph. Houwink ten Cate's suggestion to restore the verb in *B* as *me-ma*]-*i* , "[spea]ks to the Sun God [of] Hea[ven]".[175] This would be the *me-ma-i* which *A* has in line 10, and it would imply a shorter version in *B* i 10: [*na-aš A-NA* ᵈUTU *ŠA-ME-E ki-iš-ša-an me-ma*]-*i*. The only problem with this otherwise good solution is that *B* i 11 would have to begin with the appeal itself – [ᵈUTU *ŠA-ME-E Ù* ᵈUTU ᵁ]ᴿᵁTÚL-na etc. – and this does not fill out the gap at the beginning of the line (of ca. 11 or 12 signs). Finally, the best solution at the present, which would fill out the gaps and keep the two versions close to each other would be: (10) [*na-aš ne-pí*(*-ša*)*-aš* ᵈUTU]-*i* // (11) *ki-iš-ša-an me-ma-i* ....] (cf. iii 19), but this would entail the insertion of the paragraph divider in the middle of the sentence. Although this happens in *B* (e.g.: iii 22), here it would be somewhat peculiar because the scribe had plenty of space at the end of line 10; I cannot think of any reason why he would move the last words of the sentence to the next paragraph. The upshot is that only a join or another duplicate will provide a conclusive answer as to how *B* differed from *A* in this passage.

i 10 ff. For the following list of (main) Gods of Ḫatti ("Short List") , see Ch. XII.

i 12 The use of BAD (=BE; *HZL* 13), apparently as an abbreviation for *BE-LU*, is very rare.[176] The few clear occurrences seem to belong to pre-Imperial texts, including a letter from Maşat. Both *A* and *B* agree on this unique writing, whereas elsewhere in the text they normally write EN and rarely *BE-LU*(ᴹᴱŠ). I wonder why both scribes use this writing for the title of the Storm-god of Ḫatti, whereas two lines later, in the corresponding title of the Storm-god of Ziplanda, they both use EN. Are perhaps "BAD/BE of the Ḫatti land" and "EN of the Ḫatti land" two different titles? R. Borger *apud HZL* suggests taking BE in the sense of "source" (Akk. *nagbu*), but this has no parallels in the Hittite documentation. Could this be a rare error shared by both scribes? See Ch. V. 2. 1.

i 14 f. The phrase on Šeri provides a rare insight into the process of text editing. Both texts initially had Šeri's epithet – "the bull, the champion (lit.: "the one who steps in front") in Ḫattuša, the land" – ignoring his regular companion, Ḫurri. For reasons explained in Ch. V, *A* corrected his version by deleting Šeri's lofty epithet and inserting Ḫurri's name instead (in "absolute case").[177]

"oil", see now, H.A. Hoffner, Jr., "The Hittite Word for 'Oil' and Its Derivatives", *Historische Sprachforschung* 107 (1994), 222-230; "Oil in Hittite Texts", *BA* 58 (1995), 108-114.

172 For this sense rather than "to prostrate" see C. Kühne, in B. Janowski - K. Koch - G. Wilhelm (Hg.), *Religionsgeschichtliche Beziehungen zwischen Kleinasien, Nordsyrien und dem Alten Testament. Internationales Symposion Hamburg* (*OBO* 129, Freiburg & Göttingen 1993), 260 ff.

173 For this rare verb, mostly appearing in iterative or medial forms, see *HW*, 3. Erg., 13; Neu, *StBoT* 5, 33 f.; Otten, *StBoT* 11, 24; J. Siegelová, *StBoT* 14, 58 f..

174 H. Otten, *ZA* 50, 236; E. von Schuler, *Fs. Friedrich* (1959), 446; *HW*, 359.

175 "The Sun God of Heaven", *Effigies Dei* (1987), 20. For a similar context see KUB 57. 63 iii 26' *mān lukkata*[*=ma*] (27') *nu* ᴸᵁ́SANGA *INA* É ᵈUTU (28') ᵁᴿᵁ*Arinna šarā* (29') *paizzi n=ašta* ᵈUTU-*i* (30') *menaḫḫan*[*da*] *kišš*[*an*] (31') *memai*; A. Archi, *Fs. Otten*² (1988), 24.

176 The *CTH* files have the following: KBo 16.25 iii 1 (*CTH* 251); HKM 81, obv. 1, rev. 30 (BE-*TI-*(*I-*)*IA*, for *BELTIYA*); KUB 45.47 iv 37 (*CTH* 494); KUB 57.46 rev.? 11' (*CTH* 252.B); KBo 22.52 ii 6' (?)(*CTH* 832). The last two appear in fragmentary contexts and are uncertain.

177 Some of the traces left after the erasure are quite clear. I have restored the rest by calculating the available space. The *Winkelhaken* of Ḫatti's *-ti* is particularly clear, which precludes a repetition of *B*' s *Ḫattuši*. The remark of

The correct sense of Šeri's epithet is provided by i 33.

i 16-24 Translated by Houwink ten Cate, "The Sun God of Heaven", *Effigies Dei* (1987), 21 with n. 38, who considers this passage to be "a short intermittent prayer."

i 17 *A* has *ḫumanduš* for nom. pl. only here, whereas in three other cases (i 15, 16, 49) he has *ḫumanteš*. *B* has *ḫumanteš* throughout the text. Other cases of *-uš* for grammatical nom. pl. are *alpuš* and IM$^{\text{HI.A}}$-*uš* (iii 10); *B* shares the former but has *ḫuwanteš* for the latter. See further Ch. IV.5.1

i 18 ^{LÚ}SANGA-*az*, with the particle *-z(a)*[178] in a nominal sentence, with a first person subject.[179] Cf. iii 48 f. (with *-za*) and iii 26 (where *-za* is missing).

i 19 *ḫumandaz* can have an adverbial meaning "out of everything", i.e. "on every occasion","in every respect," "in full measure."[180] However, it seems to me that the sense conveyed here is that Muwatalli was chosen, out of other possible candidates, to kingship in Ḫatti.[181] *B* has only *da-az* which, as suggested to me by Hoffner, may be an abbreviated writing of the synonym *da-<pí->az*, rather than a flawed *<hu-ma-an->da-az*.

i 20 f. *memian arkuwar* of *A* could be considered as two accusatives in partitive apposition, lit. "the word, the plea," i.e., "the word of pleading". *B*, however, adds the conjunction *-a*, "word and plea" (see *CHD*, L-N, 270). In this context *memian arkuwar* must be the equivalent of the more frequent *AWATE*^{MEŠ} *arkuwar*, despite the singular vs. plural form.

i 21 f. A further clear case of *A*' s editorial work is the emendation of *am-me-el* into *šu-me-el*, and consequently, the erasure of *šumel* in the next line. Although the original version, still kept by *B*, does make sense, *A* decided to "improve" the sentence by simplifying its pronominal forms. Apparently, he went on to correct the compound "lordly gods" as well (*ŠA* is written over an erasure). The sense of "my gods", lost through the emendation of *ammel*, was regained by changing the usual EN^{MEŠ} DINGIR^{MEŠ} into the unusual EN-*LÍ* DINGIR^{MEŠ}, with an Akkadian possessive pronoun. This is a clear demonstration of *A*' s resourcefulness in achieving the desired changes in meaning through minimal corrections in the written text. See further Ch. IV.4.4.

i 24 *ma-aḫ-ḫa-na-at* probably consists of *maḫḫan=a=at*, with an adversative *-a* stressing the opposition between good and bad treatment. *maḫḫan* is employed in this text as a comparative (i 23, 24 and esp. iii 72) and as a temporal conjunction (i 8 iv 45, 47).

i 25 "the matters of my (own) soul" is paralleled by "the matters in His Majesty's heart" in iv 46 (see there, and Ch. VII).

i 26 For the occasional conflation of the two semantically and phonetically similar verbs *aruwai-* , "to bow before" (see above on i 9) and *arkuwai-* "to plead", see H. Otten & Ch. Rüster, *ZA* 67 (1977), 61 f.; A. Kammenhuber, *HW*^{2} I 311, sub 1d; J. Puhvel, *HED*, 151. *B* apparently hesitated between the two and eventually wrote *-u-* over an erasure, thus creating an otherwise unattested form *ar-u-wa-ar-ri*$^{\text{HI.A}}$. Collation shows that in both texts the plural was marked with ḪI.A.

H.G. Güterbock, *Cahiers d'Histoire Mondiale* 2 (1954), 389, n. 59, that "a reference to Ḫurri-land is erased in 45 i 14..." is invalidated by the collated reading of the line.

[178] Not ablative *-az*, as listed in C. Kühne, *Fs. Otten*^{2} (1988), 227, n. 106. The writing *-az*, which is rare in Late Hittite, only occurs here and in i 21; *-za* appears thirteen times.

[179] See, H. A.Hoffner, *JNES* 28, 230; *Fs. Güterbock*^{2} (1986), 90.

[180] A. Goetze. *Hatt.*, 72; cf. H. Otten, *StBoT* 24, 9.

[181] Note that according to Ḫattušili's Apology (i 9) the oldest son of Muršili was a certain Ḫalpa-šulupi, whose fate is unknown.

i 28 "accept and hear them!" *B* has both verbs in the present, though the second is defective. *A* has the first verb in imperative (*dattin*), the second in present (*ištamaštini=ia=at*; could the omission of *-i* in *dattin* be affected by *sandhi* ?). On the other hand, from the context one would expect imperatives, as in i 27 and elsewhere in the text. Craig Melchert has suggested to me that the intended phrase was indeed an imperative *dattin ištamaštin=ya=at*, with a transition vowel between *n* and *ya*. For the"incorrect" use of the allomorph *-ya* after a consonant, he compares the Puduḫepa Letter KUB 21.38 obv. 54, 57, where we find both *iyat=ya* and *iyatt=a*.

i 30 f. UN-*az*/ *antuḫšaš* KAxU-*az*: *A* has a partitive apposition, lit. "from the man, from the mouth"; *B* used a more regular genitive dependence "from the mouth of a man", in other words "from my human mouth." The same idea of the irresponsible human mouth is expressed more elaborately in Muwatalli's other prayer, KBo 11.1 rev. 15 f.: "But as we are human beings, the words that we know, [that came up] from our mouth, [ ] and those (words) that we do not know, that did not come up from our mouth ..." (Houwink ten Cate & Josephson, *RHA* 25, 119).

i 31 Lit.: "let forth in respect to hearing." The actual meaning of this phrase has often been debated: does it mean that the gods should let the unworthy words pass through, i.e. permit them, despite their reservations, or rather, that they should simply let them pass by, i.e., ignore them. A. Goetze (*AM*, 209; *ANET*, 398a) opted for the second possibility and rendered: "refrain from hearing." On the other hand, F. Ose, *Supinum und Infinitiv im Hethitischen* (Leipzig 1944), 13, as well as the English dictionaries (*HED*, 457; *CHD*, P, 125) prefer the first: "permit/allow them to be heard." I think that the basic meaning of *para tarna-* allows for both interpretations, but I prefer Goetze's, because it is hard to assume that the suppliant would want to impose his unworthy words on the gods despite their wish. It is more conceivable that the gods are asked to decide themselves what is and what is not worthy of their hearing and acceptance.

i 33 *B* adds GUD to the divine determinative. In *B* iv 67 (= *A* iv 36) ^{d}*Še-ri* is written over an erasure, and I assume that there too he first wrote GUD, but then erased it and was content with DINGIR. My understanding of Šeri's epithet differs from previous interpretations: A. Goetze, *ANET*, 398a: "...thou bull who standest in the presence of the Storm-god of the Hatti-land"; H. G. Güterbock, *Cahiers d'Histoire Mondiale* II (1954), 389: "bull of the Weather-god of Ḫatti ..."; H. Otten, *HdO* 8 (1964), 108: "Stier, der du vor dem Wettergotte von Ḫatti stehst"; R. Lebrun, *Hymnes et prières*, 274: "taureau du dieu de l'orage du pays hittite, après t'etre avancé/presenté". These renderings take Ḫatti as depending on the Storm-god, but in the similar phrase in i 14 = *B* i 15 (omitted in *ANET*) the Storm-god is not present. Therefore, I take "bull of the Storm-god" as an apposition to Šeri, and the rest of the line as the expression "champion of Ḫatti".

peran[182] *tianza* , lit. "the one who steps in front", is treated as a noun, taking the genitive "of the Land of Ḫatti". It may be rendered as "front-runner", "champion", or the like; German *Vorsteher/Vortgesetzte* comes closest to the Hittite construction.[183] The image recalls the leaping bulls at the head of the procession of gods in Yazılıkaya. See further Ch. XIV.

i 35 *kē/ki:* for *B*' s preference for *i* vocalization, see Ch. IV. 3.1.1.

i 36 *B* seems to have the better text, with *arkuwar ti[yauw]aš* as in l. 34. *A* probably omitted *tiyauwaš* (or eliminated it on purpose), and was left with a somewhat aberrant asyndetic pair, "words (and) plea."

B' s *dagazipaš<šaš>* is a simple dittography, or perhaps it is a flawed attempt to distinguish the

[182] For the vocalization *pé-ra-an* (not *pí-ra-an*), see Neu, *StBoT* 18 (1974), 38; H. C. Melchert, *Studies in Hittite Historical Phonology* (Göttingen 1984), 85.

[183] Cf. IBoT i 36 ii 48, 53 *péran ti(ya)nteš* LÚ.MEŠ SIG_5-*TIM*; L. Jakob-Rost, *MIO* 11 (1966), 187: "vorgesetzte Offiziere"; H. G. Güterbock & Th. P. J. van den Hout, *The Hittite Instruction for the Royal Bodyguard* (Chicago 1991), 21, 53: "advanced corporals"; cf. also A. Archi, *Fs. Otten*^{2} (1988), 30.

genitive and the nominative; in iii 10, however, *B* (iii 48) uses a correct genitive.

B i 38 Weber's autograph is inaccurate. *iš-ta-ma-aš-ša-du* belonged originally to line 38. Thereafter, the scribe of *B* started a new paragraph with the list of ritual offerings (which in *A* appears in iv 3 ff.), beginning with the Sun-goddess of Arinna. He then discovered that he had omitted the offerings for the Sun-god of Heaven and squeezed this in the empty space between the two words of line 38: [3 NIND]A.GUR$_4$.RA *A-NA* ^{d}UTU AN-*I* and added, at some distance, a small KI.MIN. In order to separate this additional phrase from the previous paragraph, he added a new division line, which resulted in the separation of *ištamaššadu* from its original paragraph. Finally, he added a large double-X -like mark at the end of the new division line to note this sloppy passage. See further Chs. IX and XIII.

i 37-iii 4 The "Long List" of local cults is discussed as a whole in Ch. XII. Here only limited comments are offered regarding individual entries.

i 37-39 For this entry and the solar deities in the text, see Ch. XIII.

i 40 For the intriguing variant *B*: *Tiwa* / *A*: *Šamuḫa*, see Ch. XV and my article in *Fs. Houwink ten Cate.*[184] The original text no doubt had Tiwa, which was emended (partly in *B* and fully in *A*), probably due to the influence of the following paragraphs. G. del Monte, *RGTC* 6/2, 340, does not comment on the textual variant of *B* and conceives of this and the following two paragraphs as one long entry of Šamuḫa, with the list "male gods, etc. .... of Šamuḫa" repeated twice by mistake. Although there is definitely a connection between the three paragraphs, the division is no doubt intentional and comprehensible. With an original toponym Tiwa in this paragraph, there is no repetition at all.

i 42 The first deity is neither IŠTAR (as first read by Güterbock, *Cahiers d'Histoire Mondiale* 2, 390; Garstang-Gurney, *Geography*, 116), nor ^{d}U.GUR, (as read by Lebrun, *Hymnes et prières, 259*), but rather ^{d}U DU$_6$, "Storm-god of the Ruin" (as in ii 5). See further Ch. XV.

i 43-45 Both texts have the last sign of *BE-E-LA-AT* written above the line. For the crucial significance of this omission see Ch. V. 2.

The cults of the important cult center Šamuḫa in the Upper Land, mostly of Ḫurrian origin, have been studied in depth.[185] "Lady of *AYAKKI*"[186] is probably an epithet of IŠTAR of Šamuḫa, rather than an independent deity.[187] The *ayakku* is probably a temple,[188] which is mentioned also in the great prayer to IŠTAR;[189] the parallel Neo-Babylonian fragment has É.AN.NA instead (l. 28): "Have mercy, Lady of Holy Eanna, the pure treasury". The etymology of the name remains unknown. Conspicuously missing in this list is the well-known Goddess of the Night, unless she was indeed identified with the local IŠTAR/Šaušga, as suggested by Lebrun and Wegner. For arguments against this identification, see A. Archi, *RSO* 51, 297; A. Ünal, "The Nature and Iconographical Traits of 'Goddess of Darkness'", *Fs. Nimet Özgüç* (1993), 639-644.

i 46-49 The two paragraphs are related to Katapa, but the first entry lists in fact the gods of Šaḫpina,

[184] "The Toponyms Tiwa and Tawa", in Th. P.J. van den Hout and J. de Roos (eds.), *Studio Historiae Ardens: Ancient Near Eastern Studies Presented to Philo H.J. Houwink ten Cate on the Occasion of his 65th Birthday* (Istanbul 1995), 271-274.

[185] See esp. I. Wegner, *Gestalt und Kult der Ištar-Šawuška in Kleinasien* (1981); R. Lebrun, *Samuha, Foyer Religieux de l'Empire Hittite* (Louvain-la-Neuve 1976); *RHA* 36 (1978), 135-140.

[186] The term is Akkadian, not Hittite, as incorrectly indicated in HW^2 I, 47. See H. Hoffner, *BiOr* 35 (1978), 245.

[187] Wegner, op. cit., 35 f.; see also H.-M. Kümmel, *ZA* 59 (1969), 323.

[188] *CAD* A1, 224 "a structure in a temple" ; *AHw*, 24 "ein Heiligtum, Hochtempel".

[189] *CTH* 312; E. Reiner & H.G. Güterbock, *JCS* 21 (1969), 260.

who are also venerated in the greater cult center. *Šartiyaš* is given in Laroche, *Dieux*, 76 and elsewhere as the full name of the deity, but there is definitely sufficient space to restore ᵈ[U] on which the genitive *šartiyaš*, "of help", depends.[190] The well-known Queen of Katapa is variously identified as an IŠTAR or a Ḫebat.[191] The prominent place of Katapa in the list is explained by KUB 17. 14 "obv." 4'-6', where it is one of four important royal towns, the others being Ḫattuša, Arinna, and Zip(pa)landa.[192]

i 50-56 As one would expect, the entry of Ḫatti/Ḫattuša is the longest in the list, representing the different layers of Hittite religion: Hattian (Ḫalmašuit, Karzi, Ḫapantaliya), Neshite (Pirwa and Ašgašipa[193]), Hurrian (the "Prominent Calf", perhaps representing Šarruma; see Ch. XIV), and various "imported" cults from Syria (Storm-god and Ḫebat of Ḫalab, Kubaba) and Mesopotamia (Ea and Damkina, IŠTAR of Nineveh). It is of interest to note the persistence in Ḫattuša of the old cult of the throne-goddess Ḫalmašuit, the patron goddess who delivered the city to Anitta half a millennium earlier.[194] Allatum, the Akkadian goddess of the Underworld, probably stands for Lelwani.[195] I cannot explain why the entry is divided into two paragraphs and why only the *lulaḫḫi*-gods are mentioned, but not the *ḫabiru*-gods, who always appear together in the witness lists of Hittite treaties (Laroche, *Dieux*, 122 f.; Klengel, *RlA* 7, 164 ff.). The appearance of the capital in a mere sixth place in the list is explained in Ch. XII.

i 57-58 The latest study on Zip(pa)landa and its cults is that of M. Popko, *Zippalanda, Ein Kultzentrum im hethitischen Kleinasien* (*TdH* 21, 1994). He identifies this important cult center with Alaca Hüyük.[196]

i 59-60 *A*' s corrections of *B*' s version are clearly demonstrated in this paragraph. *B* initially had a single line for Zitḫara (ii 24). With the division line already drawn, he then decided to squeeze in an additional line (ii 25) which came out in disarray. He first erased something (perhaps another *kur*]-*ša-aš*); then he repeated *Zitḫariyaš* and finished with "the rivers of Zitḫara", leaving out the rest of the recurring formula. Having discovered his omission he squeezed in above the line "the mountains", but not the "male gods and the female gods." *A* first followed *B*' s corrected version, then returned and erased two of the names which he deemed superfluous: ᵈLÍL[197] and

190 Cf. KBo 17.85, 16': ᵈU *šar-di*[-

191 See G. del Monte, *RGTC* 6, 199 with refs.; H.Otten, *RlA* 5, 486.

192 H.-M. Kümmel, *StBoT* 3 (1967), 58 f.; V. Haas, *Gesch. der heth. Religion* (1994), 584.

193 For a recent study on the "god on the horse"and his connection to Ašgašipa and to IŠTAR see, V. Haas, "Das Pferd in der hethitischen religiösen Überlieferung", in B. Hänsel und A. Hintze (eds.), *Die Indogermanen und das Pferd: Fs. Bernfried Schlerath* (Budapest 1994), 79 ff.

194 For ᵈ*Ḫalmašuit*- see now Kammenhuber, *HW*² II, 65 ff. (with previous refs.). The identification of this deity as the deified throne of Proto-Hattian origin has been questioned by F. Starke, *ZA* 69 (1979), 104-12; but cf. the responses of A. Archi, *Fs. Otten*² (1988), 13 f., n. 35, and I. Singer, " 'Our God' and 'Their God' in the Anitta Text", in O. Carruba, M. Giorgieri, C. Mora (eds.), *Atti del II Congresso Internazionale di Hittitologia* (*Studia Mediterranea* 9, Pavia 1995), 343-350.

195 For Lelwani and Allatum see H. Otten, *JCS* 4 (1950), 119-36; A. Kammenhuber, *Or* 41 (1972), 299; E. Laroche, *Fs. Güterbock*¹ (1974), 185; E. von Schuler, *Wörterbuch der Mythologie*, 186; O.R. Gurney, *Some Aspects of Hittite Religion*, 16; V. Haas, *Gesch. der heth. Rel.*, 245 n. 46. Lelwani is listed as a deity of Ḫattuša also in KBo 9.98+KUB 40.46 i 7, for which see Ch. XI.

196 Also V. Haas, *Gesch. der heth. Religion*, 591; idem, "Das Pferd...", in *Fs. Schlerath* (1994), 78 n. 17 (identifying Mount Taḫa with Kalehisar, some 5 kms. from Alaca). Cf., however, the differing views of O. R. Gurney, *AnSt* 15 (1995), 71, and R. Gorny, *JAOS* (forthcoming).

197 As pointed out by Houwink ten Cate, *JNES* 27, 208, the deity following ᵈLAMMA ᴷᵁŠ*kuršaš* should have been ᵈLAMMA LÍL, the Protective god of the Field. For these protective deities, see G. McMahon, *The Hittite State Cult of the Tutelary Deities* (Chicago 1991), and esp. *Appendix B*, on *kurša*-.

the second *Zitḫariyaš*.[198] He finished the paragraph with "the mountains (and) the rivers of Zitḫara", omitting, as had *B*, the "male gods and female gods." This is one of the clearest proofs that *A* copied and edited *B*' s version (see Ch. V. 2). As suggested in Ch. XI., the entry of Zitḫara follows that of Zippalanda because both towns have a son of the Storm-god. DUMU ᵈU must be an apposition to the Storm-god of the Army.

i 61 Urauna is always associated with the Sun-goddess of Arinna and Mezzulla; thus the restoration of the first deity in the entry remains unknown.[199] Urauna must be located not too far from Kummanni.[200]

i 62-65 Kummanni, the most important cult center of Kizzuwatna (see Kümmel, *RlA* 6, 335 f.), has a large entry which includes two pairs of Tešub and Ḫebat (of the city itself and of the nearby Mount Manuziya), NIN.GAL, Pišanuḫi[201] and Mount Kallištapa . One misses other important cults of Kummanni, like that of Išḫara and Lelwani. Kummanni is the only place in the list whose gods are specifically attributed to both the city and the land, the latter being a synonym for Kizzuwatna.

The term *šinapši* (with É and GIŠ determinatives)has often been discussed during recent years.[202] It is a typically Kizzuwatnean architectural term related to various chthonic cults. A location in the mountains, or some other connection to mountains, is shown by several passages; e. g. the juxtaposition of the two in KBo 11.1 obv. 32 (see Ch. X): "But if a mountain or a *šinapši* or a holy pit[203] has been offended and it has pleaded with the Storm-god ....". The present text shows that the patron deities of the *šinapši* were Tešub and Ḫebat, or rather Ḫebat-Šarruma, taking into account *B*' s addition of LUGAL above the line. On Ḫebat-Šarruma see further under i 78.

i 66-67 The Storm-god *piḫaimi/piḫam(m)i* is not a "doublet" of the Storm-god *piḫaššašši* (Laroche, *Dieux*, 71; also Haas, *Gesch. der heth. Religion*, 326 n. 90). The etymologies of the two may be related, but there is nothing else to show an equation of the two "shining" deities (for the etymology of *piḫaššašši* see Ch. XV). Besides the entry of Šanaḫuitta, a town located in the Halys Basin,[204] the Storm-god *piḫa(i)mmi*[205] occurs in lists of *ḫuwaši*'s,[206] in an Anatolian ritual from Emar[207], in a cult

[198] Two deities called Zitḫariyaš also occur next to each other in the festival of IŠTAR of Šamuḫa, KUB 27.1 i 64: 1 NINDA.SIG LUGAL ᵈ*Zittaḫariyaš* KI.MIN 1 NINDA.SIG *ŠA* SAL.LUGAL ᵈ*Zitḫariyaš* KI.MIN. Laroche, *Dieux*, 40 (omitting the *ŠA*) took this reference to mean that there were a male and a female form of the deity. However, McMahon, op. cit., 23 convincingly demonstrated that these are protective deities of the king and the queen respectively. Perhaps the repetition of Zitḫariya in our text had a similar significance.

[199] The available space and the traces would pass for [ᵈU ḪI.Ḫ]I, and the region of Kummanni would suit the surmised origins of the Storm-god *piḫaššašši* (see Ch. XV), but there is no textual evidence to support such a restoration.

[200] *RGTC* 6, 459. In *RGTC* 6/2 del Monte distinguishes betwen two towns with that name, without explaining his reasons.

[201] ᵈPišanuḫi is a gentilicon derived from a city Pišana (*RGTC* 6, 316). KUB 30.31+ iii 17 has ᵈNupatik ᵁᴿᵁPišanuḫi, which may suggest that ᵈNupatik is identical to ᵈPišanuḫi. The latter also appears in the *ḫišuwa* festival (KUB 20. 23 iv 5 = KUB 47.73 iii 1; cf. also KUB 48. 93, 6).

[202] V. Haas - G. Wilhelm, *Hurrische und luwische Riten aus Kizzuwatna* (1974), 36-38; F. Gentili Pieri, "L'edificio "šinapši" nei rituali Ittiti", *Atti Acc. Tosc.* 47 (1982), 1-37; G. Beckman, *Hittite Birth Rituals* (1983), 113; E. Masson, *Les douze Dieux de l'immortalité* (1989), 111 ff.; P. Negri-Scafa, *SMEA* 29 (1992), 189 ff.; J. Börker-Klähn, "Ahnengalerie und letzte Dienste derer von Ḫattuša", in H. Gasche, a.o. (eds.), *Mesopotamian History and Environment: Hommage à Léon de Meyer* (Leuven 1994), 362 f.; V. Haas, "Ein hurritischer Blutritus und die Deponierung der Ritualrückstände nach hethitischen Quellen", in B. Janowski, K. Koch & G.Wilhelm (Hg.), *Religionsgeschichtliche Beziehungen zwischen Kleinasien, Nordsyrien und dem Alten Testament. Internationales Symposion Hamburg* (*OBO* 129, Freiburg & Göttingen 1993), 70.

[203] For the sense of *AŠRU* in this context (KBo 11.1 obv. 32) – "pit, hole, cistern", rather than "(holy) place", see F. Gentili Pieri, op.cit., 32.

[204] M. Forlanini, *Hethitica* 6 (1985), 47, suggests an identification with Alişar Hüyük.

[205] See Ph. Houwink ten Cate, "The Hittite Storm God", *Natural Phenomena* (1992), 146, n. 64. Cf. also the PN

inventory of Karaḫna,[208] and in the list of witness gods to the Ulmi-Tešub treaty.[209] The proximity between the two "shining" Storm-gods in the last two contexts only shows an associative thought but not an equation or confusion between the two deities.

i 68-70 The cult of the lost city of Nerik is perpetuated in neighboring places, such as Kaštama (see, e.g., Haas, *Gesch. der heth. Religion,* 594-607). Mount Zaliyanu appears twice in the entry, but not as a flawed repetition. Rather, it is first listed among the gods of Nerik (together with the Storm-god, ZABABA and Zaḫapuna) and then (with a prepositioned genitive: "of Kaštama") among the gods of Kaštama (together with Tazzuwaši). It is perfectly conceivable that the same mountain would be sacred for two neighboring towns (or towns on opposite slopes of a mountain) and that therefore, for the sake of completeness, it would be mentioned with each of the two.

i 71-72 Takupša/ta appears to be an important district capital in the north, the seat of an AGRIG who supplies provisions for the cults of nearby centers such as Nerik and Ḫatenzuwa (I. Singer, *AnSt* 34, 115).

i 73 Šarišša was probably one of the main centers of the Anatolian IŠTAR-*liš,* to be distinguished from the Hurrian IŠTAR/Šaušga. In the Kumarbi myth, in the King of Battle legend, and in the so-called "Hurrian-Hittite" hymn to IŠTAR (*CTH* 717) the name of this goddess is written with the same phonetic complements.[210] The city was overrun by the Kaška for a certain period (von Schuler, *Kaškäer*, 28). It has recently been suggested that Šarišša be identified with the site of Kuşaklı near Başören in the province of Sıvas.[211]

i 74-75 Ḫantidaššu ("the mightiest") is the exclusive local goddess of Ḫurma (Otten, *RlA* 4, 110), but *B* nevertheless found it expedient to add "of Ḫurma" above the line (in sloppy characters). *A* took on the correction and he also added a *ŠA* after the divine couple of Ḫalab. For other cults of Ḫurma, see Otten, *RlA* 4, 502 f.

i 76-77 For the importance of the scribal error in the spelling of Lawazantiya repeated in both manuscripts see Ch. V. 2. It is intersting to note that only the so-called "Asianique" deities (to use Laroche's terminology in *Dieux*, Ch. IV), are listed, but not the typically Hurrian ones like Tešub, IŠTAR/Šaušga, Ḫebat-Šarruma, etc.[212]

i 78-9 The restoration [*Pitiy*]*arik*(*a*), a town situated near the Euphrates, is probable but not certain. Its inclusion in the same paragraph with Uda, a city located somewhere in northern Kizzuwatna

---

Piḫami and other names beginning with *Piḫa*-. Laroche, *Les Noms des Hittites* (1966), 139 ff.

206 KUB 12.2 i 18, iii 1; KUB 51. 88 r. col. 3'; AT 454 l. edge vi 1. See C. W. Carter, *Hittite Cult Inventories* (Diss. Chicago 1962), 76, 84.

207 Emar VI/3 (1986), 472, 24 : ^{d}IM *pí-ḫa-im-mi*. See E. Laroche, "Observations sur le rituel anatolien provenant de Meskene-Emar," in F. Imparati (ed.), *Studi di storia e di filologia Anatolica dedicati a Giovanni Pugliese Carratelli*, Firenze 1988, pp. 114-117; R. Lebrun, "Divinités Louvites et Hourrites des Rituels Anatoliens en langue Akkadienne provenant de Meskene," *Hethitica* 9 (1988), 148-150.

208 KUB 38. 12 iii 18 f.: ^{d}U *piḫaššaššiš* ^{d}U ḪI.ḪI ^{d}U *piḫaimi* ^{d}U *miyannaš*. For the juxtaposition of the first two names see Ch. XV.

209 KBo 4. 10 i 53: ^{d}U *piḫaimmiš* ^{d}U ḪI.ḪI-*aššiš* . The Bronze Tablet iii 86 replaces the two names with a single ^{d}U *piḫaššaššiš*. See Ch. XV.

210 G. Wilhelm, "Hymnen der Hethiter", in W. Burkert & F. Stolz (eds.), *Hymnen der Alten Welt im Kulturvergleich* (*OBO* 131, Freiburg Schweiz 1994), 70, n. 31, suggests *walliwalli*, an epithet of IŠTAR, as the possible Anatolian designation of the deity. For *CTH* 717 see also, I. Singer, "Some Thoughts on Translated and Original Hittite Literature", *Israel Oriental Studies* 15 (1995), 123-128.

211 G. Wilhelm, *MDOG* 127 (1995). For the first season of excavation conducted by A. Müller-Karpe, see AJA 99 (1995), 220 f.

212 For the pantheon of Lawazantiya see, R. Lebrun, *Hethitica* 4 (1981), 95-107; I.Wegner, *Gestalt und Kult der Ištar-Šawuška in Kleinasien*, (1981), 170-174; *RlA* 6, 436.

(see below), also supports the restoration.

The compound ᵈHebat-Šarruma (with only one divine determinative) is well-known in the region of Kizzuwatna.[213] They are conceived as one distinct entity, (compared by Laroche to "Madonne à l 'Enfant"), which recalls of course Yazılıkaya, where Šarruma is depicted standing behind his mother in the line of goddesses. In this text ᵈHebat-Šarruma only occurs in this entry and in the entry of Kummanni, where LUGAL is added above the line, in *B* only (i 68-70).[214]

For a balanced discussion on the location of Uda, see E. Laroche, *Syria* 40 (1963), 293 ff. Laroche pointed out the difficulties in the traditional location of Uda at Hyde in the Konya Plain (Garstang-Gurney, *Geography*, 293), and argued for a location in northern Kizzuwatna, which would explain its typically Hurrian/Kizzuwatnean cult. Recently M. Forlanini, *Hethitica* 10 (1990), 109-127, has suggested that we distinguish between a western and an eastern Uda, which he would locate in the region of Fıraktın.

ii 1-2 The Deity of Parša also appears in the Bronze Tablet (iii 50) and in the small fragment KUB 44. 51, 11'. In the former text it is listed together with the Storm-god *piḫaššašši* and with IŠTAR of Inuita; all three deities are in possession of localities outside the Land of Tarḫuntašša, which are exempted from the *šaḫḫan luzzi* service. This establishes a close relationship between the three deities, but we lack evidence for the localization of Parša.

The Sun-god(dess) of the Earth/Underworld is usually identified with Lelwani and with the Akkadian *ALLATUM*.[215]

ii 3-4 The Storm-gods of Ḫiššašḫapa and of Kuliwišna are listed as the gods of a royal palace. In KUB 19. 9 ii 19' (*CTH* 83.1) a Hittite king recounts that his father had a palace (ᴱ*ḫa-li-in-du-wa*) in Ḫiššašḫapa.[216] It may very well be the same palace as the one mentioned here. Ḫiššašḫapa apparently fell victim to a Kaška attack in the reign of Muwatalli, but it was later reconquered by Ḫattušili (Goetze, *Ḫatt.*, 21, l. 57).

ii 5-6 Karaḫna was probably the most important cult center of the Protective-god.[217] Together with Marišta and Šatupa it was occupied for a while by the Kaška in this period, which may explain the appearance of the Storm-god of the Ruin(-town) in this list. ᴰᴵᴺᴳᴵᴿ.ˢᴬᴸAlāš is not erased (so Haas, *Gesch. der heth. Religion* , 450) but written over an erasure in both manuscripts. The scribes apparently hesitated over where to put the long *ā* and finally got it in the wrong place.[218]

ii 7 Zulima is probably identical with Zulumma (H. Otten, *ZA* 53, 179).

ii 8-9 Liḫš/zina was an important cult center in the far north of Ḫatti (G. Frantz-Szabó, *RlA* 7, 18 f.). Its goddess,Tašimi, also appears as the consort of the Storm-god of Nerik (V. Haas, *Gesch. der*

---

213 See E. Laroche, "Le dieu Anatolien Sarruma", *Syria* 40 (1963), 292; V. Haas, *Gesch. der heth. Religion*, 387 f.

214 Since it is clearly attested in a text of Muwatalli II, the mention of ᵈḪebat-Šarruma cannot serve as a proof for a Ḫattušili III or Tudḫaliya IV dating of a religious text (KBo 21.34+), as claimed by R. Lebrun, *Hethitica* 2 (1977), 135. Generally speaking, there seems to be a tendency to date any text that deals with Kizzuwatnean cults to the age of Puduḫepa or later, partly ignoring the involvement of earlier kings in southern affairs. For Muwatalli and Kizzuwatna see Ch. X and Epilogue.

215 See O.R. Gurney, *Some Aspects of Hittite Religion*, 5 n. 6 (with refs.); Houwink ten Cate, "The Sun God of Heaven...", *Effigies Dei* (1987), 15; J. Börker-Klähn, *Fs. Nimet Özgüç* (1993), 345 ff. For *ALLATUM* and Lelwani see above on i 50-56.

216 The father of the king is probably Muršili II (see G. del Monte, *RGTC 6*, 112). For *ḫalentuwa*, "palace", see n. 164 above.

217 H. Otten, RlA 5, 403; V. Haas, *Gesch. der heth. Religion* (1994), 458.

218 The name is normally spelled *A-a-la*. This protective deity may have Mesopotamian origins. See G. McMahon, *Tutelary God* (1991), 98-115; V. Haas, *Gesch. der heth. Religion* (1994), 449.

heth. Religion , 446).

ii 10-11 Quite often *B* uses a Hittite word-order with prepositioned genitive, whereas *A* prefers an Akkadian construction (see Ch. iv. 4.4). For the location of Durmitta southwest of the Halys Basin (rather than in the east), see n. 375.

ii 12-14 Together with the Ḫulaya River, the Maraššantiya (= Halys) is the only deified river mentioned in the list by name. For the cluster of names Nenašša, Ḫupišna, Tuwanuwa see Ch. XII.2.

ii 15-17 GAZ.BA.IA (also spelled with A and A.A) is to be read Ḫuwaššanna, an important Luwian deity whose cult is described by numerous texts (*CTH* 690-694). Ḫupišna is usually identified with Kybistra/Ereğli, and its mountain Šarlaim(m)i ("the lofty one") must be one of the nearby peaks of the Bolkar Mountains.

ii 18-19 The omission of *ŠA* is the only variant in the small fragment C (against both *A* and *B*).

ii 20-21 Illaya is one of the few places (cf. Ḫurniya, ii 26) that has two male gods as its main deities – the Storm-god and the War-god; the latter appears regularly in the witness lists of Hittite treaties.

ii 22-23 Šuwanzipa of Šuwanzana is the prime example for a deity deriving its name from a location (or vice versa). *B* confused the two in the second occurrence and was corrected by *A*. The cult of this city[219] is described in KUB 57.108 iii 6-10 (*RGTC* 6/2,150).

ii 26-27 For the difficulty in reading the word after "king" see transliteration, n. 69. If the suggested solutions are valid, it would seem that neither scribe was able to come up with a real name for the "Kingly God" of Ḫurniya (lit.: "the king, the god"). It is difficult to decide whether this is a separate deity or simply an apposition to the Storm-god of Ḫurniya. KUB 57.87 ii 1-6 (transliterated in Ch. XI) provides a list of deities of Ḫurniya, including Tarupšaniš, Muwattiš, Pipiraš, and Nawatiyalaš. Ḫurniya also appears in the Bronze Tablet (iii 48) as the name of a land situated beyond the confines of both Ḫatti and Tarḫuntašša. For the general localization of this and the following places see Ch.V.2.

ii 28-29 Zarwišša appears in the Bronze Tablet (i 48) in relation to Mount Šarlaimmi.

ii 30-31 DINGIR.MAḪ, "the mighty god(dess)", is probably Ḫannahanna. She appears as the deity of Šaḫḫaniya also in KUB 57. 87 ii 3 (Ch. XI) and in KUB 54. 1 ii 40 ff.[220]

ii 32-33 For Mallitaškuriya, the place to which Alluwamna and Ḫarapšili were exiled (KUB 26. 77 obv. 10-12), see M. Forlanini, *Vicino Oriente* 7 (1988), 137, n. 39. The name is also restored in KUB 48. 105+KBo 12. 53 obv. 42' (A. Archi - H. Klengel, *AoF* 7, 145).

ii 34-35 For Ḫarziuna see M. Forlanini, *SMEA* 18 (1977), 214 f. The vocalization of the first syllable is not certain.

ii 36-37 Garstang-Gurney, *The Geography,* 118, render "Zanduza Lord of Šallapa", but EN-*aš* is an apposition to Zanduza of Šallapa (correctly G. del Monte, *RGTC 6*, 333). Ḫarziuna is followed by Šallapa also in KBo 4.13+ i 10.

ii 38-40 For the purportedly flawed spelling Ḫuwa*la*nuwanda (instead of Ḫuwa*t*nuwanda) see Ch. V.2.6. The Lower Land is situated south of the Tuz Gölü. Its exact extent depends on the identification of the River Ḫulaya (see Ch. XII.2) and the localization of Parašḫunta, the seat of the important Assyrian *kārum*.The new geographical data provided by the Bronze Tablet render the traditional identification with Acem Höyük near the Salt Lake unlikely; a more (south-)westerly location

---

219 Located by M. Forlanini, *Hethitica* 10 (1990), 118, in the region of Ereğli.

220 V. Haas, *Gesch. der heth. Religion* (1994), 434, 109, maintains that although Ḫannaḫanna is adopted in city pantheons, she never appears as a city goddess. This distinction requires clarification.

should be sought.[221]

ii 41-42 In Wašuduwanda two great goddesses are worshiped (cf. Illaya and Ḫurniya with two male gods). Innuwita is now attested in the Bronze Tablet (iii 51: *In-ú-i-ta*); its IŠTAR is one of three deities associated with townships outside Tarḫuntašša exempted from *šaḫḫan luzzi* taxes (see above on Parša, ii 1-2).

ii 43-45 *B* has a slightly unusual order, inserting Mount Takurga in the midst of the otherwise closed sequence "male gods, etc." *A* corrected this error, but, contrary to his usual skills, he introduced a few errors of his own (see Ch. V.3). (1) As elsewhere, *A* changed the Hittite into Akkadian genitive constructions, but then was unsure how many *ŠA* URUḪ. were needed and erased the last one; (2) He added the lost nasal *n* in the first Ḫanḫana, but failed to do so in the following occurrences (see Ch. IV.3.2.3); (3) he left out DINGIR in DINGIR.SAL (also in ii 61).
For the localization of Ḫanḫana, see H. Otten, *RlA* 4, 104. Alazḫana is attested only in this text.

ii 46-47 Contrary to the previous paragraph, Here *A* left the Hittite genitive construction unchanged. He added the nominative ending to Kataḫḫa. The same goddess, "the Queen", is written in ii 60 with initial Ḫ.

ii 48-49 Wašḫaniya appears as a Land in *A*, but not in *B*. On the other hand, the two scribes treat Tupazziya (ii 70) in an opposite manner, and it appears as a land only in *B*.

ii 50-51 The "Lord of Landa" must be Kunniyawanni, one of the "two lords" of the city evoked by Muršili in his "Fourth Plague Prayer" (KUB 14. 13 i 1; *RGTC 6*, 243). He is usually preceded by his consort, the "Lady (*BĒLAT*) of Landa."[222]
This unique association of Landa with Ḫattina, a toponym located in the Halys Basin (*RGTC 6*, 101; 6/2, 36), has led to erroneous localizations of Landa in the same region (Garstang-Gurney, *Geography*, 22). The weight of all the other geographical indications leads towards a localization in the southern Konya Plain, as first suggested by E. Forrer (see *RGTC 6*, 242 f. and Forlanini, *Vicino Oriente* 7, 136 f., with refs.).

ii 52-54 I suspect that Ḫarpiša is followed in the next paragraph by Ḫakpiša because of the phonetic resemblance (see Ch. XII.1). According to KUB 30.29 obv. 10, Ḫarpiša had a cult of Ḫalmašuit; this probably indicates a location in northern Anatolia. Kalimuna on the Kaška frontier is one of the towns mentioned in connection with Hattušili's realm (Otten, *RlA* 5, 323). Its deity, Karmaḫi, may be identical with Karmaḫili who appears in several ritual fragments, one of them mentioning Ḫakmiš and Muwatalli (Otten, *RlA* 5, 447).[223]

ii 55 Although the gods of Ḫakpiša,[224] the capital of Ḫattušili's sub-kingdom, are often mentioned in other texts (see *RGTC* 6, 66 f.), it is rather surprising that here we have only the plain formula "the male gods, etc." Was the text written before Ḫakp/miš rose to a prominent political role? Note, however, that this entry is immediately followed by the ancestral gods of the king (see Ch. XII.1).

ii 56-58 *B* listed the royal ancestors in the order *father, grandfather, grandmother* (but then erased by mistake the first *ABI* of *grandfather*). This seems to me to be the original ("chronological") order,

[221] See V. Haas, *MDOG* 109 (1977), 15 f.; I. Singer, *AnSt* 34 (1984), 125.

[222] O. R. Gurney, *Some Aspects of Hittite Religion*, 5, n. 5, considers the possibility that the name concealed behind the Akkadogram might be Hurrian Allani,"the Lady". However, as he admits, her consort, Kunniyawanni, bears a Luwian name. According to KUB 57.87 ii 1 (see Ch. XI), the Lady of Lanta could be an "IŠTAR-type" goddess. See further Ch. VIII.

[223] The restoration of the same name in KUB 38. 2 ii 4 (Bo 2383), the description of a male figurine, is not certain. See C.-G. von. Brandenstein, *Bildbeschr.*, 7; see also V. Haas, *Gesch. der heth. Religion* (1994), 812, n. 214.

[224] For the development of the spellings of Ḫakmiš, see Hoffner, *JNES* 31 (1972), 31.

which was then reversed by *A*. Curiously, the gods of the mother are missing; mere oversight or deliberate omission?

The Protective-god of the Field/Countryside (^{d}LAMMA.LÍL) is represented in texts and in iconography as a god standing on a stag (McMahon, *Tutelary God*, 44 ff). He is the guardian of hunters, and thus, his association with the Protective-god of the King (see ib. 47) is natural. In one text ^{d}LAMMA LÍL appears in the king's dream requesting offerings (KUB 48. 122+KUB 15.5 iv 7-8).

ii 59 The "House of Gazzimara" was an important royal storehouse (*RGTC 6*, 205), and probably for this reason it is listed after the royal ancestors.

ii 60-61 Ḫataḫḫa is a variant of Kataḫḫa, "the Queen" (Laroche, *Dieux*, 28; Ünal, *RlA* 5, 477 f.). On the basis of dated occurrences H. Otten & C. Kühne (*StBoT* 16, 49 f.) suggested the following phonetic development: Kataḫḫa > Kataḫga > Ḫataḫḫa > Ḫataḫga > Ḫatagga. According to their "chronology" Ḫataḫḫa would fall neatly between Muršili II and thirteenth century texts. But then, how are we to account for the spelling Kataḫḫa(š) in the entry of Tawiniya (ii 46)? Are we dealing with a purely chronological phonetic development, or are perhaps dialectal variants also to be taken into account?
The festival of the Storm-god of the Rain is celebrated in the ANTAḪŠUM-festival immediately after the celebrations which take place in Ankuwa (Güterbock, *JNES* 19, 84). The colophon of KBo 22. 214 also mentions the "Rain festival of Ankuwa." IŠTAR of the Field also appears among the gods of Šamuḫa.

ii 62-63 The phonetic resemblance may have attracted Niniša<n>kuwa after Ankuwa. The place also occurs in a Maşat letter (*HKM* 71, 19), but its location remains unknown. Neither do we know much about Duruwaduruwa and Ikšun(uw)a, clearly grouped together on account of their common cult of Pirwa (Forlanini, *Fs. Alp*, 177, 179). Besides this cluster Pirwa only occurs in the entry of Ḫatti/Ḫattuša.

ii 64-65 Šullama and Ḫatrā must have been important cult centers of Išuwa. The Storm-god of Ḫatrā is worshiped in the festival of IŠTAR of Šamuḫa. Šullamma is attested also as the name of a mountain (*RGTC 6/2*, 148).

ii 66-67 For the location of Tegarama in the region of Elbistan see refs. in *RGTC* 6, 384; *RGTC* 6/2, 154.

ii 68 An IŠTAR of Paliya occurs in an offering list for Hurrian deities (*RGTC 6/2*, 119). Could this IŠTAR /Šaušga be the "Queen of Paliya" mentioned here ?

ii 69-70 *B* considered Tuppaziya as a "land", and this is supported by a Maşat letter (*HKM*, 96, 19'). *A* omitted the KUR (cf. ii 49). An Arzawan attack from Tuppaziya seems to locate this place not far from Tuwanuwa (*DŠ* 15 F iv 13' ff.; *RGTC 6*, 441).

ii 71 Kariuna of Karuna is another case of a DN derived from a GN or vice versa (cf. Šuwanzana/Šuwanzipa). Note the different rendering of the *u*-vocalism in the two duplicates (see Ch. IV.3.1.2).

ii 72-73 For the Storm-god of Growing, see V. Haas, *Gesch. der heth. Religion* (1994), 327, n.98; see also *CHD*, M, 238. Ap(a)zišna appears with places located in the north (*RGTC 6*, 27 f.). However, if it is indeed identical with Azpišna, as suggested by Forlanini , *Hethitica* 10 (1990), 113 f., a more southerly location is more likely.

iii 1 Kalašmitta (= Karašm/tita; Otten *RlA* 5, 407) is located according to KUB 48.105 + KBo 12. 53 rev. 14 in the province of Durmita, near the eastern course of the Halys. It should thus be distinguished from Kalašma further to the east.

iii 2-3 For Tapiqqa and its identification with Maşat Hüyük, see n. 373.

iii 4 "The house of the *tawannanna*" seems to be attested only in this text, but "the house of the queen" (É SAL.LUGAL) appears in a list of institutions which provide cultic provisions.[225]

The Storm-god *ḫulaššaššiš* is probably identical with the Storm-god of the town Ḫulašša (*RGTC* 6, 115; 6/2, 41; cf. Starke, *StBoT* 31, 108). He had a cult of his own (KUB 44.1) and was also worshiped in the festival of IŠTAR of Šamuḫa (KUB 27. 1 i 54). According to KUB 40. 2 obv. 30' Ḫulašša must be located near Tarša/Tarsus (Goetze, *Kizzuwatna*, 62 f., 69). The appearance of the Storm-god *ḫulaššaššiš* just before "the gods and the goddesses of the king and the queen" seems to indicate some special relationship between this deity and the royal house. Muwatalli's connections to southern Kizzuwatna are best attested by his Sirkeli relief (see also Epilogue with n. 445).

iii 5 "of the king and the queen"; *A* corrected *B*' s flawed Akkadian complements. See Ch. IV.4.4.4.6.

iii 6 ff. Goetze, *ANET*, 398a, renders: "in whose temples king and queen worship officiating as priests", taking LÚ.MEŠ SANGA as referring to the king and queen and *kuedaš* to the temples. I understand *kuedaš* as referring to the gods. The distinction is between temples which are frequented by the royal couple itself (obviously in their capacity as high priests of the kingdom) and those that are not, but whose cult is maintained by (regular) priests (similarly Lebrun, *Hymnes*, 280).

iii 7 *peran appa iya-* lit.:"walk forth and back", meaning "to frequent" or perhaps even "to attend to, take care of" (cf. *HW* 80; *HED*, Vol. 1 & 2, 332 f.).

iii 9-12 As in the lists of divine witnesses in Hittite treaties, the Long List of invoked deities is concluded by the cosmic elements. *B*'s preference for phonetic spellings, some of them quite rare, is best exemplified in this section.

iii 9 f. Forrer's ingenious solution for the fragmentary beginning of iii 10 (= B iii 48) seems to have been ignored by most subsequent commentators.[226] Only by taking "[hea]ven" (*A:* [A]N-*aš*; *B:* [*ne-p*]*í-aš*) as a genitive depending on "gods and goddesses" in the previous line is a sensible meaning obtained without a superfluous repetition of the "sky".

The "dark netherworld"[227] is treated differently in the two manuscripts. *B* takes it as a genitive (*dankuyaš*[228]), providing a twofold division of the pantheon into "male gods and female gods of [hea]ven (and) of the dark earth."[229] I assume that this was the original meaning, followed by a

[225] KUB 52.98 ii 2; see Otten, *StBoT* 13, 23. According to Sh. R. Bin-Nun, *The Tawananna in the Hittite Kingdom* (Heidelberg 1975), 51, 278, this house may have belonged to Danuhepa who remained queen during Muwatalli's reign but was not his wife.

[226] E. Forrer, *ZDMG* 76/NF 1 (1922), 244 . Witzel, *Keilschr. Studien IV* (1924), 92, restored [U]D-*aš* "day" and translated the following GE_6-*iš* as "night". Goetze, ANET 398a, left it untranslated. Lebrun, *Hymnes et prières*, 280, renders "[c]iel", but in the nominative case, which results in a repetition of "sky." Forrer's solution was acknowledged by Güterbock *apud* Houwink ten Cate, *JNES* 27, 207.

[227] For the concept of the "dark earth/netherworld", see, recently, N. Oettinger, "Die 'dunkle Erde' im Hethitischen und Griechischen", *WdO* 20/21 (1989/90), 83-98 (with previous lit.). The same expression has now turned up in the Hurrian – Hittite bilingual from Boğazköy (KBo 32. 83, 4'), and E. Neu suggests a Hurrian, i.e. Near Eastern, rather than an Indo-European origin for this Hittite cosmological concept: "Knechtschaft und Freiheit; Betrachtungen über ein hurritisch-hethitisches Textensemble aus Ḫattuša," in B. Janowski, K. Koch & G.Wilhelm (Hg.), *Religionsgeschichtliche Beziehungen zwischen Kleinasien, Nordsyrien und dem Alten Testament: Internationales Symposion Hamburg* (*OBO* 129, Freiburg & Göttingen 1993), 343 f. See also J. Klinger, *OLZ* 88 (1993), 506, n. 5.

[228] Usually spelled *dankuwayaš* , but cf. the ablative *da-an-ku-ia-az-za* in the Alakšandu Treaty § 21 (iv 36).

[229] For the underworld pantheon see, e.g., M. Vieyra, "Ciel et enfers Hittites", *RA* 59 (1965), 127-130; H. Otten, "Eine Beschwörung der Unterirdischen aus Boğazköy", *ZA* 54 (1961), 114-157; A. Archi, "The Names of the Primeval Gods", *Or* 59 (1990), 114-129. The gods of the underworld, collectively designated as the Anunnaki, appear in Muwatalli's other prayer (KBo 11.1 rev. 17). Incidentally, I understand this passage somewhat differently than did Houwink ten Cate and Josephson, *RHA* 25, 119. The Anunnaki are apparently being asked to search for (*šanḫandu*) the unworthy

similar bipartition of the universe into "heaven (and) earth."[230] On the other hand, *A* takes the "dark netherworld" as a nominative (GE$_6$-*iš* for *dankuiš*),[231] which may reflect a different cosmological perception – a tripartition of the universe into the dark netherworld, the (surface of the) earth, and heaven. A threefold division of the cosmos, with gods dwelling in heaven and in the netherworld and men inhabiting the earth, is typical for the Mesopotamian cosmogony.[232]

iii 10 *nepiš tekan* is written without any space between the two components. "Heaven-earth" often occurs as an asyndetic pair, but cf. the Alakšandu Treaty § 20, iv 26 (*nepiš tekan=a*).

alpuš IM.ḪI.A-*uš*, "clouds (and) winds", appears in opposite order in the Alakšandu Treaty (§ 20). *B* has the rare phonetic spelling *ḫuwanteš*, with the case ending in disaccord with *alpuš*.

iii 11 *tetḫima-* "thunder" and *wantewantema-* "lightning" are both nominal constructions with *-ma-* , built from the verbs *tetḫai-* "to thunder" and *wantai-* "to glow, to be warm," respectively (Götze, *KlF* 186 f.). Another derivative of *tetḫai-* is **tetḫeššar*, in ^{d}U *tetḫešnaš* Storm-god of Thunder (Friedrich, *SV* II, 33, n. 5). The Storm-god of Lightning (on whom see Ch. XV) is better known by his Luwian appelation, ^{d}U *piḫaššašši*.

iii 11 f. The last element[233] generally appearing in the divine assembly is the place of assembly itself, for which see Houwink ten Cate, "The Sun God of Heaven...", *Effigies Dei* (1987), 20 ff. In parallel passages the nominative "place" is usually expressed by the Akkadogram *AŠRU*.[234] Here we have a phonetic spelling with unusual case endings. *B* apparently hesitated for a while before finalizing his spelling. He erased his first attempt, wrote *tu-li-ya pé-di*$_{12}$[235] over it, and finally added a small *-aš* above the line for the genitive. *tuliyaš pedi* must be a case attraction from next line's dat.-loc. (rather than a vocative). On the other hand, *A* wrote a confident *pé-e-da-aš*, for which Harry Hoffner and Craig Melchert suggest an animate nominative functioning as a vocative.

iii 13-24 This short hymn to the Sun-god has been referred to in various studies dealing with prayers to solar deities, recently in Houwink ten Cate, "The Sun God of Heaven...", *Effigies Dei* (1987), 23 with n. 45. On the solar deities in this prayer see Ch. XIII.

iii 13 *B* provides the unique Hittite reading of ^{LÚ}SIPA: *weštara-*, "shepherd". Already Böhl recognized the importance of this reading and suggested an etymological connection to Latin *pastor*.[236]

---

words in the dark underworld and then get rid of them. On the meanings of *šanḫ-* see H. Hoffner in O. Carruba (ed.), *Per una grammatica ittita* (Pavia 1992), 140 f.

230 A good parallel is provided by KUB 59, 56 obv. 11' f.: 1 ^{GIŠ}BANŠUR *ANA* DINGIR^{MEŠ} LÚ^{MEŠ} DI[NGIR^{MEŠ} SAL^{MEŠ} *n*]*epiši daganzipiy*[*a* , "one table for the male go[ds (and) the female gods] in heaven and earth."

231 One could, of course, take the easy way of explaining the different case endings in the two duplicates by assuming a scribal error, but I would doubt such an assumption.

232 See, e.g., V. Haas, *Gesch. der heth. Religion* (1994), 125.

233 Note the conspicuous absence of the "great sea", which as a rule appears in the state treaties, including Muwatallli's treaty with Alakšandu.

234 CTH 379 (prayer of Muršili; see Ch. VIII), KUB 31.121+KUB 48.111 i$^{!}$ 19' DINGIR.MEŠ LÚ.MEŠ *tu*$^{!}$*-li-ia-aš ḫumanteš* (20') DINGIR.MEŠ SAL.MEŠ *tu*$^{!}$*-li-ya-aš ḫumanteš* (21') *tu-li-ia-aš AŠRU AŠAR DINI* DINGIR.MEŠ *kue*[*dani*] (22') ⸤*pí*⸥-[*di t*]*u-*[*l*]*i-ia tiškanzi* "all the male gods of the assembly, all the female gods of the assembly, place of assembly, place of judgment, [to wh]ich pl[ace] the gods are wont to step up to asse[mbly]". Lines 19' and 20' (KUB 48.11, ll. 10'-11') have *li-li-ia-aš*, which I suspect is simply a scribal error confusing two similar signs; the next line has a correct *tu-li-ia-aš* (cf. *CHD* L, 60b s.v. *lili-*). *CTH* 384 (prayer of Puduḫepa; D. Sürenhagen, *AoF* 8, 98 f.), KUB 21.19 iv 25' *nu=tta-kan* ^{URU}*Hattušaš* DING[IR.MEŠ]-*aš tu-li-ia-*[*aš AŠ*]*-RU* (26') ^{URU}*Arinnaš tuel aššianza* U[RU-*aš*] (27') ^{URU}*Neriqqaš* ^{URU}*Zippalandaš* (28') *ŠA* DUMU-*KA* URU.DIDLI.ḪI.A *uwandaru* "Let Hattuša, the pla[ce] of div[ine] assembly, Arinna, your beloved c[ity], Nerik (and) Zippalanda, the cities of your son, be visible / distinguished for you!"

235 Collation shows a clear *pí-te* (*di*$_{12}$) in both lines. For this unique spelling see Ch. IV.3.2.2.

236 *Theol. Tijdschr.* 1916, 323; Cf. E. Benveniste, *Hittite et Indo-Européen; Études comparatives* (Paris 1962), 37.

Between *weštaraš* and the previous word there is an additional sign inserted above the line, which, as suggested by Harry Hoffner, could perhaps be an ill-drawn determinative LÚ.

iii 13 f. The rise of the sun is usually expressed by *šara up-* or *šara ar-* (A. Archi, *Fs Otten*², 31). The verb is put here in initial position for stress. For the significance of this unique description of the sun emerging from the sea see Ch. XIII.

iii 14 For *B*' s distinctive spelling of gen. *nepiaš* see Ch. IV. 5.1.2.

iii 15 *A*' s UR.GI$_7$-*maš*! is probably a graphic error for the regular UR.GI$_7$-*aš* (as in *B*),[237] or possibly a unique phonetic complement for a root ending on *-ma*, for which there is no supportive evidence. For a possible Hittite reading see H. C. Melchert, "PIE 'dog' in Hittite?", *MSS* 50, 1989, 97-101.

iii 16 *A* adds the conjunction *-a* to combine the four genitives dependent on a correct Akkadian accusative *DINAM*. *B* writes *DI-šar* (for *ḫaneššar*) in the wrong place, between the two associated genitives "of the beast" and "of the field". *B'* s unique spelling *ḫu-it-ta-aš* must reflect a mistake of hearing, as noted by Houwink ten Cate (*JNES* 27, 206). The great hymn to the Sun-god has after the dog and the pig "the animals who do not speak with their mouth."[238] Is there any connection between the latter and "the beast of the field" in our text ?

iii 17 ff. For the insertion of the paragraph-dividers after *B* iii 56 and 61, see transliteration n. 80 and Ch. V.4.4.6. *B* originally had the entire invocation to the Sun-god of Heaven (*A* iii 13-24 = *B* iii 52-64) as one long paragraph, which he later broke into three sections. *A* inserted these new paragraph-dividers into his copy, moving the second one to a more suitable place, the end of a clause.

iii 21 *arai* is usually rendered "to (a)rouse" [239], but A. Kammenhuber[240] distinguishes between two verbs: 1. an intransitive *sich erheben*, "to arise" 2. a transitive *jem./etw. anhalten*, "to halt, bring to a standstill". She cites this passage as an instance of *arai-* 2, observing that the required action here is not to arouse the deities, but rather to beseech them to desist from their various occupations and attend to the presentation of the plea.

A omits the apparently superfluous *kuš*, "these" (acc.).

iii 22 "in whichever prayer" refers to the two prayers (cf. i 26 *arkuwarri*$^{\text{HI.A}}$) directed to the gods: the first dealing with their own matters, the second with Muwatalli's personal wishes. *arkuešni*, d.-l. of **arkueššar*, is defined by Laroche, *Prière*, 16, as a "resultative noun", apparently construed to deal with oblique cases. A semantic distinction from *arkuwar*, which only occurs in direct cases, is not apparent. See commentary to i 3.

iii 23 f. Embryonic evocation list consisting of three pairs of locations: heaven (and) earth, mountains (and) rivers, temples (and) thrones. The "thrones" could perhaps refer to open cult places, with natural or carved seats for the gods.[241]

iii 25 For the different spellings of *appanda* employed by the two scribes, see Ch. IV.4.4.2.

---

[237] So already E. Tenner, "Zwei hethitische Sonnenlieder", in F. Sommer – H. Ehelolf, *Kleinasiatische Forschungen* (Weimar 1930), 391.

[238] *šuppalan=a ḫanneššar iššit kuieš UL memiškanzi* ; Güterbock, *JAOS* 78, 240; Lebrun, *Hymnes et prières*, 95.

[239] A. Goetze, *ANET*, 398a; Ph. Houwink ten Cate, *Fs. Böhl* (1973), 209 with n. 53; "The Sun God of Heaven...", *Effigies Dei* (1987), 23 (with question mark); G. Kellerman, *Numen* 30 (1983), 275; *HED*, 125.

[240] *HW*² I, 244 ff. (with previous lit.); see also N. Oettinger, *Die Stammbildung des hethitischen Verbums* (Nürnberg 1979), 478 f.

[241] Cf. KBo 11.1 obv. 40, where the "throne of the Storm-god" is paired with a stele (*ḫuwaši*), a typically open-air cult place. For the possible archaeological identification of such "rock thrones" see, H. Gonnet, "Nouvelles données archéologiques relatives aux inscriptions hiéroglyphiques de Hartapusa à Kızıldağ", in R. Donceel et R. Lebrun, *Archéologie et religions de l'Anatolie ancienne: Mélanges Paul Naster* (Louvain 1984), 121 f.

iii 26 The lack of the reflexive particle *-za* in this first person nominal sentence is one of the few exceptions to the rule established by Hoffner, *JNES* 28, 230, concerning first or second person nominal sentences. Since it is missing in both copies this cannot be accidental. To be sure, the first person subject is clearly marked by the verb *ešun*, and the lack of *-za* does not produce any ambiguity in the sense of the sentence.

iii 26 f. Muwatalli stresses that his father officiated as priest of the Sun-goddess of Arinna and all the gods, a title which is attested from the reign of Muwatalli on (A. Archi, *Fs. Otten*^{2}, 6 n. 4, 10).

iii 28 f. For the motif of taking an infant from his mother and raising him under the supervision of a deity, see H. Vorländer, *Mein Gott* (*AOAT 23*), 133 ff. The same motif appears in the Kantuzzili prayer in a somewhat different form: "O my god, ever since my mother gave birth to me, you, my god, have been bringing me up."[242] In contrast, Muwatalli stresses the father's role in his birth, whereas the mother is simply the body from which he is taken by his personal god. As pointed out to me by Harry Hoffner, the use of the ablative *annaz* instead of an expected dative indicates a temporal or even locative meaning, "out of (my) mother('s womb)". Indeed, *CTH* 372 iv 24, a parallel text to the Kantuzzili prayer, has: "... I was born from the womb of my mother..." (*annaza* ŠÀ-*za*).

iii 29-31 The four verbal forms describing the Storm-god's actions – *daš, šallanut, iyat, daiš* – can grammatically be either second or third person sg. preterite, although the latter is obviously far more attested. Goetze, *ANET*, 398, and Otten, *HdO* 8 (1964), 106, render these verbs in the second person. I prefer (with Lebrun, *Hymnes et prières,* 281) a third person in this passage, in contrast to the second person imperative in the next.

iii 35 *uwaianu-* is a rare verb attested in prayers always referring to some intermediating deity who represents the suppliant in a favorable way before superior gods.[243] Goetze, *ANET*, 398b renders "intercede for me"; Laroche, *Prière,*18: "fais-moi paraître (aux yeux de tous ces dieux)." Haas, *Nerik,* 194 f.: "mache mich bemitleidenswert." The last rendering conforms with C. Melchert's tentative suggestion, to regard (*u*)*waianu-* as a causative to (*u*)*wai-* "woe, pain", i.e., "to make someone feel sorry for someone else."

iii 37 *šunni* lit. "fill (in)", refers here to the act of transmission of the words to the gods. For the distinction between *šunna-* , "to fill", and *šuniya-* , "to dip", see below, on iii 43.

iii 40 Both scribes seem to have hesitated with the sign following MUŠEN. After erasing a previous attempt, *B* wrote *-za*; the reflexive particle is indeed required by *appa ep-*[244]. *A* seems to have opted for a phonetic complement *-iš*$^?$. The identical simile in a Muršili prayer has MUŠEN-*iš=za=kan.*[245] For a possible Hittite reading of the ideogram MUŠEN (=*peri-* ?), see Singer, *StBoT* 27 (1983), 97.

---

242 *CTH* 373 ii 16 f.; H. G. Güterbock, "Some Aspects of Hittite Prayers" (1978), 133. See also H. Otten, "Die Religionen des Alten Kleinasien", *HdO* 8 (1964), 107 with n. 2.

243 Besides here, I know of only two other occurrences of this verb (quoted in Haas, *Nerik*, 194): *n=ašta* ^{d}IM EN-*IA ANA* DUMU.NITA-*KA aššiyanti paranda memi nu=mu=kan u-wa-i-nu-ut* "transmit it to the Storm-god, my lord, your beloved son, and recommend me" (KUB 36, 87 iv 11'-14'); *nu=mu=kan* DINGIR-*LUM* EN-*IA ANA* ^{d}[IM] *ABI=KA Ù ANA* ^{d}UTU ^{URU}TÚL-na *u-wa-a-i-nu-ut* "recommend me, O god, my lord, to the Storm-god, your father, and to the Sun-goddess of Arinna" (KUB 21. 27+ iv 37 f.).

244 H. G. Güterbock, *AJA* 87 (1983), 137 f., used this passage to establish the exact meaning of *-za appa ep-* , "to take refuge", which bore important consequences for the "Aḫḫiyawa Problem". See also Güterbock, *Fs. Alp* (1992), 235, 241; D. Easton, *Antiquity* 59 (1985), 189.

245 MUŠEN-*iš=za=kan* ^{GIŠ}*tap-ta-ap-pa-an* EGIR-*pa epzi n=an* ^{GIŠ}*tap-ta-ap-pa-aš ḫu-u-*[*iš-nu-zi*] (KUB 14. 8 rev. 22). As stated by G. Beckman, *JNES* 45 (1986), 22, "the use of quite similar language by the two rulers [Muršili and Muwatalli] in separate compositions again supports the interpretation of the imagery as proverbial." For similar biblical expressions see H. Vorländer, *Mein Gott* (*AOAT* 23), 245 f.

taptappa- is spelled here *tap-tap-* , whereas in the Muršili prayer (twice), *tap-ta-ap-* . This conforms with the increasing tendency to utilize CVC signs in thirteenth century texts. As for its meaning, both Goetze and Lebrun translate "nest". But can a nest really save the bird? It may perhaps diminish the beauty of the metaphor, but a cage[246] is more "realistic" and is strongly supported by the occurrence of gold and silver *taptappa-* in inventory texts.[247]

iii 41 For the 1st person sg. of the personal pronoun *A* uses both *uk* and *ammuk,* whereas *B* uses only *ammuk.* See Ch. iv. 5.2.1.

iii 42 Goetze, *ANET,* 398b, takes TI-*nut* (*ḫuišnut*) as an imperative, second person. Though possible, it seems to me (with Lebrun, *Hymnes et prières,* 281) that the king is describing an already existing situation, rather than beseeching future salvation in the future. A similar phrase occurs in the second Plague Prayer of Muršili (*CTH* 378.II), KUB 14. 8 rev. 21, where an imperative is more appropriate (Lebrun, ib., 21).

iii 43 *anda šunni* Following an observation of Friedrich, *HW,* 197 f., Laroche, *RHA* 31 (1973), 91-93, distinguished between two easily conflated verbs, *šunna-* , "to fill", and *šuniya-* , "to plunge, dip, drop" (see iv 5). What is the Storm-god *piḫaššašši* supposed to do with the words of Muwatalli? Lebrun, *Hymnes,* 287, opts here for the second verb: "inonde les dieux des paroles". I prefer Goetze's choice (*ANET,* 398b) of the first meaning ("pass them on in full to the gods"), but with a more general meaning, "emit". A juxtaposition of lines 37 and 43 seems to imply that (*ANA*) *PANI* DINGIR.MEŠ *šunni* equals *ANA* DINGIR.MEŠ *anda šunni.* I cannot detect any difference in meaning.

iii 44 For *šarlai-* / *šarliške-* see below on l. 47.

iii 46 Neither here nor elsewhere is any hint given as to the nature of the "bad thing" in the king's soul. For the purpose of the prayer, see Ch. VII.

iii 47 Instead of *A*'s correct SIG_5-*aḫ-ḫa-an-zi, B* has SIG_5-*aḫ-zi.* Rather than a flawed 3rd pers. sg. (cf. correct *šarlanzi*), this aberrant form is probably due to an omitted *-ḫa-* and a lost nasal *-n-*, typical for this scribe (see Ch. 3.2.3).

šarlai- is related to the adjective *šarli-* "superior, elevated" (Laroche, *Fs. Friedrich,* 292). The meaning here seems to be the removal or the transformation of the evil thing by lifting it or turning it over; in other words, coming out on top of it or making it turn out well.[248] H. C. Melchert suspects a Luwianism comparable to the more common Hittite *šarazziyaḫḫ-*.

iii 48 f. Usually understood as third person questions: "To whom is praise due, if praise is not due to the Storm-god *p*." (Goetze, *ANET* 398b; Sommer, *AU,* 95; Kammenhuber, *HW²*, 588; Lebrun, *Hymnes et prières,* 281). However, as demonstrated by Hoffner (*Fs. Güterbock²*, 90), the *-za* in a nominal sentence must relate to the first or second person: "Whose praise will I be? Will I not be the praise of the Storm-god *p.*, my lord?"[249] A similar concept, but formulated in the affirmative and not as a rhetorical question, is restored in Muwatalli's other prayer: *n=at* DUMU.LÚ.U_{19}.LU *išpiyanumar ešdu ANA* ᵈ*U-ma-at* EN-*IA wa-al*[*-li-ia-tar ešdu* (?)] (KBo 11. 1 rev. 21) "And may it be

---

[246] Güterbock, *JAOS* 78 (1958), 245, n. 64: "nest (or: cage)"; Laroche, *Prière* (1964), 16: "cage (?)".

[247] 5 *tap-tap-pa-aš* GUŠKIN (KUB 42.40 rev.? 8'); 1 *tap-tap-pa-aš* KÙ.B[ABBAR (KUB 42.35, 2'). Both S. Košak, *Hittite inventory texts* (*TdH* 10, Heidelberg 1982), 240, and J. Siegelová, *Hethitische Verwaltungspraxis im Lichte der Wirtschafts- und Inventardokumente* (Prag 1986), 622, translate "cage". Two further occurrences appear in fragmentary context: 1 *tap-tap-pa-an* (KUB 15.27 ii 11'); ᴳᴵŠ*tap-tap-pa-an* (KUB 57.189, 7). Note that all these occurrences share the later spelling, *tap-tap-* .

[248] H. G. Güterbock, *AnSt* 30 (1980), 44, renders the verb *šarlai-* "let prevail"; similarly R. Lebrun, *Hymnes et prières*, 281: "feront triompher"; cf. G. Kellerman, *Numen* 30 (1983), 275: "ennobliront".

[249] Cf. KUB 21. 38 obv. 48, where Puduḫepa enjoys the praise of Ḫatti. On the verb *walliya-* see also Hoffner, *AfO Beih.* 19 (1982), 135 n. 13. For prayers of praise (*walliyatar*) in general see, R. Lebrun, *Hymnes et prières*, 442 f.

saturation for mankind but for the Storm-god, my lord, [let it be] a (matter of) pr[aise] !" (Houwink ten Cate and Josephson, *RHA* 81, 119).

iii 49 f. Apparently on account of the Akkadian accusative DINGIR-*LAM*, Goetze (*ANET*, 398 f.) translates: "Then, whenever a man looks upon god and mortal, he will say...". It seems to me (with Lebrun, *Hymnes et prières*, 281) that it makes more sense to take both god and mortal as subjects who might look and express their admiration for the Storm-god *pihaššašši*. Cf. line 59, where the latter is praised by the gods of heaven, the mountains and the rivers. Deficient application of the Akkadian case endings is often found in this text (though not with accus.): DINGIR-*LIM* for grammatical nom. (iii 57, both texts; iii 58 only *B*); *AWATE*^{MEŠ} for nom. (iv 46, both texts); *ŠA* DINGIR.MEŠ *BE-LU* for gen. (i 21 only *B*). See further Ch. V. 4.4.

iii 50 Since an accusative object is missing, I render *auš-* in an intransitive meaning, "look". There is no need to restore an *-at* or a *-mu* after *mān*, as suggested by Lebrun, *Hymnes et prières*, 287.

iii 51 The epithet "King of Heaven" is also attributed in this text to the Storm-god of Heaven (i 11) and to the Storm-god of Ḫatti (i 12), besides to the Storm-god *piḫaššašši*. For the theological implications see Ch. XV. Among the goddesses only Ḫebat is called "Queen of Heaven" (i 41).

iii 52 ff. I follow Goetze (*ANET*, 398b) and L ebrun (*Hymnes et prières*, 281) in taking the chain of verbs as 3rd pers. pret., rather than 2nd pers. (Starke, *StBoT* 31, 237; *CHD* L-N, 242). It is true that EN-*IA*, "my lord" (iii 51), would better fit a 2nd pers. verb, but this is an almost mandatory addition whenever the god is mentioned, and therefore its appearance here does not establish person.

For *kaniš-* "to recognize, acknowledge, honour", see Laroche *RHA* 68 (1961), 28.

For the Luwian verb *kulanitta*, see C. W. Carter, *Hittite Cult Inventories*, (Doct. Diss., Chicago 1962), 192: "to be completed, come to end"; F. Starke, *StBoT* 31, 237: "erfolgreich machen"; H. C. Melchert, *Cuneiform Luvian Lexicon* (Chapel Hill 1993), 106: "bring to (a successful) end".[250]

H. Vorländer, *Mein Gott*, 134 n. 2, understands *meḫunaš arnut* in the sense that the prayer itself was well-timed. I think a more general meaning is intended: the god "brought (the king) through/to good times", or the like.

iii 54 ff. For a similar pledge of respect to a deity in future generations, see, e.g., *Ḫatt.* iv 86-89 (to IŠTAR of Šamuḫa). *zilatiya* appears with (single) *Glossenkeil* in *B*, without it in *A*. The Apology of Ḫattušili has *ziladuwa* with double *Glossenkeil*, but elsewhere it appears without it (Laroche, *DLL*, 115). Both are derived from Luwian *zila*, "hence", but a semantic difference has, so far, not been found.

iii 56 The small fragment *D* probably conforms with *A*' s *-šar-* , rather than *B*'s *-ša-ar-* (see Table 1).

iii 58 For *para ḫandant-* "rightly guiding (deity)", "rightly guided (human)", see *CHD* P, 111; *HED* H, s.v. *ḫantā(i)-* ; Houwink ten Cate, "The Hittite Storm God" (1992), 88.

A probably has a correct nominative DINGIR-*L*]*UM*, whereas *B* has a flawed DINGIR-*LIM*. See Ch. IV.4.4.4.

iii 59 It is somewhat surprising that only the gods of heaven (and the mountains and rivers) are mentioned. Are the gods of the netherworld (cf. iii 9 f.) omitted unintentionally, or are they not expected to praise the Storm-god of Lightning ?

iii 60 *ug=a=kan* (*A*) / *ammug=a=kan* (*B*) serves here for the dative case (*HW* 233; Sommer, *AU*, 33). The enclitic *-a-* has here the function of the emphatic conjunction, which in late texts is usually

[250] The first pers. pret. *ku-la-ni-wi*$_5$ appears in a historical fragment which mentions Muwatalli (KUB 21. 20, 1'); see F. Starke, *StBoT* 31 (1990), 237 n. 811.

replaced by *-ma*.[251] It is employed here to emphasize a change of subject – from the praises bestowed upon the Storm-god *piḫaššašši* by other mortals and deities to the joy and gratitude of Muwatalli himself.

iii 61 *-kan ištanza anda dušk-* "to be happy inside the soul" occurs in the Ullikumi Myth, "Second Tablet", i 10' (Güterbock, *JCS* 5, 28). "Inside Muwatalli's soul" is equivalent to "in His Majesty's heart" in iv 46. On the Hittite concepts of mind and soul see A. Kammenhuber *ZA* 56 (1964), 150-212 (esp. pp. 170, 204).

iii 64 *-za parā dušk- HW* 230 "sich freuen" ; *CHD* P/2 "to fully rejoice". For the semantic distinction between *dušk-* with and without the particle *-za*, "to rejoice" and "to amuse, entertain", respectively, see A. Archi, *UF* 5 (1973), 25, n. 76.

iii 64 f. The phrase "thick bread(s) and libation" represents one standard offering and is therefore considered as singular (*kuin*).

iii 66 f. *A* replaced the 2nd pers. pers. pron. *-ta* by 3rd pers. *-ši* in l.66, but failed to do the same in the following line. For the significance of this discrepancy for the redactional history of the text, see Ch. V.4.4.4.2.

iii 67 The *-ant* form *pidduliyant-* (*B*) and the *-want* form *pidduliyawant-* (*A*) are used interchangeably.[252] They are both related to the noun *pittuliya-* "tightness, tension, anguish", which, in its turn, must be related to (SíG)*pittula-*, *pittuliya-*, "noose, loop, tie" (*HW*, 172; 1. *Erg.*, 16). Perhaps "stressed" can bridge the semantic distance between a tied object and a tight spirit. In the present context, the opposite of "joyfully"[253] could be something like "grudgingly" (Goetze, *ANET*, 398b), or "reluctantly".

iii 68 A. Kammenhuber, *TdH* 7 (1976), 55 suggested a Hurrian origin for *armuwalašḫa-* "moonshine", but cf. F. Starke, *KZ* 93, 257 f. (with previous refs.) who claims a Luwian origin for the *-šḫa-* suffix. He suggests a Luwian origin for *wantai-* (iii 70) as well.

iii 69 *armuwalai-* (*hapax legomenon*) is usually understood as "to glow, shed moonlight" or the like (Friedrich, *JCS* 1, 277; Oettinger, *Stammbildung*, 32), but Puhvel, *HED*,152 f. argues for a meaning "to wax like the moon".

iii 70 The comparative *iwar* + genitive is employed here, whereas 71 f. has the comparative *maḫḫan* + dat.-loc. Goetze (*ANET*, 398b) renders the former "like (the moon/the sun)", the latter "as (with) a bull to draw (the wagon)".[254]

iii 71 f. "Walk with me at my right hand" recalls the pictorial representation of the Hittite king held by his right hand by his personal deity. The *Umarmungsszene* appears on seals of Muwatalli II and Muršili III (Urḫi-Tešub),[255] but the best known example is the Yazılıkaya relief depicting Šarruma with Tudḫaliya. The next metaphor, the teaming up with a draft bull, may allude to Šeri, the bull of the Storm-god (see Ch. XIV).

---

[251] See H. Otten and Vl. Souček, *StBoT* 8 (1969), 68; Ph. H. J. Houwink ten Cate, "The Particle -a- and Its Usage with Respect to the Personal Pronoun", *Fs. Otten* (1973), 119-139 (p. 137); J. Puhvel, *HED*, 10.

[252] For these constructions see N. Oettinger, *MSS* 40, 146 f.; idem, "Hethitisch *-uant-* ", in E.Neu & Ch. Rüster, *Festschrift H. Otten*[2] (1988), 275, 280 f.

[253] The same promise of joyful service to the god in return for his blessing can be found, e.g., in a Babylonian prayer to Marduk ; see T. Abusch, "The Form and Meaning of a Babylonian Prayer to Marduk", *JAOS* 103 (1983), 10 (with text refs. on p. 3 n. 2): "O Marduk great lord; grant me my life; decree for me a healthy life; in joyfully serving you regularly will I then find satisfaction."

[254] For comparison in Hittite, see H. A. Hoffner, "Hittite *iwar* and Related Modes of Expressing Comparison", *IstMitt* 43 (1993), 39-51.

[255] H. Otten, *Zu einigen Neufunden hethitischer Königssiegel* (Stuttgart 1993), 22 ff.

iii 73 There may be a poetic opposition between *katta iyanni-* in l. 71 and *šarā iyanni-* here, but the shades of meaning are not transparent to me.

In calling upon his god to act in a true "Storm-godly" fashion, the author expresses a concept well-known from Biblical prayers. The ground for petition lies in the very character and reputation of God, who is asked to act in accordance with the divine ways of justice and righteousness.[256]

iii 74 f. Another first person nominal sentence marked with *-za,* with three participles describing the god's blessings bestowed upon the king. The first two are in Hittite and have clear meanings. The third is a Luwian part. in *-mi,* the etymology and meaning of which has been discussed in studies on Luwian.[257] Melchert first thought of an etymological connection with *māi-* "to grow, prosper". F. Starke, *StBoT* 31 (1990), 492, understood it along similar lines: an iterative from a Luwian **miyi/mayi,* with the meaning "ständig gedeihen". Another etymology has presented itself with the identification of the cuneiform and hieroglyphic Luwian word *manā-* "to see", and its reduplicated form *mammanna-* (Hawkins, *Kadmos* 19, 1980, 123 ff., with an appendix by Starke, ib. 142 ff.). Melchert, *KZ* 101 (1988), 218 ff. and *Cuneiform Luvian Lexicon* (Chapel Hill 1993), 147, now derives the participle *mimmammi-* from a related verb, *mimma-* "to regard, to favor". The resulting "favored, well-regarded" is in fact very close in meaning to Hittite *kaniššanza.* While the Luwian origin may require *i*-vocalism in both syllables (Melchert, ib.), it is interesting to observe the *e / i* variations of the two duplicates: where one has *e,* the other has *i,* and vice versa.

iii 76 The direct speech particle indicates that the king's projected gratitude for the favors bestowed upon him by the Storm-god of Lightning is continued in this line. The sentence probably ends with a 3rd pers. pret. verb, the subject of which must be the Storm-god *piḫaššašši.*

iv 1 A new subject is introduced in this very fragmentary line. Since specification of the ritual offerings begins in the next line, this line must contain some closing sentence of the prayer. The following tentative restoration is based on a combination of the remaining traces in *B* iv 45 and in *A* iv 1. *B* iv 45 was squeezed in with minuscule characters which caused some distortion in the shape of some signs. The word after *nu=kán* begins with a peculiar sign which looks quite different on the tablet itself than in Weber's autograph (see Table 1). Despite its unusual shape, I think that it must be a GIM (cf. the ninth and the tenth variant in *HZL* 165), followed by *-an.* After a gap of some two or three signs follows *ḫal-z[i-* ,which could belong to an infinitive *ḫalz[iyauwanz]i-* , followed in *A* iv 1 by *aššanuzzi. aššanu-* with *-kan* and an infinitive is used in the sense of "to provide, to accomplish, to finish (doing something)".[258] Although I cannot quote an exact parallel for *ḫalziyauwanzi aššanuzzi, ḫalziyauwanzi zinnit* in KUB 36.28, 4' is quite similar in sense.[259] "He finishes calling" would refer to the gods who have been summoned to the divine assembly. I would thus restore iv 1:

nu-kán GIM$^{!}$*-an* [DINGIR^{MEŠ} (?)] *ḫal-z[i-ia-u-wa-an-z]i*[260] *aš-ša-nu-uz-zi*

When he finishes ca[lling the gods (?)]"

---

[256] P. D. Miller, *They Cried to the Lord; The Form and Theology of Biblical Prayer* (Minneapolis 1994), 268 f.

[257] In Laroche's Luwian dictionary (*DLL*) the vocable is not given. *CHD* L-N, 268 leaves it untranslated, but refers to H. C. Melchert, *Studies in Hittite Historical Phonology* (Göttingen 1984), 169. Certainly unacceptable is Eichner's emendation of the text in order to achieve a *MI-IM-MA* me-iš-ta "prospered in every respect" (*Die Sprache* 21, 1975, 105). See Melchert's arguments, ib.

[258] F. Ose, *Supinum und Infinitiv im Hethitischen* (1944), 23-26, 72. A. Kammenhuer, *HW*^{2}, 372, 382, questions the common interpretation according to which *aššanu-* with infinitive can mean not only "besorgen", but also "fertig werden, zu Ende bringen, vollenden", but she admits that the latter meaning is contained within the former.

[259] Cf. KUB 21.16 i 11 *nu=kan* DINGIR^{L}[^{AM}] (12) [*ḫal-z*]*i-ia-u-wa-an-zi UL namma* [*pait*] (*HW*^{2} III/12, Ḫ, 110a). Cf. also KUB 13.5+ iii 39' *nu=kan* DINGIR.MEŠ-*aš šaklain aššanuzi* .

[260] For the spelling of the infinitive *ḫal-z[i-ia-u-wa-an-z]i* cf. iv 45 *pár-ši-ia-u-wa-an-zi zi-in-na-i* (in both duplicates).

iv 2 This line probably opens the description of the ritual offerings. Houwink ten Cate, "The Sun God of Heaven", *Effigies Dei* (1987), 31, n. 36, suggests restoring here the offering for the Sun-god of Heaven on the basis of *B* i 39.[261] Although this proposal would establish a correspondence between the two tablets, there are certain difficulties entailed in it: 1) The following line (iv 3) in *A* must have had, like *B*, the introductory sentence "afterwards he breaks the thick breads", which marks the beginning of the offering ceremony. 2) It is true that *B* preceded that phrase with a short entry regarding the offering for the Sun-god of Heaven, but he clearly did this as an afterthought, squeezing in the additional line in an empty spot (see commentary on i 36). As a result this addition does not have the regular elaborate formulation, but only an opening sentence appended with KI.MIN, "ditto". There is no sign of similar corrections or additions in *A*; what remains of the first lines of col. iv is written in a normal and tidy manner. 3) Even if one would allow for a similar "disorder" in the opening of the ritual offerings in *A*, there is hardly enough space in iv 2 to insert even the condensed phrase of *B* i 39. Lebrun, *Hymnes et prières*, 269, restores *pár-š]i-ya-az-zi*$^{?}$, but this form of the verb never occurs in text *A* (only twice in *B*), and it hardly fits the traces. For these reasons I doubt that *A* iv 2 contained an offering for the Sun-god of Heaven. The rationale for the "omission" of the Sun-god of Heaven in text *A* is explained in Ch. XIII.

(*B* i 39) On this addition of *B* see commentary after i 36 and Ch. XIII. For *B*' s special spelling AN-*I* (for *ŠA-ME-E*) see Ch. IV. 3.1.1.

iv 4 There are two types of sacrificial bread descriptions: "Three thick bread(s) of moist flour of (one) *tarna-*" are given only to the Sun-goddess of Arinna and to the Storm-god of Ḫatti (iv 23); all the other deities receive white (and red) thick breads. In the rest of the offering there is no difference between the deities. See further Ch. IX.

iv 5 For *šuniya-* , "to dip", see above, iii 43 (on *šunni*). As noted by Laroche, in this text both scribes write exclusively *šu-un-ni-* instead of *šu-ú-ni-*.

iv 7 The libation of wine is normally expressed by *peran šippanti*, except for *A* iv 7, 32, and 51 (which is a later addition) where *peran* is omitted. In this line the omission may have been caused by the lack of space, but not in 32 or 51.

iv 8 *B* has throughout the unique spelling ŠÀ.PA for regular ŠÀ.BA; see Ch. IV. 3.2.2. For the use of -*ŠU* and -*ŠÚ* see Ch. IV.4.2.

iv 10 "... on the table of (DN)..." is regularly expressed in *B* as: ^{GIŠ}BANŠUR-*i ŠA* (except for a single mix up in 37). *A* has several variations: ^{GIŠ}BANŠUR-i *ŠA* (10, 37, 40, 42); ^{GIŠ}BANŠUR *ŠA* (34); ^{GIŠ}BANŠUR (15, 20); *ANA* ^{GIŠ}BANŠUR *ŠA* (25, 30, 44). See further Ch. IV. 4.4.

iv 11 In this line only *A* adds -*kan* and reverses the usual order of fat-bread and groats. I cannot suggest any connection between the two anomalies.

B has twice (out of seven occurrences) the long spelling *me-em-ma-al*; *A* never.

iv 15 According to both the introduction (i 4) and the postscript (iv 61), there are only two offering tables on the roof, whereas in the list of offerings there seem to be six. The apparent discrepancy has a simple solution, for which see Ch. IX.

iv 19 *B* unnecessarily repeats "Storm-god of Heaven" here, whereas in iv 25 and 28 he omits ^{d}U. Generally speaking, his carelessness increases the closer he gets to the end of the text. See Ch.V.4.

iv 22 Besides here, the spelling *KU-UK-KU-UB* (for regular *KU-KU-UB*) also occurs in KBo 13.135 rev. 2'. For this vessel see Y. Coşkun, *Boğazköy Metinlerinde Geçen Başlica* (Ankara 1972), 10 ff.

---

261 As explained in the commentary on i 36, *ištamaššadu* does not belong to this line.

iv 28 In *A* the offering of breads to the various deities is invariably expressed by the dative: with Hittite case ending, with *ANA*, or with both. On the other hand, *B* shifts between dative *ANA* (8, 13, 19, 36, 55) and genitive *ŠA* (28, 41, 43). See Ch. IV. 4.4.4.

iv 29 *šunniya*(*n*)*zi* in *A* is no doubt an inappropriate nasalization, rather than a misplaced plural.

iv 34 ff. From here on both texts abbreviate their description by inserting KI.MIN, "ditto". *A* already has it in l. 34; *B* only "catches up" in l. 37, adding it on the column divider. In the following five entries (ll. 33-44) KI.MIN must refer to the full description of the offerings, including the wine.

iv 36 For the inclusion of ᵈḪurri see Ch. XIV.

iv 45 The offerings to the "gods of Ḫatti" end, and the actual prayer should be inserted here (see Chs. VI and VII). Thereafter follow the offerings to the "gods of the lands".

iv 46 Nominal sentence with the predicate expressed by a noun in dat.-loc.[262] Actually, *karta* (ŠÀ-*ta*) is an archaic directive preserved here as a frozen expression.[263] In her study on the soul concepts of the Hittites, A. Kammenhuber, *ZA* 56 (1964), 170, cites this passage to show that "heart" and "soul" are interchangeable and that ZI is still used by Muwatalli in the sense of "soul" (whereas later it becomes mainly "wish" or "will").

iv 49 The beginning of the offerings to the "gods of the lands" is marked in *A* by *nu* EGIR-*ŠU* rather than by the regular EGIR-*ŠU-ma*. *B* originally had no conjunction at all, but inserted EGIR-*anda* afterwards. For the varying writings of **appanda* see Ch. IV.4.2.

The word order DINGIR.LÚ^MEŠ KUR-*eaš ḫumandaš*, compared with DINGIR.LÚ^MEŠ *ḫumandaš ŠA* ^URU*Ḫatti* in iv 33 f., shows that the correct rendering is "male gods of all the lands," rather than "all the male gods of the lands" (as rendered by Lebrun, *Hymnes et prières*, 284).

iv 50 "... upon the thick breads", which always follows after "fat-bread (and) groats", is omitted in this entry, probably in both texts.[264] At the same time, this is the only place where *A* uses the synonym *išḫuwai* instead of the regular *šer šuḫḫai*. *B* also employs *šer išḫu*(*wa*)*i* once, but in a different place (iv 58).

iv 51 The libation is added (only in *A* !) in the same handwriting as the postscript in ll. 59-61 (see below). The logographic spelling BAL-*ti* for *šippanti* occurs only here.

iv 53 "... to whom he presented a plea" must refer also to the "male gods of the lands" of the previous section. For unknown reasons *B* omits the rest of this paragraph.

iv 55 f. I have no explanation for *B*'s sudden change from medial *paršiya* to active *paršiyaz*[*zi*], attested only here and in the next line.

iv 56 *B* 's *Glossenkeil* word *ḫuwaialli* was probably replaced in *A* with its Hittite equivalent *kutrui*.[265]

iv 58 *peran laḫuwai* (in both texts), instead of the simple verb elsewhere (iv 51, 54), does not seem to basically affect the meaning of the action. Note that *B* had to squeeze in a very ill-shaped *peran*.

iv 59 ff. The last three lines were added only in *A* (cf. l. 51) in a different, smaller and shallower handwriting. See Ch. IV. 2. *B* left a large uninscribed space at the end of the column, perhaps in anticipation of some additions.

---

262 See P. Cotticelli - Kurras, "Die hethitischen Nominalsätze", in O. Carruba (ed.), *Per una grammatica ittita* (Pavia 1992), 114.

263 G. Beckman, *StBoT* 29 (1983), 163. For other examples, see N. Oettinger, *StBoT* 22 (1976), 29-30.

264 In *B*, the end of the line is broken, but the available space is too small for *A-NA* NINDA.GUR$_4$.RA^ḪI.A *še-er*.

265 Houwink ten Cate, *JNES* 27, 204. Cf. Muwatalli's other prayer, where the Sun-god of Heaven "stands to witness" (*kutriwanni artari* KBo 11.1 obv. 8). For the Luwisms in this text, see Ch. V. 4.4.2.

The offering breads saturated with the other ingredients are burnt on two GUNNI made of wood (*IṢ-ṢI*, or GIŠ-*ṢI*; misread by Lebrun, *Hymnes et prières*, 273). GUNNI is usually rendered as "hearth", but in this context "furnace" (Houwink ten Cate, *Numen* 16, 87) or "pyre" seems more appropriate.[266]

[266] Burnt offerings consisting of bread, honey, oil, and other substances are also attested in IBoT 2. 109+ iii 5'-8' (*CTH* 404 i B; first Maštigga ritual); KUB 7.41 rev. 15 (*CTH* 446.A; ritual for underworld deities); KBo 12.103 rev. 11 f. (*CTH* 456.2; purification ritual).

Chapter III: Glossaries

The glossary contains all preserved and partially preserved words according to the line numeration of text *A*, as well as the variants of text *B* (*C* and *D* do not contain variant forms). In the section of Geographical Names, *all* occurrences of *A* and *B* are given whenever there are different writings for the same name (e.g. Ḫatti, Arinna). In addition to the word itself, the immediate context is often included (e.g., modifiers, deities with their locations, etc.). Luwian forms (with or without *Glossenkeil*) are also listed separately at the end of the first section.

Hittite and Luwian

-a-	"he, she, it"	
	-aš nom. sg. c.	iii 40
	-an acc. sg. c.	iii 47,52,53(x 2), 66
	-at nom. pl. c.	i 24, iii 7
	-at nom.-acc. pl. n.	i 28,29,30,31, iii 37,39 iv 47
	-aš acc. pl. c.	i 9, iii 9,23, iv 5 (x2), 9,10,14,15, 19,20,24,25,29,30,34,37,40,42,44,60
-a/-ya	"and, also; but"	
	word-connective	i 28,36 iii 16,55,64,75
	sentence-connective	i 20,24 iii 32, 44,60,62 (x 2)
Ù	Akk. word-connective	i 5,10,17,65,72 iii 5,19,27,30
alpa - c.	"cloud"	
	al-pu-uš nom. pl.	iii 10
ammel	"mine"	
	am-me-el	i 20 iii 4; B iv 23 (A iii 54: om.)
	am-me-el(-ma)	iii 36
	am-me-el(-pát)	B i 22 (A i 21: šu-me-el-pát !)
ammuk	" I"	
(see also: uk)	am-mu-uk	iii 18 (= B), 32 (B broken) B iv 42 (= A iii 74: ú-uk)
	am-mu-uk(-ma-za-at)	i 29 (= B)

	[am]-mu-g(a-kán)	B iv 29 (= A iii 60: ú-ga-kán)
	am-mu-uk(-ma-kán)	B iv 10 (= A iii 41: ú-u[k-ma$^{?}$-z]a-[ká]n)
anna -	"mother"	
	an-na-az abl. sg.	iii 28
anda (see also ŠÀ-)	"into" (as prev.)	
	an-da šunna- "fill in"	iii 43
	an-da dušk- "rejoice"	iii 60
	"(with)in, inside" (as adv.)	
	ZI-ni an-da	iii 46
antuḫša-	"man, human being"	
	an-tu-uḫ-ša-an acc. sg.	B iv 20 (= A iii 51: UN-an)
	an-tu-uḫ-ša-aš gen. sg.	B i 31 (= A i 30: UN-az !)
	an-tu-uḫ-ši dat.-loc. sg.	B i 2 (= A i 2: UN-[ši])
*appanda	see EGIR	
apiya	"there, then"	
	a-pí-ia(-ia)	iii 44
arai-	"to halt"	
	a-ra-a-i imp. sg. 2	iii 21
arḫa	"off, away"	
	ar-ḫa BIL-nu- "burn down"	iv 60
arkueššar	"plea, argument"	
	ar-ku-u-e-eš-ni dat.-loc. sg.	iii 22 =
	ar-ku-e-eš-ni	= B iii 61

arkuwai -	"to plead, exculpate oneself, argue"	
	ar-ku-wa-nu-un pret. sg. 1	iii 35
	ar-ku-iš-ki-mi iter. pres. sg. 1	iii 19=
	ar-ku-ú-i-iš-ki-mi	=B iii 59
	ar-ku-ú-e-eš-ki-mi	iii 33
arkuwar	" plea, argument" (with iya-, dai-)	
	ar-ku-wa-ar(-) nom.-acc. sg.	i 3, 21, 22, 25, 27, 30, 34, 36
		iii 38, 42 iv 47, 48, 53
	ar-ku-wa-ar-r(a)	B i 21
	ar-ku-wa-ar-ri$^{HI.A}$ nom.-acc. pl.	i 26 =
	ar-u$^{!}$-wa-ar-ri$^{HI.A}$	= B i 27
armuwalai -	"to shine like the moon"	
	šer ar-mu-u-wa-la-i imp. sg. 2	iii 69 =
	-]mu-wa-la-a-i	= B iv 37
armuwalašḫa -	"moon shine"	
	ar-mu-wa-la-aš-ḫa-aš gen. sg.	iii 68
arnu-	"to move along, promote"	
	meḫunaš ar-nu-ut pret. sg. 3	iii 53
aruna -	"sea"	
	a-ru-na-az abl. sg.	iii 14
aruwar	see arkuwar	
aši	"this (one), the aforementioned (one)"	
	a-ši (DINGIR-*LIM*) nom. sg. c.	iii 57
aššiyant-	"favored, beloved"	
	a-aš-ši-ia-an-za sg. nom. c.	i 13 =
	a-aš-<ši>-ia-an-za	= B i 15

aššanu -	"to provide for; to finish (doing something)"		
	aš-ša-nu-uz-zi	pres. sg. 3	iv 1
	aš-ša-nu-ut	pret. sg. 3	iii 53
au(š) -	"to see, observe"		
	a-uš-zi	pres. sg. 3	iii 50
awan	adverb strengthening movement verbs		
	a-wa-an (šara iyanni)		iii 73
(dU) eḫellibi (Hur.)	"(Storm-god of) Salvation"		see DN
ep-	"to seize"		
appa ep -	"to find refuge"		
	EGIR-pa e-ip-zi	pres. sg. 3	iii 40
	EGIR-pa *AṢ-BAT*	pret. sg. 1	iii 41
(GEŠTUG) para ep-	"to hold out (the ears), listen"		
	para e-ep-tén	imp. pl. 2	i 26
eš-	"to be"		
	e-šu-un	pret. sg. 1	iii 26
	e-eš-ta	pret. sg. 3	iii 27
ḫalzāi-	"to call, to name, to invoke"		
	ḫal-zi-iḫ-ḫu-un	pret. sg. 1	iii 34, 22 =
	ḫal-zi-iḫ-ḫu-u-un		= B iii 62
	ḫal-za-a-i	imp. sg. 2	iii 24
	ḫal-z[i-ia-u-wa-an-z]i (?)	inf.	iv 1
ḫannešk-	"to decide, determine"		
	ḫa-an-ne-iš-ki-ši	pres. sg. 3	iii 17 =
	ḫa-an-ni-iš-ki-ši		= B iii 56

parā ḫandant-	"rightly guiding" (deity)	
	para ḫa-an-da-an-za part. nom. sg. c.	iii 58
ḫandan	"indeed, truly"	
	ḫa-an-da-an(-wa)	iii 50,57,73
ḫarpiya -	"to team up, to assist"	
	ḫar-pí-ia-aḫ-ḫu-ut mid. imp. sg. 2	iii 72
ḫuḫḫa-	"grandfather, ancestor"	
	(É. GAL) ḫu-uḫ-ḫa-aš gen. sg.	i 42
ḫuiš -	"to live"	
	ḫu-i-iš-zi pres. sg. 3	B iv 10 =
	TI-zi	= iii 40
	TI-nu-ut pret. sg. 3	iii 42 (= B)
ḫuitar	"animal, creature"	
	(gimraš) ḫu-it-na-aš gen. sg.	iii 16 =
	ḫu-it-ta-aš	= B iii 56
ḫuittiya -	"to draw, pull"	
	ḫu-it-ti-ia-u-wa-an-zi inf.	iii 72
(^{d}U) ḫulaššašši- (Luw.)	"Storm-god of Ḫulašša(?)"	see DN
ḫumant-	"all, every"	
	ḫu-u-ma-an-te-eš nom. pl. c.	i 15, 16, 49, B i 18, 38]
	ḫu-u-ma-an-du-uš nom. pl. c.	i 17 (B: ḫumanteš)
	ḫu-u-ma-an-da-aš gen. pl.	iii 19
	ḫu-u-ma-an-da-aš dat.-loc. pl.	iii 27,30 iv 33, 39, 50, 52
	ḫu-u-ma-da-aš	B iii 67
	ḫu-u-ma-an-da-az abl.	i 19 = (B: da-<pí->az ?)

ḫudak	"at once, first off"	
	ḫu-u-da-ak(-ma-az)	i 21
\ ḫuwaialli- (Luw.)	"witness"	
	\ ḫu-u-wa-ia-al-li ^{d}UTU-i dat.-loc. sg	B iv 53 (= A iv 56: kutrui)
ḫuwant - c.	"wind"	
	ḫu-u-wa-an-te-eš nom. pl.	B iii 49 (=A iii 10: IM$^{\text{Ḫi.A}}$-uš)
iya-	"to make"	
	DÙ-an-zi pres. pl. 3	iv 59
	i-ia-at pret. sg. 3	iii 30
	DÙ-at	iii 28 (= B: iyat)
DINGIR^{MEŠ} iya-	"to worship gods"	
	i-ia-an-te-eš part. nom. pl. c.	i 23
É^{MEŠ} DINGIR^{MEŠ} / šaklauš iya-		"to build temples; perform rites"
	i-ia-mi pres. sg. 1	iii 62, 63
-za arkuwar iya-	"to make a plea"	
	i-ia-mi pres. sg. 1	i 23, 25, 30 iii 38,42
	DÙ-mi	i 28 (= B: iyami)
	DÙ-zi pres. sg. 3	i 4 iv 47 (=B)
iya- (mid.)	"to walk"	
piran appa iya-	"to walk forth and back, take care for"	
	i-ia-an-ta-ri pres. pl. 3	iii 7, 8
iyannai -	"to go, start walking"	
	katta i-ia-an-ni imp. sg. 2	iii 71
	awan šara i-ia-an-ni	iii 73
išḫuwai- / šuḫḫai-	"to pour, scatter"	
	šer šu-uḫ-ḫa-i	iv 7, 12, 16, 21,27, 32, 54, 58
	šer iš-ḫu-u-⸢i⸣ pres. sg. 3	B iv 54 (=A iv 58: šuḫḫai)
	iš-ḫu-u-wa-i	iv 50 (B broken)

išpanduzzi -	"libation, libation vessel"		
	iš-pa-an-du-uz-zi(-ia)	nom.-acc. sg.	iii 64
ištamašš-	" to hear, to listen to"		
	iš-ta-ma-aš-te-ni	pres. pl. 2	i 29
	iš-ta-ma-aš-ša-an-zi	pres. pl. 3	iii 45
	iš-ta-ma-aš-tén	imp. pl. 2	i 21, 27
	iš-ta-ma-aš-ti-n(i-ia-at)		i 28 =
	uš[!]-ta-ma-aš-ti<-ni>(-ya-at)		= B i 29
	iš-ta<-ma>-aš-tén		B i 28
	iš-ta-ma-aš-ša-an-du	imp. pl. 3	iii 43 (=B), i 36 =
	iš-ta-ma-aš-ša-du		= B i 39
	iš-ta-ma-aš-šu-wa-an-zi	inf.	i 32
idalu-	"bad, evil"		
	i-da-lu-uš (memiaš)	nom. sg. c.	iii 46
idalawaḫḫ-	"to mistreat"		
	i-da-la-wa-aḫ-ḫa-an-te-eš	part. nom. pl. c.	i 24 =
	i-da-la-a-u-wa-aḫ-ḫa-an-te-eš		= B i 25
iwar	"like, in the manner of"		
	i-wa-ar		iii 69, 70
ka-	"this"		
	ke-e-da-ni	dat.-loc. sg.	iii 20, 21
	ki-i-da-ni		B iii 61
	ki-i	nom.-acc. sg./pl. n.	i 8
	ki-i	nom.-acc. pl. n.	i 28, B i 36 (= A i 35: ke-e)
	ke-e		i 26 (= B), 35
	ku-u-uš	acc. pl. c.	B iii 61
	ke-e-da-aš	dat.-loc. pl.	i 34

-kan	sentence particle	
	-kán	i 4,9,18,30 iii 35,37,41,43,46, 53 (x2),60,63,71, 76 iv 5 (x2),9,10, 11 (om. in B),14,15,19,20,24,25,29, 30,34,37,40, 42,44,46,47; B iv 45
kaneš -	"to honor, recognize"	
	ka-ni-iš-ta pret. sg. 3	iii 52 =
	ga-ni-iš-ta	= B iv 21
	ka-ni-iš-⌜ša⌝-[(an-za)] part. nom. sg. c.	iii 75
kariya-	"to cover"	
	[k]a!-ri-ia-an-da part. nom. pl. n.	i 5
karp-	"to be finished, completed"	
	kar-ap-ta-ri mid. pres. sg. 3	iv 48
kāša	"behold !"	
	(nu) ka-a-ša	iii 18
katta	"down; with"	
	kat-ta iyannai-	iii 71
gimraš ḫuitar	"wild animal"	
	gi-im-ra-aš-š(a) ḫuitnaš gen. sg.	iii 16 =
	gi-im-ra-aš ḫuittaš	= B iii 55
kinun	"now"	
	ki-nu-na	i 20 iii 32
kiššan	"thus, as follows"	
	ki-iš-ša-an	i 10 iii 25, 50, 57, 74

kui-	"who, which"		
	ku-iš	nom. sg. c.	iii 46 B i 15 (= A i 14: eras.)
	ku-in	acc. sg. c.	iii 65
	ku-it	nom.-acc. sg. n.	iii 42
	ku-e-el	gen. sg.	iii 48
	ku-e-da-ni	dat.-loc. sg.	iii 12,22 =
	ku-i-e-da-ni		= B iii 51,61
	ku-i-e-eš	nom. pl. c.	i 19 iii 5,6
	ku-i-e-eš	acc. pl. c.	iii 21,34, 63 =
	ku-e-eš	acc. pl, c.	= B iv 31
	ku-e	nom.-acc. pl. n.	i 27,29 iii 38,62 iv 46 (B: kui), 60
	ku-i		B iv 46 = A iv 46: ku-e
	ku-e-da-aš	dat.-loc. pl.	i 18 iv 53
	ku-e-ta-š(a-at)		iii 7=
	ku-e-da-š(a-at)		= B iii 45
	ku-e-ta-aš		iii 6 =
	ku-i-ta-aš		= B iii 44
kuiški	"someone, something"		
	ku-iš-ki	nom. sg. c.	i 3
\ kulani - (Luw.)	"to bring to (a successful) end; promote"		
	\ ku-la-a-ni-it-ta	pret. sg. 3	iii 52 =
	\ ku-la-ni-it-ta		= B iv 21
(^{d}LAMMA) ^{KUŠ}kuršaš	"(Protective-god of) fleece(?)/hunting bag(?)		
	(^{d}LAMMA) ^{KUŠ}kur-ša-aš		i 59
kutru(wa) -	"witness"		
	ku-ut-ru-i ^{d}UTU-i	dat.-loc. sg.	iv 56 (B: \ ḫuwaialli)
kuwapi	"when, where"		
	ku-wa-pí		iii 45

laḫuwai -	"to libate"		
	la-ḫu-u-wa-i	pres. sg. 3	iv 51,54
	piran la-ḫu-u-wa-i		iv 58 =
	piran la-a-ḫu-u-wa-i		= B iv 5
lē (cf. *UL*)	"not"		
	le-e		iii 39, 67
-ma- (cf. -a)	"and; but, however"		
	-ma-		i 7,21,25(x2),29,33 iii 25,26,28,31,36, 67,69,73 iv 3,4,6,8,11,13,15,18,20,23, 26,28,31,33,36,38,41,43,45,47,52,55,56 B iv10,48
maḫḫan	"how, as; when"		
	ma-aḫ-ḫa-an		B iv 40 (= A iii 72: GIM-an)
	ma-aḫ-ḫa-n(a-at)		B i 24 = (A i 24: GIM-an-na-at)
	GIM-an(-)		i 8, 23, 24 iii 72 iv 45, 47
	GIM! -an		B iv 45
mān	"when, as soon as; if"		
	ma-a-an		i 2 iii 49
meḫur	"time"		
	me-e-ḫu-na-aš	dat.-loc. pl.	iii 53 =
	me-ḫu-na-aš		= B iv 22
mema-	"to say, speak"		
	me-ma-i	pres. sg. 3	i 10 iii 25,50
	me-ma-an-zi	pres. pl. 3	iii 57
	me-mi-iš-tén	pret. pl. 2	i 19
	me-ma-al-lu	imp. sg. 1	iii 74

memal	"groats"	
	me-ma-al nom.-acc. sg.	i 7 iv 6 11,16,21,26,31,50, 54,57
	me-im-ma-al	B i 47, 51
me/immami- (Luw.)	"favored"	
	mi-im-ma-me-iš-š(a) part. nom. sg. c.	iii 75 =
	me-em-ma-mi-iš-š(a)	= B iv 44
memiya-	"word, message"	
	me-mi-aš nom. sg. c.	i 3] iii 46
	me-mi-an acc. sg. c.	i 20
menaḫḫanda	"opposite, against"	
	^{d}UTU-i me-na-aḫ-ḫa-an-da	i 4
(^{d}U) miyannaš	"(Storm-god of) Growth"	see DN
-mu-	"me, for/to me"	
	-mu- acc.	iii 28(x 2),29(x2),31,42
	-mu- dat.-loc.	i 18,20,25,26,29,30,34, 35 iii 35, 39,43,46,47, 68,69,71(x 2),73
naḫšarrišk-	"to be reverent, pious; to fear"	
	na-aḫ-šar-ri-iš-ki-u-an tiyanzi supine	iii 56 =
	na-aḫ-ša-ri-iš-ki-u-wa-an	= B iv 25
nakkiyašš-	"to oppress, burden someone's conscience"	
	na-ak-ki-ia-aš-zi pres. sg. 3	i 3
namma	"further, then"	
	nam-ma	iv 59

našma	"or"		
	na-aš-ma		iii 49
nepi(š)-	"sky"		
	ne-pí-iš (tekan)	nom.-acc. sg.	iii 10
	ne-pí-ša-aš	gen. sg.	i 36 (=B i 37) iii 14,19,20, 23,51, 69 (=B iv 38)
	ne-pí-aš	gen. sg. !	B iii 48], 53, 59(x2), 62 iv 20
	[A]N-aš		i 10
	ŠA-ME-E	gen. pl.	i 9, 10,11, 12, 37, 41 iii 13, 15, 59 iv 18, 20 B i 54
	AN-*I*		B i 38 ii 8 (A: *ŠA-ME-E*)
	ne-pí-ši	dat.-loc. sg.	iii 14
	ne-pí-ša-az	abl. sg.	iii 23
	DINGIR^{MEŠ} .... nepi(š)aš		i 36, B iii 48
	DINGIR^{MEŠ} .... [A]N-aš		iii 10
	DINGIR^{MEŠ} *ŠAMĒ*		iii 59
	nepi(š)aš ^{d}UTU		iii 14, 19, 20, 23, 51, 69
	^{d}UTU *ŠAMĒ*		i 9, 10, 37 iii 13, 15
	^{d}UTU AN-*I*		B i 39 (A om.)
	^{d}U LUGAL *ŠAMĒ*		i 11
	^{d}U *ŠAMĒ*		iv 18, 20 B i 54
	^{d}U Ḫatti LUGAL *ŠAMĒ*		i 12
	^{d}U piḫaššašši nepi(š)aš LUGAL		iii 51
	^{d}Ḫebat SAL.LUGAL *ŠAMĒ*		i 41 =
	^{d}Ḫebat SAL.LUGAL AN-*I*		= B ii 8
nu	"and"		
	nu		i 8,10,28 iii 18,20,21,34,35,44,45, 49, 50,54,57,61,64,73 iv 49, 60
	nu-kán		i 9 iii 43 iv 46; B iv 45
	nu-mu		i 25,26,34,35 iii 29(x2),42,43,68,71
	nu-mu-kán		iii 35, 46, 71

	nu-mu-za		iii 28
	nu-wa-kán		iii 76
	nu-ut-ta		iii 59
	nu-wa-ar-an		iii 52
	nu-wa-ar-an-kán		iii 53 (x2)
	nu-za		i 3,27 iii 37,42,48
	nu-za-kán		iii 63
	nu-uš-ša-an		i 6 iii 14
	na-aš		i 9 iii 9, 23, 40 iv 60
	na-aš-kán		iv 5(x2),9,10,14,15,19,20,24,25,29,30,34,37,40,42,44
	na-an-mu		iii 47
	na-an-ši		iii 66 =
	na-an-ta		= B iv 34
	na-at		i 31
	na-at-kán		iii 37
	na-at-mu		iii 39
	na-at-mu-kán		i 30
	na-at-za		iv 47
pa(i)-	"to go"		
	(šara) pa-iz-zi	pres. sg. 3	i 9 =
	(šara) pa-a-iz-zi		= B i 9
pai-	"to give"		
	pe-eš-ki-mi	iter. pres. sg. 1	iii 65, 67
	pí-iš-ke-el-lu	iter. imp. sg. 1	iii 66
parā	"forth, forward, out"		
	pa-ra-a ep-		i 26
	" ḫandant-		iii 58
	" tarna-		i 32
	" dušk-		iii 64

paršiya -	"to break, crumble (bread)"		
	pár-ši-ia-a[z-zi]	act. pres. sg. 3	B iv 52, 53
	pár-ši-ia	mid. pres. sg. 3	iv 3,9,13,19,24,29,34,37,39, 42,43, 50,53,55, 56,60
	pár-ši-ia-u-wa-an-zi	inf.	iv 45
-pat	emphatic particle		
	-pát		i 21,30,31
^{d}U piḫami- (Luw.)	"luminous(?) (Storm-god)'		see DN
^{d}U piḫaššašši- (Luw.)	'(Storm-god of) Lightning"		see DN
peran	"before, in front of"		
	pé-ra-an šipant-		iv 12,17,22,27; B i 44, 64
	" laḫuwai-		iv 58
	" tianza		i 33, B i 16]
	" EGIR-pa iya-		iii 7,8
peda -	"place"		
	tuliyaš pé-e-da-aš	nom. sg. c. (!)	iii 11 =
	tuliyaš pé-di$_{12}$(te)	dat.-loc.(?) sg.	= B iii 50
	pé-di	dat.-loc. sg.	iii 12 =
	pé-di$_{12}$(te)	"	= B iii 51
pittuliya(wa)nt -	"troubled, reluctant"		
	píd-du-li-ia-u-wa-an-za(-ma-da)	nom. sg. c.	iii 67 =
	p[ít]-tu-li-ia-an-za(-ma-ta)		= B iv 35
šaklai -	"custom, rite"		
	ša-ak-la-uš-š(a-da)	acc. pl.	iii 62

šallanu-	"to bring up, rear"		
	šal-la-nu-ut	pret. sg. 3	iii 29
	šal-la-nu-wa-an-za	part. nom. sg. c.	iii 33, 75
-šan	sentence particle		
	-ša-an		i 6 iii 14
šara	"up"		
	awan ša-ra-a iyanni-		iii 73
	ša-ra-a pai-		i 9
	ša-ra-a uwa-		i 31
	ša-ra-a-kán uwa-		iii 13
šarku -	"prominent"		
	šar-ku-uš AMAR-uš	nom. sg. c.	i 50
	šar-ku-uš UR.SAG-iš		iii 58
šarlāi -	"to praise; to rectify"		
	šar-la-a-mi	pres. sg. 1	iii 61
	šar-la-an-zi	pres. pl. 3	iii 47
	šar-li-iš-ki-mi	iter. pres. sg. 1	iii 44
(^{d}U) šartiyaš	"(Storm-god of) Help"		see DN
šēr	"above, over, upon"		
	še-er(-)		i 4 iii 69,70 iv 7,11,16,21,26,32,54,57
-ši	"to him"		
	-ši		iii 66 (B: -ta)
(^{GIŠ})šinapši	a cult building		
	^{d}U ši-na-ap-ši [^{d}Ḫ]é-pát $^{GIŠ!}$ši-na-ap-ši		i 62-63

(peran) šippant-	"to libate, sacrifice"	
	(peran) ši-ip-pa-an-ti pres. sg. 3	iv 12,17,22,27,32
	ši-pa-an-ti	iv 7
	(peran) ši-ip-pa-ti	B i 44,48,52,56,60,64
	BAL-ti	iv 51
	ši-ip-pa-an-za-kán-zi iter. pres. pl. 3	iii 9
šuḫḫa-	"roof"	
	šu-uḫ-ḫi(-) dat.-loc. sg.	i 4,9
šuḫḫai-	"to pour, scatter" see išḫuwai-	
(^{d}U) šuḫurribi (Hur.)	"(Storm-god of) Life"	see DN
šumel	"yours"	
	šu-me-el-pát	i 21 (B: ammel)
	šu-me-el	B i 23 (A: erased)
šunna-	"to fill, transmit"	
	šu-un-ni imp. sg. 2	iii 37
	anda šu-un-ni	iii 43
šuwant-	"full"	
	^{DUG}TU$_7$ šu-u-wa-an nom.-acc. sg. n.	i 7
	^{DUG}LIŠ.GAL "	i 8
šunniya -	"to plunge, dip"	
	šu-un-ni-ia-zi pres. sg. 3	iv 5, 9, 14, 19, 24 B i 62
	šu-un-ni-ia<-an>-zi pres. sg.$^{!}$ 3	iv 29
-ta-	"you, to/for you"	
	-ta- acc.	iii 59
	-ta- dat.-loc.	iii 62; B iv 34 (A: -ši), 35

	-da- dat.-loc.	iii 62, 67
da-	"to take"	
	ta-at-ti-ni pres. pl. 2	B i 29 (A: da-at-ti-in)
	da-a-aš pret. sg. 3	iii 29
	da-a imp. sg. 2.	iii 37
	da-at-ti-in imp. pl. 2.	i 28 (B: ta-at-ti-ni)
dāi-	"to put, present"	
	da-a-i pres. sg. 3	i 5,6 iv 6,10,15,20,25,31,35,37,40,42,44
	da-a-iš pret. sg. 3	iii 31 iv 53
	arkuwar ti-ia-u-wa-ar verb. subst. n.-a. sg.	iv 48
	arkuwar ti-ia-u-wa-aš " gen. sg.	i 34; B i 37[
daga(n)zipa- c.	"earth; netherworld"	
(cf. tekan)	da-ga-zi-pa-aš gen. sg.	B iii 48 (= A iii 10: KI-aš)
	da-ga-zi-pa-aš-š(a)<<-aš-ša>>	B i 37 (= A i 36: KI-aš-ša)
dankui-	"black, dark"	
	GE_6-iš (KI-aš) nom. sg. c.	iii 10 =
	da-an-ku-ya-aš (dagazipaš) gen. sg. c.	= B iii 48
tabarna-	title of Hittite kings	
	ta-ba-ar-na ^{M}NIR.GÁL	i 1
dapiya -	"all"	
	da-pí-aš dat.-loc. pl. c.	iii 35
	da-<pí>-az (?)	B i 19 (=A i 19: ḫumandaz)
^{GIŠ}taptappa -	"cage"	
	^{GIŠ}tap-tap-pa-an acc. sg.	iii 40

tar-	"to say, mention"		
	da-ra-an-te-eš	part. nom. pl. 3	iii 5[, 6
tarkummiya-	"to announce, proclaim"		
	tar-kum-ma-i	imp. sg. 2	i 35
tarna-	a capacity or weight unit		
	NINDA.GUR$_4$.RA tar-na-aš *ŠA* ZÍD.DA.DUR$_5$		i 6
	NINDA.GUR$_4$.RA *ŠA* ZÍD.DA.DUR$_5$ tar-na-aš		iv 4, 23
tarna-	"to let go"		
	parā tar-ni-iš-tén	imp. pl. 2	i 32
^{SAL}tawannanna	title of Hittite queens		
	(^{d}U *ŠA* É) ^{SAL}ta-wa-an-na-an-na		iii 4
tekan n.	"earth"		
(cf. dagazipa-)	(nepiš) te-kán	nom.-acc. sg.	iii 10
	ták-na-aš (^{d}UTU-uš)	gen. sg.	ii 1
	ták-na-az	abl.	B iii 63 =
	KI-az		= iii 23
tetḫeššar	"thunder"		
	(^{d}U) te-et-ḫi-iš-na-aš	gen. sg.	i 49
tetḫima-	"thunder"		
	te-et-ḫi-ma-aš	nom. sg.	iii 11
tiya-	"to step, take one's stand"		
	-šan ... ti-ia-ši	pres. sg. 2	iii 15
	ti-ia-an-zi	pres. pl. 3	iii 56
	ti-iš-kán-zi	iter. pres. pl. 3	iii 12

peran tianza	"champion"		
	peran ti-an-za	part. nom. sg. c.	i 33
	peran ti-ia-an-za (erased)		i 15
	[piran ti-ia-a]n-⌈za⌉		B i 16]
tuedaz	"from you, by you"		
	tu-e-da-az		iii 32
tuliya -	"council"		
	tu-li-ia-aš	gen. sg.	iii 11
	tu-li-ia	dat.-loc. sg.	iii 12 =
	tu-u-li-ia		= B iii 51
dušk-	"to be happy, rejoice"		
	parā du-uš-kat-ti	pres. sg. 2	iii 64
	anda du-uš-ga-i	pres. sg. 3	iii 61
dušgarawant-	"happy"		
	du-uš-ga-ra-u-wa-an-za	part. nom. sg. c.	iii 66
uk	"I"		
(see also ammuk)	ú-uk		iii 74 (B: am[-mu-uk)
	ú-u[k-ma?-z]a-[ká]n		iii 41 (B: am-mu-uk-ma-kán)
	ú-ga-kán		iii 60 (B: [am]-mu-g(a-kán)
utne (see KUR)			
uwa-	"to come"		
	šarā-kan ú-wa-ši	pres. sg. 2	iii 14
	-kan šarā ú-iz-zi(-pát)	pres. sg. 3	i 31
	ú-wa-an-zi	pres. pl. 3 (phras.)	iii 54

uwaianu -	"to intercede, to convince"		
	ú-wa-ia-nu-ut	imp. sg. 2	iii 35
-wa(r)-	direct speech particle		
	-wa-		iii 50, 57, 74, 76
	-wa-ar-		iii 52, 53 (x 2)
waḫnu -	"to (make) turn, reject"		
	appa wa-aḫ-nu-wa-an-zi	pres. pl. 3	iii 39
walla -	"to praise"		
	wa-li-ia-an-zi	pres. pl. 3	iii 59
walliyatar	"praise"		
	wa-al-li-ia-tar	nom.-acc. sg.	iii 48, 49
wantāi -	"to heat, warm"		
	wa-an-ta-a-i	imp. sg. 2	iii 70
wantewantema -	"lightning"		
	wa-an-te-wa-an-te-ma-aš	nom. sg.	iii 11
weštara -	"shepherd"		
	$^{\text{LÚ?}}$ú-e-eš-ta-ra-aš	nom. sg.	B iii 52 =
	^{LÚ}SIPA-aš		= iii 13
-z(a)	reflexive particle		
	-za(-)		i 3, 25, 27, 29 iii 28, 37, 41, 48(2), 63, 74 iv 47, 53
	-az		i 18, 21
zik	"you"		
	zi-ik		iii 17

(\) zilatiya	"in the future, henceforth"	
	zi-la-ti-ia	iii 54 =
	\ zi-la-ti-ia	= B iv 23
zinna -	"to finish, end"	
	zi-in-na-i pres. sg. 2	iv 45

***Glossenkeil* and Luwian words**

\ ḫuwaialli-	"witness"	
	\ ḫu-u-wa-ia-al-li ^{d}UTU dat.-loc. sg.	B iv 53 (A: kutrui)
\ kulani -	"to honor"	
	\ ku-la-a-ni-it-ta 3. sg. pret.	iii 52 =
	\ ku-la-ni-it-ta	= B iv 21
memmami-	"to elevate, exalt"	
	mi-im-ma-me-iš-ša part. nom. sg. c.	iii 75 =
	me-im-ma-mi-iš-ša	= B iv 44
^{d}U piḫami-	Luminous(?) Storm-god	see DN
^{d}U piḫaššašši-	Storm-god of Lightning	see DN
(\) zilatiya	"in the future, henceforth"	
	zi-la-ti-ia	iii 54 =
	\zi-la-ti-ia	= B iv 23

Sumerograms

AD.KID	"reed"	
	2 ^{GIŠ}BANŠUR AD.KID	i 4
ALAM	"statue, image"	
	ALAM-*KUNU*	i 22
AMA.AMA	"grandmother, ancestor"	
	ŠA AMA.AMA ^{d}UTU-*ŠI*	ii 58
AMAR	"calf"	
	šarkuš AMAR-uš nom. sg.	i 50
AN	"sky"	see *nepiš*
BABBAR	"white"	
	NINDA.GUR$_4$.RA BABBAR	iv 8,13,18,28,33,36,38,41,43,49,52
BAD	"lord"	see *BĒLU*
BAL	"to libate, sacrifice"	see *šipant-*
^{GIŠ}BANŠUR	"table"	
	^{GIŠ}BANŠUR	i 4,5,6 iv 15,20,25,30,34,44,61
	^{GIŠ}BANŠUR-i d.-l. sg.	iv 5,10,37,40,42, B i 50,55,59,62,66,74
BIL	"to burn"	
	BIL-nu-zi pres. sg. 3	iv 61
^{DUG}DÍLIM (LIŠ).GAL	" bowl"	
	memal=ma ^{DUG}LIŠ.GAL šuwan	i 8
^{DUG}DÍLIM (LIŠ).GAL SIG	"thin bowl"	
	[^{DUG}DÍLIM.G]AL SIG	i 7

DINGIR	"god, deity"	
	[DINGIR-*L*]*UM* nom.	iii 58
	DINGIR-*LAM* nom. !	iii 49
	DINGIR-*LIM* nom. !	iii 57; B iv 27
	DINGIR-*LIM* ^{URU}Parša nom.	ii 1
	ŠA ^{URU}Ḫurniya LUGAL-uš DINGIR-*LUM*$^{!}$-uš	ii 26 =
	" " " DINGIR-*LIM*$^{!}$-uš	= B ii 66
	DINGIR.SAL-*TUM* *ŠA* ^{d}U piḫami	i 66
	DINGIR^{MEŠ}-aš d.-l. pl.	iii 35
	DINGIR^{MEŠ}	i 3,16,17,20,21,23,25,27,28,30, 31, 35(x2),36 iii 12,19, 21(x2),27,30,34, 35,37(x2),42,43,45,47 iv 47
	DINGIR^{MEŠ} LÚ^{MEŠ}	i 5
	DINGIR.LÚ^{MEŠ}	i 15,38,40,44,46,48,55,57,61,64,67,70, 71,73,75,77,78 ii 1,3,6,7,8,10,13,17,19, 20,22,24,26,29,[(30)],35, 36,39,45,47, 48,50,51,52,53,55,56,57,58,59,61,64, 66,69,73 iii 2,[(4)],9 iv 33,49
	DINGIR.SAL^{MEŠ}	i 15,38,40,45,46,48,55,57,61,64,67,70, 71,73,75,77,79 ii 1,4,6,7,8,10,13,17,19, 21,22,24,27,29,31,35,37,39,47,48,50, 51,52, 53,55,56,57,58,59,65,66,69,73 iii 2,5,9 iv 38, 52 B iii 12,28
	<DINGIR.>SAL^{MEŠ}	ii 45, 61
	DINGIR^{MEŠ} lulaḫiyaš	i 53
	DINGIR^{MEŠ} *ŠAMĒ*	iii 59
	DINGIR^{MEŠ} *ŠA* É.GAL ḫuḫḫaš	i 42
	É^{MEŠ} DINGIR^{MEŠ}	iii 6,8,62
	É^{MEŠ} DINGIR$^{\textit{LIM}}$-*KUNU*	i 22
	É^{MEŠ} DINGIR$^{\textit{LIM}}$-*ŠUNU*	B iii 64 =
	É^{MEŠ} DINGIR^{MEŠ}-*ŠUNU*	= iii 24
DÙ	"to do, prepare"	see iya-
(^{d}U) DU_6	"(Storm-god of the) Ruin"	see DN

DUG	see ^{DUG}LIŠ.GAL	
DUMU	"son"	
	DUMU-aš nom. sg. c.	i 13
	DUMU	i [2], 59
	DUMU-*IA*	iii 54
DUMU.DUMU	"grandson"	
	DUMU.DUMU-*IA*	iii 54
DUMU.LUGAL	"prince"	
	DUMU^{MEŠ} LUGAL	iii 55
DUMU.LÚ.U_{19}.LU	"mortal, mankind"	
	DUMU.LÚ.U_{19}.LU-aš nom. sg.	iii 26
	DUMU.LÚ.U_{19}.LU	iii 13
	DUMU.LÚ.U_{19}.LU-*TI*	iii 15, 49
	DUMU.LÚ.U_{19}.LU-*UT-TI*	B iii 52, 55 iv 18
DUR_5	"moist"	
	ZÌ.DA DUR_5 tarnaš	i 6 iv 4, 23
É	"house, estate"	
	É ^{URU}Gaz-zi-ma-ra	ii 59
	É ^{SAL}ta-wa-an-na-an-na	iii 4
É.DINGIR	"temple"	
	É^{MEŠ} DINGIR^{MEŠ}	iii 8, 62, 6 =
	É$^{EŠ!}$ [ ]	= B iii 44
	É^{MEŠ} DINGIR^{LIM}-*KUNU*	i 22
	É^{MEŠ} DINGIR^{MEŠ}-*ŠUNU*	iii 24 =
	É^{MEŠ} DINGIR^{LIM}-*ŠUNU*	= B iii 64

É.GAL	"palace"	
	É.GAL ḫuḫḫaš	i 42
	É.GAL ^{d}UTU^{ŠI}	ii 4
EGIR-anda / -*ŠU*	"thereafter"	
	EGIR-an-da	B iii 65 iv 50 (= A: EGIR-*ŠU*-ma)
	EGIR-an-ma$^{!}$	B iv 52 (= A: EGIR-*ŠU*-ma)
	EGIR-an<<-na>>-da(-ma-za)	B i 26 (= A: EGIR-*ŠU*-ma-za)
	nu EGIR-*ŠU*	iv 49 (= B: EGIR-*ŠÚ*-ma)
	EGIR-*ŠU*-ma	iii 25 iv 3,4,8 iv 13,15,18,26, 28,31,33, 36,38,41,43,52,55,56 B i 43,47,55, 57
	EGIR-*ŠÚ*-ma	iv 6, 20, 23; B i 45, 49 iv 48
	EGIR-*ŠU*-ma-kán	iv 11
	EGIR-*ŠU*-ma-za	i 25
EGIR-pa	"back, again"	
	EGIR-pa ep- / *ṢABATU*	iii 40, 41
	peran EGIR-pa iya-	iii 7, 8
	EGIR-pa waḫnu-	iii 39
	EGIR-pa SIG$_5$-aḫ-	iii 47
EME	"tongue"	
	EME-*IA*	iii 22, 34, 36
EN	"lord"	see *BĒLU*
EN-*UTTU*	"lordship"	
	EN-*UT-TA*	i 19
GAŠAN	"lady"	see *BĒLAT*
GE$_6$	"dark, black"	see dankui-

GÉŠPU	"fist"	
	ZAG-ni GÉŠPU	iii 71
GEŠTIN	"wine"	
	KUKUB GEŠTIN	i 8 iv 7, 12, 16, 22, 27, 32, 51
GEŠTUG	"ear"	
	GEŠTUG-an acc. sg.	i 26
GIM-an	"when, how"	see maḫḫan
^{GIŠ}GU.ZA	"throne"	
	^{GIŠ}GU.ZA^{MEŠ}-*ŠUNU*	iii 24
GUD	"bull"	
	GUD-i GIM-an d.-l. sg.	iii 71
	^{d}Šeriš... GUD *ŠA* ^{d}U	i 33 =
	$^{\text{DINGIR.GUD}}$Šeriš	= B i 34
	[Š]e-r[i-iš] GUD	B i 15 (A: erased)
GUNNI	"hearth, pyre"	
	ŠA IṢṢI 2 GUNNI	iv 59
(^{d}U) ḪI.ḪI	"(Storm-god of) Lightning"	see DN
ḪUR.SAG	"mountain"	
	ḪUR.SAG^{MEŠ}-az abl. pl.	iii 23
	ḪUR.SAG^{MEŠ}	i 15, 38, 40, 45, [(47)], 48, 55, 57, 60, 61, 65, 67, 75, 77, 79 ii 2, 6, 9, 11, 14, 17, 19, 21, 23, 25, 27, 29, 31, 35, 37, 39, 45, 47, 48, 50, 51, 52, 54, 55, 61, 65, 66, 69 iii 3, 59 iv 41, 55

Ì.DÙG.GA	"fine oil"	
	LÀL Ì.DÙG.GA	iv 5, 9, 14, 19, 24, 29, 51, 54, 58
	[^{DUG}LIŠ.G]AL SIG LÀL ŠÀ.BA Ì.DÙG.GA	i 7
ÍD	"river"	
	ÍD^{MEŠ}-az abl. pl.	iii 24
	ÍD^{MEŠ}	i 16, 39, 40, 45, 47, [(49)], 55, 58, 60, 61, 65, 67, 75, 77, 79 ii 2, 6, 9, [(11)], 14, 17,19, 21, 23, 25, 27, 29, 31, 35, 37, 39, 45, 47, 49, 50, 51, 52, 54, 55, 61, 65, 67, 70 iii 3, 59 iv 43, 55
IM	"wind"	see ḫuwant-
ÌR	"servant"	
	ÌR-*KA*	iii 36, 60
	ÌR-*KU-NU*	i 20
KAxU	"mouth"	
	UN-az KAxU-az abl. sg.	i 31
(^{d}U) KARAŠ	"(Storm-god of the) Army"	see DN
KI	"earth"	see daganzipa-
KI.MIN	"ditto"	
	KI.MIN	i 68, 75; B i 39 ii 27(x 2), 51,55, 57(x2), 60, 71 iii 3, iv 34, 37, 39, 42, 44, 55
KUR	"land"	
	^{URU}Ḫattuši KUR-e d.-l. sg.	B i 15 (A: erased)
	DINGIR.LÚ/SAL^{MEŠ} KUR-e-aš gen. pl.	iv 49, 52
	ḪUR.SAG^{MEŠ} ÍD^{MEŠ} KUR	B iv 52 (A om. KUR)
	KUR ^{URU}GN	see GN

LÀL	"honey"	
	LÀL Ì.DÙG.GA	iv 5, 9, 14, 19, 24, 29, 51, 54, 58
	[^{DUG}LIŠ.G]AL SIG LÀL ŠÀ.BA Ì.DÙG.GA	i 7
LUGAL	"king"	
	LUGAL-uš nom. sg. c.	i 9 iii 18, 25, 32
	ŠA LUGAL-*RI* gen. sg.	iii 5 =
	ŠA LUGAL	= B iii 42
	LUGAL KUR ^{URU}Ḫatti	i 1, 2
	LUGAL SAL.LUGAL	iii 7
	LUGAL^{MEŠ}	iii 54
	DUMU^{MEŠ} LUGAL	iii 55
	^{d}U piḫaššaššiš ... nepišaš LUGAL-uš	iii 51
	^{d}U LUGAL *ŠAMĒ*	i 11
	^{d}U ^{URU}Ḫatti LUGAL *ŠAMĒ*	i 12
	ŠA ^{URU}Ḫurniya LUGAL-uš	ii 26
	LUGAL-maš see	DN Šarruma
LUGAL.GAL	"great king"	
	LUGAL.GAL	i 1,2
LUGAL-uiznatar	"kingship"	
	LUGAL-iz-na-an-ni d.-l. sg.	iii 31
MUŠEN	"bird"	
	MUŠEN-iš$^{?}$ nom. sg.	iii 40 =
	MUŠEN-za	= B iv 9
NINDA.GUR$_4$.RA	"thick bread"	
	NINDA.GUR$_4$.RA	i 6 iii 64 iv 4, 8, 13, 18, 23, 28, 33, 36, 38, 41, 43, 49, 52, 55, 56, 60 B i 39
NINDA.GUR$_4$.RA$^{ḪI.A}$		iv 3, 7, 11, 16, 21, 26, 31, 45, 54, 57, B i 57 iv 33

NINDA.Ì.E.DÉ.A	"fat bread"	
	NINDA.Ì.E.DÉ.A	i 7 iv 6, 11, 15,20, 26, 31, 50, 53, 57
NIR.GÁL	Muwatalli	see PN
(^{d}U) NIR.GÁL	"Valiant (Storm-god)"	see DN
SA_5	"red"	
	NINDA.GUR_4.RA ... SA_5	iv 8, 13, 18, 28, 33, 36, 38, 41, 43, 49
SAL.LUGAL	"queen"	
	ŠA SAL.LUGAL-*TI* gen. sg.	iii 5 =
	ŠA SAL.LUGAL-*UT-TI*	= B iii 42
	SAL.LUGAL^{MEŠ}	iii 54 =
	SAL.LUGAL$^{ḪI.A}$	= B iv 24
	LUGAL SAL.LUGAL	iii 7
	^{d}UTU ^{URU}Arinna ... SAL.LUGAL	i 10
	^{d}Ḫebat SAL.LUGAL	i 12
	^{d}Ḫebat SAL.LUGAL *ŠAMĒ*	i 41
	SAL.LUGAL ^{URU}Paliya	ii 68
^{LÚ}SANGA	"priest"	
	^{LÚ}SANGA(-)	i 18 iii 27, 30
	ŠA ^{LÚ}SANGA-*KUNU*	i 20
	LÚ^{MEŠ}SANGA	iii 9
SIxSÁ	"to prepare"	
	S[IxSÁ?-z]i pres. sg. 3	i [8
SIG	"thin"	
	[^{DUG}LIŠ.G]AL SIG	i 7

SIG$_5$-aḫḫ-	"to make right (again), to alleviate"	
	EGIR-pa SIG$_5$-aḫ-ḫa-an-zi pres. pl. 3	iii 47 =
	SIG$_5$-aḫ-zi	= B iv 16
^{LÚ}SIPA	"shepherd"	see weštara-
ŠÀ	"heart; within, therein"	
	ŠÀ-ta dir./d.-l. sg.	iv 46
	ŠÀ.BA	i 7 iv 8, 13, 18, 28, 33, 36, 38, 41,43, 49
	ŠÀ.PA	B i 45, 49, 53, 61, 65, 67, 69, 71, 73
	ŠÀ-*BI*	iv 5, 9,1 4, 19, 24, 29
ŠAḪ	"swine, pig"	
	ŠA ... UR.GI$_7$-aš ŠAḪ-aš gen. sg.	iii 16
TI	"to live, to stay alive"	see ḫuiš-
^{DUG}TU$_7$	a (cooking) pot	
	NINDA.Ì.E.DÉ.A ^{DUG}TU$_7$ šuwan	i 7
UD(^{KAM})	"day"	
	kedani UD-ti d.-l. sg.	iii 21, B iii 60 =
	kedani UD^{KAM}-ti	= iii 20
	UD^{KAM}-tili	"daily"
	UD-ti-li	iii 16
	UD^{KAM}-li	B iii 56
UN	"man"	see antuḫša-
UR.GI$_7$	"dog"	
	ŠA...UR.GI$_7$-(m)aš$^!$ ŠAḪ-aš gen. sg.	iii 15

UR.SAG	"strong, valiant"	
	šarkuš UR.SAG-iš nom. sg.	iii 58
	UR.SAG	i 2
^{d}UTU-*ŠI*	"His Majesty"	
	A-NA ^{d}UTU-*ŠI* ŠÀ-ta	iv 46
	ŠA É.GAL ^{d}UTU-*ŠI*	ii 4
	ŠA A-BI ^{d}UTU-*ŠI*	ii 57
	ŠA A-BI A-BI ^{d}UTU-*ŠI*	ii 56
	ŠA AMA.AMA ^{d}UTU-*ŠI*	ii 58
ZAG	"right"	
	ZAG-ni GÉŠPU d.-l. sg.	iii 71
ZI	"soul, mind"	
	ZI-an-za nom. sg.	iii 60 =
	ZI-za	= B iv 29
	ZI-ni anda d.-l. sg.	iii 46
	ŠA ZI-*IA* gen. sg.	i 2
ZÌ.DA DUR$_5$	"moist flour"	
	ŠA ZÌ.DA DUR$_5$ tarnaš	iv 4, 23
	tarnaš *ŠA* ZÌ.DA DUR$_5$	i 6

Akkadograms

ABU	"father"	
	A-BU-IA nom. sg.	iii 26,28
	ŠA A-BI ^{d}UTU-*ŠI* gen. sg.	ii 57, B iii 24
ABU ABU	"grandfather, ancestor"	
	ŠA A-BI A-BI ^{d}UTU-*ŠI* gen. sg.	ii 56

AYAK(K)I	a temple in Šamuḫa	
	^{d}*BE-E-LA-AT A-IA-AK-KI*	i 44 =
	^{d}*BE-E-LA-AT A-IA-KI*	= B ii 10
ANA	"to" (sign of dat.)	
	A-NA	i 3, 5, 9, 27, 30, 34, 35 iii 6, 8, 26, 27, 30, 29, 31, 35, 37, 42, 43, 55, 60(x2), 65 iv 4, 7, 8, 11, 13, 16, 18, 21, 23, 25, 26, 28, 30, 31, 36, 41, 43, 44, 46, 47, 49, 52, 54, 55, 57 B i 39, 54 iv 4
ANA PANI	"before, in front of"	
	A-NA PA-NI	iii 37 (B: *PA-NI*)
(EGIR-pa) *AṢBAT*	"I found refuge"	see EGIR-pa ep-
AWATU	"thing, word"	
	A-WA-TE^{MEŠ}	i 25, 27, 28, 29, 34, 35 iii 36, 38, 43, 45 iv 46
BĒLU	"lord"	
	BE-LU^{MEŠ}	iii 55 =
	EN^{MEŠ}	= B iv 24
	ŠA DINGIR^{MEŠ} *BE-LU*	B i 22 =
	ŠA EN-*LÍ* DINGIR^{MEŠ}	= i 21
	^{d}U Ḫatti ... BAD(BE) KUR Ḫatti	i 12
	^{d}U Ziplanda ... EN KUR Ḫatti	i 14
	^{d}Zanduza EN-aš nom. sg. c.	ii 36
	EN ^{URU}Lanta	ii 50
	EN-*IA*	i 11, 12, 13, 33 iii 13, 15, 20, 26, 41, 49, 51, 56, 61, 63, 65, 68
	EN^{MEŠ} DINGIR^{MEŠ}	i 16, 17, 18, 26, 27, 28, 31, 35, 36

EN-*UTTU*	"lordship"	
	EN-*UT-TA*	i 19
BĒLAT	"lady"	
	d*BE-E-LA-AT AIAK(K)I*	i 44
	GAŠAN-*IA*	i 10, 11, 12, 17
DĪNU-	"verdict"	
	DI-NAM acc. sg.	iii 16 =
	DI-šar	= B iii 55
- *IA*	"my, mine"	
	-*IA*-	i 10, 11(x2), 12 (x2), 13, 17, 25, 33 iii 13, 15, 20, 22, 26 (x2), 28, 34, 36, 41, 49, 51, 54 (x2), 56, 61, 63, 65, 68
IṢṢU	"wood"	
	ŠA IṢ-ṢI 2 GUNNI gen. sg.	iv 59
IŠTU	"from, by means of" (sign of inst. or abl.)	
	IŠ-TU	iii 22, 24, 33], 34, 74
-*KA*	"yours"	
	-*KA*	iii 36, 60
DUG*KUKKUBU*	libation vessel	
	DUG*KU-KU-UB*	i 8 iv 7, 12, 16, 27, 32, 51, B i 56
	DUG*KU-UK-KU-UB*	iv 22
-*KUNU*	"yours"	
	-*KU-NU*	i 20(x2), 22(x2)

PANI	"before, in front of"	
	PA-NI	iv 61
	A-NA PA-NI	iii 37 (B: *PA-NI*)
QATI	"ended"	
	QA-TI	iv 61
ŠA	"of"; sign of gen.	
	ŠA	i 6, 11], 13, 16, 17, 18, 20, 21, 22, 23, 25, 33 (x2), 39, 40, 42, 44, 45, 47, [(49)], 55, 58, 60, 61, 65(x2), 66(x2), 67, 69, 70, 72(x2), 73, 74, 75, 76, 77, 79 ii 2, 4, 6, 7, 9, 10, [(11)], 12, 14, 17, 18, 19, 20, 21, 22, 23, 25, 26, 27, 28, 29, 31, 34, 35, 36, 37, 40, 43, 44(x2), 45, 46, 47, 49, 51(x2), 52, 53, 54, 55, 56, 57, 58, 59, 60, 61, 62(x2), 63, 65, 67, 70, 71, 73 iii 2, 3, 4, 5 (x2), 13, 15, 18, 36(x2), 48, 55 iv 4, 6, 10, 23, 25, 30, 35, 37, 39, 40, 42, 44, 59 B i 15, 50, 55, 61, 65, 71, 73 B ii 56, 69 iii 16, 58
ŠAMĒ	"sky, heaven"	see nepiš
KUR *ŠAPLITI*	Lower Land	
-ŠU	"his, her"	
	-ŠU	i 25 iii 25 iv 3], 48, 11, 13, 15, 18, 26, 28, 31, 33, 36, 38, 41, 43, 49, 52, 55, 56 B i 43, 55, 57
	-ŠÚ	iv 6]$^{?}$, 20, 23 B i 45, 49 iv 48
-ŠUNU	"their"	
	-ŠU-NU	iii 24 (x2)

Ù	"and"	see -a/-ya
UL	"no, not"	
(see also *lē*)	*Ú-UL*	i 29 iii 6, 8, 48
UŠKĒN	"he bows"	
	[*UŠ-KE*]*-EN* pres. sg. 3	i 9
(^{d}U) *ZUNNI*	"(Storm-god of the) Rain"	
	^{d}U *ZU-UN-NI*	ii 60

Personal Names

Muršili	^{M}Mur-ši-i-li	i 2
Muwatalli	^{M}NIR.GÁL	i 1 iii 18, 32, 36, 60

Divine Names

Most of the DN in the list appear in the nominative case. The case ending will only be indicated where multiple endings are attested. The domicile of each deity according to the entries in the Long List of local gods is indicated in parantheses; in addition, the explicit relation of a deity to a locale is fully quoted.

^{d}Aya- (in Ḫatti)	^{d}A-a-aš	i 52
^{d}Ala- (in Karaḫna)	$^{DINGIR.SAL}$A-la-a-aš	ii 5
^{d}Allatum (in Ḫatti)	^{d}Al-la-tum	i 52
^{d}Ammama- (in Ḫaḫana)	^{d}Am-ma-ma-aš	ii 44
^{d}Apara- (in Šamuḫa)	^{d}A-pa-a-ra-aš	i 44
^{d}Ašgašipa- (in Ḫatti)	^{d}Aš-ga-ši-pa-aš	i 54
^{d}Ḫantidaššu- (in Ḫurma)	^{d}Ḫa-an-ti-da-aš-šu-uš	i 74 =
	^{d}Ḫa-an-ti-<da-aš->šu-uš	= B ii 39

^{d}Ḫapandaliya- (in Ḫatti)	^{d}Ḫa-pa-an-da-li-ia-aš	i 56 =
	^{d}Ḫa-pa-an-ta-li-ia-aš	= B ii 21
^{d}Ḫāšigašnawanza- (in Lawazantiya)	^{d}Ḫa-a-ši-ga-aš-na-wa-an-za	i 76
^{d}Ḫataḫḫa- (in Ankuwa)	see Kataḫḫa	
^{d}Ḫebat	^{d}Ḫé-bat	i 11 iv 13, 15
	of É.GAL ḫuḫḫaš	i 41
	in Apzišna	ii 72
	in Kadapa	i 46
	in Kummanni	i 62
	in Šamuḫa/Tiwa	i 40/B ii 7
	in Wašuduwanda	ii 41
^{d}Ḫebat–Šarruma	in Uda: ^{d}Ḫé-bat LUGAL-ma-aš	i 78
	in Kummanni: Ḫe-bat LUGAL	B ii 27 =
	Ḫe-bat ^{GIŠ}šinapši	= i 63
^{d}Ḫebat of Ḫalab	^{d}Ḫebat ^{URU}Ḫalab *ŠA* ^{URU}GN	
	in Ḫatti	i 51
	in Ḫurma	i 74
	in Šamuḫa	i 43
^{d}Ḫulla- (in Arinna)	^{d}Ḫu-ul-la-aš	i 38
^{d}Ḫurri- (in Ḫatti)	^{GUD}Ḫur-ri	i 14
	A-NA ^{d}Še-ri ^{d}Ḫur-ri	iv 36
^{d}Karmaḫi- (in Kalimuna)	^{d}Kar-ma-ḫi-iš	ii 53
^{d}Karuna- (in Kariuna)	^{d}Ka-ru-na-aš	ii 71
^{d}Karzi- (in Ḫatti)	^{d}Kar-zi-iš	i 55
^{d}Kataḫḫa- (in Tawiniya)	^{d}Ka-taḫ-ḫa-aš	ii 46 =
	^{d}Ka-taḫ-ha	= B iii 14
^{d}Ḫataḫḫa- (in Ankuwa)	^{d}Ḫa-taḫ-ḫa-aš	ii 60
^{d}Kubaba- (in Ḫatti)	^{d}Ku-pa-pa-aš	i 53 =
	$^{DINGIR.SAL}$ Ku-pa-a-pa-aš	= B ii 18
^{d}Lušiti- (in Nenašša)	^{d}Lu-ši-ti-iš	ii 12
^{d}Mizzulla- (in Arinna)	^{d}Mi-iz-zu-ul-la-aš	i 37 =
	^{d}Me-ez-zu-ul-la-aš	= B ii 2

^{d}Mulliyara- (in Lawazantiya)	^{d}Mu-ul-li-ia-ra-aš	i 76
^{d}Nawatiyala- (in Zarwiša)	^{d}Na-wa-ti-ia-la-aš	ii 28
^{d}Pirwa -	^{d}Pí-ir-wa-aš	
	in Ḫatti	i 54
	in Ikšun(uw)a	ii 63
	in Neniša(n)kuwa	ii 62
	in Duruwaduruwa	ii 63
^{d}Pišanuḫi- (in Gallištapa)	^{d}Pí-ša-nu-ḫi-iš	i 64
^{d}Šaḫḫaššara- (in Tuwanuwa)	^{d}Ša-aḫ-ḫa-aš-ša-ra-aš	ii 18
Šarruma-	^{d}Ḫé-pát LUGAL-ma-aš (in Uda) ^{d}Ḫé-pát LUGAL (in Kummanni)	ii 78 B ii 27
^{d}Šeri- (in Ḫatti)	*A-NA* ^{d}Še-ri ^{d}Ḫur-ri	iv 36 (= B)
^{DINGIR}Še-ri-iš EN-*YA* GUD *ŠA* ^{d}U *ŠA* KUR Ḫatti peran tianza		i 33 =
$^{DINGIR.GUD}$Še-ri-iš etc.		= B i 34
^{d}Š[e-r]i-uš$^{!}$ ~~GUD *ŠA*~~ ^{GUD}Ḫur-ri ~~KUR ^{URU}Ḫatti kuiš peran tianza~~		i 14-15 =
[$^{DINGIR.GU}$]^{D}[Še]-r[i-iš] GUD *ŠA* ^{URU}Ḫattuši KUR-e kuiš [peran tia]nza		= B i 15-16
^{d}Šuwanzipa- (in Šuwanzana)	^{d}Šu-wa-an-zi-pa-aš	ii 22
^{d}Tamišiya - (in Tapiqqa)	^{d}Ta-mi-ši-ia-aš	iii 2 =
	^{d}Ta-mi-iš-ši-ia-aš	= B iii 39
^{d}Damkinna- (in Ḫatti)	^{d}Dam-ki-in-na-aš	i 52
^{d}Tašimi- (in Liḫšina)	^{d}Ta-ši-mi-iš	ii 8
^{d}Tazzuwaši- (in Gaštama)	^{d}Ta-az-zu-wa-ši-iš	i 70
^{d}Telipinu-	^{d}Te-li-pí-nu-uš	
	in Ḫa(n)ḫana (B om. -uš)	ii 43
	in Kadapa	i 68
	in Tawiniya	ii 46
	in Durmitta	ii 10
^{d}Wašḫaliya- (in Ḫarziuna)	^{d}Wa-aš-ḫa-li-ia-aš	ii 34
^{d}Zaḫapuna- (in Gaštama)	^{d}Za-ḫa-pu-na-aš	i 68
^{d}Zanduza (in Šallapa)	^{d}Za-an-du-za EN-aš	ii 36
$^{DINGIR.SAL}$Zinduḫiya- (in Arinna)	$^{DINGIR.SAL}$Zi-in-du-ḫi-ia-aš	i 38 =
	$^{DINGIR.SAL}$Zi-in-<du->ḫi-ia-aš	= B ii 3
^{d}Zitḫariya- (in Zitḫara)	^{d}Zi-it-ḫa-ri-ia-aš	i 59, B ii 25

^{d}Zūlima- (in Šugazziya)	^{d}Zu-ú-li-ma-aš	ii 7
^{d}*BĒLAT AYAK(K)I* (in Šamuḫa)	"lady of *AYAKKI*-temple"	i 43
^{d}DAG (in Ḫatti)	^{d}DAG-iš	i 52 =
	^{d}DAG-ti-iš	= B ii 17
DINGIR of Ḫurniya	*ŠA* ^{URU}Ḫ. LUGAL-uš DINGIR-*LUM*$^{!}$-uš$^{!}$	ii 26 =
	" DINGIR-*LIM*$^{!}$-uš$^{!}$	= B ii 66
DINGIR (deity) of Parša	DINGIR-*LIM* ^{URU}Parša	ii 1
EN of Lanta	EN ^{URU}Lanta	ii 50
^{d}GAZ.BA.IA (in Ḫupišna)	^{d}GAZ.BA.IA	ii 15
^{d}IŠTAR	^{d}IŠTAR	
	in Ḫaddarina	i 54
	in Innuwita	ii 42
	in Ninuwa	i 53
	in Šariššа (^{d}IŠTAR-li-iš)	i 73
	in Šullama	ii 64
	in Wašuduwanda	ii 41
^{d}IŠTAR.LÍL	^{d}IŠTAR.LÍL	
	in Ankuwa	ii 60
	in Šamuḫa	i 43
^{d}LAMMA "Protective-god"	^{d}LAMMA	
	in Ḫatenzuwa	i 71
	in Ḫatti	i 51
	in Kalašmitta	iii 1
	in Karaḫna	ii 5
^{d}LAMMA ^{KUŠ}kuršaš (in Zitḫara)	^{d}LAMMA ^{KUŠ}kur-ša-aš ^{d}LÍL	(i 59) B ii 24
^{d}LAMMA.LÍL	^{d}LAMMA.LÍL... *ŠA ABI ABI* ^{d}UTU-*ŠI*	ii 56
^{d}LAMMA.LUGAL	^{d}LAMMA.LUGAL...*ŠA ABI ABI* ^{d}UTU-*ŠI*	ii 56
^{d}LÍL	^{d}LAMMA ^{KUŠ}kur-ša-aš ^{d}LÍL	B ii 24 (A i 59 om.)
LUGAL-uš ("King of GN")	see DINGIR of Ḫurniya	
^{d}MAḪ (in Šaḫḫaniya)	DINGIR.MAḪ	ii 30

^{d}NIN.GAL (in Kummanni)	^{d}NIN.GAL		i 63
SAL.LUGAL ("Queen of GN")	SAL.LUGAL ^{URU}Kadapa		i 48
	SAL.LUGAL ^{URU}Paliya		ii 68
	SAL.LUGAL *ŠAMĒ* (see Ḫebat)		
^{d}U "Storm-god"	^{d}U		i 13
in Storm-god fashion	^{d}U-ni-li		iii 73
all the Storm-gods	^{d}U$^{ḪI.A}$ ḫu-u-ma-an-te-eš		i 49
Storm-god of Salvation	^{d}U e-ḫi-el-li-bi (in Arinna)		i 39
Storm-god of Ḫulašša(?)	^{d}U ḫu-la-aš-ša-aš-ši-iš		iii 4
Storm-god of Growth	^{d}U mi-ia-an-na-aš (in Apzišna)		ii 72
Luminous(?) Storm-god	^{d}U pí-ḫa-mi-iš (in Šanahuitta)		i 66
Storm-god of Lightning	^{d}U ḪI.ḪI (in Šamuḫa / Tiwa)		i 40
	^{d}U pí-ḫa-aš-ša-aš-ši-iš	nom.	i 41 iii 25, 28, 51, 63, 68
	[^{d}U pí-ḫ]a-aš-ša-aš-ši		B ii 8 (A: -iš)
	^{d}U pí-ḫa-aš-ša-aš-ši-in	acc.	iii 41, 44, 61
	ŠA ^{d}U pí-ḫa-aš-ša-aš-ši	gen.	iii 48 iv 10, 35, 37, 44 ; B i 72
	ŠA ^{d}U pí-<<pí>>ḫa-aš-ša-aš-ši		B iv 17
	ŠA ^{d}U $^{URU!}$pí-ḫa-aš-ša-aš-ši		iv 42
	ANA ^{d}U pí-ḫa-aš-ša-aš-ši	dat.	iii 55,65 iv 8
	IŠTU ^{d}U pí-ḫa-aš-ša-aš-ši	instr.	iii 33, 74
Storm-god of Help	^{d}[U] šar-ti-ia-aš (in Kadapa)		i 48
	^{d}U ši-na-ap-ši (in Kummanni)		i 62
Storm-god of Life	^{d}U šu-ḫur-ri-bi (in Arinna)		i 39
Storm-god of Thunder	^{d}U te-it-ḫi-iš-na-aš		i 49
Storm-god of Ruin(-town)	^{d}U ^{URU}DU$_{6}$ (in Karaḫna)		ii 5
Storm-god of Ruin	^{d}U DU$_{6}$ (in É.GAL ḫuḫḫaš)		i 42
Storm-god of the Army	^{d}U KARAŠ		
	in Ḫatti		i 50
	in Zitḫara		i 59
Storm-god king of Heaven	^{d}U LUGAL *ŠAMĒ*		i 11
Storm-god of Heaven	^{d}U *ŠAMĒ*		iv 18,20,B i 54

Valiant Storm-god	^{d}[U] NIR.GÁL (in Kadapa)	i 46
Storm-god of the Rain	^{d}U *ZU-UN-NI* (in Ankuwa)	ii 60
Storm-god of GN	Alazḫana	ii 43
	Apzišna (^{d}U miyannaš)	ii 72
	Arinna	i 37
Storm-god of	Ḫalab in Ḫatti	i 51
Storm-god of	Ḫalab in Ḫurma	i 74
Storm-god of	Ḫalab in Šamuḫa	i 43
	Ḫarziuna	ii 34
	Ḫatti	i 12,33,50 iv 23,25
	Ḫatrā	ii 64
	Ḫiššašḫapa	ii 3
	Ḫupišna	ii 15
	Ḫurma	i 74
	Ḫurniya	ii 26
	Illaia	ii 20
	Karaḫna	ii 5
	Kuliwišna	ii 3
	Kummanni	i 62
	Liḫšina	ii 8
	ḪUR.SAG ^{URU}Ma-nu-zi-ia	i 63
	Nenašša	ii 12
	Neriqqa	i 68
	Paḫtima	ii 32
	Parašḫunta	ii 38
	[Pitiy]arik (?)	i 78]
	Šaḫḫaniya	ii 30
	Šaḫḫuwiya	ii 32
	Šaḫpina	i 46
	Šallapa	ii 36
	^{d}U piḫami *ŠA* Šanaḫuitta	i 66
	Šarišša	i 73

	Šugazziya	ii 7
	Tegarama	ii 66
	Tupazziya	ii 69
	Tuwanuwa	ii 18
	Ušša	ii 38
	Uda	i 78
	Zarwiša	ii 28
	Ziplanda	i 13,57 iv 28,30
^{d}UTU "Sun-god(dess)"		
Sun-god of Heaven	nepi(š)aš ^{d}UTU-uš nom.	iii 14,17,20,23
	nepi(š)aš ^{d}UTU-aš gen.	iii 70
	nepišaš ^{d}UTU-i d.-l.	iii 19
	^{d}UTU-i	i 4
	^{d}UTU *ŠAMĒ*	i 9,10,37 iii 13,15
	^{d}UTU AN-*I*	B i 39 (=A: *ŠAMĒ*)
Witness Sun-god	kutrui ^{d}UTU-i d.-l.	iv 56 =
	\ḫuwaialli ^{d}UTU-i	= B iv 53
Sun-goddess of the Earth	taknaš ^{d}UTU-uš nom. sg.	ii 1 (in Parša)
Sun-goddess of Arinna	^{d}UTU Arinna	i 5,10,17,37, 41, 61 iii 18, 26, 29 iv 4, 6, 40
Sun-god(dess) of GN	Ḫatti	i 50
	Malitaškuriya	ii 33
	Wašḫaniya	ii 48
^{d}ZA.BA$_4$.BA$_4$ "War-god"	^{d}ZA.BA$_4$.BA$_4$	
War-god of GN	Arziya	ii 24
	Ḫatti	i 52
	Ḫupišna	ii 16
	Illaya	ii 20
	Neriqqa	i 68

Geographical Names

In all the cases where different spellings of a name are used, all occurrences are listed for both *A* and *B*.

Towns and Lands (URU and KUR ^{URU}GN)

Alazḫana	A-la-az-ḫa-na	ii 43
Ankuwa	An-ku-wa	ii 60,61
Apzišna	Ap-zi-iš-na	ii 72[, 73[, B iii 37
	A-pa-zi-iš-na	B iii 38
Arinna	A-ri-in-na	i 39, B i 41, 42, 70 ii 4 iii 58, 67, 70
	TÚL-na	i 5, 10,17, 37 (x 2), 41, 61 iii 18, 26, 29 iv 4, 6, B i 11, 17 ii 26 iv 40
Arziya	Ar-zi-ia	ii 24,25
Ḫakpišša	Ha-ak-pí-iš-ša	ii 55
Ḫalab	Ḫa-la-ab	i 43 (x 2), 51 (x 2), 75
Ḫa(n)ḫana	Ḫa-an-ḫa-na	ii 43
	Ḫa-ḫa-na	ii 44, 45, B iii 11, 12, 13 (x 2)
Ḫarpiša	Ḫa-ar-pí-ša	ii 52
Ḫarziuna	Ḫar-zi-ú-na	ii 34 (x 2), 35]
Ḫaddarina	Ḫa-ad-da-ri-na	i 54
	Ḫa-at-ta-ri-na	B ii 19
Ḫatenzuwa	Ḫa-te-in-zu-wa	i 71[
Ḫatti / Ḫattuša	^{URU}Ḫa-at-ti	i 1, 2, 11, 18 iii 31, 55 B i 17, 18, 19, 24, 34, 58, 59, 69 ii 15 (x 2),16, 17, 20 iii 55
	^{URU}Ḫa-<at->ti	B iii 72
	$^{URU\ GIŠ}$Ḫat(GIDRU)-ti	i 12 (x 2), 14, 16, 23, 50 iv 39
	^{URU}KÙ.BABBAR-ti	i 17, 33, 50, 51 (x 2), 55 iv 23, 25, 34 B i 13, 65
	ŠA ^{URU}Ḫa-at-tu-ši KUR-e	B i 15
Ḫattina	Ḫa-at-ti-na	ii 51
Ḫatra	Ḫa-at-ra-a	ii 64
Ḫiššašḫapa	Ḫi-iš-ša-aš-ḫa-pa	ii 3
Ḫupišna	Ḫu-u-pí-iš-na	ii 15 (x 2),16, B ii 56 (x 2)
	Ḫu-u-piš-na	ii 17

Ḫurma	Ḫur-ma	i 74, 75
	TIN(sic)-ma	B ii 39 (x 2)
Ḫurniya	Ḫur-ni-ia	ii 26 (x 2),27
Ikšuna	Ik-šu-na	ii 63
	Ik-šu-nu-wa	B iii 30
Illaia	Il-la-ia	ii 20 (x 2),21
Innuwita	In-nu-wi_5-ta	ii 42
Išuwa	I-šu-wa	ii 65
Kalašmitta	Ka-la-aš-mi-it-ta	iii 1
Kalimuna	Ka-li-mu-na	ii 53,54
Garaḫna	Ga-ra-aḫ-na	ii 5 (x 2)
	Ka-ra-aḫ-na	ii 6; B ii 48 (x 2),49
Kariuna	Ka-ri-u-na	ii 71
	Ka-ri-ú-na	B iii 36
Gaštama	Ga-aš-ta-ma	i 69, 70
	Ka-aš-ta-ma	B ii 34, 35
Kadapa	Ka-da-pa	i 47,48, 49
	Ka-ta-pa	B ii 12
	Ka-a-ta-pa	B ii 13,14
Gazzimara	Gaz-zi-ma-ra	ii 59
Kuliwišna	Ku-li-wi_5-iš-na	ii 3
Kummanni	Kum-ma-an-ni	i 62 (x 2), 65 (x 2)
Lanta	La-a-an-ta	ii 50, 51
	La-a-an-da	B iii 18, 19
Lawazantiya	La-u-wa-an-a$^{!}$-[ti-i]a	i 76, B ii 41]
	La-u-wa-za-an-ti-ia	i 77
	La-u-wa-za-ti-ia	B ii 42
Liḫšina	Li-iḫ-ši-na	ii 8,9
Lower Land	see *Lands*	
Malitaškuriya	Ma-li-ta-aš-ku-ri-ia	ii 33
Manuziya	$^{\text{ḪUR.SAG}}$Manuziya	B ii 28 (A: without URU)
Nenašša	Ne-na-aš-ša	ii 12 (x 2),14
	Ne-na<-aš-ša>	B ii 54

Nenišakuwa	Ne-ni-ša-ku-wa	ii 62
	Ne-ni-ša-an-ku-wa	B iii 29
Neriqqa	Ne-ri-i[q(-qa?)	i 68[, 72[
	Ne-ri-iq-qa	B ii 37
	Ni-ri-iq-qa	B ii 33
Ninuwa	Ni-nu-wa	i 53
Paḫtima	Pa-aḫ-ti-ma	ii 32
Paliya	Pa-li-ia	ii 68
Parašḫunta	Pár-aš-ḫu-un-ta	ii 38
Parša	Pár-ša	ii 1,2
(Piḫaššašši)	dU URU!pí-ḫa-aš-ša-aš-ši	iv 42 (B without URU)
[Pittiy]arik (?)	]-ik	i 78
	-i]a-ri-ka	B ii 43
Šaḫḫaniya	Ša-aḫ-ḫa-ni-ia	ii 30 (x 2),31[
Šaḫḫuwiya	Ša-aḫ-ḫu-wi$_5$-ia	ii 32
Šaḫpina	Ša-aḫ-pí-na	i 46
Šallapa	Šal-la-pa	ii 36(x 2), 37
Šamuḫa	Ša-mu-ḫa	i 40 (x 2), 43, 44, 45
Šanaḫuitta	Ša-na-ḫu-it-ta	i 66, 67
Šarišša	Ša-ri-iš-ša	i 73 (x 2)
Šugazziya	Šu-gaz-zi-ia	ii 7(x 2)
Šullama	Šul-la-ma	ii 64
Šuwanzana	Šu-wa-an-za-na	ii 22, 23, B ii 62
	Šu-wa-an-zi-pa (!)	B ii 63
Takupša	Ta-ku-up-ša	i 72
Tapiqqa	Ta-pí-iq-qa	iii 2, 3, B iii 40
	Ta-pí-iq-aš (!)	B iii 39
Tawiniya	Ta-wi$_5$-ni-ia	ii 46, 47
Tegarama	Te-ga-ra-ma	ii 66, 67
URUTÍL (ruin)	URUTÍL	ii 5
Tiwa	Ti-wa	B ii 7 (A has Šamuḫa !)
Tupazziya	Tu-u-pa-az-zi-ia	ii 69, 70
	Tu-u-up-pa-zi-ia	B iii 34, 35

Durmita	Dur-mi-it-ta	ii 10, 11
Duruwaduruwa	Du-ru-wa-du-ru-wa	ii 62
	Du-ru-ud-du-ru-wa-aš	B iii 29
Tuwanuwa	Tu-wa-nu-wa	ii 18 (x 2), 19; B ii 58
	Tu-u-wa-nu-wa	B ii 58, 59
Urauna	U-ra-u-na	i 61
Uššа	U-uš-ša	ii 38
Uda	U-da	i 78,79
Wašḫaniya	Wa-aš-ḫa-ni-ia	ii 48,49
Wašuduwanda	Wa-šu-du-wa-an-da	ii 41(x 2)
Zarwiša	Za-ar-wi$_5$-ša	ii 28(x 2), [29]
Zippalanda	Zi-ip-la-an-da	i 13], 57, 58 iv 28
	Zi-ip-pa-la-an-da	iv 30, B i 63 ii 22
	Zi-ip-pa-la-an-ta	B i 61 ii 23
Zitḫara	Zi-it-ḫa-ra	i 60
KÙ.BABBAR-ti	see Ḫatti	
TÚL-na	see Arinna	

Lands only (KUR $^{(URU)}$); for spellings see above.

KUR ^{URU}Ḫatti		all occurrences have KUR except:
		i 12, 50(x2), 51(x2) iii 55 iv 23, 25, 34, 39
KUR ^{URU} Išuwa		ii 65
KUR ^{URU}Kummanni		i 65
KUR ^{URU}Takupša		i 72
KUR ^{URU}Tegarama		ii 67
KUR ^{URU}Tuppaziya		B iii 35 (A without KUR)
KUR ^{URU}Wašḫaniya		ii 49 (B without KUR)
KUR *ŠAPLITI* (Lower Land)	KUR *ŠAP-LI-TI*	ii 40
	KUR *ŠAP<LI-TI>*	B iii 8

Mountains (ḪUR.SAG)

Ḫaḫarwa (in Takupša)	Ḫa-a-ḫar-wa	i 71
Ḫuwalanuwanda (in Lower Land)	Ḫu-wa-la!-nu-wa-an-da	ii 38
Gallištapa (in Kummanni)	Gal-li-iš-ta-pa-aš	i 64
Manuziya (in Kummanni)	Ma-nu-zi-ia	i 63
	ḪUR.SAG URUMa-nu-zi-ia	B ii 28
Piškurunuwa (in Ḫatti)	Piš-ku-ru-nu-wa	i 54
Šarlaimiš (in Ḫupišna)	Šar-la-i-mi-iš	ii 16
	Šar-la-im-mi-iš	B ii 57
Šummiara (in Ḫatti)	Šum-mi-ia-ra	i 56
Daḫa (in Zippalanda)	Da-ḫa	i 57
	Ta-ḫa	B ii 22
Takurga (in Ḫanḫana)	Ta-ku-úr-ga	ii 44
Tatta (in Ḫatti)	Ta-at-ta	i 56
Zaliyanu (in Kaštama)	Za-li-ia-nu-uš	i 69 (x 2)

Rivers (ÍD)

Ḫulaia (in Lower Land))	Ḫu-u-la-ia	ii 39
	Ḫu-la-ia	B iii
Maraššantiya (in Nenašša)	Ma-ra-aš-ša-an-ti-ia-aš	ii 13

Part Two

THE SCRIBES

Chapter IV: Writing Features

1. The Tablets

The two main exemplars of *CTH* 381 were found in the early years of Winckler's excavations at Boğazköy and were registered at the Vorderasiatisches Museum in Berlin as VAT 7456 and VAT 7512. F.M.Th. Böhl, who transliterated the two tablets in 1910, designated them as exemplars *A* and *B* respectively, an appellation kept in all successive studies (*Theol. Tijdsch.* 50, 303-326). Otto Weber, director of the Deutsche Orient-Gesellschaft, published the two tablets in 1923 as KUB 6. 45 and KUB 6. 46, respectively.

A join to *A* ii 1-2, iii 62-76 was published in 1939 as KUB 30.14 (Bo 3282). The original fragment is kept in the Istanbul Museum, but a cast of it is loosely attached to the main tablet in Berlin. Another small join, without a Bo-number, has been glued to *A* i 68-78 (still missing in KUB 6). It appears in the photographs prepared by Frau Ehelolf. A third join, 1111/z (*A* i 9, ii 2-9), was found in the debris of Makridy's excavations near the eastern magazines of the Great Temple and was published in transliteration by H. Otten & Ch. Rüster, *ZA* 64 (1975), 242 f. This establishes the original find-place of *A* and probably also of *B*, since the two tablets were most probably found together. No joins to tablet *B* have turned up so far.

A third duplicate (*C* = *A* ii 13-23) was published as KUB 12. 35 (Bo 526), and a fourth small fragment, 1785/u (= *A* iii 55-61), was kindly put at my disposal for publication by Professor Otten. It was found in the same area as the large tablets, namely, in Magazine 16 east of the Great Temple.[267] Both fragments are preserved on one side only. It is theoretically possible that Bo 526 and 1785/u belong to the same tablet; the former is in Istanbul, the latter in Ankara, and until this possibility is verified 1785/u will be designated as duplicate *D*.

I collated *A* and *B* in Berlin in July 1994. The Vorderasiatisches Museum also provided me excellent photographs of *A*, *B* and *C* (see Plates). From Professor Otten I received his handcopies of *D* and of 1111/z.

Tablet *A* measures 29 x 18.5 cms. It is made of a very fine clay with shiny surface. Tablet *B* is more squat, 27x 19.5 cms., and has a more porous and matt texture. *A* has a pinkish colour, with large dark, burnt surfaces. *B* is more yellowish and does not have dark surfaces. Both tablets have an almost flat obverse and a convex reverse, but *B* has a somewhat sharper angle.

A has somewhat larger and more deeply incised script, with straight, upward slanting lines. Except for the "Postscript" in iv 59-61 and the addition in iv 51 (see below), *A* has relatively few corrections and additions, and the scribe rarely uses the column-dividers for writing.

On the other hand, *B* has many crooked lines and numerous erasures, corrections, and additions between the lines and on the margins. The general impression is that the scribe of *B* is relatively careless and inexperienced, and he writes on a tablet of lesser quality than that of *A*.

---

[267] Note that Muwatalli's other prayer, KBo 11.1 (*CTH* 382), was found in Building K on the Büyükkale.

2. Ductus

An initial paleographic study of the two main duplicates was carried out by A. Archi in 1975.[268] He compared the script of these tablets and of three duplicates of Muwatalli's treaty with Alakšandu (*CTH* 76) with that of earlier and of later texts and concluded that the texts of Muwatalli II represent the "watershed" between an older ductus, which has a continuity from the Old Kingdom down to Muršili II, and a younger one, which is systematically employed from Ḫattušili "III" on.[269] In texts of Muwatalli II, a certain number of old forms continue to be employed together with newer ones. Archi duly emphasized that exceptions to this general paradigm are fairly common, and one still encounters old forms in some late thirteenth century texts.

The corpus of paleographic studies has continued to grow in the last two decades, including a second volume of *Hethitische Keilschrift-Paläographie* (*StBoT* 21, 1975),[270] in which E. Neu and Ch. Rüster put together a comparative chart of eleven Late Hittite (*Junghethitisch*) texts.[271] Incidentally, none of them belongs to Muwatalli. Whereas this and other studies have considerably broadened our basis for a diachronic paleography, some scholars have emphasized the urgent need for more synchronically oriented investigations, in which the writing habits (*Schreibergewohnheiten*) of individual scribes and, where possible, of scribal schools are studied and compared.[272] *CTH* 381, with its two almost completely preserved duplicates, provides an excellent opportunity for such an investigation.

One of the most important results of my collation of the main tablets in Berlin is the observation that the last three lines on *A* (iv 59-61) were added in a different handwriting. The wedges are smaller, shallower, and quite different in shape from the rest of the tablet (note in particular the signs *ni, ti, qa,* DÙ in Table 1). Probably the same hand also added the end of line iv 51: 1 ^{DUG}*KU-KU-UB* GEŠTIN BAL-*ti*.[273] It is noteworthy that both of these additions are missing in *B* . I would suggest that the "Postscript" in *A* iv 59-61 and the augmentation in iv 51 were added by another scribe, possibly an instructor or supervisor, who deemed it necessary to give instructions for the burning of the sacrificial breads and to add a wine libation to the "male gods of the land". The implications of this discovery for the redactional history of the text will be taken up in Ch. V.

The comparative chart in Table 1 includes 43 diagnostic signs arranged in the order of Ch. Rüster & E. Neu, *Hethitisches Zeichenlexikon* (Wiesaden 1989). Distinctive variants of a sign occurring in the same tablet were counted and noted in parentheses, and the same applies to some of the rare signs. Such statistical data provide more reliable information than a simple juxtaposition of the variant forms.[274] In other cases, the less frequent forms are set in parentheses. The line references in *A* usually refer to the "Postscript" in iv 59-61.

---

[268] "Sur la forme des signes cunéiformes hittites de l'époque de Muwatalli", *Oriens Antiquus* 14 (1975), 321-324.

[269] This slightly contradicts A. Kammenhuber's observation of a *Scriftreform* under Muršili II: *ZA* 23 (1965), 179 f. ; *KZ* 83 (1969), 262. Cf. O. Carruba, *Fs. Otten*² (1988), 68 n. 21.

[270] See reviews by A. Archi, *ZA* 67 (1977), 129-132; H. A. Hoffner, *BASOR* 226 (1977), 78-79; G. Frantz-Szabó & S. Heinhold-Krahmer, *Kratylos* 21, 97-102.

[271] With the possible exception of the first column, KUB 24. 4, which is an early version of the Plague Prayers, possibly dated to Šuppiluliuma I; see *StBoT* 21, 3, 7 and H. G. Güterbock, "Some Aspects of Hittite Prayers", in T. T. Segerstedt (ed.), *The Frontiers of Human Knowledge* (Uppsala 1978), 136. Texts dated to Šuppiluliuma I are usually still written in a Middle Hittite ductus; see E. Neu, *KZ* 93 (1979), 64-84.

[272] E. Neu & Ch. Rüster, *StBoT* 21, 13; Ch. Rüster, *Fs. Otten*² (1988), 306; G. Frantz-Szabó & S. Heinhold-Krahmer, *Kratylos* 21, 102.

[273] The ideographic spelling BAL-*ti* is only employed in this addition; in the rest of the tablet *šipanti* is always spelled phonetically.

[274] For statistical data on the paleography of thirteenth century texts, see in particular Th. van den Hout, *KBo IV 10 + (CTH 106); Studien zum Spätjunghethitischen Texte der Zeit Tudhaliyas IV* (Doct. Diss. Amsterdam 1989), 326-343. See also J. Siegelová, *Hethitische Verwaltungspraxis im Lichte der Wirtschafts- und Inventardokumente* (Praha 1986), 535-546.

A has a very distinctive, confident handwriting, which combines older and younger signs.[275] He writes almost exclusively the younger forms of *li* (x 25, with a single exception) and *ik* (x 6), but only the older form of *šar* (6) and *zu* (x 4), and almost always the older form of URU. For *ak* he uses both the older (x 3) and the younger (x 2) forms, and the same holds for KÙ (2 : 4). No pattern can be discerned in the distribution of these older and younger forms. In signs that combine a vertical and a diagonal wedge (*ni, ir, in*), *A* consistently crosses them (in contrast to *B*). His *al* is remarkable, with no exact match in the charts of *StBoT* 20-21: a long wedge crosses the two verticals obliquely.

A employs three variants of MEŠ: the regular MEŠ, ME.EŠ with *Winkelhakens*, and ME.EŠ with three combined horizontals, which seems to be typical for texts of Muwatalli.[276] A recurrent pattern can be observed in the frequent sequence DINGIR.LÚ.MEŠ, DINGIR.SAL.MEŠ, ḪUR.SAG.MEŠ, ÍD.MEŠ: in about half of the 43 preserved occurrences, the first two have the older MEŠ (with *Winkelhakens*), whereas the last two the younger ME.EŠ (with horizontals).[277] The opposite pattern never occurs, but the scribe may occasionally use the younger form in the first pair, or the older form in both pairs. In other contexts (e.g., in EN.MEŠ DINGIR.MEŠ) no clear pattern can be discerned.

As mentioned above, the **"Postscript"** in iv 59-61 is written in another hand, whose salient features include not only its smaller size, but several sign forms that never occur in the rest of *A*: *ni* with the two wedges not touching, *qa* with three wedges,[278] and a conspicuous DÙ (like MAŠ+U). The last two differ from *B*'s handwriting as well. It seems quite certain that these lines (and the addition in iv 51) were written by a third hand.

B has a smaller, less confident hand, which differs considerably from that of *A*. For most of the diagnostic signs he uses the younger forms only: *ak* (x 3), *šar* (x 7), *zu* (x 4), URU and MEŠ (with three horizontals; also used as $eš_{17}$). For *ki* he uses the older form only three times and the younger form (with two verticals) 27 times.[279] On the other hand, he employs the older KÙ (x 1), and the older *li* more often (x 19) than the younger one (x 7). There is no obviously distinctive pattern (though the last nine *li* in rev. iv are all older); he may use the older and the younger *li* in the same word a few lines apart (e.g., *Kalimuna* in iii 21, 22; *Telipinu* in iii 11, 14).[280] It is noteworthy that he employs the younger *ik* for GÁL (x 4), but the older form for *ik* (x 2), as if he considered them two different signs. The horizontal and the oblique in his *ni, ir,* and *in* do not touch, and his *al* is "normal" (compared to *A*' s unusual variant).

C has a younger *šar* and a younger URU which conform with *B*, but an older MEŠ which is only found in *A*. The few preserved signs of ***D*** (according to H. Otten's autograph) show a similar picture: traces of a younger *šar* (as in *B* and *C*), an older *ki* and a younger *ik* (found in both *A* and *B*), and an older MEŠ (as in *A* and *C*). These few diagnostic signs in the small fragments are hardly sufficient for reliable comparisons, but it is worth pointing out that: (1) *C* and *D* agree with each other on two preserved diagnostic signs (MEŠ and *šar*),which leaves open the possibility that they belong to the same tablet. (2) None of the small fragments fully agrees in ductus with either of the main tablets; in orthography, however, both of them

---

275 I am using the terminology often employed by Otten, Neu and Rüster in their studies on ductus (*älter, jünger*). I think that at this stage of Hittite paleographic research it is more appropriate to employ a relative terminology, supplemented with comparative charts, than to become entrenched in an absolute dating, the details of which still remain to be refined.

276 Th. van den Hout, op. cit., p. 339 with n. 2. It is worth noting that this particular form of MEŠ is apparently missing in late thirteenth century texts.

277 The same pattern can be observed on KBo 9.98+ i 2 f. See Ch. XI.

278 This variant of *qa* is typical of late thirteenth century texts, and, other than this "Postscript", is not found in texts of Muwatalli. See Th. van den Hout, op. cit., n. 342.

279 The "late" KI is already found in KUB 24.1, a prayer of Muršili II. The two forms of KI appear together also in KUB 57.63, a text dated more or less to the same period as *CTH* 381. See A. Archi, "Eine Anrufung der Sonnengöttin von Arinna", *Fs. Otten*[2] (1988), 7 with n. 7.

280 Cf., e.g., the data on KUB 21.19+, exemplar A of the Prayer of Ḫattušili and Puduḫepa to the Sun-goddess of Arinna (*CTH* 383), as provided by D. Sürenhagen, *Altorientalische Forschungen* 8 (1981), 87: The older *li* appears six times, the younger one seven times; the names Ḫattušili and Muršili are written with the younger *li*, the prohibitive *lē* exclusively with the older *li*, and *tuliya-* with both.

HZL	A = KUB 6.45	B = KUB 6.46	C=KUB 12.35	D = 1785/u
7 tar				
21 qa	(iv 61)			
30 gi				
37 ti	(iv 61)			
39 nam				
40 en				
67 ik		2×ik 4×GÁL		
69 KÙ	(×2) (×4)	(×1)		
72 ni	(iv 61)			
75 DÙ	(iv 59)			
77 ir	(×1) (×3)			
81 ak	(×3) (×2)	(×2) (×1)		
89 SA_5				
92 az				
93 uk				
113 ḫé				
126 EGIR				
128 du				
131 GEŠTIN				
133 ka				
152 up	(iv 51)			
165 GIM		! iv 45		

Table 1: Paleographical comparison of the duplicates

HZL	A = KUB 6.45	B = KUB 6.46	C=KUB 12.35	D = 1785/u
183 al				
187 e				
192 SAG				
197 un				
205 ba				
209 zu				
214 da				
215 it				
229 URU	( )			
233 ra				
237 DUMU				
249 te				
250 kar				
298 dam				
313 ki	( )	(x27) (x3)		
332 aḫ				
343 li	(x25) (V 34)	(x19) (x7)		
353 šar	(x6)	(x 7)		
354 in				
367 ḫa				
360 meš,eš$_{17}$				

agree with *A* and disagree with *B*.[281] The significance of these data for the relationship between the various duplicates will be evaluated in Ch. V.

If to judge by the majority of diagnostic signs, one would probably consider *B*' s script as generally younger than that of *A*. On the other hand, if one were to consider only the form of *li*, which is the most frequently quoted diagnostic sign, one would deduce that *A* is the younger manuscript. This distribution of older and younger forms in the two manuscripts once again demonstrates how unreliable a paleographic diagnosis can be if it depends on a few signs only. Even with a large sample as is the case here, I would still hesitate to conclude on paleography alone which tablet was written before the other or whether they are contemporary. Other criteria, discussed in Ch. V, may prove more helpful in establishing the relative dating of the two main tablets and their possible interdependence.

As for the absolute dating of the two tablets on the basis of their paleography, it is generally assumed that both were written during the reign of Muwatalli.[282] Actually, A. Archi (op. cit.) utilized this text and the Alakšandu Treaty to establish the sequence of transition from the older to the younger ductus in the early thirteenth century. To be sure, Muwatalli's authorship provides only a *terminus post quem* for the date of the manuscripts. Theoretically at least, one or both could be later copies, and indeed, C. Kühne suggested in passing that (at least) duplicate *A* should be dated to the second half of the thirteenth century (*Fs. Otten*², 1988, 226, n. 104).

To provide a firmly grounded answer on the absolute dating of the two manuscripts one would need a thorough comparison with the corpora of texts written in the reigns of Ḫattušili "III", of Tudḫaliya "IV" and of Šuppiluliama II. Even with such a comprehensive study, it would still be almost impossible to separate texts written under Muwatalli from those written under Ḫattušili, since only a few years separate one reign from the other.[283] Although I have not made a thorough comparison of *A* and *B* with other imperial texts, my general impression is that their ductus indeed falls between fourteenth century texts (Šuppiluliuma I and Muršili II) and late thirteenth century texts (Tudḫaliya "IV" and Šuppiluliama II). As already mentioned, the paleographic comparison by itself does *not* point to a definite priority of one duplicate over the other, and I would tentatively suggest that both tablets were indeed written during the reign of Muwatalli II in the early thirteenth century. A reconstruction of the redactional history of the text may provide further data for an absolute dating of the manuscripts (Ch. V).

3. Orthography

3.1 Vowels

3.1.1: e / i[284]

ḫa-an-ne-iš-ki-ši (*A*)	ḫa-an-ni-iš-ki-ši (*B*)
ké-e (*A*)	ki-i (*B*)
ké-e-da-ni (*A*)	ki-i-da-ni (*B*)
ku-e (*A*)	ku-i (*B*)
ku-e-ta-aš (*A*)	ku-i-ta-aš (*B*)
ku-e-da-ni (*A*)	ku-i-e-da-ni (*B*)

[281] *C* has *ŠA* in ii 17, 20 and *Šuwanzana* in ii 23; *D* has *na-aḫ-ša*]*r-ri-iš-ki-u-a*[*n* in iii 56. In one case (ii 18), *C* omits a *ŠA* where both *A* and *B* have it.

[282] E.g., I. Hoffmann, *TdH* 9, 95; Th. van den Hout, op. cit., 340 f. A Muwatalli dating for both manuscripts is also inferred from Houwink ten Cate's reconstruction of the text's redactional history.

[283] As observed by Th. van den Hout, op. cit., 342, there is no real difference in ductus between texts of Muwatalli and of Ḫattušili. A noticeable change can only be observed from Tudḫaliya "IV" on, type III c in his refined division of the Late Hittite ductus.

[284] For the distinction between *e* and *i* in Hittite see C. H. Melchert, *Studies in Hittite Historical Phonology* (Göttingen 1984), 78-156; "Hittite Vocalism" in O. Carruba (ed.), *Per una grammatica ittita* (Pavia 1992), 183 f.

mi-im-ma-me-iš-ša (*A*)	
me-em-ma-mi-iš-š[a] (*B*)	
Me-zullaš (*B*)	Mi-zzullaš (*A*)
pé-te(di_{12}) (*B*)	pé-di (*A*)

With two exceptions (*Mezzulla* and *pedi*), *B* prefers an *i*-vocalism , whereas *A* prefers *e*. This contrast is particularly clear in the pronominal forms. In the Luwian participle *me/immami-* , the two scribes reverse their choice of vowel coloring. The case of *B*' s *pé-te*(di_{12}) versus *A*' s regular *pé-di* is more ambiguous. It could be caused by a confusion of the somewhat similar signs *di* and *te*, or, more likely, it could be a result of *B*' s generally poor distinction between *e* and *i*. This is probably also the reason for *B*' s unique spelling AN-*I* for Akkadian *ŠAMĒ*, where *A* has a correct *ŠA-ME-E*.[285] In some cases the *e*-vocalism is considered to be older than *i*, e.g. in *kedani/kidani*.[286] However, in this text I would attribute the different spellings to the phonetic idiosyncracies of the scribes, especially of *B*, rather than to a chronological factor.[287]

3.1.2: u / ú [288]

The only variation between *u* and *ú* is ^{URU}*Ka-ri-u-na* of *A* vs. ^{URU}*Ka-ri-ú-na* of *B*.

3.1.3 "Plene Writing" [289]

The following comparative table lists all the variant spellings of "plene writing" versus the shorter spelling, first in *A* and then in *B*.

ar-ku-u-e-eš-ni (*A*)	ar-ku-e-eš-ni (*B*)
ku-la-a-ni-it-ta (*A*)	ku-la-ni-it-ta (*B*)
me-e-ḫu-na-aš (*A*)	me-ḫu-na-aš (*B*)
Ḫu-u-la-ia (*A*)	Ḫu-la-ia (*B*)
ar-ku-ú-i-iš-ki-mi (*B*)	ar-ku-iš-ki-mi (*A*) (also: ar-ku-ú-e-eš-ki-mi)
ḫal-zi-iḫ-ḫu-u-un (*B*)	ḫal-zi-iḫ-ḫu-un (*A*)
i-da-la-a-u-wa-aḫ-ḫa-an-te-eš (*B*)	i-da-la-wa-aḫ-ḫa-an-te-eš (*A*)
ku-i-e-da-ni (*B*)	ku-e-da-ni (*A*) (see also under *e* / *i*)
la-a-ḫu-u-wa-i (*B*)	la-ḫu-u-wa-i (*A* and *B*)
na-aḫ-ša-ri-iš-ki-u-wa-an (*B*)	na-aḫ-šar-ri-iš-ki-u-an (*A*)
pa-a-iz-zi (*B*)	pa-iz-zi (*A*)
tu-u-li-ia (*B*)	tu-li-ia (*A* and *B*)
[zi-in-n]a-a-i (*B*)	zi-in-na-i (*A*)
Ka-a-ta-pa (*B*)	Ka-ta / da-pa (*A* and *B*)
Ku-pa-a-pa-aš (*B*)	Ku-pa-pa-aš (*A*)
Tu-u-wa-nu-wa (*B*)	Tu-wa-nu-wa (*A* and *B*)
ar-mu-u-wa-la-i (*A*)	

[285] Cf. KBo 11.1 obv. 7 (*CTH* 382) which has the correct spelling AN-*E*.

[286] Melchert, "Hittite Vocalism" (1992), 189. Melchert found evidence for this change (which reflects a raising of *ē* from old *i*-diphthongs to *ī*) in texts of the late thirteenth century B.C. However, in view of the evidence provided by this text, he would now argue that the transition had already taken place in the spoken language (reflected by *B*, which was probably dictated) somewhat earlier, and that it penetrated only later into the standard written language.

[287] *B*'s odd *ku-i-e-da-ni* (iv 12, 22) is explained by Melchert as an attempt to "correct" *ku-i-da-ni* into *ku-e-da-ni*, i.e. some sort of a "compromise" between the dictated form and the written standard (written communication).

[288] See Melchert, "Hittite Vocalism" (1992), 186 f.

[289] On the state of the art on the so-called Hittite "Scriptio Plena", see Melchert, "Hittite Vocalism" (1992), 185 (with references to the debate over this controversial issue).

[ar-]mu-wa-la-a-i (*B*)

Clearly, *B* has more "plene writings" than *A*, but both scribes are inconsistent in their fuller spelling of a certain word. *A* has *ar-ku-iš-ki-mi* alongside *ar-ku-ú-e-eš-ki-mi*. *B* has once *la-a-ḫu-u-wa-i*, twice *la-ḫu-u-wa-i*, once *tu-u-li-ia* and once *tu-li-ia-aš* ; twice *Tu-u-wa-nu-wa* but once *Tu-wa-nu-wa* ; twice *Ka-a-ta-pa* but once *Ka-ta-pa*.[290] On the other hand, both scribes have consistent *ḫu-u-mant-* , *ḫu-u-da-ak*, *Ḫu-u-pišna* ; *B* also has *ḫu-u-wanteš* and \ *ḫu-u-waialli*. *B*' s preference for "longer" spellings is also evident in consonantal doubling.

3.1.4 *"Vowel syncope"*

Two place-names appear with a shorter or with a longer spelling containing an additional vowel.[291] As in other cases, *B* uses the "longer" spellings more often.

Ap-zi-iš-na (*A* x 2; *B* x 1)	A-pa-zi-iš-na (*B* x 1)
Zi-ip-la-an-da (*A* x 4)	Zi-ip-pa-la-an-da / ta (*A* x 1; *B* x 4)

3.2 *Consonants*

3.2.1 *Consonantal doubling*

me-em-ma-al (*B* in 2 out of 8)	me-ma-al (*A* and *B*)
Šar-la-im-mi-iš (*B*)	Šar-la-i-mi-iš (*A*)
Ta-mi-iš-ši-ia-as (*B*)	Ta-mi-ši-ia-aš (*A*)
Tu-u-up-pa-zi-ia (*B*)	Tu-u-pa-az-zi-ia (*A*)

Again, *B* shows a preference for a "longer" spelling, but not as frequently as in the case of "plene writing". On the other hand, *A* gives a correct double consonant in Akkadian *A-IA-AK-KI*, as well as a single spelling *KU-UK-KU-UB*, against seven times *KU-KU-UB*.

3.2.2 *"Voiced" and "voiceless"*

When the two scribes use variant spellings of the dental, *A* usually prefers the "voiced" *d*, and *B* usually prefers the "voiceless" *t*. The opposition primarily concerns the signs *da* / *ta*, only once in the case of *di* / *te*(di_{12}) and once in the case of *du* / *tu*. As in previous oppositions, the preference is not carried through consistently. For the personal pronoun second person *A* twice employs *-ta* and twice *-da*, whereas *B* perseveres with *-ta*. For the verb *da-*,"take", both scribes employ the usual "voiced" sign, with a single exceptional *ta-at-ti-ni* of *B*. On the other hand, for the relative pronoun, dat.-loc. plural *A* twice uses the usual *kuedaš* and once *kuetaš*, contrary to his regular tendency. *Zip(pa)landa* is always written by *A* with *-da*, whereas *B* writes it twice with *-da* and twice with *-ta* (in two passages, each with both spellings!).

d	*t*
pé-di (*A*)	pé-te(di_{12}) (*B*)
píd-du-li-ia-u-wa-an-za-ma-da(*A*)	p[ít]-tu-li-ia-an-za-ma-ta (*B*)
-da- (*A* x 2)	-ta- (*B* x 4; *A* x 2)
da-at-ti-in (*A*)	ta-at-ti-ni (*B*; but dā, dāš)
Ḫa-ad-da-ri-na (*A*)	Ḫa-at-ta-ri-na (*B*)
Ka-da-pa (*A*)	Ka(-a)-ta-pa (*B*)

290 The latter is written over an erasure which may have concealed a different spelling originally.

291 One may adduce a third case: *Du-ru-wa-du-ru-wa* (*A*) vs. *Du-ru-ud-du-ru-wa-aš* (*B*), but the similarity of the signs *wa* and *ut* leaves open the possibility of a scribal error.

Da-ḫa (*A*)	Ta-ḫa (*B*)
Zi-ip-(pa-)la-an-da (*A* and *B*)	Zi-ip-pa-la-an-ta (*B*)
^{d}Ḫa-pa-an-da-li-ia-aš (*A*)	^{d}Ḫa-pa-an-ta-li-ia-aš (*B*)
ku-e-da-ša-at (*B* x 3; *A* x 2)	ku-e-ta-ša-at (*A* x 1)
La-a-an-da (*B*)	La-a-an-ta (*A*)

To be sure, the preference for *d* or *t* does not necessarily express a real phonetic opposition of voiced and voiceless. It is interesting to observe, however, that the two scribes have the same preferences of "voiced" and "voiceless" in the much rarer oppositions *b*/ *p* and *g*/ *k*. For the former, I can only point to *B*' s unique habit of writing ŠA.PA instead of the normative ŠA.BA "therein". For the latter, *g* is chosen twice by *A*, once by *B* .

g	*k*
Ga-ra-aḫ-na (*A* x 2)	Ka-ra-aḫ-na (*B*; *A* x 1)
Ga-aš-ta-ma (*A*)	Ka-aš-ta-ma (*B*)
ga-ni-iš-ta (*B*)	ka-ni-iš-ta (*A*)

3.2.3 *Loss of nasal consonant*

B has a clear tendency to drop the nasal *n* before obstruents (*t*/*d*, *z*). Each separate case may be seen as a "scribal error", but the accumulation of examples leaves little doubt that this recurring omission is an idiosyncracy of this scribe. The clearest example is *šipanti* which is written seven times without *n*, only once with *n* (but with a single *p* !).

A		*B*	
	ḫu-u-ma-an-da-aš		ḫu-u-ma-da-aš (x1; ḫumant- *passim*)
	iš-ta-ma-aš-ša-an-du		iš-ta-ma-ša-du (x 1; with *n* x 1)
	La-u-wa-za-an-ti-ia		La-u-wa-za-ti-ia (x 1)
	ši-ip-pa-an-ti		ši-ip-pa-ti (x 7; ši-pa-an-ti x 1)
	KI-aš		da-ga-zi-pa-aš- (x 2)

A further case which may be added to this list is *B*' s SIG_5-*aḫ-zi* instead of pres. pl. 3rd pers. SIG_5-*aḫ-ḫa-an-zi* (*A* iii 47). I assume that *-ḫa-* was omitted, but the missing *n* reflects a pronunciation in which the nasal was weakened or lost. At any rate, I would not analyze this as 3rd pers. sg., especially in view of the following *šarlanzi*.

In marked contrast to their regular spelling habits, *B* has in a single case the more "correct" form *Ne-ni-ša-an-ku-wa*,[292] whereas *A* has either an assimilated *Ne-ni-ša-ku-wa* or simply a scribal error.

An opposite case of "nasalization" is the single occurrence in *A* iv 29 of *šu-un-ni-ia-an-zi* for a grammatical singular. In five identical contexts *A* has a correct *šu-un-ni-ia-zi*.

3.3 *CVC vs. CV-VC*

CVC signs, which are widely used in late thirteenth century texts, are rare in *A* and almost absent in *B*.[293]

na-aḫ-šar-ri-iš-ki-u-an (*A*)	na-aḫ-ša-ri-iš-ki-u-wa-an (*B*)
^{URU}Ḫu-u-piš-na (*A* x 1)	^{URU}Ḫu-u-pí-iš-na (*A* x 2; *B*)
$^{URU.GIŠ}$Ḫat-ti (*A* x 6)	^{URU}Ḫa-at-ti (*B*) (see below)

292 *Ni-ni-ša-an-ku-*[is attested now also in a Maşat letter (HKM 71, 19).

293 Note that both texts spell *tap-tap-pa-an*, whereas a Muršili prayer spells *tap-ta-ap-pa-an* (KUB 14.8 rev. 22). See commentary on iii 40.

4 Ideograms

4.1 Determinatives

$^{\text{DINGIR.GUD}}$Šeriš (*B* x 2)	^{DINGIR}Šeriš (*A* x 3; *B* x 1 on erasure!)
$^{\text{DINGIR.SAL}}$Kupapaš (*B*)	^{DINGIR}Kupapaš (*A*)

In these two cases *B* uses more expanded determinatives than *A*. Note that both texts have the determinative DINGIR.SAL for two other goddesses: *Alāš* and *Zintuḫiyaš.*

4.2 Ideographic vs. phonetic spellings

A		*B*	
	DÙ-at (x 1; iyat x 1)		iyat
	EGIR-ŠU		EGIR-anda (see discussion below)
	GE_6-iš		dankuyaš
	GIM-an		maḫḫan (x 2; GIM-an x 2)
	IM.ḪI.A-uš		ḫuwanteš
	KI-aš (x 2)		dagazipaš(šaš) (x 2)
	^{LÚ}SIPAD-aš		weštaraš
	TI-zi		ḫuišzi (but TI-nut)
	UN-a- (x 3)		antuḫša- (x 3)

^{URU}KÙ.BABBAR-ti / $^{\text{URU.GIŠ}}$PA-ti, ^{URU}Ḫa-at-ti (see discussion below)
^{URU}TÚL-na / ^{URU}Arinna (see discussion below)

A uses ideographic writing far more often than *B*. The latter employs phonetic spellings not only for commonly attested words (*antuhša-, ḫuiš-, iya-, maḫḫan*), but also for rare ones such as *weštara-*, "shepherd" and *ḫuwant-* "wind". Generally speaking, the use of ideographic spellings gradually increases towards the end of the empire. However, the marked difference in the employment of ideograms between these two manuscripts (see in particular Ḫatti and Arinna) was interpreted by Houwink ten Cate (*JNES* 27, 206) as an indication that *B* was dictated.

The spelling of **appanda*, "thereafter", presents an interesting pattern. Both scribes prefer an Akkadian phonetic complement, but *B* also employs a Hittite complement four times; twice he manages a correct EGIR-*an-da*, but twice he apparently misspells it: EGIR-*an-<<na->>da(-ma-za), EGIR-an-ma*$^!$. The distribution of *ŠU* vs. *ŠÚ* is also noteworthy:

	EGIR-*ŠU*	EGIR-*ŠÚ*	EGIR-*anda*
A	20	14	–
B	3	3	4

The rare use of -*ŠÚ*, a typically late feature,[294] is not synchronized between the two manuscripts. This fact speaks against a "mechanical" copying from one tablet to the other. *A* has two consecutive and a third separate occurrence of -*ŠÚ* (iv 6, 20, 23); *B* has two close -*ŠÚ* 's with a "regular" -*ŠU* sandwiched between them (i 45, 49) and a third one in an addition above the line (iv 48).

B' s predilection for phonetic spellings is best exemplified by the two most frequent toponyms, Ḫatti and Arinna. *B* spells the latter *A-ri-in-na* seven times, and TÚL-*na* three times. On the other hand, *A* employs the ideographic writing thirteen times (all the occurrences with ^{d}UTU or ^{d}U) and only once the

[294] The prayers of Ḫattušili and Puduḫepa (*CTH* 383-4), e.g., employ -*ŠÚ* almost exclusively. See D. Sürenhagen, *Altorientalische Forschungen* 8 (1981), 163.

phonetic (i 39; "...mountains, rivers of Arinna"). For Ḫatti, *B* uses almost exclusively the older spelling *Ḫa-at-ti* (once misspelled *Ḫa-ti*), never the typical thirteenth century spelling $^{URU.GIŠ}$*Ḫat-ti*.[295] Of interest is *B*' s unique ^{URU}*Ḫa-at-tu-ši* KUR-*e* (i 14), where *A* has an (erased) KUR ^{URU}*Ḫa-at-ti* (i 14). *A* is more diversified, with a more-or-less balanced ratio between the three standard spellings. A clear distribution pattern is not discernible, but there are some clusters of occurrences with the same spelling: e.g., four out of six $^{URU.GIŠ}$*Ḫat-ti* are clustered in i 12-16. Noteworthy is the employment of the older spelling *Ḫa-at-ti* (twice) in the introductory genealogy (i 1-2). Coupled with the phonetic spelling *Mur-ši-i-li*, this may show a (conscious ?) inclination to use more traditional spellings in the genealogical formula.

	^{URU}Ḫa-at-ti	^{URU}KÙ.BABBAR-ti	$^{URU.GIŠ}$Ḫat(GIDRU)-ti	^{URU}Ḫa-at-tu-ši
A	7	9	6	–
B	17	2	–	1

4.3 Phonetic complements

^{d}DAG-ti-iš (*B*)	^{d}DAG-iš (*A*)
UD^{KAM}-ti (*A* x 1)	UD-ti (*A* x 1; *B* x 2)
UD-ti-li (*A*)	UD^{KAM}-li (*B*)
ZI-an-za (*A*)	ZI-za (*B*)
ŠA LUGAL-*RI* (*A*)	*ŠA* LUGAL (*B*)
SAL.LUGAL-*UT-TI* (*B*)	SAL.LUGAL-*TI* (*A*)
DUMU.LÚ.U$_{19}$.LU-*UT-TI* (*B* x3)	DUMU.LÚ.U$_{19}$.LU (*A* x 1)
	DUMU.LÚ.U$_{19}$.LU-*TI* (*A* x 2)

More expanded phonetic complements, Hittite or Akkadian, are occasionally used by both scribes, without a clear edge of one duplicate over the other. *B* seems to be more consistent in his choices, especially with the Akkadian complement *-UT-TI* which he employs both as a feminine marker (flawed for "queen"; see below) and as an abstract suffix ("mortal, mankind"). *A* seems to be more flexible in his choices, especially with Akkadian complements, which may indicate a better command of Akkadian (see below).

4.4 Akkadograms

As is the case in Late Hittite texts, the Akkadian case endings are often grammatically incorrect, but *A* seems to have mastered Akkadian better than *B*. (See Commentary for details on the following examples.)

1. In iii 16 *A* employs a correct accusative *DI-NAM*, whereas *B* has *DI-šar* (*ḫaneššar*) inserted in the wrong place.

2. In iii 57 both scribes write DINGIR-*LIM* for a grammatical nominative. In the next line *B* repeats DINGIR-*LIM*, whereas *A* probably has a correct nominative [DINGIR-*LU*]*M* (restoration not certain).[296]

3. Reading is problematical also in ii 26, where again *A* seems to have a correct nominative DINGIR-*LUM*$^{!}$-*uš*$^{?}$ (for *šiuš* ?), whereas *B* has DINGIR-*LIM*$^{!}$-*uš*$^{?}$ (see further Ch. V.2).

4. *B* uses *LIM* as a plural marker in É^{MEŠ} DINGIR^{LIM}-*ŠU-NU*, whereas *A* iii 24 has a more conventional MEŠ (É^{MEŠ} DINGIR^{MEŠ}-*ŠU-NU*).

5. In iii 49 both scribes have an accusative DINGIR-*LAM* for what I understand to be a grammatical nominative.

---

[295] A similar picture emerges from the prayers of Ḫattušili and Puduḫepa (*CTH* 383-4): thirteen occurrences use the older *Ḫa-at-ti*, only two the younger ^{GIŠ}PA-*ti*. See ibid.

[296] Cf. KBo 11.1 (*CTH* 382) obv. 14 and 18, with DINGIR-*LUM* and DINGIR-*LIM*, respectively, both in the same nominative function.

6. In iii 5, *A* understood, probably correctly, "male gods (and) female gods of the king and the queen", providing the correct Akkadian complements *ŠA* LUGAL-*RI* for *šarri* and *ŠA* SAL.LUGAL-*TI* for *šarrati* (*CAD*, Š II, 73). In *B*, LUGAL was left uncomplemented, followed by *ŠA* SAL.LUGAL-*UT-TI*. Although one may take this to represent an abstract *šarratuti*,"queenship" (*CAD*, Š II, 76), I suspect that this is merely evidence of *B*' s unawareness of the correct ending of "queen".

7. *A*' s flexibility in the employment of Akkadian case markers is best exemplified in the recurring formula of the offering ritual at the end of the text. For the expression " (he puts them) on the table of DN" *B* uses invariably ^{GIŠ}BANŠUR-*i* *ŠA* DN (only once out of ten with a flawed *ŠA* ^{GIŠ}BANŠUR-*i* DN). On the other hand, *A* has four variants for the same expression: ^{GIŠ}BANŠUR-*i* *ŠA* DN (x 5); *ANA* ^{GIŠ}BANŠUR *ŠA* DN (x 2); ^{GIŠ}BANŠUR DN (x 2); ^{GIŠ}BANŠUR *ŠA* DN (x 1).

8. For the expression "(he breaks breads) to DN" both texts usually employ *ANA* DN. In some cases in which the recipient is marked with a Hittite dative ending, the Akkadian case marker *ANA* is omitted (iv 33, 39: *ḫumandaš*; iv 56: *kutrui*/ \ *ḫuwaialli*; but cf. iv 52). In three cases out of eleven *B* writes *ŠA* DN instead of the usual *ANA* DN. Houwink ten Cate (*JNES* 27, 206), in demonstrating that *B* was probably dictated, suggested that the reason for this change was that *B* apparently interpreted -*aš* as gen. plur. instead of dat. plur.; *A* corrected the "flawed" *ŠA* to *ANA*. This is certainly a possible explanation, but I would rather consider these as variants. Actually, breaking the breads *of* DN, instead of *to* DN, is hardly a "mistake," and in the majority of cases *B* also chooses the dative, through *ANA* or through a Hittite case ending.

9. In several cases, *B* has a Hittite word order with a prepositioned genitive followed by its governing noun, whereas *A* has an Akkadian genitive formation with *ŠA*. This again may show that *B*' s version is closer to the Hittite formulation than *A*′ s. *B* is not consistent in marking the Hittite nominative ending, but *A* is.

B ii 52	*ŠA* ^{URU}*Durmitta* ^{d}*Telipinuš*	*A* ii 10	^{d}*Teli*[*ŠA* ^{UR}]^{U}*Durmitta*
iii 11	*ŠA* ^{URU}*Ḫaḫana* ^{d}*Telipinu*	ii 43	^{d}*Telipinuš* *ŠA* ^{URU}*Ḫanḫana*
iii 12	*ŠA* ^{URU}*Ḫaḫana* ^{d}*Ammamaš*	ii 44	^{d}*Ammamaš* *ŠA* ^{URU}*Ḫaḫana*
iii 13	*ŠA* ^{URU}*Ḫaḫana* $^{ḪUR.SAG}$*Takurga*	ii 44	$^{ḪUR.SAG}$*Takurga* ~~*ŠA* ^{URU}*Ḫaḫana*~~
ii 9	^{URU}*Šamuḫa* ^{d}IŠTAR.LÍL	i 43	^{d}IŠTAR.LÍL ^{URU}*Šamuḫa*

5 Grammar

5.1 Noun

1. *B* has two unusual gen. sg. forms: *dagazipašaš(=a)* in i 37 (= *A* i 36 KI-*aš-ša*) may be a dittography, especially in view of the normal gen. sg. *dagazipaš* in iii 48 (= *A* iii 10 KI-aš).

2. On the other hand, *ne-pí-aš* (x 6), as distinguished from the normal *ne-pí-ša-aš* (x 2), must be considered an idiosyncracy of *B*.[297] Already E. Tenner, *Kleinas. Forsch.* (1930), 391, suggested a transfer into the *i*-class (**nepi-* like *ḫalki-*). Güterbock (*apud* Houwink ten Cate, *JNES* 27, 206) added the possibility of a kind of "shorthand" abbreviation comparable to *pé-an* instead of *pé-ra-an* (cf. *da-<pí?->az* in *B* i 19).

3. *antuḫšaš* KAxU-*az* in *B* i 31, as opposed to *A*' s UN-*az* KAxU-*az*, was explained by Houwink ten Cate (*JNES* 27, 206) as a misundertanding by *B* who wrote from dictation. This explanation is by no means necessary: *B* used a regular genitive construction, "from the mouth of a man", whereas *A* preferred a more distinct construction with a partitive apposition, lit. "from the man, from the mouth."

4. For nom. pl. (of substantives, adjectives and participles) *B* uses, with one exception (*alpuš*), only the traditional -*eš* ending. *A* uses both -*eš* and -*uš* in similar proportions; note the occurrence of *ḫumanteš* and *ḫumanduš* in two consecutive lines (i 16-17).

---

[297] This spelling also occurs in KBo 11. 32 obv. 31 (*ne-pí-aš* ^{d}U-*aš*); Neu - Otten, *IF* 77 (1972), 184 f.; *CHD*, L-N, 448; O. Carruba, "Der Stamm für 'Frau' im Hethitischen", in P. Vavroušek, *Iranian and Indo-European Studies: Fs. Otakar Klíma* (Praha 1994), 14.

daranteš (*A* and *B*)	alpuš (*A* and *B*)
ḫuwanteš (*B*)	IM.ḪI.A -uš (*A*)
ḫumanteš (*B* x 5; *A* x 2)	ḫumanduš (*A* x 1)

5. In the only occurrence of an acc. pl. both scribes have *šaklauš*(-).

5.2 *Pronoun*

1. For the independent personal pronoun 1st person *B* uses *ammuk* exclusively, both for the nominative and the dative.[298] On the other hand, *A* uses *ammuk* three times and the older *uk* three times, once for the dative (iii 60). I cannot discern any pattern in his employment of the older ("archaic") and the younger forms, except for the fact that the first three occurrences have *ammuk*, the last three have *uk*. The enclitic *-a-* attached to both *A*' s *uk* and *B*' s *ammuk* in the dative case is probably the emphatic, adversative *-a-* (see Commentary on iii 60).

		nominative	
A i 29	am-mu-uk-ma-za-at	*B*	am-mu-uk-ma-za-at
iii 18	am-mu-uk		am-mu-uk
iii 32	am-mu-uk		[ ]
iii 41	ú-u[k-ma?-z]a-kán		am-mu-uk-ma-kán
iii 74	ú-uk		am[-mu-uk]
		dative	
iii 60	ú-ga-kán		[am]-mu-ga-kán

2. *A* appears to be more "economical" in his use of the genitive of the independent personal pronoun. In iii 54 he omits an *ammel* which is redundant in combination with the Akkadian enclitic pronouns:...*zilatiya* (*B* adds *ammel*) DUMU-*IA* DUMU.DUMU-*IA*...

3. In i 21-22, *A* skillfully eliminates one pronoun and corrects another, thus slightly modifying the sense of the sentence. This case shows that *A* has a good command of both Hittite and Akkadian pronominal forms.

4. Another pronominal correction by *A* is in iii 66 where he replaces the enclitic 2nd pers. pron. *-ta* with the 3rd pers. *-ši*, without however carrying through the correction in the next line as well (see further Ch. V.4.4).

5. The two texts employ *kuieš* for both the nom. and the acc. pl. common gender of the relative pronoun.

5.3 *Verb*

There are relatively few discrepancies between *A* and *B* in the verbal forms.

1. Both texts usually employ the medio-passive form *paršiya* for "breaking bread", but *B*, after writing it a dozen times, suddenly switches in the last two occurrences to an active *paršiyazzi*.[299]

2. For "pour, scatter, sprinkle," relating to groats (*memal*) and fat bread (NINDA.Ì.E.DÉ.A), both texts normally use *šer šuḫḫai*, only once the synonym (*šer*) *išḫuwai*. In iv 58 the two texts are not synchronized; in iv 50 *B* is broken.

3. For the opposition *pidduliyant-* / *pidduliyawant-* (iii 67) and the apparent disagreement in tenses in i 28 see respective commentaries.

4. It has already been noted in Ch. IV. 4.2 that *A* employs more ideographic writings than *B* (verbs: DÙ / *iya-*, TI / *ḫuiš-*). It is worth noting the full agreement between *A* and *B* on the Hittite and Akkadographic rendering of *appa ep-*: EGIR-*pa epzi* (iii 40), EGIR-*pa AṢBAT* (iii 41). Two ideographic writings, BAL and BIL, are only found in the "Postscript" and in the addition to *A*, written by a third hand (see Ch. IV. 2).

[298] The same applies to two prayers of Ḫattušili and Puduḫepa, *CTH* 383-4. D. Sürenhagen, *Altorientalische Forschungen* 8 (1981), 145.

[299] Although in both occurrences the end is missing, part of *-az* is clearly visible.

5.4 *Particles and Conjunctions*

The two texts almost always agree on the employment of the particles *-pat* (x 3), *-šan* (x 2), *-kan* (a single omission in *B* out of 45 occurrences), and the reflexive *-az/-za* (only twice *-az*, 13 times *-za*).[300] *-ašta* never occurs. The same applies to the conjunctions *-a/-ya, Ù, -ma, nu* and *našma.*

6 *Conclusions*

As already indicated in the discussion on ductus, it is not easy to determine the relative dating of the two main manuscripts. Some of the orthographic and the grammatical evidence seems to be contradictory. On the one hand, *A* uses more CVC signs and more ideograms, which one would usually take as an indication that this manuscript is later. Such a conclusion would also be supported by *B'* s tendency to use "plene spellings" more frequently and his almost exclusive use of the *-eš* ending for the nom. pl., in contrast to *A'* s use of both *-eš* and *-uš*. But on the other hand, *B* only uses *ammuk* for the nominative and dative of the personal pronoun, whereas *A* uses both the younger *ammuk* and the older *uk*. One could argue, of course, that his reverting to *uk* is a deliberate archaism (as in late thirteenth century texts), but I see no grounds for such an assumption. Also, Luwian *ḫuwaialli* in *B* vs. Hittite *kutrui* in *A* would *a priori* speak for *A* being earlier.

I tend to ascribe the paleographic, orthographic, and grammatical differences between *A* and *B* to unequal scribal skills and circumstances of writing, rather than to chronological factors. As often repeated in the above sections, *A* seems more resourceful, more versatile, and more knowledgeable than *B*. In all fairness, part of *B's* lack of "sophistication" should no doubt be attributed to the pressures of writing hastily from dictation. This explains many of *B'* s features: more phonetic spellings, less complex employment of Akkadographic compounds, more frequent use of "ditto", and, of course, far more misspellings and other mistakes (see Ch. V). However, dictation does not account for other idiosyncracies, such as more "plene writings" and more use of genitive personal pronouns. I have the general impression that the scribe of *B* was less experienced and skilled and therefore less imaginative and more conservative. In contrast, the scribe of *A*, who exhibits a more confident hand-writing, is more variegated and "daring" in his spelling and grammar. Then again, since he probably copied his text, he would have had considerably more time to think and to experiment with alternative modes of expression and spelling, both in the first writing and in the subsequent "proof-reading" (see further below).

---

[300] *-az* for the reflexive becomes very rare in thirteenth century texts. See H. A. Hoffner, *JNES* 31 (1973), 32; *JAOS* 103 (1983), 190b; C. Kühne, "Über die darstellung der hethitischen Reflexivpartikel -z, besonders in postvokalischer Position", *Fs. Otten*^{2} (1988), 226. The proportion in this text between *-az* (twice, including i 18 which is listed as ablative by Kühne) and *-za* (x 13) could well reflect a transitional phase of the early thirteenth century.

Chapter V: Redactional History

1. Previous studies

The question of the relationship between the two main manuscripts was first dealt with in depth by Houwink ten Cate in 1968.[301] His observations and conclusions may be summarized as follows:
1. The type of mistakes made by *B* strongly suggests that the scribe worked hastily under dictation (unfinished signs; dislocated words; assimilation of adjacent words; considerably more syllabic writings versus *A*' s logograms; omission of paragraph-dividers or their abbreviated notation; misunderstanding or misinterpretation of dictated words). On the other hand, there are no indications that *A* was dictated.
2. *A* and *B* share some common mistakes (*errores coniunctivi*), which establish a direct dependence between the two manuscripts. This seems to rule out the possibility that both manuscripts rely on a third archetype.
3. *B* has far more errors than *A*, and therefore it is most unlikely that *B* copied from *A*. In fact, there are some clear indications that *A* corrected *B*' s errors and edited the latter's text, including a major change in the arrangement of the offering lists. In several cases *A* first copied *B*' s version, but later erased or corrected it, leaving traces of the earlier formulation.
4. In the process of editing, *A* introduced a few mistakes of his own, which are absent from *B* (*errores separativi*).
5. In conclusion, *B* probably represents an original draft dictated at the very moment that the text was composed, while *A* is a "revised edition". *C* is based on the "revised edition" since in most cases it sides with *A* against *B*.

As far as I can see, Houwink ten Cate does not take an explicit stand as to how much time passed between the completion of *B* and the writing of *A*' s corrected version, but the very terminology of "draft" and "revised edition" suggests that Houwink ten Cate posits a very short interval between the two manuscripts. (This does not necessarily apply to *C* which according to Houwink ten Cate is a copy of the "revised edition".) In other words, on the question of absolute dating Houwink ten Cate shares the commonly held opinion that both exemplars were written under Muwatalli.

A somewhat different reconstruction of the redactional history was briefly formulated in the unpublished doctoral dissertation of Harald Winkels, where he deals with the general question of drafts and dictated texts.[302] Though accepting Houwink ten Cate's thesis that *B* is a dictated version and *A* is a revised version based on it (leaving plenty of mistakes), Winkels raises the possibility that both manuscripts are school exercises: the teacher first dictated the text to one pupil (*B*) and later assigned a second pupil (*A*) to correct and edit it. This assumes the existence of an original archetype used by the teacher for dictation.

Before taking a stand on these proposals, it is necessary to provide a detailed comparison between the two main manuscripts, particularly on those points which may be of value for the reconstruction of the redactional history. Most of these have already been noted by Houwink ten Cate, but several have not, including some crucial cases. Also, the discovery of a "third hand" that wrote the "Postscript" in tablet *A* is highly relevant to the redactional history of the text.

---

301 "Muwatallis' 'Prayer to be Spoken in an Emergency,' an Essay in Textual Criticism," *JNES* 27 (1968), 204-208. His conclusions are followed by R. Lebrun, *Hymnes et prières* (1980), 292.

302 *Das zweite Pestgebet des Mursili (KUB XIV 8 und Duplikate). Eine methodologische Untersuchung zur Datierung hethitischer Texte des 14. Jahrhunderts v. Chr.* (Diss. Universität Hamburg 1979), 15.

2. Errors (or particular spellings) shared by *A* and *B* (*errores coniunctivi*)

1. *A* i 12 = *B* i 13: BAD(=BE), a very rare spelling for *BE-LU*, "lord". Elsewhere in the text both scribes write either EN, or, more rarely, *BE-LU*(^MEŠ^). Unless this is a different title than the regular "lord" (see Commentary), this could be either an error (omission of *-LU* ?) or an idiosyncracy shared by both manuscripts.

2. *A* i 44 = *B* ii 10: Both texts insert the *-AT* of ^d^*BE-E-LA-AT* above the line. This very conspicuous connective error (not noted by Houwink ten Cate) lends itself to several possible explanations: 1) One scribe copied automatically from the other his inserted correction. 2) Both scribes copied the corrected word from a third text , without pulling down the inserted sign into the line. 3) Both scribes wrote from dictation, misheard or misunderstood this word, and later returned to correct it.[303] 4) One scribe copied from the other a flawed ^d^*BE-E-LA*. Later, both texts were proofread by the scribe(s) or by supervisor(s), and the missing *-AT* was added above the line in both texts. If one were to consider this unusual error separately from the rest of the text, I think that the third and the fourth options would appear to be the most likely. However, in view of other data, I would definitely opt for the fourth explanation, especially in view of the new evidence for proofreading in both texts (see below). If so, this shared crux would strongly argue for the contemporaneity of the two manuscripts, both corrected while the clay was still soft.

3. *A* i 59 f. = *B* ii 24 f.: The paragraph listing the gods of Zitḫara contains erasures and corrections in both manuscripts (see Commentary). Both texts had a repetitive ^d^*Zitḫariyaš*, but *A* later erased the second occurrence. On the other hand, he too left out "the male gods and the female gods." This is the only omission of its kind in the entire text, and the fact that it is shared by the two manuscripts proves their mutual dependence.

4. *A* i 76 f. = *B* ii 41 f.: Both texts have a double error in the first occurrence of the toponym Lawazantiya: *La-u-wa-an-a*^!^*-ti-ia* , with *a* instead of *za*[304] and with metathesis of *an* and (*z*)*a*.[305] In the following line both texts have *za*, and *A* reversed the order to a correct *-za-an-*, whereas *B* omitted *an*. This unique double error and its ensuing correction in the next line is, in my view, the strongest evidence that one of the manuscripts directly depends on the other. I doubt that if the text had been dictated to both scribes, or if one scribe had written from dictation and the other had copied from an archetype, exactly the same double error would appear in both manuscripts.

5. *A* ii 26 = *B* ii 66: Both scribes had difficulty in providing the name of the deity who is "the King of Ḫurniya", and they both corrected what they had first written. I tentatively suggest reading DINGIR-*LIM*^!^*-uš*^!^ in *B* and DINGIR-*LUM*^!^*-uš*^!^ in *A*. It would seem that *B* first wrote down a name or an epithet of this deity, but being uncertain about it, he corrected it to simply "deity" (*šiuš*). *A* copied *B*' s version, but then corrected the Akkadian phonetic complement to *-LUM*.[306]

6. *A* ii 38 = *B* iii 7: ^ḪUR.SAG^*Ḫu-wa-la-nu-wa-an-da*. Elsewhere this toponym is usually spelled *Hu-ut-nu-wa-an-ta* or *Ḫu-wa-at-nu-wa-an-da*, which would seem to indicate that both texts have a flawed spelling here with *la* instead of *at*.[307]

---

303 This would imply that Akkadograms were pronounced, at least on occasion, as Akkadian words.

304 Although the two signs are similar, collation leaves no doubt that both texts have *a*.

305 The name in *A* appears on the unnumbered fragment glued to VAT 7456, which does not appear in KUB 6.46 (and was apparently not seen by Houwink ten Cate).

306 This example is cited by Houwink ten Cate under his category (*a*), a shared crux, but in fact, if the reading I suggest is valid, it should rather belong to category (*c*), corrections introduced by *A*.

307 For references, see *RGTC* 6, 132; *RGTC* 6/2, 46, and note the same "mistake" also in KUB 48, 15 i 10, where this mountain appears next to ÍD SÍG, the River Ḫulana. Could there be an etymological connection between the two

7. *A* iv 50 = *B* iv 49: Probably both manuscripts omit the standard "... upon the thick breads," which is found eight times in other occurrences of this formula. (Although the line is broken in *B*, the available space does not allow restoring this omission.)

3. Errors introduced by *A* (*errores separativi*)

Houwink ten Cate found about thirteen instances where the reading of *B* should be preferred over the reading of *A*; these few mistakes were introduced by *A* in the course of his revision of *B*. But a closer look at these cases may reduce the number of errors introduced by *A*. (For details see Commentary.)

One case is eliminated by collation: ii 7 *Šu-gaz-zi-ia* as in *B*. Several "errors" are in fact ambiguous. In iv 15, 20, *A* has an uncomplemented Akkadian construct state: *na-aš-kán* ^{GIŠ}BANŠUR DN *dāi*, compared to *B*' s ^{GIŠ}BANŠUR-*i ŠA* DN, which is also used by *A* in other places. This is hardly a grammatical error, and, as pointed out above, *A* has a better command of Akkadian forms and hence is able to use them more flexibly. The same applies to iii 19 where *A* eliminates a superfluous *ŠA* before the gen. pl. DINGIR^{MEŠ} *ḫumandaš* (but has *ŠA* before the unmarked Sun-goddess of Arinna).

In two cases *A* omits a Hittite word which is not really necessary for the understanding: i 37 f., *tiyawaš* and *ḫumanteš*. In two others he eliminates two pronouns which are indeed superfluous: iii 21 *kuš* ; i 22 *šumel*.

There remain a few cases in which *A* indeed omitted something: twice he left out DINGIR in DINGIR.SAL (ii 45, 61); in two cases out of six he omitted *peran* before *šippanti* (iv 7, 32); he omitted *an* in *Nenišankuwa* in ii 62 and KUR after "the mountains and the rivers" in iv 52. Of all these, only the last really affects the meaning.[308] To these omissions one should add one misspelling (iv 29) and one "hyper-correction" (iii 66). About half a dozen mistakes in a text of nearly three hundred lines is quite a commendable achievement, and one can only reinforce Houwink ten Cate's conclusion that *A* is a "revised edition," hardly a "school exercise" as suggested by H. Winkels (unless by a brilliant pupil indeed).

4. Corrections and changes introduced by *A*

B has innumerable errors that are absent from *A*, and it would be pointless to simply list these errors as they can easily be recognized in the partiture-transliteration.[309] I will rather indicate those discrepancies which establish and illustrate the editorial work of *A* over *B*. (For details see Commentary.)

4.1 Restored and corrected words or sentences

1. *A* corrected the following omissions in *B*: ii 63 ^{d}*Pirwaš*; iv 25 ^{d}U; iv 29 *paršiya*; iv 30 ^{URU}.

2. In i 19, *B* has the crux *da-az*, which was meant to be either *da<p>iaz* or, less likely, *<ḫuman>daz*, the latter being *A*' s version.

3. In ii 23 *A* corrected *B*' s flawed ^{URU}*Šuwanzipa* (assimilated from ^{d}*Šuwanzipa*) to ^{URU}*Šuwanzana*.

---

toponyms (Ḫulana > *Ḫuwalana?)? In that case *CTH* 381 would have the correct reading and this example should be removed from the list of common errors. Incidentally, the same confusion between *at* and *la* appears, for example, in the name *Kuwatna-/Kuwalana-ziti*, where the issue has been decided in favor of *la*. See M. Poetto, *Kadmos* 21 (1982), 101-103; *Athenaeum* 61 (1983), 528 f.

308 It is hard to decide who has the "better" text in i 63. After *Ḫebat*, *B* inserted LUGAL above the line (probably for the compound *Ḫebat-Šarruma*). *A* ignored this addition, leaving a simple *Ḫebat*.

309 For a classification of frequently recurring scribal errors in Hittite texts see, H. Eichner, "Einige Fehlschreibungen und Fehllesungen in hethitischen Texten", *Die Sprache* 21 (1975), 157-165; Ch. Rüster, "Materialien zu einer Fehlertypologie der hethitischen Texte", *Fs. Otten*^{2} (1988), 295-306. Cf. also M. Marazzi – H. Nowicki, "Vorarbeiten zu den hethitischen Gebeten (*CTH* 372, 373, 374)", *Oriens Antiquus* 17 (1978), 257-278 (especially p. 277), for a similar close reading and evaluation of scribal errors.

4. In ii 56 f., *B* originally had *ABI* and then *ABI ABI*, but he later mistakenly erased half of "grandfather". *A* restored the word and changed the order.

5. In ii 63, *B* wrote ^{URU}*Ikšunuwa*, probably under the influnce of the previous toponym. *A* corrected it to ^{URU}*Ikšuna*, which is attested elsewhere.

6. In iv 54, *A* restored a whole recurring phrase which is left out in *B*. (Unlike the later addition in iv 51, this phrase was written in the first pass.)

7. In 15 out of 17 cases, *A* replaced *B*' s abbreviation KI.MIN, "ditto", with a fully spelled word. He copied KI.MIN only in i 68, 75.

4.2 *Luwisms*

In a single case, *B* (iv 53) has a Luwian epithet with *Glossenkeil* (*ḫuwaialli* ^{d}UTU), where *A* has a Hittite one (*kutrui* ^{d}UTU). Another word, (\)*zilatiya*, has a *Glossenkeil* in *B* but not in *A*. *kulanitta* is defined with a *Glossenkeil* in both texts. Several Luwian words are not indicated as such in either text: the adjectival genitive *piḫaššašši-* and the participles *piḫami-* and *memmami-*.

If indeed *B* is the original dictated text and *A* is a revised version, the "correction" of a Luwian into a Hittite word may have important bearing on the issue of the employment of the two languages in thirteenth century Ḫatti, which is beyond the scope of this study.

4.3 *Word order*

1. In iv 18 f., *A* restored *ANA* ^{d}U *ŠAMĒ* to its proper place before the verb and eliminated its repetition.

2. In iv 23 f., *A* moved the verb to the end of the sentence.

3. In iv 11, *A* inverted the "normal" order of the pair NINDA.Ì.E.DÉ.A *memal* (attested eight times) for no apparent reason.

4.4 *Grammatical changes*

1. In i 21 f., *A* performed a series of changes intended to simplify the pronominal forms: he emended *ammel* to *šumel*, erased the superfluous *šumel* in the next line, and changed EN^{MEŠ} DINGIR^{MEŠ} into EN-*LÍ* DINGIR^{MEŠ}. This is one of the best examples of *A*' s resourcefulness in improving *B* 's text.

2. In iii 66, *A* suddenly switches from the 2nd pers. pers.pron. *-ta* (iii 59, 62, 67) to the 3rd pers. *-ši* (only here !). This might be considered a *lectio difficilior* proving the primariness of *A*, but I doubt it. Throughout this invocation the Storm-god *piḫaššašši* is addressed in the second person (with verbs in 2nd pers. imperative), and this sudden deviation from the norm seems to me more like an ill-construed attempt of *A* to "improve" this sentence (as he did in the previous example). However, he failed to carry through his "improvement" into the next contrasting sentence, with a dissonant result: "...let me give it to *him* joyfully, let me not give it to *you* reluctantly."

3. To these specific pronominal changes one should add *A*' s more skillful treatment of Akkadographic writings, which were discussed above in Ch.4.4. Some of them are improved Akkadian case endings; others are simply alternative, more diversified ways of expression (e.g., genitive expressed by either construct state or by a *ŠA* construction).

4.5 Thematic changes

1. i 14-15: As will be explained in Ch. XIV, *A* performed a major contextual correction here. He erased the epithet of *Šeri* and inserted the name *Ḫurri* instead. This is one of the clearest examples of the editorial activity *A* performed on the text of *B* (see further below).

2. i 40: *B* originally had the toponym ^{URU}*Tiwa* twice; he later erased the first occurrence and wrote^{URU}*Šamuḫa* instead, leaving the second occurrence untouched. *A* completed the correction by writing ^{URU}*Šamuḫa* in both cases. For the significance of this change, the only substitution of a toponym in the entire text, see my article in *Fs. Houwink ten Cate.* This is a clear case of *lectio difficilior* in *B*, one of the best proofs for *B*' s primariness (not noted by Houwink ten Cate).

3. In ii 49, *A* added KUR to *B*' s ^{URU}*Wašḫaniya;* conversely in ii 69, *A* omitted KUR from ^{URU}*Tuppaziya*. It is hard to tell whether these are simple "graphic" variants or perhaps reflect real geographical observations.

4. *B* i 39 (after *A* iv 2) inserted an extra offering to the Sun-god of Heaven, which *A* deliberately omitted (for reasons that will be explained in Ch. XIII).

5. Mention should be made here of the "Postscript" in *A* iv 59-61 and the addition in iv 51, although these are written in a different hand (see below).

4.6 Paragraph dividers

Discrepancies in the position of the paragraph-dividers in different manuscripts can be a most valuable tool in the reconstruction of the redactional history of a text. Houwink ten Cate used this as evidence in support of his assertion that *B* wrote from dictation, in some cases abbreviating his paragraph-dividers and in others omitting them altogether.

In seven instances *B* omits a paragraph-divider found in *A* (following ii 54, 56, 57, 58, 59, iv 51, 55).[310] A glance at the respective paragraphs shows that these "omissions" are not necessarily in conspicuous places where the context would strongly require the opening of a new paragraph.
1. In ii 52-54, *B* grouped together the gods of Ḫarpiša, of Kalimuna, and of Ḫakpiša, whereas *A* set the last one in a separate paragraph.
2. In ii 56-61, *B* grouped together the gods of the ancestors (father, grandfather, grandmother) with the gods of the (store-)house of Gazzimara and of the city of Ankuwa. *A* set each of these in a separate paragraph. Whereas I can see the logic in listing all the ancestors together, I am less confident about the last two entries.[311]
3. In iv 51, *B* omits the division between the male gods and the female gods of the land.
4. In iv 55, *B* omits the division between the offerings to the mountains and the rivers of the land and to the "Witnessing Sun." Note, however, that he begins the latter entry not with the normal *appanda*, "afterwards," (as in *A*) but rather with the conjunction *-ma*, which entails a less stressed transition.

Of more consequence for the redactional history are those instances in which *B* uses a single *Glossenkeil* as an abbreviation for a paragraph-divider (i 78, ii 63, 67, 71, 73, iii 44, iv 48).[312] Houwink ten Cate took these abbreviations to indicate that *B* was working in haste and under stress in attempting to keep pace with the dictation. In other words, the scribe was told to begin a new paragraph (or understood so himself

[310] References, as usual, are to *A*' s lines. Houwink ten Cate's references (one omitted) are to the line numbers of *B.*

[311] The ancestors may perhaps be related here to cult institutions which would then be paralleled with the (store-)house of Gazzimara (see Commentary). Could this apply somehow to Ankuwa as well ?

[312] The first six are long wedges crossing over to the next line. The one after iv 48 is shorter, resembling more the *Glossenkeil* before Luwian words.

from the context), but in order to save time he did not draw the paragraph-divider, but simply indicated it with the *Glossenkeil*. *A* took up all except one of these abbreviations and actually inserted the dividing lines. The only exception is in i 78, where both *A* and *B* have a *Glossenkeil* after the Storm-god of [*Pitiy*]*arik*(*a*), followed by the gods of *Uda*. For some reason, *A* did not deem it necessary to transform this abbreviation into a dividing line.[313] I can think of two possible explanations for this, of which I prefer the latter: (1) Being close to the bottom of the column, he wanted to accomodate both entries in the remaining space, which he would not manage if he drew a paragraph line. (2) On the assumption that *A* had *B* before his eyes, this was his first encounter with *B*' s abbreviation "system", and he copied it automatically, realizing only when he encountered it again that he should transform it to an actual paragraph-divider.

Finally, a particular case of paragraph marking is found in *B* iii 52-64 = *A* iii 13-24. Weber's copy shows two clear paragraph dividers after *B* iii 56 and 61. Collation shows that in both places there are actually only very faint lines which do not run through the entire width of the column. In other words, *B* originally had the three sections containing the invocation to the Sun-god of Heaven as a single paragraph. Only after the paragraph was already written were the two new paragraph-dividers inserted into the middle of it, or better said, they were faintly marked on the tablet so as not to erase the written text. To better mark these new divisions, a horizontal wedge was added (later?), slightly below each of the two lines, with its head protruding into the column-divider.[314] One result of this somewhat forced insertion of new divisions into an existing paragraph was that the second paragraph-divider cuts a relative clause in its middle: ... *kuedani arkuešni* \\ *IŠTU* EME-*YA ḫalziḫḫun*. *A*, who adopted these paragraph-dividers right from the beginning, moved the second one to the end of the clause.

The remarkable procedure which emerges here is extremely important for the reconstruction of the redactional history of the text. How can this afterthought of *B* be explained? It seems to me that this spot almost entirely eliminates the possibility that *B* copied from *A*. If he had, why would he not have inserted *A*' s paragraph-dividers right from the beginning, and why would he have marked them afterwards? The only way one could possibly account for this is to assume that the text was dictated to him from *A*, and that he then proofread his text, checking it against tablet *A*, and inserted the missed paragraph-dividers. However, this seems to me a most farfetched and unlikely explanation. It is much easier to assume that *B* is the primary text, in which the entire section on the Sun-god of Heaven was first written as a single paragraph. Later, the scribe himself or his supervisor deemed it necessary to break up this paragraph into three sections. Finally, *A* inserted the new paragraph-dividers into his copy, moving the second one to a more suitable place. He could only have done so by copying from *B* or from another manuscript which already had the new paragraph-dividers.

In conclusion, the comparison of the paragraph-dividers in the two main manuscripts strongly suggests that *B*, in which some of the paragraph-dividers are only hastily marked is the primary text. *A* picked up these abbreviated marks and inserted them as real paragraph-dividers in their proper places. The only exception to the rule, where *A* simply copied the *Glossenkeil* marker of a paragraph-divider (i 78), only reinforces this conclusion, which conforms with other observations on the redactional history of the text.

4.7 Text arrangement

The only basic difference in the arrangement of the two manuscripts is in the location of the offerings for the great gods of Ḫatti. In *B* these offerings (i 39-ii 1) follow immediately after the invocation of the main gods of Ḫatti (i 11-38); thus, they are separated from the offerings to "the gods of the lands" (iv 48-55) which are listed at the end of the text. *A* moved the first list of offerings next to the second, the two lists being separated only by the prospective prayers (iv 45-48).

As pointed out by Houwink ten Cate (p. 205), *A*' s apparently better organization of the text is misleading. In fact, *B*' s order, which places the respective offerings immediately after the invoked deities

[313] *A* also uses a long diagonal wedge for this abbreviation, whereas his only *Glossenkeil*, preceding Luwian *kulanitta* (iii 52), is a very short diagonal wedge.

[314] Similar horizontal wedges were also added to reinforce the beginnings of faint lines after *B* iii 28, 31, 35, 37, 40. These, however, were added to paragraph-dividers that were already marked in the first writing.

makes better sense. As discussed in Ch. XII, there is a basic distinction made between the "gods of Ḫatti" and the "gods of the lands", and *B*' s arrangement follows this distinction. Once again, *B* appears to be the original text, with a more "authentic" arrangement, whereas *A* attempted to improve on this arrangement by grouping together the two lists of offerings.

5. Conclusions

Cumulative evidence shows that Houwink ten Cate's 1968 textual criticism was basically correct: *B* appears to be the original version, probably written from dictation, whereas *A* visually copied from *B*, introducing numerous corrections and other editorial changes. Fragments *C* and *D* are too small to enable a reliable placement in the redactional history of the text. However, both fragments (which could belong to the same tablet) clearly side with *A* and could thus belong to (an)other "revised edition(s)," written either before, after, or at the same time as *A*. The additional data supplied by collation and a more detailed study of the two manuscripts further reinforce these conclusions.

A major addition to the redactional history of the text, provided by collation, is the discovery of more than one stage in the writing of each of the two manuscripts, i.e., a tablet was first fully written down and was later "proofread" and corrected by the same or by another scribe. This procedure is much better evidenced in manuscript *A*, but I believe it can also be demonstrated for *B*.

The best evidence for "proofreading" in *B* is the addition of paragraph-dividers in the invocation to the Sun-god of Heaven. It is most unlikely that *B*, who apparently wrote by dictation in much haste and under stress, added these new paragraph-dividers immediately after completing the paragraph. It is much more likely that he added them after the end of the dictation, when he had sufficient time to reread the entire tablet and insert necessary corrections. Obviously, it is equally possible that someone else, e.g., the person who dictated the text, inserted these paragraph-dividers, as well as numerous other corrections, additions, and erasures.[315] I could not discern a different hand-writing in the corrections and additions of *B*, comparable to the additional hand in *A*.

On tablet *A*, I believe I have found actual proof for a "stratigraphy" of scripts.[316] The "Postscript" in iv 59-61 and the addition in iv 51 are written in a hand-writing which differs considerably from the rest of *A*. In all probability, these lines were added by another person who proofread the tablet, perhaps an instructor or a supervisor. The same person may have executed some of the major corrections in the rest of the tablet, for example, the erasure of Šeri's epithet in i 14 f. and the insertion of Ḫurri instead. As will be argued in Ch. XIV, this adjustment was required for the sake of conformity with the list of offerings in rev. iv, where Šeri and Ḫurri appear as a pair. If so, it is evident that the correction in i 14 f. was made only after the entire tablet had been completed.

I assume that the proofreading of each of the two manuscripts was done not long after the first writing, when the clay was still soft enough to insert corrections. As for the time that elapsed between the writing of *B* and its revised edition in *A*, theoretically a wide range is possible. Paleography can certainly not distinguish between a few minutes and several years. There is one clue, however, which leads me to suggest that one manuscript was written immediately after the other: the insertion of *-AT* in *BE-E-LA-AT* above the line in both manuscripts. If the interpretation suggested above (Ch. V.2.2) is valid, this unique spot would indicate that *A* started to copy from *B*, *before* the addition of *-AT* in *B*, in other words, when tablet *B* was still soft.

315 The horizontal wedges added to strengthen some faint paragraph-dividers in col. iv (see previous note) could also belong to this proofreading.

316 Tablets that contain different hand-writings have already been observed in the past, e.g., the opening lines of the reverse of Text A of The Acts of Ḫattušili I (KBo 10, 1); see H. Craig Melchert, *JNES* 37 (1978), 11. Also, colophons which mention both the name of the scribe who wrote the tablet and the name of his supervisor ("chief scribe") indicate that the process of composing a written tablet could involve more than one person. It is more difficult, however, to actually reconstruct the process and to distinguish the various layers of writing and the contribution of each scribe. I believe that the two manuscripts of *CTH* 381 contribute some valuable insights to the study of "proofreading" in Hittite texts.

In conclusion, I suggest the following stages in the redactional history of *CTH* 381:

a) The prayer was dictated to scribe *B* (by the king himself ? see Ch. X).

b) Tablet *B* was proofread and corrected by the scribe himself or by another scribe (possibly *A*), who added the new paragraph-dividers in *B* iii 54 and other corrections.

c) *A* copied from tablet *B* while editing it. He corrected many mistakes (V.4), ignored others (e.g.: V.2.4 *La-u-wa-an-a* ! *-ti-ia*), and introduced some of his own (V.3). He also introduced some thematic changes in the text (V.4.5; V.4.7).

d) A third person, probably a supervisor, proofread both *A* and *B*,[317] corrected *BE-E-LA-AT* in both texts, and introduced other corrections and changes in *A*, including the addition in iv 51 and the "Postscript" in iv 59-61.

e) Perhaps the improved text was again recopied to a "clean" manuscript. The fragments C and/or *D* could be parts of this last copy, but not necessarily. One of them, or both, could also come after (*b*) or (*c*), although this seems to me less likely. Future joins (and duplicates) may better define the relative placement of these small fragments in the redactional history of *CTH* 381.

The redactional history outlined above suggests that texts *B* and *A* were written at the same time, both in the reign of Muwatalli. A more precise dating is of course impossible on the basis of script and language alone. However, historical and geographical considerations, to be dealt with in Ch. XII, strongly suggest that the text was written before Muwatalli' s transfer of the capital to Tarḫuntašša.

---

317 It is not impossible that it was in this second proofreading that the extra offering to the Sun-god of Heaven was added in *B* i 39, and that therefore it could not be included in *A*. See further Ch. XIII.

Part Three

THE PRAYER

Chapter VI: Structure

CTH 381 is probably the best preserved text in the corpus of Hittite prayers, affording a comprehensive view of its structure and layout.

The ***Preamble*** (i 1-3) presents the author, the occasion, and the type of prayer employed: an *arkuwar*, i.e. a "pleading" or "argumentation" of the suppliant's case before the addressed deities (see Commentary).

Instructions for the ***Ritual Offerings*** frame the body of the prayer, with preparations at the beginning (i 4-9) and the performance itself at the end of the text (rev. iv). This ritual part, rarely found or preserved in other prayers, is not specifically designated in the text; it is simply referred to as the "breaking of the breads" (iv 45 NINDA.GUR$_4$.RA$^{HI.A}$ *paršiyauwanzi*).

The ***First Invocation*** is addressed to the (main) "gods of Ḫatti", who appointed Muwatalli as king in their land and whom he serves as priest (i 10-19 "Short List"). These divine entities receive the first and the most copious offerings.

The ***Agenda of the Prayers*** is presented to the great gods immediately after their invocation (i 20-32): first a report regarding the gods and their treatment, thereafter a pleading of the suppliant's case. The gods are asked to listen only to those parts of the prayer that they find acceptable to their ears.

The ***First Intercessory*** is directed towards Šeri, the bull of the Storm-god, who, in his capacity as herald of Ḫatti, is asked to intercede for the sake of a successful audience with the gods (i 33-36).

In *B*, which probably has the original version, the ***(First List of Offerings)***, presented to the gods of Ḫatti invoked above, follows here. *A* moved this list next to the second list of offerings at the end of the text.

The ***Second Invocation*** is directed to the "gods of all the lands" (i 37-iii 9) and to the cosmic forces (iii 10-12). This "Long List" includes a more detailed list of the gods of Ḫatti proper, as well as the gods of all the other lands, listed in separate entries, with the recurring formula "male gods, female gods, mountains (and) rivers of GN."

The ***Second Intercessory*** is addressed to the Sun-god of Heaven, who is asked to summon all the gods (iii 13-24). This intercessory includes a short hymnic part (iii 13-17) and an even shorter evocation (iii 23-24), specifying the whereabouts of the summoned gods.

The ***Third Intercessory*** (iii 25-76), which is the longest, is directed towards the Storm-god of Lightning (*piḫaššašši*), the king's personal god, who is asked to intercede with the gods addressed in the prayer. In a hymnic style, this intercessory emphasizes the god's direct involvement in Muwatalli's upbringing, protection, and success. In return the king pledges to his god the veneration of future generations of royalty, as well as improvements in his present worship. This part, the centerpiece of the text in style and originality, is a quasi-independent prayer by itself, reminiscent of other hymns dedicated to great gods.

The ***Ritual Offerings*** are divided into two parts, separated (in *A*) by a notation indicating where the ***Personal Prayer*** should be inserted (iv 45-48). The ***First List of Offerings*** is to the divine entities of Ḫatti (iv 1-44); the ***Second List of Offerings*** is to the "gods of all the lands" (iv 49-55) and to the Witness Sun-god (iv 56).

A ***Postscript,*** added by a different hand, gives instructions for the burning of the offerings. The text is defined as "complete".

Obviously, the prayer has a perfectly clear and logical composition. It is addressed to the Assembly of Gods (see Ch. VIII), who are divided into two groups: "the gods of Ḫatti" and "the gods of all the lands". This twofold division is the key to the structure of the text and is a quintessential principle in its theological concept: an appeal to the totality of the Hittite pantheon, which consists of an inner circle of the main gods of Ḫatti surrounded by a larger circle of the gods of the lands (see Ch. XII).

The offerings are divided between the two groups, and so are the invocations and the intercessories. The gods of Ḫatti, the "divine lords," are approached first, with Šeri, "the champion of Ḫatti," acting as an intercessor. The gods of all the lands are invoked next, with the Sun-god of Heaven, the supreme judge, and the Storm-god of Lightning, Muwatalli's personal god, serving as intercessors.

The three intercessories,[318] in which the suppliant petitions intermediating gods to prepare for him a successful audience with the divine assembly, appear in an escalating order, from the lesser to the superior deity: Only four lines are dedicated to Šeri, twelve lines to the Sun-god of Heaven, and 52 lines to the Storm-god *piḫaššašši*. The three intercessors are asked, respectively, to *introduce* the suppliant and his prayer, to *summon* the gods, and to *intercede* for the king in the assembly of the gods (all in the second person imperative). The last intercessory, to the king's personal god, is manifestly the climax of the entire prayer, followed only by the ritual offerings. It is in itself a self-contained prayer within the larger one, with a petition formulated in hymnic style. Nevertheless, it serves here as an elaborate intercessory, in which the Storm-god of Lightning is invoked as a supreme intermediator between the suppliant and all the gods, who are expected to put right the "bad thing" in the soul of the king (iii 45-47). Therefore, the appropriate title for the text is Muwatalli's prayer to the Assembly of Gods, rather than the traditional designation, the prayer to the Storm-god *piḫaššašši*.

As far as I can see, this structure is unique among Hittite prayers. Obviously, each of its components may be compared to respective passages in other prayers. E. g., the relatively short intercessory to the Sun-god of Heaven has much in common with other Hittite prayers to solar deities, which follow Babylonian models (see n. 383). Some of the imagery is duplicated in prayers of Muršili II (iii 40). Still, the composition as a whole has an original and clear layout, which redounds to the credit of its author, Muwatalli II (see Ch. X).[319]

What remains to be established is the *purpose* of the prayer itself. Consideration of this intriguing issue will be followed by an overview and discussion of Hittite prayers to the Assembly of Gods and a short discussion on the ritual offerings.

---

[318] For intercessories in Mesopotamian prayers see, e.g., T. Jacobsen, in H. A. Frankfort a.o., *The Intellectual Adventure of Ancient Man* (Chicago 1946), 203-207; T. Abusch, "The Form and Meaning of a Babylonian Prayer to Marduk", *JAOS* 103 (1983), 13.

[319] I cannot accept Güterbock's categorical statement (*JAOS* 78, 245) that "it is obvious that Muwatalli's prayer is much inferior to those of Kantuzzili and Mursili."

Chapter VII: Purpose of the Prayer

One of the striking particularities of this prayer is the absence of any specific request by the suppliant. As discussed above, the prayer consists of a series of invocations to intercessors who are asked to convene the Assembly of Gods and to grant a sympathetic audience for the suppliant's pleadings. Almost nothing, however, is said about the nature of these pleadings. As far as I can see, the only clue to the *raison d'être* of the prayer may be deduced from the title phrase – *If some problem burdens a man* (i 3) – and from the prayer agenda announced in i 20-25:

First, I shall make a plea with regard to yourselves, my divine lords,
about your temples, about your statues;
how the gods of Ḫatti are treated and also how they are mistreated.

Thereafter, I shall make the matters of my (*own*) *soul into a plea.*

The latter phrase is taken up again towards the end of the prayer:

... *the bad thing which is in my soul, the gods will put it right, etc.* (iii 46 f.)
... *the things which are in His Majesty's heart, he makes them into a plea, etc.* (iv 46 f.)

Is this two-stage plan carried out in the text ? H. G. Güterbock (*JAOS* 78, 245) identified the long invocation of all gods, arranged by cult places, as the first prayer, whereas the short prayer to the Sun-god of Heaven and the longer prayer to the Storm-god *piḫaššašši* make up a second set. I find it difficult to accept this interpretation. The long invocation ("Long List") is nothing but an enumeration of the gods who are supposed to listen to the prayer, and the three invocations – to Šeri, to the Sun-god of Heaven and to the Storm-god *piḫaššašši* – are, as mentioned before, simply intermediary pleadings for a favorable hearing. None of these contains any information on the reason behind the two-staged prayer – neither on the gods' matters nor on His Majesty's problems.[320]

A clue to the nature of the first part of the projected prayer is provided by the opposition "how the gods are treated and also how they are mistreated." The latter usually refers to neglect of cults due either to ravages inflicted by an enemy (e.g., *CTH* 375 on the Kaška) or to the shortcomings of a (usually previous) king (e.g., *CTH* 378.II on neglect of River Mala; *CTH* 380 on Lelwani; *CTH* 382 on Kummanni). That would imply that the suppliant is required to insert a report on the condition of the state cults, probably excusing himself for any deficiencies due to his or, more often, others' faults.

As for the king's personal prayer, the actual meaning depends largely on the understanding of the nature of the *oppression* indicated in the opening sentence of the prayer. The verb *nakešš-* / *nakiyašš-* with an accusative or dative object is rendered by *CHD*, L-N, 371 f. as "to become troublesome to, bother, trouble, haunt, urge someone". Most of the quoted examples refer to deities or sins *burdening one's*

[320] This is apparently also the viewpoint of R. Lebrun, *Hymnes et prières*, 288 ff. Although this is not explicitly stated, his remark "le rituel [de la plaidoirie] devait faire l'objet d'une tablette séparée" (p. 290) seems to indicate that he too does not recognize an actual prayer in the text. I doubt, however, that there was another tablet containing the actual prayer.

conscience,[321] and I suspect that this is the meaning required in the present context as well. That is, "the bad thing(s)" in His Majesty's soul (iii 46) and heart (iv 46) are not just any problems, but rather things that burden *his guilty conscience* and need to be repented in a prayer. I am aware, of course, that such a distinction between *regular* problems and *bad conscience* problems would hardly have existed in the mind of the believer. Any problem would ultimately have been seen as caused by some sin or misconduct. I have tried to convey in my translation this sense of *nakkiyašzi* by rendering the opening sentence "If some problem burdens a man('s conscience)" instead of a more neutral "If some problem oppresses a man." Such an interpretation would be more in line with the corpus of Hittite prayers, practically all of which promise to make amends for some admitted sin(s) or implore to be informed about sins of some unknown nature. It would also provide a logical link between the two parts of the prayer, the suppliant's *problem* caused by the *mistreatment* of some god(s).

Whereas the interpretation above provides a theoretical *raison d'être* for the prayer, it is perhaps well to reassert that the text does not contain any concrete reference to sins or to resulting problems. It is in fact a *model prayer*, or a *framework for a prayer*, the actual causes to be inserted whenever the occasion arises. This sense was aptly conveyed by the title given to the prayer by A. Goetze in his *ANET* translation – *A Prayer to be Spoken in Emergency.* As such, this prayer is unique in the extant corpus of Hittite prayers. It is an attempt to provide a ready, one could say "canonized" format of an all-purpose prayer not only for the reigning king, but for future generations as well. To what extent this model prayer was indeed utilized by successive monarchs still remains to be discovered. To judge by the extant material, it would seem that the model was not adopted in the prayers of the following kings of Ḫatti, perhaps because of their different religious concepts (see Epilogue). The last recorded prayers, which are addressed to the Sun-goddess of Arinna and her family (see below), return to earlier models.

[321] E.g.: "the affair of Tudḫaliya the Younger, the son of Tudḫaliya, began to *trouble* me"; "that act of bloodshed *troubles* that person"; "at that time Ḫebat of Kummanni *troubled* me with regard to the festival of invocation" (see refs. in *CHD*). A similar understanding of *nakkeš-* in these contexts was already suggested by G. Furlani, "Muršiliš II e il concetto de peccato preso gli Hittiti", *Studi e Materiali di Storia delle Religioni* 10 (1934), 19-37 (esp. p. 22).

Chapter VIII: Prayers to the Assembly of Gods

A glimpse at the concise table of relatively well preserved Hittite prayers (Table 2)[322] shows that more than half, including the oldest examples, are addressed to solar deities: the Sun-goddess of Earth (*CTH* 371), the Sun-god of Heaven (372-4), and, first and foremost, the Sun-goddess of Arinna (375-6, 378 iii, 383-5). The obvious reason, often discussed in relevant literature, is the Sun's central function as "shepherd of mankind" who sees everything and exerts his judgment over all living creatures. A suppliant who is uncertain of the reason for which he is being punished by the gods, naturally directs his prayer to the all-seeing Sun, who can reveal his sin and can also soften his punishment. Obviously, the Sun is best informed not only on "terrestrial" matters, but, as the "Sun-god of the gods," he is also aware of all that happens up in heaven and can reveal the cause for the anger of other gods. In grave offenses the Sun deity is the one who summons the Assembly of Gods and presides over it as supreme judge. As stated by Houwink ten Cate ("The Sun God of Heaven", *Effigies Dei*, 24), "the Sun God functioned as an intermediary agent between the King who represented his people and the Divine World at large." Thus, it is only natural that most royal prayers should be directed to solar deities.[323]

The first prayers directed to gods other than the Sun are attributed to Muršili II, the most prolific of Hittite authors of prayers. Specific gods are usually approached when the cause of a certain calamity is known to the suppliant. In that case he would naturally try to appease the offended deity, or else, he would turn to the god(s) in whose "professional" domain the specific calamity is found. E.g., Iyarri, a god of war and pestilence, occupies a prominent place in the Assembly of Gods addressed in the Fourth Plague Prayer of Muršili II (*CTH* 378.IV, obv. i 2).

The sins confessed in prayers intended to appease a particular offended deity range from personal insults, where the sin and its punishment are restricted to a certain person, to grave national offenses and calamities. An example of the former is *CTH* 380, a prayer directed to Lelwani on behalf of Gaššuliyawiya, Muršili's ailing wife, who neglected the offerings due to this deity. Of the latter, the obvious example is the series of prayers dealing with the terrible plague that decimated Ḫatti for more than twenty years (*CTH* 378-9). Various sins were acknowledged as the possible causes for the disaster, and the prayers were addressed to the deities that were thought to be most offended by the respective sins. The First Plague Prayer, which admits the murder of Tudḫaliya Junior, is addressed to the assembly of oath gods who were present when the Hittite nobility swore allegiance to the legitimate king. The Storm-god of Ḫatti is the main addressee in the Second Plague Prayer because he was the guarantor of the Kuruštama treaty with the Egyptians, which was violated by Šuppiluliuma. In the Third Plague Prayer directed to the Sun-goddess of Arinna and the gods and in the Fourth Plague Prayers directed to the Divine Assembly, the identification of the sin is not preserved on the tablet.

---

[322] The concept is based on the similar chart composed by Ph. H.J. Houwink ten Cate in "Hittite Royal Prayers", *Numen* 16 (1969), 84-6. Practically all Hittite prayers are royal. *CTH* 373 is the only prayer attributed not to a king, but to prince Kantuzzili, a contemporary of Šuppiluliuma I. The suppliant in *CTH* 372 is any "mortal", but clearly the prayer must have had a more "noble" authorship, as shown by its close affinity with the Kantuzzili Prayer and with *CTH* 374 composed by an unnamed king (see H.G. Güterbock, "Some Aspects of Hittite Prayers", 130 ff.). In my chart I have replaced Houwink ten Cate's *Subject* column with two columns defining the confessed sins and the petition. My terminology in these chapters has been influenced by literature on Biblical prayers, notably, M. Greenberg, *Biblical Prose Prayer* (University of California Press 1983); S. E. Balentine, *Prayer in the Hebrew Bible* (Fortress Press, Minneapolis 1993); P.D. Miller, *They Cried to the Lord; The Form and Theology of Biblical Prayer* (Minneapolis 1994).

[323] In Egypt too, most hymns are dedicated to the Sun-god. See J. Assmann, "Ägyptische Hymnen und Gebete", *Texte aus der Umwelt des Alten Testaments* II/6 (Gütersloh 1991), 827 ff.

Table 2: *Analytic chart of Hittite prayers*

CTH	Suppliant	Addressed God(s)	Confession	Petition
371	unnamed king	Sun-goddess of Earth (& her entourage)		ignore calumny of family members
375	Arnuwanda & Ašmunikal	Sun-goddess of Arinna & gods	neglect of cults in Kaška occupied area	punish the Kaška
374	unnamed king	Sun-god	not known to suppliant	recover from illness caused by some deity
373	prince Kantuzzili	"	"	"
372	"a(ny) mortal"	"	"	"
376.A,C	[Šuppi. I (?)[324]]	Sun-goddess of Arinna & gods		divert plague from Ḫatti to enemy lands
376.B,D,E	Muršili II	"		"
378.iii	"	"	[not preserved]	stop the plague
378.iv	"	Assembly of Gods (listed geographically)	[not preserved]	"
378.i	"	Assembly of male & female oath gods	murder of young Tudḫaliya	"
378.ii	"	Storm-god of Ḫatti & gods	neglect of offerings to R. Mala violation of Egyptian treaty	"
379	"	Assembly of Gods (listed typologically)	violation of Egyptian treaty	["]
377	"	Telipinu	not mentioned (or not preserved)	cure, prosperity, punish enemies
376.F	"	Sun-goddess of Arinna	[not preserved]	cure for Gaššuliyawiya
380	[" (?)[325]]	Lelwani	Gaššuliyawiya neglected cult of Lelwani in Šamuḫa	cure for Gaššuliyawiya

[324] Middle Hittite version probably dated to Šuppiluliuma I. See Houwink ten Cate, *Records of the Early Hittite Empire*, 8 ff. (text "283 C"); Güterbock, "Some Aspects of Hittite Prayers" (1978), 136 ff.

[325] A. Ünal, "Hethitische Hymnen und Gebete", *Texte aus der Umwelt des Alten Testaments II: Religiöse Texte; Lieder und Gebete II* (Gütersloh 1991), 811, identifies Gaššuliyawiya in this prayer as the daughter of Ḫattušili and Puduḫepa, rather than the queen of Muršili II as usually assumed. For the problem of distinguishing between the two Gaššuliyawiyas see also I. Singer, *UF* 23 (1991), 328-330.

CTH	Suppliant	Addressed God(s)	Confession	Petition
381	Muwatalli II	Assembly of Gods & S.-g. of Lightning	neglect of cults (?)	not specified
382	"	Storm-god (& intercessors)	neglect of cults of Kummanni	prosperity for Kummanni
383	Ḫattuš. & Pudu.	Sun-goddess of Arinna	prosecution of Tawanana; prosecution of Danuḫepa; Urḫi-Tešub affair	not specified
384	Puduḫepa	Sun-goddess of Arinna (& intercessors)	Urḫi-Tešub affair	well-being of Ḫattušili
386	Ḫattuš. or Tudḫ.	Storm-god of Nerik	not specified / preserved	prosperity
385.9	Tudḫaliya	Sun-goddess of Arinna	neglect of festivals	help against unnamed enemy

The Hittite prayers addressed to the Assembly of Gods are exceptional within the corpus of ancient Near Eastern prayers. Prayers are normally addressed to one god at a time.[326] The simple logic of this is the worshiper's belief that it is in the power of a certain god to grant his request, and therefore all his efforts are concentrated in appeasing and supplicating that god, occasionally extending the prayer to that god's acolytes (e.g., *CTH* 371, 382, 384). To be sure, on another occasion the same suppliant may petition some other god, with the same piety and fervor.[327] Quite often a general appeal to "All Gods" is appended to the name of the specific god approached (*CTH* 375; 376; 378 ii-iii), but prayers explicitly directed towards an entire pantheon are almost absent in the ancient Near Eastern literature.[328]

What intellectual climate could motivate such an exceptional form of prayer? I think the answer is quite simple. When all the individual prayers and propitiations have failed to bring salvation, the desperate suppliant would, as a last resort, turn collectively to all the "thousand gods of Ḫatti", hoping to reach even the remotest and least prominent of offended deities. A collective prayer would also cover the eventuality that some large-scale misconduct had angered the entire divine world. I think that such a line of thought would be quite consistent with Hittite mentality, well-known for its scrupulous meticulousness.

---

326 See, e.g., Morton Smith, "The Common Theology of the Ancient Near East", *Journal of Biblical Literature* 71 (1952), 135-47; repr. in Frederick E. Greenspahn (ed.), *Essential Papers on Israel and the Ancient Near East* (New York University Press 1991), 50 f. Smith's conclusion is based on a perusal of the prayers and the rituals translated in *ANET*, with possible exceptions discussed on p. 57 f., n. 9.

327 As rightly pointed out by M. Smith (p. 51), the exaltation of a single god in a prayer or hymn, often with exaggeration of his omnipotence, does not mean that he is actually thought to be the only god. The same worshipper may use similar flattery when appealing to another god.

328 Prof. Robert Biggs and Prof. Edward Wente of the Oriental Institute in Chicago advised me that "All Saints" type prayers are virtually absent in the Mesopotamian and Egyptian corpora. On the other hand, the Ugaritic corpus seems to provide the closest parallels to the Hittite prayers addressed to an assembly of gods, although, as pointed out to me by Prof. Dennis Pardee, the evidence is scant and controversial. RS 4.474 (=*KTU* 1.16) and RS 24.271 (=*KTU* 1.123) contain lists of deities, who are perhaps approached in a kind of prayer. For the latest comprehensive discussion of these texts with references to previous literature, see D. Pardee, *Les textes rituels*, Chs. 16 and 49 (respectively). For a prayer to Baʿ l embedded within a ritual text (RS 24.266), see idem, "Poetry in Ugaritic Ritual Texts" in J. C. de Moor & W. G. E. Watson (eds.), *Verse in Ancient Eastern Prose* (Neukirchen-Vluyn 1993), 213-218.

A forerunner to the prayers directed to the Assembly of Gods is found in the Middle Hittite prayer of Arnuwanda and Ašmunikal (*CTH* 375). The opening address is directed "[to the gods (and)] to the Sun-goddess of Arinna".[329] The prayer itself is addressed (in the second person plural) to the gods who have been deprived of their cult places and offerings by the sacrileges of the Kaška. It stands to reason that in a situation in which numerous gods are affected the prayer should be addressed to the entire pantheon, headed by the Sun-goddess of Arinna. This early example does not yet contain a detailed list of gods, but the list of ravaged lands headed by Nerik (ii 20-25) is in fact a precursor of that idea. Since it is the gods of these lands that are petitioned in particular, this is only a step away from supplying a full list of the addressed gods.

The first prayers addressed explicitly to the Assembly of Gods belong to the age of Muršili (*CTH* 378.IV and 379). Faced with the national catastrophe of the devouring plague, every approach to appeasing the angry gods was tried, resulting in an unprecedented proliferation of prayer types. Prayers were addressed to the great gods of the pantheon – the Sun-goddess of Arinna (*CTH* 376), the Storm-god of Ḫatti (378.II), Telipinu (377). Then, in an attempt to reach out to all the divinities of the kingdom capable of offering salvation, prayers were directed to All Gods. *CTH* 378.I is addressed to "a[ll the ma]le [gods] (and) all the female gods [...], all the male gods of the oath (and) all the female gods of the oath [...], all the ancient male gods (and) all the ancient female gods, all you gods who have been summoned to witness in this [matter] in the assembly of oath, mountains, rivers, springs, underground waters." This address already contains all elements of the Assembly of Gods, except the actual listing of the gods' names. It also introduces the separation of the gods into male and female, a distinction maintained in later prayers.

In a recent article Houwink ten Cate discussed the origins and the development of the Assembly of Gods in the Hittite world, a concept frequently found in other Near Eastern religions, including biblical theology.[330] Following up on earlier observations made by Goetze, Gurney, and Laroche, he points out that this celestial court which is convened by the Sun-god of Heaven closely resembles the assembly (*tuliya-*) of Hittite nobility (*panguš*) which was convoked by the king. The Assembly of Gods, consisting of a systematically organized list of deities concluding with cosmic forces and the place of assembly itself, appears in a variety of texts – mythology, rituals, instructions, prayers, and most prominently in treaties, where it acts as witness and guarantor to the agreement. Houwink ten Cate distinguished two forms in which the Assembly of Gods appears in prayers: typologically, by categories of deities, and geographically, by cult centers. In fact, a closer look shows that functional and geographical dimensions are present in both categories.

The former type is exemplified by *CTH* 379, a Muršili prayer, probably belonging to the series of plague prayers (Fifth ?).[331] The gods in the fragmentary first(!)[332] column are arranged by "functional" types, but most entries are also associated with a certain locality which is the main cult center of the particular deity. This list has much in common with the lists of the Muwatalli prayer. The table below is analytical, disregarding lines and paragraph dividers:

[329] KUB 31, 123 i 2: [*A-NA* DINGIR^{MEŠ} (Ù)]x *A-NA* ^{d}UTU ^{URU}A-ri-in-na [. Cf. iii 21: *šu-ma-a-aš A-NA* DINGIR^{MEŠ} ^{d}UTU ^{URU}A-ri-in-na. Cf. the introductory lines of *CTH* 381, with two offering tables prepared for the Sun-goddess of Arinna and the male gods.

[330] Ph. H. J. Houwink ten Cate, "The Sun God of Heaven, the Assembly of Gods and the Hittite King", in D. van der Plas (ed.), *Effigies Dei: Essays on the History of Religions* (Leiden 1987), 13-34. For the "Divine Court " in Israel and in Ugarit, see F. M. Cross, "The Council of Yahveh in Second Isaiah", *JNES* 22 (1953), 274-277; W. Herrmann, "Die Göttersöhne", *Zeitschrift für Religions- und Geistesgeschichte* 12 (1960), 242-251; O. Cooke, "The Sons of (the) God(s)", *Zeitschrift für Altestamentliche Wissenschaft* 76 (1964), 22-47. For the Assyrian assembly of gods see, S. Parpola, "The Assyrian Cabinet", in M. Dietrich & O. Loretz (eds.), *Vom Alten Orient zum Alten Testament: Fs von Soden* (Neukirchen-Vluyn 1995), 379-402.

[331] KUB 31.121 + 121a + KUB 48.111. See H. G. Güterbock, *RHA* 18/66-67 (1960), 57-63; R. Lebrun, *Hymnes et prières*, 240-247; M. Marazzi, "Inni e preghiere ittite: A proposito di un libro recente", *Studi e materiali di storia delle religioni* 49 (1983), 327; Houwink ten Cate, "The Sun God of Heaven...", *Effigies Dei* (1987), 19 f.

[332] According to the collation by H. G. Güterbock the sides as given in the edition (also in Lebrun's transliteration) must be reversed.

Solar gods & court (Arinna) :	[Sun-god of Heav]en, Storm-god [of Arinna(?)[333]], [Sun-goddess of Arin]na, Mezzulla,[Ḫulla(?)/Zintuḫi(?)]
Storm-gods & court (Ḫatti) :	Storm-god of Ḫatti, [Storm-god of Zippa]llanta, [ ] Šeri, Ḫurri, [Storm-god *piḫai*]*miš* (?)[334] All the Storm-gods
Ḫebats (Kummanni), Ḫalki :	[-]*eš* , Ḫebat of Kummanni Al[l Ḫebats], Ḫalki
[Šarrumas ?], Ḫebat-Šarrumas :	All [Šarruma]*s* [ ], all Ḫebat-Šarruma*s*
Protective-gods (Ḫatti) :	[LA]MMA, [LAMMA of Ḫat]ti, all LAMMA*s*
IŠTARs (Šamuḫa):	IŠTAR, [IŠTAR.LÍL(?) of] His Majesty, IŠTAR of Šamuḫa, a[ll] IŠTAR*s*
Telipinus :	Telipinu, a[ll] Telipi<nu>*s*
War-gods :	ZABABA, all ZABABA*s*
Underworld & other gods :	Sun-goddess of Earth, [Le]lwani, Pirwa, Marduk, Iyarri Ḫašammeli, [-]šu, [ ]

"All the male gods of the assembly[335], all the female gods of the assembly,the place of assembly, the place of judgment of the gods, to whi[ch] pl[ace the gods] step up in [assembly]."

The first geographically oriented list of the Assembly of Gods is found in the Fourth Plague Prayer of Muršili.[336] The text opens with "My divine lords" followed by a list of some two dozen cult centers (i 1-16). Most of them are simply indicated as "Gods of GN"; a few add the name of a specific local deity.

As might be expected, first in the list is Muršili's personal god,[337] the Valiant Storm-god.[338] He is followed by the "two lords of Landa"[339] and Iyarri, a god of war and pestilence who regularly assists

[333] Houwink ten Cate, ib., 21 restores "Storm God, K[ing of Heaven]" , but the parallel passage in the Muwatalli prayer, KUB 6.45 i 37, shows that the first group includes the Sun-god of Heaven and the Sun-goddess of Arinna.

[334] The traces conform with a *-m]i-iš* . For this deity see Commentary on i 66 f.

[335] The text (KUB 48.11, 10'-11') in fact has *li-li-ya-aš* twice, which I suspect is simply a scribal error for *tu-li-ya-aš*, as correctly written in the next line. Cf., however, *CHD* L, 60 b s.v. *lili.* For the parallel formula in the Muwatalli Prayer iii 11 f. see Commentary on iii 11f..

[336] A: KUB 14.13 + KUB 23, 124; B: KBo 22, 71. See Lebrun, ib., 220 ff.

[337] It is interesting to note that in *CTH* 377, Muršili's prayer to Telipinu, the latter is designated *anzel* EN-*NI* DINGIR-*LAM ŠA* SAG.DU-*NI*, "our Lord, our personal god" (lit.: "the god of our head"). Elsewhere, Telipinu does not appear as Muršili's personal god, and this particular epithet may be employed here only because the prayer is directed to Telipinu.

[338] Muršili is designated as "beloved of ^{d}U NIR.GÁL/Muwatalli" in KBo 1. 28 obv. 3 and on a seal from Ugarit (*Ugaritica* III, 103, seal 1). This deity regularly appears in texts dated to Muršili (historical texts, treaties, prayers), and is practically unknown before his time. No wonder that Muršili names one of his sons after his personal deity.

[339] The "two lords of Landa" must be Kuniyawani and the "Lady (*BĒLAT*) of Landa," who is probably an IŠTAR-type goddess (see Commentary on ii 50 f.).

Muršili in his wars. The prominent place in which the gods of Landa appear in this list must indicate either some personal connection to Muršili himself or an association with the plague which is the subject of this prayer. After this group, which here occupies the initial position normally reserved for solar deities, follow some two dozen cult centers and a few individual deities: Ḫatti/Ḫattuša, Arinna, Zippalanda, Tuwanuwa, Ḫupišna, Durmitta, Ankuwa, Šamuḫa, Storm-god of Šariššа(!) and gods of Šarišša, Ḫurma, Ḫanḫana, Karaḫna, Ellaya, Kamrušepa of Taniwanda, Zarwiša, Liḫzina, Protective-god of the army of His Majesty's father which is in Marašantiya, Uliliyašši of Parmanna, Kattila, Storm-god of Ḫašuna, Muwa[ni(?)], Zazziša, Telipinus (of?) the temples that are destroyed within the land, Šalpa, Storm-god of [ ].

Most of these places can also be found in the much longer list of the Muwatalli Prayer, but some of the rare names at the end of the list are peculiar to this prayer: Taniwanda (*hapax legomenon*), Maraššantiya,Parmanna, Kattila, Ḫašuna, Muwa[ni?] and Zazziša. As pointed out by Lebrun (*Hymnes et prières*, 236), Muršili's list covers the Ḫatti Land, the Lower Land and the Upper Land, conspicuously omitting the great cult centers of Kizzuwatna. This omission becomes all the more noteworthy when compared to the typological list in *CTH* 379 (see above), which includes Ḫebat of Kummanni and her son Ḫebat-Šarruma.

The full development of the prayers to the Assembly of Gods is found in the Great Prayer of Muwatalli (*CTH* 381). The Long List of cult centers, which, with its eighty-three toponyms, is probably the most detailed description of the divine assembly, will be dealt with in Ch. XII. In this context, which deals with the linkage between the addressed god(s), the confessed sins, and the request(s) of the suppliant, suffice it to note that, as shown in the previous chapter, this text is in fact a *model for a prayer*, without a specific occasion or request. Since the parameters of the prayer are deliberately not specified, it is only natural that it should be addressed to the entire pantheon acting as an all-purpose court capable of dealing with any eventuality in the future. It seems that the list of the Assembly of Gods was "updated" by Muwatalli himself in a later text (see Ch. XI).

After having reached its high point in the Muwatalli Prayer, the genre of prayers to the Assembly of Gods seems to disappear. The last recorded prayers, of Ḫattušili, Puduḫepa, and Tudḫaliya (*CTH* 383-6), are addressed to the Sun-goddess of Arinna and her family.

Chapter IX: The Ritual Offerings

An important asset of *CTH* 381 is the fully preserved record of the offering rituals accompanying the prayer. This provides important insights on the relationship between the two.

The preparations for the ritual are described in i 4-9. Two covered offering tables are placed on the roof; on them are breads and vessels filled with oiled-honey, fat-bread, groats, and wine. When everything is ready the king goes up to the roof and begins to pray.

The first invocation (i 10-19) is directed towards the great gods of Ḫatti, consisting of eleven divine entities: Sun-god of Heaven, Sun-goddess of Arinna, Storm-god of Heaven, Ḫebat, Storm-god of Ḫatti, Storm-god of Ziplanda, Šeri and Ḫurri, male and female gods of Ḫatti, mountains and rivers of Ḫatti. After a preliminary agenda of the prayers to follow and a short invocation to Šeri, text *B* (i 39-74) introduces here the list of offerings to these gods of Ḫatti (not necessarily in the same order). A twelfth deity, the Storm-god *piḫaššašši*, is added to the list of offerings (after the Sun deities).[340] Text *A* moved this list to the end of the text (iv 3-44), next to the list of offerings to the "gods of the lands" (iv 49-58). This second list consists of the male gods, the female gods, and the mountains and the rivers of the lands. Finally, the Witness Sun-god also receives an offering (iv 56-58). Altogether, there are 17 divine entities that receive offerings according to *B*, which is the original text (see Ch. V): the Storm-god *piḫaššašši* plus eleven entities of Ḫatti, four entities of the lands, and the Witness Sun-god. Text *A* has only 16 divine entities, excluding the Sun-god of Heaven.[341]

The two offering tables placed on the roof at the beginning of the text are identified as the table of the Sun-goddess of Arinna and the table of the male gods, respectively (i 5 f.). In the ritual itself, however, six different tables are mentioned. This apparent discrepancy has a simple solution: the two tables are conceived as serving male deities and female deities respectively, and their designation alters according to the deity being served. One table serves the Sun-goddess of Arinna (iv 4-7), Ḫebat (13-17) and the female goddesses of Ḫatti (38-40). Whereas in the first and in the third case the table is referred to as "the table of the Sun-goddess of Arinna", in the offering to Ḫebat the table is referred to as "the table of Ḫebat". I doubt that additional tables were brought up to the roof. Rather, the two designations refer to the same table, on which goddesses are served, just as the tables of the Storm-god *piḫaššašši* (iv 10), the Storm-god of Heaven (iv 20), the Storm-god of Ḫatti (iv 25), and the Storm-god of Ziplanda (iv 30) are all one and the same table, on which male gods are served. It is interesting to note that contrary to these Storm-gods, in the case of Šeri and Ḫurri the table is designated as belonging to the Storm-god *piḫaššašši*, a further demonstration of the close relationship between the Storm-god and his sacred bulls. It is somewhat surprising that the mountains and the rivers of Ḫatti are both served on the table of the Storm-god *piḫaššašši.* Rivers are usually conceived of as feminine entities (Laroche, *Noms des Hittites*, 275; Lebrun, *Hymnes et prières*, 54). No tables are mentioned in the offerings to the "gods of the lands" and to the Witness Sun-god (iv 49-58). I assume that the same two offering tables are used, though I cannot explain why this is not explicitly mentioned.[342] Finally, the two (!) offering tables reappear in the "Postscript" in *A* iv 61.

---

[340] He may have been omitted from the first invocation because he later re-appears as the main mediator between the suppliant and the petitioned gods. Another, more significant reason may be, that although he is a major deity in this prayer, strictly speaking, he is *not* a god of Ḫatti. For the Storm-god *piḫaššašši* see Ch. XV.

[341] In text *B* the Sun-god of Heaven was inserted at a later stage; this extra offering was not taken up in text *A*. See Commentary on iv 2 (*B* iv 45) and discussion in Ch. XIII.

[342] I doubt that this is a simple omission, even though text *B* shows definite signs of "fatigue" towards the end of the text and omits a whole line (iv 54; re-inserted in *A*).

Table 3: *Offerings to the gods*

Deity	Table of	Thick breads	Honey-oil, fat-bread& groats	Pitchers of wine
dUTU AN-*I* (added only in *B* !)	–	[3] N.G.R.	KI.MIN	→ (?)
dUTU URUArinna	dUTU URUArinna	3 N.G.R. *ŠA* ZÌ.DA DUR_5 *tarnaš*	specified	1
dU *piḫaššašši*	dU *piḫaššašši*	3 N.G.R. BABBAR ŠÀ.BA 1 SA_5	"	1
dḪebat	dḪebat	"	"	1
dU *ŠAMĒ*	dU *ŠAMĒ*	"	"	1
dU URUḪatti	dU URUḪatti	3 N.G.R. *ŠA* ZÌ.DA DUR_5 *tarnaš*	"	1
dU URUZippalanda	dU URUZippalanda	3 N.G.R. BABBAR ŠÀ.BA 1 SA_5	"	1
DINGIR.LÚ.MEŠ *ḫumandaš ŠA* Ḫatti	dU *piḫaššašši*	"	KI.MIN	→ (?)
Šeri & Ḫurri	dU *piḫaššašši*	"	KI.MIN	→ (?)
DINGIR.SAL.MEŠ *ḫumandaš ŠA* Ḫatti	dUTU URUArinna	"	KI.MIN	→ (?)
ḪUR.SAG.MEŠ	dU *piḫaššašši*	"	KI.MIN	→ (?)
ÍD.MEŠ	dU *piḫaššašši*	"	KI.MIN	→ (?)
DINGIR.LÚ.MEŠ KUR-*eaš ḫumandaš*	–	3 N.G.R. BABBAR ŠÀ.BA 1 SA_5	specified	1 (only in *A* !)
DINGIR.SAL.MEŠ KUR-*eaš ḫumandaš*	–	3 N.G.R. BABBAR	"	
ḪUR.SAG.MEŠ ÍD.MEŠ (KUR)	–	2 N.G.R.	KI.MIN	
kutrui / *ḫuwaialli* dUTU	–	1 N.G.R.	specified	

The ritual offering is performed by the king. He breaks the breads, dips the pieces in a mixture of honey and oil, puts them on the offering-table, and pours fat-bread and groats over the pile. Finally, he pours out a pitcher of wine in front of this pile of food.

Three types of bread are offered: "thick breads of moist flour of (one) *tarna-*"[343] (NINDA.GUR$_4$.RA *ŠA* ZÌ.DA DUR$_5$ *tar-na-aš*) and white and red thick breads (e.g., 3 NINDA.GUR$_4$.RA BABBAR ŠÀ.BA 1 SA$_5$). It is interesting to note that the former type is offered only to the Sun-goddess of Arinna (iv 4) and to the Storm-god of Ḫatti (iv 23), i. e., the supreme divine couple of the pantheon of Ḫatti. All the other gods receive white (and red) thick breads, in differing quantities. In the preparations for the ritual only "35 thick breads of (one) *tarna* of moist flour" are mentioned; therefore, I assume, that the white and the red breads are included in this general designation.

The numbers of offered breads and the pitchers of wine do not seem to add up to the quantities specified at the beginning of the text. The gods of Ḫatti receive three breads each, which adds up to 36 breads. The gods and the goddesses of the lands also receive three breads each (group), whereas the mountains of the lands, the rivers of the lands, and the Witness Sun-god receive one bread each. Altogether, 45 breads according to *B*, 42 breads according to *A* (which omits the Sun-god of Heaven). The only solution I can offer for this discrepancy is a scribal error in the introduction – 35 instead of 45 breads (i.e., omission of one *Winkelhacken* out of four).

The number of wine pitchers poured is even more problematic: only six pitchers are explicitly mentioned in *B* (the first six gods of Ḫatti), seven in *A* (with the addition of one pitcher to the male gods of the lands, in iv 51). Even if we were to extend the "ditto" in iv 33-44 to include a pitcher of wine as well, we would still have only thirteen pitchers, much less than the 30 pitchers prepared on the roof. I can offer no explanation for these numbers, except to recall that similar discrepancies are not uncommon in other texts.

The "Postscript" added to text *A* (in a different hand) provides for the burning of the offerings on two pyres of wood erected in front of the two tables. Burnt offerings – usually of animals, only rarely of other ingredients[344] – are mostly associated with the Hurrian-Luwian milieu of southern Anatolia and northern Syria.[345]

In his analysis of ritual activities associated with incantation prayers, E. Gerstenberger[346] distinguished four stages: (1) Purification rituals in the place of prayer; (2) Presentation of gifts to the addressed god(s); (3) Apotropaic rituals to dispel evil forces; and (4) The disposal of the cultic apparatus and the presented offerings. Of these, only the second and the fourth stages are represented in this prayer, the latter added in a postscript.

---

343 The exact measure or weight of the *tarna-* is difficult to establish. See Th. P.J. van den Hout, "Masse und Gewichte", *RlA* 7 (1990), 524.

344 E.g., KUB 45.23 rev., with burning of birds, lambs, broken breads and other ingredients over a hearth. See, V. Haas, a.o., *Corpus der hurritischen Sprachdenkmäler* I/5, no. 95.

345 See V. Haas, *Gesch. der heth. Religion* (1994), 661-665 (with further bibliography).

346 *Der bittende Mensch: Bittritual und Klagelied des Einzelnen im Alten Testament* (Neukirchen-Vluyn 1980), 78-93.

Part Four

THE AUTHOR

Chapter X: CTH 382: Muwatalli's Prayer to the Storm-god

The authorship of *CTH* 381 is clearly indicated in the preamble: "Thus (says) *tabarna* Muwatalli...". Although the occasion for the prayer is more generally phrased – "if some problem burdens a man('s conscience)"– it is quite obvious from the following quotations that the troubled suppliant is the king himself: "... I shall make my (own) personal wishes into a plea" (i 25); "... the things which are in His Majesty's heart, he makes them into a plea to the gods" (iv 46 f.). Obviously, once the prayer was created, other persons could also have used it.[347]

The colophon of Muwatalli's other prayer, *CTH* 382, is even more explicit as to the king's authorship: "... written down from the m[outh] of His Majesty" (rev. 24 f.; Houwink ten Cate and Josephson, *RHA* 25, 113, 119). If this restoration (suggested by Güterbock) is correct, it would seem that the text was actually dictated to a scribe by Muwatalli. It is quite possible that the same is true for *CTH* 381, one duplicate of which was most probably dictated (see Ch. V).

A third text, restored from a number of fragments containing lists of local gods, is tentatively attributed to a further prayer (or other type of religious text) of Muwatalli (Ch. XI). It seems that Muwatalli, like his father Muršili, was quite active in the composition of prayers. This is particularly remarkable in view of the scarcity of texts attributed to Muwatalli II, who must have taken part of the royal archives to his new capital in Tarḫuntašša.[348] Moreover, Muwatalli is the only monarch whose direct authorship in the composition of his prayers is explicitly mentioned.[349]

CTH 382 was edited by Ph. Houwink ten Cate and F. Josephson in 1968.[350] For the sake of comparison with *CTH* 381 it is worth describing the main features of this text briefly, with some remarks on its interpretation. It is a typical prayer of confessional penitence to the Storm-god, somewhat resembling Mesopotamian "incantations for appeasing an angry god".[351] Nowhere in the text is this Storm-god (^{d}U) identified more explicitly, but because the text deals with the cult of Kummanni and the other gods mentioned in it are Kizzuwatnean (Ḫebat, Šarruma, Ḫuzzi, Ḫutanni), it has generally been assumed that the Storm-god of Kummanni is meant. I would rather opt for a more universal hypostase of the Storm-god,

[347] Compare *CTH* 372-374, a prayer preserved in three parallel versions, attributed to an unnamed king, to Kantuzzili, and to a(ny) "mortal", respectively. See Güterbock, "Some Aspects of Hittite Prayers" (Upsala), 130 ff.

[348] Since the discovery of a seal impression of Muwatalli I, a king of the "Middle Kingdom," the texts and the references to Muwatalli must be closely scrutinized for their ascription to this or the other king, or other namesakes; see O. Carruba, "Muwatalli I.", *X. Türk Tarih Kongresi, Ankara 1986* (Türk Tarih Kurumu Basimevi, Ankara 1990), 539-554, Taf. 297-300; H. Otten, *Das hethitische Königshaus im 15. Jahrhundert v. Chr. – Zum Neufund einiger Landschenkungsurkunden in Boğazköy* (Wien 1987). This may limit even more the number of texts attributed to the king who fought at Qadesh: the Talmi-Šarruma Treaty (*CTH* 75), the Alakšandu Treaty (*CTH* 76), and possibly the letters KUB 23.102 and KBo 18.24 written to Assyrian kings (*CTH* 171; Otten, *AfO* 22, 113. For other datings of these letters, see A. Harrak, *Assyria and Hanigalbat*, 138-149, with bibliography). The so-called Tawagalawa Letter must be attributed to Ḫattušili III, a dating which is now supported by indirect evidence from an Egyptian letter of Ramses II; see I. Singer, "New Evidence on the Last Decades of the Hittite Empire" (forthcoming). It is more difficult to attribute religious texts to Muwatalli, but in view of later references to his activities in the cultic domain (see Epilogue), it stands to reason that some of the undated texts were composed during his reign.

[349] R. Lebrun, "Observations sur la prière hittite" (1980), 42.

[350] "Muwatallis' Prayer to the Storm-god of Kummanni (KBo XI 1)", *RHA* 25 (1968), 101-140. Cf. also R. Lebrun, *Hymnes et prières hittites*, 294-308.

[351] See W. G. Lambert, "Dingir.šà.dib.ba Incantations", *JNES* 33 (1974), 267-322, with an appendix on "Hittite Parallels" by H. G. Güterbock (pp. 323-327). For Biblical prayers of penitence see, S. E. Balentine, *Prayer in the Hebrew Bible* (Fortress Press, Minneapolis 1993), 103-117; P.D. Miller, *They Cried to the Lord; The Form and Theology of Biblical Prayer* (Minneapolis 1994), 244-261.

especially in view of his epithets in obv. 1: "Lord of Heaven (and) Earth" (EN AN.KI), "King of the Gods" (LUGAL DINGIR.MEŠ). I would not even exclude the possibility that the addressed deity is Muwatalli's personal deity, the Storm-god of Lightning (*piḫaššašši*). As will be argued in Ch. XV, this Storm-god probably had eastern origins before he became the head of the pantheon of Tarḫuntašša.

The prayer begins with a confession of offenses and sins to the Storm-god.[352] Thereafter, several divine entities are invoked to dispel the Storm-god's anger: Ḫebat, [Šarruma ?], the gods of the lands (DINGIR.MEŠ KUR.KUR.ḪIA), the mountains, the rivers, the w[ells and the springs], Ḫuzzi (and) Ḫutanni, [ ], Heaven (and) Earth (AN.KI).

The body of the prayer consists of a systematic search for the cause of the Storm-god's anger and the king's solemn promise to make amends. The Storm-god might be angry with a local god (lit.: "god of a land") or with some geographical element (mountain, river, etc.). Another possibility would be that a complaint was transmitted to the Storm-god by an angry local god, a mountain, a *šinapši,* a holy pit, a throne, a stele, an orphan, or a poor man. The sin may also have been caused by the mistreatment of an oracle bird; by the pollution of the bread of the dead spirits; by some inappropriate words expressed by humans. Finally, the Storm-god may be angry because some "good things" were expropriated from Kummanni. The prayer concludes with a final appeal to the Storm-god to restore his grace upon the Land of Kummanni, which in its turn will offer to the gods an abundance of sacrificial bread and libation wine. The colophon identifies the scribe who wrote down His Majesty's words as Lurma(-ziti),[353] junior physician ($^{(\mathrm{LÚ})}$A.ZU.TUR), apprentice of [.....], son of Aki-Tešub.[354]

Besides the various theoretical offenses and derelictions, the only concrete wrongdoing mentioned in the text is the expropriation of goods from Kummanni (# 12; rev. 12-14). The ends of lines are unfortunately missing, but the passage may nevertheless offer some important clues on the historical background of the text:

mān ŠA KUR ^{URU}*Kummanni aššawa AWATĒ*^{MEŠ} *kī pešta našma=at=kan* ^{d}*/an*[-
našma ANA DINGIR-*LIM* ^{URU}*Arušna ḫalzaiš kinun kāša apedani memini ABI ŠA* LUGAL[
šanḫa ⌈*a*⌉*-ra-wa-an-na-aš-ša-ia* SISKUR *ŠA* DINGIR-*LIM* ^{URU}*Arušna* BAL-*anzi na=at*[

If he has given these good things of the Land of Kummani, and if a g[od(?) demanded (??)] them, and if he appealed to the Deity of Arušna, behold now! In that matter the king's father [is responsible; on him] take vengeance! And they also perform the *arawanna-* ritual of the Deity of Arušna. ...

pešta in l. 12 has usually been translated as a second person singular, but to my mind a third person makes more sense here.[355] I suspect that the person who gave (away) the "good things" (perhaps the temple property ?) of Kummanni is none other than the king's father who is held responsible in the next line. An offended god may have complained to the Deity of Arušna, a highly respected deity of Kizzuwatna,[356] who could have brought a calamity over the entire land. Muwatalli blames his father for this grave

352 The Hittite phrase – "...we confess (our) offense and sin (*ḫaratar waštulla*) to him" (i.e. the Storm -god)," recalls biblical formulations of confession, such as "we have sinned, we have done wrong, we have acted wickedly" (e.g., 1 Kgs. 8: 47; Ps 106: 6; Dan 9: 5); see Miller, op. cit., 252 ff.

353 The sign LÚ stands closer to the name and could be part of it, rather than the determinative for A.ZU.TUR.

354 A scribe Aki-Tešub (*Á-ki-TEŠUB-pa* SCRIBA) appears in the hieroglyphic inscription ALEPPO 1, dated to Talmi-Šarruma, a contemporary of Muwatalli. Could he be the father of the instructor who supervised Lurma's work?

355 Note that *CHD* P/1, 42 cites only this occurrence for a second person preterite; all the other examples (from older texts) have *paitta.*

356 For the Deity of Arušna see M. Forlanini, *Vicino Oriente* 7 (1988), 139, who locates this important shrine at Sirkeli, near Adana. According to E. Edel, *Biblische Notizen* 11 (1980), 67 f., the toponym *ʾrwsn* appearing in Egyptian topographical lists (after *Tnyw* = Danuna in Cilicia ?) is identical with Arušna. KBo 22.70, the oracle text dealing extensively with the Deity of Arušna, has been variously dated either to Muršili II or to Ḫattušili "III". See I. Singer, *Ugarit-Forschungen* 23 (1991), 330 f. (with further references).

offense and promises to make amends by appropriate ritual offerings. In this respect *CTH* 382 fully accords with a recurring theme in Hittite penitential prayers: the suppliant blaming his predecessors for various sins.

Both in this unique reference to a concrete offense commited by Muwatalli's father as well as in all the other more general religious offenses listed in the prayer, there is hardly any intimation of a disaster that fell suddenly upon the Land of Kummanni. Houwink ten Cate and Josephson (pp. 101 f.) have found evidence in the wording of paragraphs 4 and 6 "that the country had been severely damaged by a foreign invasion," which they would relate to "the Gasgaean attack which took place after the royal residence had been transferred from Hattusas to Tarhuntassas."[357] This would date the prayer to the period when Muwatalli already resided in his new capital. Without even raising the question as to how the text (one manuscript only) was found in Ḫattuša if it was composed in Tarḫuntašša, I would simply say that I see no reference whatsoever to a "foreign invasion" in the entire text. The relevant paragraphs speak about a general decline of the land (obv. 19), a neglect of its cults, and possibly some depopulation of towns (obv. 24, 36). Such a deterioration *could* be caused by foreign intervention, but could just as well be the result of deliberate or unintentional neglect of a certain part of the kingdom. I assume that this is what Muwatalli had in mind when he criticized his father's conduct and promised an improved maintenance of the Land of Kummanni and its important cults. If the subject of the prayer were a calamity caused by the Kaška, I would expect more direct references to it, just as in the prayer of Arnuwanda and Ašmunikal (*CTH* 375) which goes into extensive detail in describing the ravages inflicted by the Kaška upon Hittite temples in the north.

The well-being of the lands and their deities seems to be the connecting thread between Muwatalli's prayers. In KBo 11.1 obv. 11 he refers to himself as "lord/patron of the lands" (EN.KUR.KUR.ḪI.A). Houwink ten Cate (p. 121) suggested that this title may refer to Muwatalli's relation to the sanctuary of Kummanni, basing this idea on KUB 21.16 i 17 f., where Ḫebat of Kummanni tells Muršili that she had given to his father all the lands. I think that Muwatalli's epithet rather refers to his overall concern for the lands, not in a military sense but rather as their patron. He apparently saw himself as the benefactor of *all* the provinces of his kingdom, including those that had been neglected by his predecessors. "All the lands" and their gods are addressed at length in *CTH* 381 with the purpose of making amends for their neglect in the past. The meticulous listing of all the gods of the kingdom, both in *CTH* 381 and in KBo 9.98+ (see below), was in itself an expression of repentance for this sin of neglect. As will be tentatively suggested in the Epilogue, this sense of "opening a new page" in the relationship between the gods and the king, rather than military considerations, was the main reason for Muwatalli's transfer of the capital to the south.

If, as argued above, *CTH* 382 is dissociated from a Kaška attack, its dating within the reign of Muwatalli remains open to consideration. A paleographic[358] and linguistical comparison with *CTH* 381, on the assumption that both were written in the reign of Muwatalli, would hardly decide their relative order. In their structure they differ considerably: *CTH* 381 is a "model" prayer (see Ch. VII), with no confessions of actual offenses and requests; *CTH* 382 concentrates on the subject matter itself, and it lacks the hymnic invocations, the long lists of local deities and the ritual offerings. Nevertheless, there is a basic thematic agreement between the two prayers in that they both seek the reconciliation of the Storm-god with the "gods of the lands," i.e. with the local pantheons of the provinces and naturally with the king and his subjects. It is of interest to note that Muwatalli is the only Hittite king who dedicates his prayers to male deities only. Though in *CTH* 381 the entire pantheon is addressed, the three intercessory invocations are all addressed to male deities – Šeri, the Sun-god of Heaven and the Storm-god *piḫaššašši*.

[357] The idea that a Kaška invasion is alluded to in this prayer seems to originate with E. Laroche, *Prière*, 18. See also R. Lebrun, *Hymnes et prières*, 306.

[358] KBo 11.1 (found in Building K on the Büyükkale) is a large one-column tablet, written in a remarkably neat and confident hand. If it was indeed written from dictation, as indicated in the colophon, it demonstrates the high skill of the scribe Lurma(-ziti). I have not seen the tablet itself, but Güterbock's excellent handcopy enables some tentative observations. The scribe uses both the old and the new *li* in equal proportions (5: 5). The *ki* and the *ik* have the older forms, and the same applies to *qa*, except for one example (rev. 20) with three wedges. Note the exceptional form of *lu* in the name of the scribe. As for orthography, one may note the use of some late CVC signs (*gul, túl, šir*).

Finally, as aptly put by Houwink ten Cate and Josephson (pp. 103 f.), the two prayers share a common spirit of "meticulous precision," an almost obsessive preoccupation with covering all possibilities, a tendency towards perfectionism characteristic of Muwatalli.

Chapter XI: A List of Local Gods: KBo 9.98 +

KBo 9.98 + KUB 40.46 was listed by Laroche under *CTH* 212 as a fragment of a list of witness gods of a treaty or a protocol. In his doctoral dissertation Theo van den Hout correctly observed that the structure of this list closely resembles that of the long list of local gods in *CTH* 381 and suggested that the fragment may belong to a further prayer of Muwatalli, rather than to a treaty.[359] More specifically, since the gods of Tarḫuntašša are listed here but not in *CTH* 381, this could be a prayer composed after the transfer of the capital from Ḫattuša to Tarḫuntašša.

Van den Hout also drew attention in passing to KUB 57. 87 (Bo 521), a fragment containing a similar list of gods. A closer look at KBo 9.98 + KUB 40.46 and KUB 57.87 has led me to think that they could in fact join as the left and the right hand columns respectively of a single tablet. I asked Dr. Cem Karasu from Ankara University to check the fragments at the Ankara Museum, and he kindly confirmed to me (14. 12. 1994) that KUB 40.46 (Bo 1956) joins directly with KUB 57.87 (but is too thin to enable gluing them together). KBo 9.98 (372/n) was found on Büyükkale, near Building H (square u/17), and a find-place on the Büyükkale is also plausible for the two Bo-fragments.

Searching for more joins in the files of the Chicago Hittite Dictionary, I came across KUB 40.52 (Bo 5705) which shares the same structure. Dr. Karasu again confirmed (14. 2. 1995) that the fragment could belong physically to the same tablet, but without a direct join. KUB 40.52 was copied by H. Klengel as rev. iii and iv, but I would explore the possibility of a join with either side of the tablet.

Following are a tentative transliteration of these fragments and some preliminary comments. A more thorough study of the originals may provide improved readings:

obv. i (KBo 9.98 + KUB 40.46)

1 [^{d}]U[TU] ^{URU}TÚL-na ^{d}Mi-iz-zu-⸢ul⸣-l[a-aš

2 [$^{\text{ḪUR.S}}$]^{AG}Ḫu-ul-la-aš DINGIR$^{\text{ME.EŠ}}$ LÚ$^{\text{ME.EŠ}}$ DINGIR[$^{\text{ME.EŠ}}$ SAL$^{\text{ME.EŠ}}$]

3 [Ḫ]UR.SAG⸤^{MEŠ}⸥ ÍD^{MEŠ} ḫu-u-ma-an-ta-a[š *ŠA* ^{URU}TÚL-na]

4 ^{d}U ^{URU}⸤KÙ⸥.B[ABBAR-t]i ^{d}LAMMA ^{URU}KÙ.⸤BABBAR-ti⸥ ⸢^{d}ZA.BA$_4$.BA$_4$⸣

5 ^{d}L[i-i]l-w[a-ni-i]š DINGIR$^{\text{M[E].EŠ}}$ LÚ[$^{\text{ME.EŠ}}$ DINGIR$^{\text{ME.EŠ}}$ SAL$^{\text{ME.EŠ}}$

6 ḪUR.⸢SAG⸣$^{\text{ME.EŠ}}$ ⸤ÍD⸥$^{\text{ME.EŠ}}$ *ŠA* ^{URU}[K]Ù.BABBAR-ti ^{d}U pí-ḫa-aš-š[a-aš-ši-iš]

7 ^{d}Ḫe-bat ⸢^{URU}⸣^{d}U-aš-ša DINGIR.[^{ME}]$^{\text{.EŠ}}$ LÚ$^{\text{ME.EŠ}}$ DINGIR$^{\text{ME.EŠ}}$ SAL$^{\text{ME.EŠ}}$

8 ḪUR.SAG^{MEŠ} ÍD^{MEŠ} da[-pí-aš] ŠA KUR ^{URU} ^{d}U-aš-š[a]

9 ^{d}GAZ.BA.⸤A$^{!}$⸥.A ^{U}[^{RU}Ḫu]-⸤ú⸥-piš-na

10 ^{d}LAMMA ^{URU}Ḫu-u-[piš-na DINGIR.^{M}]^{EŠ} SAL$^{\text{! ME.EŠ}}$ DINGIR$^{\text{ME.EŠ}}$ SAL^{ME}[^{EŠ}]

11 ḪUR.SAG$^{\text{ME.EŠ}}$ Í[D^{M}]$^{\text{E.EŠ}}$

12 *ŠA* KUR ^{URU}Ḫ[u-u-piš-na ^{d}Mu-w]a-[at-t]i-iš(?)

13 ^{d}Mu-u-wa-a[t-tiš(?)/-talliš(?)

14 x [ ]x [

---

359 *KBo IV 10 + (CTH 106); Studien zum Spätjunghethitischen Texte der Zeit Tudhaliyas IV* (Doct. Diss. Amsterdam 1989), 60 f.

obv. ii (KUB 57.87 ii)

1 ⌜^{URU}⌝U-uš-ša ^{d}IŠTAR ^{URU}La-a-an-ta
2 ^{d}Ta-ru-up-ša-ni-iš ^{d}Mu-wa-at-ti-iš
3 ^{d}Pí-pí-ra-aš DINGIR.MAH̬ ^{URU}⌞Ša-ḫa⌟-ni-ia
4 ^{d}Na-wa-ti-ia-al-la-aš DINGIR$^{ME.}$[^{EŠ} LÚ^{M}]$^{E.EŠ}$
5 DINGIR$^{ME.EŠ}$ SAL$^{ME.EŠ}$ KUR.KUR.$^{ME.EŠ}$ ÍD$^{ME.EŠ}$ [ḫu-u-]ma-⌞an⌟-te-eš
6 ^{URU}Ḫur-ni-ia ^{d}GAZ.BA.A.A
7 ^{d}LAMMA ^{d}GAZ.BA.A.A DINGIR.$^{ME.EŠ}$ LÚ$^{ME.EŠ}$
8 [DI]NGIR$^{ME.EŠ}$ SAL$^{ME.EŠ}$ KUR.KUR$^{ME.EŠ}$ ÍD$^{ME.EŠ}$ ḫu-u-ma-an-te-eš
9 [^{URU}]Ḫu-piš-ša-na-aš ^{URU}Du-un-na-aš
10 [^{URU}Za]-al-la-ra-aš $^{ḪUR.SAG}$Ša-pa-ra-a[š-ša-na-aš]
11 [^{d}IŠTA]R[360] ^{URU}Ša-pa-ra-aš-ša-na-aš
12 [DINGIR-*LIM*] ^{URU}A-ru-uš-ša-na ^{d}U ^{d}L[AMMA$^{?}$]
13 ⌜^{d}LUGAL⌝-ma-aš URU $^{.f}$[^{D}Ḫu-u-la-ia-aš(?)[361]]
14]x[

rev. iii (KUB 57.87 iii)

x+1 -]te$^{?}$-e[š$^{?}$
2']x
3' Ḫe-]bat ^{URU}Šu-lu-p[a-aš-ša]
4' [DINGIR.$^{ME.EŠ}$ LÚ$^{ME.EŠ}$ DINGIR$^{ME.EŠ}$ SAL^{M}]$^{E.EŠ}$ KUR.KUR.$^{ME.EŠ}$ ÍD$^{ME.EŠ}$
5' [ḫu-u-ma-an-te-eš ^{UR}]^{U}Ša-pí-nu-wa
6' ^{URU}Ša-mu-]ḫa ^{d}IŠTAR ^{URU}La-wa-za-ti-ia
7' [DINGIR$^{ME.EŠ}$ LÚ$^{ME.EŠ}$ DINGIR$^{ME.E}$]^{Š} SAL$^{ME.EŠ}$ ^{URU}Ša-mu-ḫa
8' ⌜^{d}⌝LUGAL-ma-aš
9']-aš ^{d}U ^{URU}Ma-nu-zi-ia
10']-aš ^{d}Al-la-a-ni-iš
11' ⌞^{d}⌟NIN.GAL ^{d}U ^{d}Ḫe-bat

end of column

KUB 40. 52 rev. iii

x+1 ^{d}U ^{URU}⌜Ne⌝-[rik(a)
2' ^{d}Ta-ši-x[
3' ^{d}Da-z[u-wašiš
4' $^{ḪUR.SA}$[^{G}Zaliyanuš(?)
5' ^{d}Ti[-lipinuš(?)
6' KUR.KUR^{ME}[$^{.EŠ}$ ÍD$^{ME.EŠ}$ ḫumanteš ^{URU}Nerik(a)]
7' ^{d}U[
8' ^{URU}Ḫ[a-tenzuwa(?)
9' $^{ḪUR.}$[^{SAG}Ḫaḫarwa(?)
10' DINGIR^{M} [$^{E.EŠ}$

---

360 Cf. KUB 48. 93, 8'-13' (*RGTC* 6/2, 139).

361 Cf. H. Otten, *Bronzetafel*, i 67, 86 iii 45. So with del Monte, *RGTC* 6/2, 44, rather than ^{URU}*A-d*[*a-ni-ia*] as restored by Forlanini, *Vicino Oriente* 7 (1988), 135.

KUB 40. 52 rev. iv

x+1 [KUR.KUR$^{ME.EŠ}$ ÍD] ⸢$^{ME-EŠ}$⸣

2' [ḫumanteš ^{URU}U]-ra-u-na ^{d}U ⸢^{d}⸣[x]-x-x-x

3' [DINGIR$^{ME.EŠ}$ LÚ$^{ME.EŠ}$ DINGIR$^{ME.EŠ}$ SAL$^{ME.EŠ}$ KUR.]KUR$^{ME.EŠ}$ ÍD$^{ME.EŠ}$

4' [ḫumanteš ^{URU} -]x-na ^{d}UTU ^{URU}Ša-pu-ḫa

5']x ^{d}LIŠ.LÍL

6' DINGIR$^{ME.EŠ}$ LÚ^{M}]$^{E.EŠ}$ DINGIR$^{ME.EŠ}$ SAL$^{ME.EŠ}$

7' [KUR.KUR$^{ME.EŠ}$ ÍD$^{ME.EŠ}$ ḫumanteš ^{UR}]^{U}Ša-mu-ḫa

8' ^{U}]^{RU}Pít-ti-ia-ri-qa

9' ^{URU}Š]a-ri-iš-ša

10']x

11' ^{URU}Te-g]a-ra-ma

12]x

These fragments share with *CTH* 381 the recurring formula "male gods, female gods, mountains, rivers of GN." It is of interest to note, however, that whereas KBo 9.98 + KUB 40.46 uses the regular ḪUR.SAG$^{ME.EŠ}$ for "mountains", both KUB 57.87 and KUB 40.52 substitute the rare KUR.KUR$^{ME.EŠ}$ for it. This idiosyncracy establishes a strong bond between the last two fragments and apparently contradicts their join with the former. However, it is not impossible that the same scribe would substitute for it a synonymous expression in the second column of his tablet.

Another apparent difficulty in joining these fragments is the repetition of two of the toponyms in different parts of the tablet: Šamuḫa(KUB 57.87 iii 7'; KUB 40.52 iv 7') and Ḫupiš(ša)na (KBo 9.98+, 9 ff.; KUB 57.87 ii 9). I cannot explain these repetitions without a fuller insight into the text structure, but in view of both physical and thematic rapport between the fragments, I would tentatively suggest that they belong to the same tablet (or at least to the same text).

The most significant geographical observation is, as already noted by Theo van den Hout, the separate entry for the gods of the Land of Tarḫuntašša (i 6-8), which follows after the gods of [Arinna] and the gods of Ḫatti. The entry includes the Storm-god *piḫaššašši* and his consort Ḫebat of Tarḫuntašša (see Ch. XV). This most probably dates the text after the transfer of the capital to Tarḫuntašša. One recalls that according to KBo 6. 28, ll. 30-33, the gods of Arinna, of Ḫatti, and the Cedar Gods were also transferred to the new capital. If the latter are identified with the gods of Kizzuwatna, they would seem to be represented in KUB 57.87 iii 8'-11' by Šarruma, the Storm-god of Manuziya, Allani, NIN.GAL, Tešub and Ḫebat – probably constituting the entry of Kummanni/Kizzuwatna.

The entry of Tarḫuntašša is immediately followed by that of Ḫupišna, a city situated not far from the land of Tarḫuntašša (see Ch. XII). The next entry belongs to Ḫurniya, another neighboring land according to the Bronze Tablet (iii 48). More intriguing is the appearance of a "town (of the) River [Ḫulaya]", if indeed this is the correct restoration in KUB 57.87 ii 13.

Finally, it should be pointed out that the identification of this text as a prayer is entirely based on the parallel with *CTH* 381. It is of course possible that it represents another type of religious text, not necessarily a prayer. The main point of interest, however, is the very fact that these comprehensive lists of deities, arranged by their respective lands and towns, were "updated" after the sweeping religious-political changes introduced by Muwatalli (see further Epilogue).

Part Five

GEOGRAPHY and THEOLOGY

Chapter XII: The Long List of Gods

With 83 names, the list of local deities in the Muwatalli Prayer (i 37-iii 9) is probably the longest preserved list of toponyms in a single Hittite text. It has often been consulted in studies dealing with Hittite historical-geography, notably in Garstang-Gurney's, *The Geography of the Hittite Empire* (London 1959), which provides a full, but not entirely accurate translation of the list (pp. 116-119). Individual entries have been incorporated into G. F. del Monte – J.Tischler, *Die Orts- und Gewässernamen der hethitischen Texte* (*RGTC* 6), Wiesbaden 1978.

One purpose of the following observations is to try to delineate the geographical scope of the list, thereby providing some insight into the Hittite theological doctrine. The question to be examined is: where are the limits between "inland" and "outland" in the Hittite divine world, which is truly but a reflection of earthly conditions.[362] With this purpose in mind, it is not exact geographical locations that are sought here, but rather a rough tracing of the limits of the territory covered by the list. Besides the theological aspect, the emerging map may of course say something on the boundaries of the kingdom at a certain point in time, and thus provide a clue as to the date of the composition. A pivotal question in this respect is whether the text was written before or after Muwatalli's transfer of the capital to Tarḫuntašša.

Another basic question to be considered is the order in which the cities are listed. It has been noted by Garstang-Gurney (p. 116) that "the order in which the cities occur evidently depends partly on the status of the deities worshiped in them and partly on their geographical situation, and it is not easy in any given instance to determine which of these considerations has been decisive." Although an all-purpose key to deciphering the order of the toponyms is hard to find, it is nevertheless worthwhile trying to discern certain "clusters" of names along the two lines suggested by Garstang–Gurney. Before turning to these questions, a few general remarks on the composition of the list are in order.

Duplicates *A* and *B* (and as far as one can tell, also *C*) show almost full agreement in the names and their order of appearance. The only exception is found in the second paragraph (*A* i 40 = *B* i 7), where *B*' s ^{URU}*Tiwa* is replaced in *A* by ^{URU}*Šamuḫa.*[363] All other differences between the texts are basically spelling variants or very similar forms such as *Ikšuna/Ikšunuwa.*

The basic unit of a local cult consists of a male god, a female god,[364] a mountain and a river. The names of the gods are often indicated, but sometimes the entry merely consists of the recurring formula "male gods, female gods, mountains, rivers of GN." The names of eleven mountains are mentioned, but only of two rivers – the Maraššantiya (in the paragraph of Nenašša) and the Ḫulaya (in the Lower Land). The local cults usually relate to towns (^{URU}GN), more rarely to lands (KUR ^{URU}GN): Ḫatti, Išuwa, Kummanni, Takupša, Tegarama, Tupazziya (only in *B*), Wašḫaniya (only in *A*) and the Lower Land. Only one toponym is specifically referred to as both a city and a land: ... *ŠA* ^{URU}*Kummanni Ù ŠA* KUR ^{URU}*Kummanni.* In a few cases, a local god is included in a paragraph about another place, e.g., the Storm-god of Alazḫana is one of the gods of Ḫanḫana; the Lord of Lanta is a god of Ḫattina; the Storm-god of Neriqqa is one of the gods of

---

[362] See I. Singer, "The Thousand Gods of Ḫatti: The Limits of an Expanding Pantheon", *Israel Oriental Studies* 14 (1994), 81-102.

[363] For the significance of this variant see I. Singer, "The Toponyms Tiwa and Tawa", in Th. P.J. van den Hout and J. de Roos (eds.), *Studio Historiae Ardens: Ancient Near Eastern Studies Presented to Philo H.J. Houwink ten Cate on the Occasion of his 65th Birthday* (Istanbul 1995), 271-274.

[364] Laroche, *Noms des Hittites*, 275; Lebrun, *Hymnes et prières*, 54. The recurring formula DINGIR^{MEŠ} LÚ^{MEŠ} DINGIR^{MEŠ} SAL^{MEŠ} corresponds to DINGIR *pišeneš* and DINGIR *kuwanšeš*, a rare phonetic spelling in KUB 43. 30 iii 36 ff. See E. Neu – H. Otten, *IF* 77 (1972), 184 f.; O. Carruba, "Der Stamm für 'Frau' im Hethitischen", in P. Vavroušek, *Iranian and Indo-European Studies: Fs. Otakar Klíma* (Praha 1994), 14 ff.; H. G. Güterbock, "The Hittite Word for 'Woman' Again", *Historische Sprachforschforschung* 108 (1995). Irrespective of the controversial *kuinnaššan* (KUB 12. 60 i 24), the interpretation of DINGIR *kuwanšeš* as "female gods" is agreed upon by all.

Kaštama.[365] In the latter case the reason is obvious: Nerik was occupied by the Kaška, and its cult was carried on elsewhere (see below).

1. The Order of the List

The question of the order in which the list is presented has puzzled many scholars. It is difficult to assume that such an important theological treatise incorporated in a royal prayer would list the cult centers in a random order, especially in the opening paragraphs. A short while ago I still expressed my wonder over the fact that the capital Ḫattuša occupies a mere sixth place in the list and suggested that this may already reflect the transfer of the political center of gravity to the south (*Fs. Houwink ten Cate,* 273). After more intensive research into the structure of the text, I now believe that I have found a much better explanation for the order in the first paragraphs of the list.

It is easy to recognize that the gods in the first list of offerings (iv 4-44) correspond with those appearing in the first invocation (i 10-17), directed to the main gods of Ḫatti ("Short List"). I would now suggest that the beginning of the "Long List" of cult centers also conforms with this order, although the correspondence is more complex and elaborate (see Table 4 below). I will concentrate here only on demonstrating this shared order, whereas more in-depth comments on individual deities and cult centers will be given in the following chapters.

It is most convenient to follow the List of Offerings, where each deity (or divine category) receives a separate offering. The bold numbers (1 to 12) are based on this list. The first entry in the Long List is dedicated to the **(1) Sun-god of Heaven** and to the **(2) Sun-goddess of Arinna** and her court. (On the omission of the Sun-god of Heaven in the List of Offerings, see Ch. XIII). The next two entries are respectively dedicated to the **(3) Storm-god *piḫaššašši*** of Šamuḫa/Tiwa (see comment on i 40 f.) and of the Palace of the Grandfather and his consort. The Storm-god *piḫaššašši* is second also in the List of Offerings, but in the Short List he is missing because he functions as the main intermediary to these very gods, and *stricto sensu* he is not a god of Ḫatti (see Ch. XV). Next come three paragraphs which correspond to the **(5) Storm-god of Heaven and (4) Ḫebat** in the List of Offerings and in the Short List. First is the entry of Šamuḫa, introduced by the Storm-god and Ḫebat of Ḫalab. This is followed by the entry of the Valiant Storm-god and Ḫebat (of Šaḫpina/Katapa; see comment on i 46-49). The third entry has the Storm-god of Help and the Queen of Katapa. I assume that the connecting thread between these entries is the town of Katapa. These three Storm-gods must be conceived as corresponding to the Storm-god of Heaven in the other lists. The correspondence of the next paragraphs with the **(6) Storm-god of Ḫatti, (7) Storm-god of Zippalanda, (9) Šeri and Ḫurri, (8) male gods, (10) female gods, (11) mountains and (12) rivers of Ḫatti** in the Short List and in the List of Offerings is quite obvious. The Long List has two paragraphs with a detailed list of the gods of Ḫatti. (The role of the division line between the two is not clear to me.) Then follows the entry of his son, the Storm-god of Ziplanda. The next entry has a further "son of the Storm-god" , the Storm-god of the Army. I assume that by way of association another god of war, Zitḫara, was also included at this point. Šeri and Ḫurri are conspicuously missing in the Long List, but one may perhaps relate them to the Prominent Calf (*šarkuš* AMAR-*uš*) immediately following the Storm-god of Ḫatti (see Ch. XIV). Table 4 below sums up the correspondence between the three lists.

If the opening paragraphs of the Long List reflect the twelve divine entities of Ḫatti in the First List of Offerings, the Second List of Offerings, dedicated to "the male gods, etc... of all the lands" (KUR-*eaš ḫumandaš*), must correspond to the remaining entries in the Long List. There is a clear distinction in this text between "the gods of Ḫatti" and "the gods of all the lands", which appears to be based on importance rather than geography. I can see no other reason why the Storm-god of Zippalanda should be considered as a "god of Ḫatti", whereas other local deities in the vicinity of Ḫattuša (e.g. Ankuwa) should be "gods of the lands." The combination of the two groups constitutes the entirety of the Hittite pantheon.

[365] The same applies apparently to the Storm-god of Šaḫpina who is listed in the paragraph on Katapa (i 46 f.). However, there follows another paragraph on Katapa (with its well-known Queen), and I can only explain this duplication as an error in the first paragraph, probably caused by the close association between the two cults (see *RGTC* 6, 328 f.).

Thus, so far as the beginning of the "Long List" of cult centers is concerned, the perfect symmetry between all the divine lists in the prayer is clearly evident. What remains to be examined is the order of "the gods of all the lands", i.e. the bulk of the Long List. This is a far more difficult task, and the "bottom line" is that I cannot identify a coherent order for the entire list. Nevertheless, some recurring patterns grouping together "clusters" of toponyms may perhaps be discerned.[366]

I was first tempted to look for a repetitive pattern based on the order of the main gods of Ḫatti. The mooted "second circle" would open with Urauna because it has a cult of the Sun-goddess of Arinna. The next entries, of Kummanni and Šanaḫuitta, should then contain some reflection of the Storm-god *piḫaššašši*. Šanaḫuitta indeed has a cult of the Storm-god *piḫami*, who often appears together with the Storm-god *piḫaššašši* (see commentary on i 66 f.). For Kummanni the connection is less evident,[367] but perhaps the order has to be reversed, and Kummanni, with its important cult of the Hurrian triad, is in fact paralleled by the Storm-god of Heaven and Ḫebat. The following entries are associated with the Storm-god of Nerik, which could be a reflection of his "brother", the Storm-god of Zippalanda. But thereafter, a meaningful pattern is no longer evident. Although such a repetitive pattern may have served as a useful mnemonic device, I now have serious doubts about its validity here.

A few clusters seem to be governed by a shared deity: IŠTAR of Wašuduwanda and of Innuwita (ii 41 f.); Telipinu of Ḫanḫana and of Tawiniya (ii 43, 46); Pirwa of Nenišankuwa, of Duruwaduruwa, and of Ikšun(uw)a (ii 62 f.). It should immediately be added that not all the places that have a cult of IŠTAR, of Telipinu, or of Pirwa are listed in these clusters.

A phonetic resemblance may occasionally have served as an associative factor: Ankuwa is followed by Neniša(n)kuwa; Ḫakpiša appears after the entry which includes Ḫarpiša.

One case of clustering is clearly related to royal ancestors and institutions: the gods of the grandfather, the father, and the grandmother of His Majesty (ii 56 ff.) are followed by the House of Gazzimara, a well-known royal storehouse (*RGTC 6*, 205). I suspect that this whole chain was "triggered" by the preceding Ḫakpiša, a town which by the time this text was composed may already have served as the regional capital of His Majesty's brother, Ḫattušili.

The most common cause of clustering is obviously geographical proximity. To establish such "geographical clusters" convincingly one would of course need a much better knowledge of Hittite geography, but even in our present state of information several plausible cases may be presented. For small clusters one may refer to Ḫurma and Lawazantiya (and possibly [Pittiy]arik and Uda) in the Antitaurus (i 76 ff.) and to the places situated in the region of Nerik (i 68 ff.). A long cluster, or rather chain, may be the one started by Durmitta (ii 10; for location see n. 375 below), followed by the often recurring group of Nenašša, Ḫupišna and Tuwanuwa in the Tyanitis, possibly continued by a series of poorly known places (such as Arziya, Ḫurniya, Zarwiša, Šaḫḫaniya, Ḫarziuna, Šallapa), and ending (?) in the Lower Land. The "chain" apparently includes places that are situated generally south and southwest of Ḫatti, between the Salt Lake and the Mediterranean (see below).

Although geographical proximity is no doubt one of the governing principles in the list, clearly, this principle cannot be universally applied. E.g., Landa and Ḫattina are included in the same paragraph, and this has led scholars to search for both places in the Halys Basin (Garstang-Gurney, *Geography*, 22). Other sources, however, clearly indicate that Landa was located in the southern part of the Anatolian plateau (see com. on ii 50 f.). It should be reiterated that the search for some geographical rationale in this and other lists will become increasingly meaningful with advances in our knowledge of Hittite geography. In any case, it is my belief that we should not simply explain our failure to discern an order by assuming a Hittite lack of sense and system, and a rationale should be sought even if the results are for the time being quite restricted and tentative.

---

[366] For the existence of such "clusters" in other lists of toponyms, see H. G. Güterbock, *JNES* 20 (1961), 96; I. Singer, *AnSt* 34 (1984), 115 f.

[367] Unless one accepts the idea of a two-stage transfer of the capital, the first being Kummanni (see Epilogue). If so, the association with the personal god of the king may explain the connection. However, this is highly hypothetical, and I am not at all convinced by the mooted two-stage transfer.

Table 4: Comparative table of the three lists of divinities

	List of Offerings (iv 1-58)	Short List (i 10-16)	Long List (i 37-iii 9)
1.	^{d}UTU AN-*I* (only in *B* !)	^{d}UTU *ŠAMĒ*	^{d}UTU *ŠAMĒ*,
2.	^{d}UTU Arinna	^{d}UTU Arinna	^{d}UTU Arinna, ^{d}U Arinna, Mezzulla, Ḫulla, Zinduḫi, gods of Arinna, ^{d}U eḫelibi, ^{d}U šuhurribi
3.	^{d}U piḫaššašši	–	^{d}U ḪI.ḪI Ḫebat of Šamuḫa, gods of Šamuḫa (*A*) / Tiwa (*B*)
			^{d}U piḫaššašši, ^{d}UTU Arinna, Ḫebat, ^{d}U DU$_{6}$, gods of É.GAL ḫuḫḫaš
4.	Ḫebat	^{d}U LUGAL *ŠAMĒ*	^{d}U & Ḫebat of Ḫalab, ^{d}IŠTAR.LÍL of Šamuḫa *BĒLAT AYAKKI*, Apara, gods of Šamuḫa
5.	^{d}U *ŠAMĒ*	Ḫebat	^{d}U NIR.GÁL, Ḫebat, ^{d}U Šaḫpina, gods of Katapa
			^{d}U šartiyaš, SAL.LUGAL Katapa, gods of K. ^{d}U tetḫišnaš, ^{d}U$^{\text{ḪI.A}}$ ḫumanteš
6.	^{d}U Ḫatti	^{d}U Ḫatti	^{d}U Ḫatti, šarkuš AMAR-uš, ^{d}U KARAŠ, ^{d}UTU Ḫatti, ^{d}LAMMA Ḫatti,
8.	Šeri Ḫurri	Šeri Ḫuri	^{d}U & Ḫebat of Ḫalab of Ḫatti, Aya,Damkina, ZABABA, DAG-ti, Allatum, IŠTAR Ninuwa
9.	male gods of Ḫatti	male gods of Ḫatti	DINGIR.MEŠ lulaḫiyaš, Kupapa
10.	female gods of Ḫatti	female gods of Ḫatti	
11.	mountains of Ḫatti	mountains of Ḫatti	IŠTAR of Ḫattarina, Pirwa, Ašgašipa,
12.	rivers of Ḫatti	rivers of Ḫatti	$^{\text{ḪUR.SAG}}$Piškurunuwa, gods of Ḫatti Karzi, Ḫapantaliya, $^{\text{Ḫ.S}}$Tatta, $^{\text{Ḫ.S.}}$Šummiyara
7.	^{d}U Zippalanda	^{d}U Zippalanda	^{d}U Zippalanda, $^{\text{ḪUR.SAH}}$Taḫa, gods of Zippa.
			Zitḫariya, ^{d}U KARAŠ DUMU ^{d}U ^{d}LAMMA ^{KUŠ}kuršaš (^{d}LÍL), gods of Zitḫara
13.	male gods of all the lands	–	The rest of the Long List
14.	female gods of all the lands	–	"
15–16.	mountains & rivers	–	"
17.	Witness Sun-god	–	

2. The Geographical Extent of the List

The following survey seeks merely an approximate location of the toponyms, mainly those that are situated at the perimeter of the territory covered by the list.

The central Halys Basin is represented with well-known cult centers such as Arinna, Katapa, Zippalanda, Ankuwa, Tawiniya, Šanaḫuitta, Ḫattena – all of which must be situated fairly close to the capital. A clustering of neighboring place-names is not evident. Their order of appearance is apparently dictated by theological or political considerations.

The northernmost[368] cities in the Long List appear to be places that were firmly held by the Hittites during the reign of Muwatalli, before the transfer of the capital to Tarḫuntašša. As far as I can see, settlements of the Kaška or Hittite towns dominated by them at this stage are not represented in the list.[369]

The status of Nerik and its vicinity is, of course, a special case. As is well known, the city itself was lost to the Hittites for centuries until it was reconquered by Hattušili "III". However, its important cult was kept in neighboring places, and this is well reflected in the long list. The gods of Neriqqa are listed together with the gods of Kaštama, and so is Mount Zaliyanu which is closely associated with both cities. The next entry, with the Protective-god of Ḫatenzuwa and Mount Ḫaḫarwa, is defined as the gods of Neriqqa and of the land of Takupša. Kaštama, Takupš/ta and Ḫatenzuwa form a cluster of places located on the road leading to Nerik.[370] They probably served as the northernmost Hittite strongholds in an area constantly threatened by the incursions of the Kaška tribes. Ḫakpišša, the seat of Ḫattušili's sub-kingdom, whence his offensive for the liberation of Nerik originated, appears elsewhere in the Long List. Another northern town whose Storm-god was raised to a prominent position is Liḫšina, the location of which is still unknown.[371]

It is noteworthy that the twin provinces of Pala–Tumanna, beyond the northern course of the Halys, are missing from the list.[372] That this is not an accidental omission is further confirmed by the fact that none of the traditional gods of Pala (see *RGTC* 6, 297) is mentioned in the Long List. It might be that in this period the province, which as already admitted by Muršili, was "not a well-protected land" (KBo 5.8 ii 22 f.), had fallen prey to the Kaška hordes. But it is equally possible that the omission of Pala–Tumanna is based strictly on theological grounds, i.e., their gods simply did not count among the gods of Ḫatti. One may recall the old threefold division of Anatolia into Ḫatti, Pala, and Luwiya (Friedrich, *Die hethitischen Gesetze*, 91 f.). The gods of Luwiya, later Arzawa, are also not represented in the list.

In the northeastern Halys Basin the farthest places represented in the list seem to be Karaḫna, Ḫiššašḫapa, and Kuliwišna, which appear in two adjacent entries. Both Karaḫna and Ḫiššašḫapa were attacked by the Kaška, perhaps even occupied temporarily, during the reign of Muwatalli, but eventually the Hittites managed to regain control over both cities (E. von Schuler, *Kaškäer*, 54). The latter is listed among the provinces governed by Ḫattušili. The Storm-gods of Ḫiššašḫapa and Kuliwišna are listed in the same paragraph as the gods of the Palace of His Majesty (see commentary on i 42). Could this indicate that one of the two places had a palace erected by Muwatalli ?

Not very far from these northeastern frontier towns was situated Tapiqqa, identified by S. Alp with

368 For recent studies on the historical-geography of northern Ḫatti, see E. von Schuler, *Die Kaškäer* (Berlin 1965); S. Alp, "Remarques sur la géographie de la région du haut Yeşil-Irmak d'après les tablettes hittites de Maşat Höyük", *Fs. Laroche* (1979), 29-35; J.Freu, *Les archives de Maşat Höyük, l'histoire du Moyen Empire Hittite el la géographie du Pays Gasga* (Nice 1983); M. Forlanini, "L'Anatolia nordoccidentale nell'impero Eteo", *SMEA* 18 (1977), 197-224; "Le spedizioni militari ittite verso Nerik i percorsi orientali", *Rendiconti Istituto Lombardo* 125 (1991), 277-308. The latest studies have integrated the valuable new data obtained from the texts from Maşat Höyük.

369 For example, none of the Kaškean *tapariyalleš* listed in the Prayer of Arnuwanda and Ašmunikkal appear in the text. See Forlanini, *Rend. Ist. Lomb.*, 125, 285 ff.

370 See, e.g., the maps in Forlanini, *Rend. Ist. Lomb.*, 125, 307 f. in which these places are located south of Nerik (= Oymaağaç), with Ḫatenzuwa as the northernmost among the three.

371 I doubt that Liḫš/zina is situated in the land of Zalpuwa in the Pontic region (so *RGTC* 6/2, 95), an area which was never really regained by the Hittites.

372 Paliya has of course nothing to do with Pala; it probably should be located somewhere in the east.

Maşat Höyük.[373] According to the Apology of Ḫattušili (ii 48 f.), Tapiqqa was fortified (together with Anziliya) by Muwatalli himself. It is perhaps significant that Tapiqqa appears as the last place-name in the Long List, and it is immediately followed by the Storm-god of the House of the Tawannanna.

The Upper Land, beyond the eastern reaches of the Halys, is represented by Ḫurma, Šug(az)ziya, Tegarama, [Piti]yarika(?), and the important cult center of Šamuḫa. The gods of the Land of Išuwa, east of the Euphrates, are also considered as gods of Ḫatti for the purpose of the Long List.

Kizzuwatna is represented by its two foremost cult centers, Kummanni and Lawazantiya, and possibly further places in its northern part, such as Uda (see commentary on i 78 f.). I cannot recognize any places from the southern part of Kizzuwatna, in the Cilician Plain.[374]

Moving westward we arrive at the Land of Wašḫaniya, south of the Halys, and then Durmitta and Ḫanḫana near its western course.[375] Durmitta is immediately followed by the cluster of Nenašša (with River Maraššantiya), Ḫupišna, and Tuwanuwa, important centers of the Tyanitis. To the west of that cluster lies the Lower Land which appears in the list as a separate paragraph, including the Storm-gods of Ušša and of Parašḫunta, Mount Ḫuwalanuwanda (sic), and River Ḫulaya. This brings us to the question of the geographical correspondence between the Ḫulaya River Land and the future kingdom of Tarḫuntašša, the borders of which are described in detail in the Kurunta Treaty (Bronze Tablet) and in the Ulmi-Tešub treaty. Without delving into the complicated issues involved, suffice it to say that either way – with the Ḫulaya River as the Calycadnos/Gök Su[376], or as the Çarsamba Çay[377] – its appearance here can only mean that at least some of the territory of Tarḫuntašša is included in the Long List. In other words, the gods of the Lower Land are considered here as gods of Ḫatti. It is also quite evident, that at the time when this list was composed, a Land of Tarḫuntašša still did not exist as a separate geo-political entity. This conclusion gains full support when one compares this list with the partially preserved list in KBo 9.98+, where the gods of the Land of Tarḫuntašša are listed as a distinct group after the gods of [Arinna] and the gods of Ḫatti (see Ch. XII).

A cluster of place-names preceding the paragraph of the Lower Land – Ḫurniya, Zarwiša, Šaḫḫaniya, Paḫtima, Šaḫuwiya, Malitaškuriya, Ḫarziuna, and Šallapa – are probably all situated in the area of the central Anatolian plateau, the last two in its northwestern end, west of the Salt Lake. Most of these places, which previously had been very scarcely documented, are now attested in KUB 57, 87 (see Ch. XI), in the Bronze Tablet, or in both (see Forlanini, *Vicino Oriente* 7, 135 ff.). They seem to be located in the vicinity of the future state of Tarḫuntašša, some of them possibly inside its confines. Two further cults, those of Parša and of Innuwita, now appear, in close association with the state cult of Tarḫuntašša (iii 47-53), in the Bronze Tablet, where their exemption from the *šaḫḫan luzzi* duties is recorded. Although the details remain to be defined, all this seems to point towards a concentration of cults from regions situated southwest of the Ḫatti Land, perhaps anticipating the ensuing transfer of the capital to that region.

The results of this general geographical survey may be summarized as follows. For the author of this list of local deities, the Hittite Assembly of Gods comprises the deities of the central districts of the Hittite

---

373 *Fs. Laroche* (1979), 31 ff.; *Belleten* 173 (1980), 58 f.; cf., however, Ph. Houwink ten Cate, "The Hittite Storm God", *Natural Phenomena* (1992), 134 ff., n. 17.

374 Especially noteworthy is the absence of the Deity of Arušna, whose cult is rising to eminence precisely in this period. Muwatalli mentions this deity in his other prayer(s) (See Chs. X-XI). It has been suggested that Arušna be located at Sirkeli, near the famous relief of Muwatalli ; see M. Forlanini in O. Carruba (ed.), *Studia Mediterranea Piero Meriggi dedicata* (Pavia 1979), 168 ff.; cf. idem, *Vicino Oriente* 7 (1988), 139.

375 Durmitta has usually been located in the eastern Halys Basin (see, e.g., Garstang-Gurney, map 2 on p. 15), but according to KUB 48.105+KBo 12.53 (A. Archi & H. Klengel, *AoF* 7, 143 ff.; Forlanini, *Hethitica* 6, 48 ff.; del Monte, *RGTC* 6/2, 175) the province of Durmitta included, among other places, Ninaša, Uwalma, Malitaškuriya, and Kalašmita. The last two also appear in the Long List of gods. Kal/rašm/tita should be distinguished from the western land of Kalašma.

376 F. Cornelius, *Gescichte der Hethiter* (1973), 8; I. Singer, *AnSt* 34 (1984), 122 f.

377 J. Garstang, *JNES* 3 (1944), 14-37; Garstang - Gurney, *Geography*, 69 f.; E. Gordon, *JCS* 21 (1967), 81 with n. 29; M. Forlanini, *VO* 7 (1988), 149 ff.; D. Hawkins, The Hieroglyphic Inscription of the Sacred Pool Complex at Hattuša (Südburg), *STBoTBeih.* 3 (Wiesbaden 1995).

kingdom – Ḫatti proper (the Halys bend), the Upper Land, Išuwa, Kizzuwatna, and the Lower Land. None of the cults of the Arzawa Lands or the Lukka lands in western Anatolia is included in the list. The same applies to the territories extending east of the Upper Land and Išuwa. Even in north-central Anatolia, in areas situated relatively close to the inner core of the kingdom, the list extends only as far as does the Hittite presence, with the notable exception of the cult of Nerik. As for the south and southeast, the significant presence of Ḫurrian, Mesopotamian, and Syrian gods should in no way be interpreted as an extension of the Hittite Assembly of Gods into these distant territories. These gods were adopted into various Anatolian cults and throughout the centuries became integral members of these cults. They were not considered as "foreign" gods of Syro-Mesopotamian origins, but rather as representatives of their respective places of worship, first and foremost of the capital Ḫattuša.[378] Although the composition of this large Assembly of Gods had changed in the course of time, it was never identical with the territorial extent of Hittite rule. It rather coincided with a basic concept of the territories that were "inherently" Hittite and whose gods were consequently considered to be Hittite as well. This somewhat abstract notion, which was evidently clear to the Hittites themselves, is less flexible than one might expect. A clear example is Kargamiš, which by the time of this prayer was a Hittite city in every respect. Nevertheless, the city *per se* is not included in the list, although its goddess Kubaba is listed among the gods of Ḫattuša.

378 For the modes of adoption of foreign gods in Ḫatti see I. Singer, "The Thousand Gods of Ḫatti: The Limits of an Expanding Pantheon", *Israel Oriental Studies* 14 (1994), 81-102. For the attitudes towards foreign gods in Mesopotamia, Egypt, and Israel, see the articles of J. Bottéro, C. Zivie, and Y. Hoffman, respectively, in the same volume.

Chapter XIII: Sun Deities

As in the lists of witness gods in Hittite treaties, all three divine lists in this prayer ("Short List", "Long List" and "Offering List"; see table 4 above) are headed by the Sun-god of Heaven and the Sun-goddess of Arinna. The characterization of these deities usually conforms with what we learn about them from other prayers, but this text may provide some interesting insights on the relationship between the two.

In the preparations for the ritual two offering tables are placed on the roof, facing the Sun (^{d}UTU-*i menaḫḫanda*). When the preparations for the ritual are completed, the king goes up to the roof and prostrates himself to the Sun-god of Heaven, who must be conceived here as the celestial star itself (see Commentary to i 4).[379]

The Sun-god of Heaven and the Sun-goddess of Arinna appear together at the head of the invocation of the great gods of Ḫatti (i 10) and in the opening paragraph of the Long List, dedicated to the deities of Arinna (i 37-39). Besides the two solar deities, the entry also lists the Storm-god of Arinna, Mezzula and Ḫulla, the daughters of the Sun-goddess, and Zintuḫiya, her granddaughter. The entry closes with two Hurrian hypostases of the Storm-god: the Storm-god of Salvation (*eḫelibi*) and the Storm-god of Life (*šuḫurribi*). The connection between these Storm-gods and the Sun-goddess of Arinna is not self-evident, but it is worth noting that the Storm-god of Salvation (^{d}IM *ḫi-el-li-pí*) appears after ^{d}UTU also in the cuneiform legend of *SBo* I 38, a royal seal of Muwatalli. The fact that these Storm-gods are listed after the recurring formula "the male gods, etc." may show that they do not really belong to the regular pantheon of Arinna.

After the joint appearance of the two solar deities in these entries, it is all the more surprising to observe the "treatment" given to the Sun-god of Heaven in the ritual part. A scrutiny of the two duplicates provides a significant observation concerning the redactional history of the text and its theological background.

B originally opened the List of Offerings (*B* i 40=*A* iv 3) and the Long List of local deities (*B* ii 2=*A* i 37) with the Sun-goddess of Arinna. At some point, probably after he had already finished writing the tablet, he discovered (or was told) that he had omitted the Sun-god of Heaven. Lacking sufficient space, he inserted this deity in both places in small characters and had to content himself with a much abbreviated offering (*B* i 39; after *A* iv 2; see Commentary).

A, who probably had before him text *B* (see Ch. V), corrected only one of the two omissions. In the Long List the two solar deities open the first entry. In the List of Offerings, however, which was transposed to the end of the text, the Sun-god of Heaven is apparently missing. Unfortunately, the beginnings of the lines in the first entries are broken (iv 2 ff.), but I can hardly see where an independent offering for the Sun-god of Heaven could have been inserted. Unless a future join or duplicate will prove me wrong, I believe that scribe *A* simply did not follow *B*' s correction at this point. This could be a simple omission, but I would rather suggest that *A* had a good (theo)logical reason for omitting the Sun-god of Heaven from the List of Offerings, namely, the Witness Sun-god (*A*: *kutrui* / *B*: \ *ḫuwayalli* ^{d}UTU-*i*) who receives the last offering. Who is this Witness Sun-god if not the all-seeing Sun-god of Heaven himself or at least a hypostase of this deity? *A* must have realized this repetition of *B* and therefore did not insert a separate

379 Spelled *nepi(š)aš* ^{d}UTU- , ^{d}UTU *ŠAMĒ*, and ^{d}UTU AN-*I* (in *B*). For a recent study on the Sun-god of Heaven and his role in Hittite religion, see Ph. H. J. Houwink ten Cate, "The Sun God of Heaven, the Assembly of Gods and the Hittite King", in D. van der Plas (ed.), *Effigies Dei: Essays on the History of Religions* (Leiden 1987), 13-34.

offering for the Sun-god of Heaven.[380]

Besides the importance of these omissions and additions for reconstructing the redactional history of the text, they probably reveal something about the nature of the Sun-god of Heaven.[381] In his capacity as a universal, cosmic deity, his "geographical domicile" must have been quite obscure. I assume that the scribe, or rather the original author of the prayer, could not be clear as to just where the Sun-god of Heaven would "fit" into this list of local cults. He eventually inserted him in the most "natural" place, in the entry of Arinna, next to the most important solar deity of Anatolia.[382] Perhaps the vagueness of his territorial affinities may also explain the curious fact that the Witness Sun-god receives only one bread, whereas all the other divinities in the list of offerings receive three, or at least two loaves.

Whereas the Sun-god of Heaven may be somewhat "overshadowed" in the company of regular territorial deities, his real status as supreme judge of the world emerges in his invocation (iii 13-24). This short prayer repeats some of the motifs of the great hymn to the Sun-god (Ištanu), which, as often pointed out, follows Babylonian models.[383] The Sun-god as the "shepherd of mankind"[384] is originally a Mesopotamian concept, but the inclusion of the dog, the pig, and the beast of the field among those judged by him is a Hittite addition.[385] As in other prayers, the Sun-god of Heaven is asked to halt the gods wherever they are and to call them to assembly. The list of places to be searched has the appearance of a brief evocation.

The most salient feature in Muwatalli's address to the Sun-god is that the god is depicted rising from the sea (iii 14). This unparalleled expression has intrigued scholars from the earliest days of Hittitology, some seeking in it a distant echo of an original Hittite habitat somewhere on an eastern littoral. F. Sommer envisaged a Hittite homeland west of the Caspian Sea and consequently argued for a Hittite immigration from the east, through the Caucasus ranges.[386] A more "homely" geographical background was put forward by F. Cornelius, who pointed out that for a Luwian living in Cilicia Aspera a sunrise from the sea would have been quite a mundane sight.[387] Finally, A. Goetze sought the meaning of the metaphor in cosmology rather than geography.[388] Be that as it may, the fact remains that the idea of the sun rising from the sea is foreign to Mesopotamia, where the sun is normally depicted as rising from the mountains.[389] It remains then that the idea was either brought by the Hittites or was originally Anatolian. In favor of the latter possibility one could refer to the myth of Telipinu and the Daughter of the Sea where the deified Sea

380 This affects of course the general count of the offering breads, for which see Ch. IX.

381 I cannot dwell here on the complex issues involved in the identification of this deity and its sex. For the vast bibliography on the subject see A. Archi, *Fs. Otten*^{2} (1988), 12, n. 30; V. Haas, *Gesch. heth. Relig.*, 377 ff.; Ph. Houwink ten Cate, "The Sun God of Heaven", *Effigies Dei* (1987), 15.

382 Other local cults of a solar deity in this text are in Ḫattuša (i 50), Malitaškuriya (ii 33), Wašḫaniya (ii 48) and Ḫatti. A "Sun-god(dess) of the Earth" is venerated at Parša (ii 1).

383 E. Tenner, "Zwei hethitische Sonnenlieder", in F. Sommer & H. Ehelolf, *Kleinasiatische Forschungen* (1930), 387; O. R. Gurney, "Hittite Prayers of Mursili II", *Annals of Archaeology and Anthropology* 27 (1940), 10 and *passim*; H.G. Güterbock, *JAOS* 78 (1958), 239-241; *Some Aspects of Hittite Prayers* (1978), 131 f.; *AnSt* 30 (1980), 41-50; G. Wilhelm, "Hymnen der Hethiter", in W. Burkert & F. Stolz (eds.), *Hymnen der Alten Welt im Kulturvergleich* (*OBO* 131, Freiburg 1994), 62 ff.

384 Besides hymns and prayers, the Sun-god as "shepherd of mankind" also recurs in the Tale of Appu; J. Siegelová, *StBoT* 14, 22 f.; H. A. Hoffner, *Hittite Myths*, 64. For the problem of the origin of this legend see I. Singer, "Some Thoughts on Translated and Original Hittite Literature", *Israel Oriental Studies* 15 (1995), 123-128.

385 Güterbock, *JAOS* 78, 242. Cf., however, G. Wilhelm, ib., 67 f.

386 *OLZ* 1921, 200; *Hethiter und Hethitisch* (Stuttgart 1947), 2 f. . See also J. Puhvel, "The Sea in Hittite Texts", *Studies Presented to Joshua Whatmough on his Sixtieth Birthday* (1957), 228.

387 *Geschichte der Hethiter* (Darmstadt 1973), 224. Cornelius could personally testify seeing such a sunrise from out of the sea in October 1959. On the basis of a misreading of DUMU.LÚ.U$_{19}$.LU-*aš*, Cornelius (p. 223, p. 336, n. 3) was convinced that Muwatalli was born in a Luwian region.

388 *Kleinasien* (1957), 137 n. 4; see also G. Wilhelm, *RlA* 8 (1993), 3; V. Haas, *Gesch. heth. Religion* (1994), 143.

389 The legend of the hunter Keššì, which is generally considered to be of Hurrian origin, also shares this Mesopotamian concept: ^{d}UTU-*uš=kan kalmaraz uit* "the sun came from the mountain"' (KUB 17.1 ii 14; *HED*, 181).

swallows the Sun-god and releases him only under the pressure of the Storm-god and his son Telipinu (Hoffner, *Hittite Myths*, 25 f.). Although Muwatalli's explicit phrase has no parallels in Hittite literature, the imagery of a "marine" Sun-god is by no means unique. It is paralleled by a "Sun-god in the water" [390] and by the description of a figurine of the Sun-god with a fish on his head.[391]

---

[390] ^{d}UTU *ú-i-te-e-ni* (KBo 5. 2 ii 13); ^{d}UTU ^{d}*ME-E* (KUB 5.6 i 6, ii 14).

[391] J. Friedrich apud C.-G. von Brandenstein, *Hethitische Götter nach Bildbeschreibungen* (Leipzig 1943), 77. In a postcard sent by Friedrich from Leipzig to Güterbock in Ankara (27. 5. 1943) the former suggested the following interpretation of this passage: "Bei Lektüre Ihres Aufsatzes [*Belleten* 7, 1943, 295-317] kam ich nun gleich auf die etwas kühne Idee, dass mit den Fischen vielleicht die geflügelte Sonnenscheibe gemeint sein könne; die zwei Flügel ähneln ja schliesslich zwei Fischen und könnten von den Hethitern so umgedeutet sein (??). Was meinen Sie dazu? ..." (quoted with permission of Prof. Güterbock). Cf. H. G. Güterbock, "Hethitische Götterbilder und Kultobjekte", *Fs. Bittel* (1983), 206.

Chapter XIV: Šeri and Ḫurri, the Divine Bulls

The sacred bulls of the Storm-god seem to have caused some redactional problems for the scribes of both tablets, and their corrections may be valuable for determining the redactional history of the text and the character of these bovine deities.[392] First we shall attempt to understand how each of the two scribes dealt with the matter and then derive more general conclusions.

Text *B* refers to Šeri alone in the first two occurrences. In the Short List, in which the main gods of Ḫatti are invoked, the epithet of Šeriš is "the bull, the champion (lit.: "the one who steps in front") of Ḫattuša, the land" (*B* i 15 f.= *A* i 14 f.). We encounter Šeri again in the invocation directed to him (*B* i 34 = *A* i 33). His epithet here is almost identical: "Šeriš, my lord, the bull of the Storm-god, the champion of Ḫatti". He is asked to introduce (*tarkummai*) the words of the prayer to the gods of heaven and earth. In none of these passages does *B* exhibit any hesitation as to whether he should include Šeri's longstanding companion, Ḫurri. There is a discrepancy between Šeri's solo appearance in the Short List of deities and the joint appearance of Šeri and Ḫurri in the list of offerings (*B* i 67 = *A* iv 36).[393]

As suggested in Ch. V, the scribe of *A* had tablet *B* before his eyes. At some point he became aware of the "omission" of Ḫurri in i 14 and tried his best to cope with the problem, not quite satisfactorily. He first copied the name of Šeri[394] with an epithet similar to the one employed by *B*. Then he erased Šeri' s epithet and added Ḫurri (without case-ending) instead, leaving a long erasure in lines 14-15. It stands to reason that he corrected this line not immediately after writing it, but rather at a later stage, when he "discovered" the missing bull Ḫurri in the list of offerings. Had he been aware of the omission from the start, he could have written an appropriate epithet for the pair of bulls and then continued writing without any concern for insufficient space. The grounds for the correction in line i 14 apparently did not apply for line i 33 as well. The appeal is addressed to Šeri alone, and there is no sign of correction or hesitation in *A*' s handwriting. The reason, I think, is that the first occurrence is in a list of the great gods of Ḫatti which has a close correspondence to the ritual offerings (see Ch. XII), whereas the second is in a separate address with no parallels elsewhere in the text. Thus, a discrepancy was felt only where the exclusive appearance of Šeri clashed with the joint appearance of the two bulls in the offering list. It remains to be asked why did *A* not simply "eliminate" Ḫurri in the list of offerings, which would have solved the entire problem and would have provided a coherent treatment of Šeri throughout the text. Although I cannot confidently answer this question, it would seem that the pair of bulls was considered as a necessary divine entity at least for the sake of ritual offerings, and therefore scribe *A* considered it more expedient to correct the first list, even in a clumsy manner, than to renounce Ḫurri altogether.

Besides the important clues that *A*' s correction provides for the redactional history of the text (see Ch. V), it raises an interesting theological question: What was the relative status of each of the two bulls in Hittite cult and religion, and is there any diachronic development in their status? I can only offer here

[392] For Šeri and Ḫurri see, H.Otten, *Kumarbi* (1950), 22 ff.; E. von Schuler, *WdM*, 195 f.; V. Haas, RlA 4, 506 f.; *Gesch. heth. Relig.* (1994), 138, 319 ff.; 471 ff.

[393] *B* erased something before he wrote the first name, but I assume that it was the composite determinative DINGIR.GUD, which he used in the previous passages.

[394] ᵈ*Š[e-r]i-uš*. Is this indeed a scribal error , or did he perhaps attempt to construe a plural form of Šeri ?! This would have provided him with an optimal solution to cope with the "problem of the twin bulls", but I have no parallels for such a daring conjecture.

some very tentative thoughts which would need to be investigated in depth in a separate study. In Hittite art the two bulls seem to have maintained an equal footing until the end of the thirteenth century.[395] This text, however, suggests that Šeri assumed a more prominent role than his mate in religious doctrine. It is also remarkable that whereas Šeri is a constant participant whenever the two sacred bulls are mentioned together, Ḫurri is occasionally replaced by other names. In the Ullikummi myth Šeri(šu)' s companion is Tella,[396] whereas in Mesopotamian lists of deities a certain Māgiru is the other bull of the Storm-god.[397]

If indeed my impression that Šeri overshadowed his companion bull is correct, I wonder whether this has anything to do with the growing influence of Kizzuwatnean theological doctrines in which a holy triad plays a prominent role. Šarruma, the son of Tešub and Ḫebat, is aptly described in rituals from Kizzuwatna as "the calf of Tešub,"[398] a designation which is almost identical with the standard epithet of the sacred bull(s).[399] A superficial phonetic resemblance between Šarruma and Šeri may also have contributed to some assimilation between the two descendants of Tešub and to the partial suppression of Ḫurri. An intermediate form could be Šarrumanni, a dyad of gods who (together with Allanzunni) are asked to intercede for Puduḫepa before Šarruma.[400] Again, all this needs thorough verification, but if valid, it may help to explain another crux of this text, for which I have not been able to provide any other solution.

Another unsolved problem is the absence of the divine bulls from the Long List. As shown in Ch. XII, there is a close correspondence between the three lists of deities in the text - the Short List, the Long List and the List of Offerings. Each of the main divine entities of Ḫatti is represented, more-or-less in the same order, in the three lists. Yet in the entry of Ḫatti there is no mention of Šeri (and Ḫurri), unless he is represented somehow by the "Prominent Calf" (*šarkuš* AMAR-*uš*) who follows immediately after the Storm-god of Ḫatti (i 50). A refutation of this possibility based on the writing "calf" instead of the expected "bull" would lose its weight if the presumed association between Šarrumma and Šeri proves to be valid. In that case, the author of the list may have alluded to both the human and the bovine offspring of the Storm-god by using an oblique epithet applicable to both.

---

395 Šeri and Ḫurri are shown in Yazılıkaya no. 42 as the leaping bulls behind the Storm-god and Ḫebat; see, E. von Schuler, *WdMyth.* I,196; V. Haas, *RlA* 4, 507. I prefer this interpretation to that of E. Laroche, *Syria* 40 (1963), 285 ff.; *RHA* 27/84-85 (1969), 79,106, who identified both bulls with Šarruma, whereas Šeri and Ḫurri he saw in the bullmen nos. 28 and 29. (Against this identification see Otten, *Anatolia* 4, 34). In fact, I believe that the first two signs in inscription 42a (see *Syria* 40, 286), the god sign and the bull-head, correspond exactly to the cuneiform determinative DINGIR.GUD occasionally found with Šeri and Ḫurri (but never with Šarruma).

396 KUB 33. 87+ iii 16. H. Otten, *Kumarbi* (1946), 22 ff.; E. Laroche,*RHA* 26/82 (1968), 70; V. Haas, *Gesch. der heth. Religion* (1994), 91

397 R. Frankena, *Tākultu* (1954), 92 no. 75; Haas, *RlA* 4, 507.

398 ᵈU-*ubbi* / ᵈ*Teššubbi* AMAR-*ti* / *ḫubiti* ᵈ*Šarrumma* . For references see Laroche, *Syria* 40, 292 n. 1.

399 The only difference – "calf" for Šarruma , "bull" for Šeri (and Ḫurri) – which in itself is not an ontological one, might be further obscured by the close similarity of the two cuneiform signs (*HZL* 155, 157; note also that AMAR sometimes has the determinative GUD !).

400 KUB 15. 1 ii 28-31. See J. de Roos, *Hettitische geloften* (Diss. Amsterdam 1984), II, 11 f.; V. Haas, *Gesch. der heth. Religion* (1994), 472.

Chapter XV: The Storm-god of Lightning (*piḫaššašši*)

Although the prayer is addressed to the Assembly of Gods, the dominant protagonist in the prayer is manifestly the Storm-god *piḫaššašši*, Muwatalli's personal god. He is approached as the main mediator between his protégé and the Hittite pantheon. Before turning to the characterization of the deity in this text, it is necessary to deal with some basic questions concerning the etymology of his epithet, his origins and his role in the state cult of thirteenth century Anatolia.

As briefly summarized up by M. Forlanini (*Vicino Oriente* 7, 148, n. 91), there are two current interpretations on the origins of the Luwian epithet *piḫaššašši-*. The first is based on the interchange with the ideographic writing ḪI.ḪI-*(š)ašši-*, which provides the meaning "Storm-god of Lightning".[401] The second interpretation, based on the fact that the determinative URU is occasionally appended to *piḫaššašši-*, derives the epithet from an otherwise unattested toponym, "Storm-god of **Piḫašša.*" Forlanini joins the majority opinion which favors the first possibility, but he does not entirely rule out the second.

The first etymology has recently been defended by F. Starke (*StBoT* 31, 103 ff.), who supplied a full survey of the textual data, including the fresh evidence from the Bronze Tablet. Although the interchange *piḫaššašši-* = ḪI.ḪI was already clearly attested in the Alakšandu Treaty (see below), some doubts were raised because in (at least) one text the two names are listed next to each other: .... ᵈU *piḫaššaššiš* ᵈU ḪI.ḪI ᵈU *piḫaimi* .... (KUB 38. 12 iii 18' f.). However, as pointed out by Starke, this single divergence[402] should not be given more weight[403] than the solid evidence from the other sources, in particular the juxtaposition of the two Tarḫuntašša treaties: where the Kurunta treaty (Bronze Tablet ii 16) has *ANA* ᵈU ḪI.ḪI-*ašši*, the Ulmi-Tešub treaty (KBo 4.10 obv. 36) has *ANA* ᵈU *piḫaššašši*. The Luwian noun **piḫaš-*[404] developed, according to Starke, a wider semantic range which includes besides "shine" and "lightning",[405] also "powerful" and "courageous". Starke's follow-up of the root in first millennium dialects is beyond the scope of the present discussion.[406] The "lightning" etymology is also supported by iconographic and hieroglyphic

[401] For ḪI.ḪI = *barāqu(m)*, "shine, lightning" see, *AHw*, 106; *CAD* B, 103. The equation ḪI.ḪI-*ašši* = *piḫaššašši* goes back to Friedrich, *SV* II (1930), 84 f., 101 f.; followed by F. Sommer, *IF* 55 (1937), 294 f.; Laroche, *Dieux*, 109; H. M. Kümmel, *StBoT* 3 (1967), 84; Ch. Rüster - E. Neu, *HZL*, no. 335. Meanings other than "(flash of) lightning" were suggested by E. Forrer, *Klio* 30, 149 ("melt down metals"), and by A. Goetze, *JCS* 5 (1951), 72 n. 5.

[402] *CTH* 517 is a cult inventory of ᵈLAMMA of Karaḫna, probably composed in the framework of Tudḫaliya IV's religious reform. As correctly pointed out by Starke, in the Muwatalli Prayer ᵈU ḪI.ḪI and ᵈU *piḫaššašši* appear in two different entries (i 40 f.) and should therefore not be regarded as a further argument against the equation.

[403] Such duplications of the same name in enumerations must not necessarily be regarded as errors, but could just as well be deliberate repetitions to avoid any possible omissions, i.e. a sort of "pseudo-apposition". A similar case is the listing of KÁ.DINGIR.RA (Bāb-ili) and Šanḫara one next to the other in an evocation list (KUB 15. 34 i 57), which some have considered as an argument against the equation of the two names of Babylonia. See Güterbock, *Ugaritica* 3 (1956), 103 n. 3.

[404] ᵈU *piḫaimmi* has a similar etymological origin, but is a different deity, who is worshiped in Šanaḫuitta (see Commentary on i 66 f.).

[405] A similar meaning is suggested by F. Starke, *BiOr* 46 (1989), 655, for *ḫaršann(i)* ("Blitzstrahl, -bündel") which forms the epithet of (another?) Storm-god, ᵈU *ḫaršanašši-* . In addition to these Luwian stems, there is another Hittite word for "lightning", *wantema-* / *wantewantema-* , derived from the verb *wantai-* "to shine" (see iii 70).

[406] H. Bossert, *JKF* 2 (1953), 333 f. suggested deriving from this Luwian root Greek Pegasus, the winged horse,

evidence. The Storm-god is often depicted as holding a bundle of lightning-bolts, and the recently clarified hieroglyphic symbol L 200 (FULGUR), which stands for **pihassa-*, shows "a jag of lightning attached to either side of the Storm-god symbol."[407]

The second suggested etymology, which allows for a hypothetical toponym *Piḫašša (without necessarily rejecting the first etymology),[408] was squarely rejected by Starke (*StBoT* 31, 105, n. 280), who considers the few occurrences of *piḫaššašši*/ḪI.ḪI with URU as "fehlerhaft". But it is not that easy to dispose of this determinative, which appears in two of the oldest occurrences of the name dating to Muwatalli II. It is perhaps well to reproduce the evidence from three duplicates of the Alakšandu Treaty (*CTH* 76):

A (KUB 21. 1) iv 41: DINGIR. MEŠ (*sic*) ^{URU}*pí-ḫa-aš-ša-aš-ši-iš* *ŠA* SAG.DU [^{d}]UTU-*ŠI*
B (KUB 21.5) iv 46': ^{d}U ^{URU}*pí-ḫa-aš-ša-aš-š*[*i*]*-iš* *Š*[*A*
C_2 (KUB 21.4) iv 10: ^{d}U ḪI.Ḫ[I(-)[409] *ŠA* SAG.]DU ^{d}UTU[-*ŠI*

It seems that two of the scribes did consider *piḫaššašši* to be a toponym, whereas the third made use of the ideographic writing. Elsewhere in that text, which seems to record all the possible writings of this intriguing name, we find an opposite interchange:

A (KUB 21. 1) iv 2 f.: ^{d}U *pí-ḫa-aš-ša-aš-ši-iš* ...
E (HT 8), 9': ^{d}U ^{URU}ḪI.ḪI ...

All in all, the scribes who copied the treaty seem to have hesitated time and again between a determined and an undetermined form. The scribes of the Muwatalli prayer were more unequivocally in favor of the undetermined form, but in one case (out of twenty), *A* added an URU (iv 42). To account for these occurrences of ^{URU}*p.* in two independent texts of Muwatalli one would have to admit that the possibility of a toponym at least "crossed the mind" of scribes writing in this period. As far as I can see, this confusion does not recur in later texts. Keeping these data in mind before reaching conclusions about the etymology of *piḫaššašši*, we should first attempt to reconstruct the theological profile of this deity.

To the best of my knowledge, the Storm-god *piḫaššašši* is never attested before Muwatalli II. Clearly, this deity was "discovered" (not to say "created") by Muwatalli and was adopted by him as his "personal god".[410] In the Alakšandu treaty the king describes himself as "beloved of the Storm-god *piḫaššašši*,"[411] and a lyrical description of the mutual love between the king and his god is found in this prayer.[412] It stands to reason that this should be the embracing god shown on Muwatalli's seals (*SBo* I 38-41), but the hieroglyphic legend identifies him as the GREAT STORM.GOD (of) HEAVEN.

The question of when the connection between Muwatalli and the Storm-god *piḫaššašši* was established depends on the relative dating of Muwatalli's texts. The Alakšandu Treaty has traditionally been dated to the beginning of his reign because Ḫattuša still appears as the capital.[413] However, Houwink ten Cate has

who according to Hesiod's "Theogony" carried the lightning of Zeus. For this connection see now P. Frei, "Die Bellerophontessage und das Alte Testament", in B. Janowski, K. Koch & G. Wilhelm (Hg.), *Religionsgeschichtliche Beziehungen zwischen Kleinasien, Nordsyrien und dem Alten Testament* (*OBO* 129, Freiburg & Göttingen 1993), 48 f.

[407] D. Hawkins, "What does the Hittite Storm-God Hold?", in D. J.W. Meijer (ed.), *Natural Phenomena* (Amsterdam 1992), 71 ff. The sign appears in KARATEPE 297: FULGUR-*ha-sá.*

[408] E. Laroche, *Dictionnaire de la langue louvite* (1959), 81; *Les Noms des Hittites* (1966), 273; see also Lebrun, *Hymnes et prières*, 286. Laroche compared names like Ḫattuša-muwa to Piḫašša-muwa (A.A).

[409] The space on the column-divider could perhaps allow for a restoration ḪI.Ḫ[I-*aš-ši-iš.*

[410] *ŠA* SAG.DU ^{d}UTU-*ŠI*, lit.: "of the head of His Majesty"; Alakšandu Treaty, iv 2, 41.

[411] *NARAM* ^{d}U *piḫaššašši-* ; i 1, iv 29.

[412] There is nothing in the long invocation to the Storm-god *piḫaššašši-* (iv 25-76) that would throw light on the origins of this god and the circumstances of his adoption by Muwatalli. Naturally, Muwatalli proclaims that the god took him from his mother, raised him, and appointed him to kingship in Ḫatti.

[413] See, e.g., S. Heinhold-Krahmer, *TdH* 8, 164 and n. 204.

recently argued for a later date on the basis of other related historical documents.[414] The Aleppo Treaty (*CTH* 75), originally written by Muršili II and ratified by Muwatalli, does not mention ^{d}U *piḫaššašši* at all, and the same applies to Muwatalli' s prayer to the Storm-god (*CTH* 382).[415] I am not at all certain whether these data are decisive for an absolute dating of the texts, and one can easily fall into a circular argument. However, the adoption of the "new" deity, with all its theological corollaries, is intimately connected with the transfer of the capital, and the two events cannot be separated by many years. Such complex processes which affect many aspects of life do not occur overnight. I assume that the move was planned quite early in Muwatalli's reign (see Epilogue).

It is none the easier to establish the origin or the "homeland" of the Storm-god *piḫaššašši*. Even if one were to accept the existence of a place called *Piḫašša, one would still have to discover its location.

Perhaps the best place to seek the origins of this deity is in the present prayer, where he appears in two consecutive entries of the Long List of cult centers. In the first (i 40), ^{d}U ḪI.ḪI is followed by his consort Ḫebat of Šamuḫa. The paragraph refers to the deities of ^{URU}*Tiwa* in text *B*, of ^{URU}*Šamuḫa* in text *A*. I have dealt in a separate article with this curious variant, which is the only real divergence between the toponyms listed in the two duplicates.[416] It is clear that *B* has the original name, which is otherwise unattested. There could be a connection to Tawa, another *hapax legomenon*, the place where the Kurunta treaty was ratified. The location of both toponyms is unknown, but the fact that *A* corrected Tiwa into Šamuḫa could indicate a proximity between the two places. An eastern location for this obscure Tiwa and for the origins of the Storm-god *piḫaššašši* is also supported by his association with Ḫebat, here and in other texts (see below), and with the "Palace of the Ancestor(s)."

In the next entry (i 41 f.), the Storm-god *piḫaššašši*, the Sun-goddess of Arinna, Ḫebat queen of Heaven, and the Storm-god of the Ruin appear as the gods of the "Palace of the Ancestor(s)" (É.GAL *ḫuḫḫaš*). The juxtaposition of the two great goddesses does not necessarily indicate some sort of syncretism.[417] Any royal institution would naturally be associated with the Sun-goddess of Arinna, who grants royalty in Ḫatti. The only known consort of the Storm-god *piḫaššašši* is Ḫebat,[418] but of course, from this period on the two great goddesses became increasingly syncretized.

The "Palace of the Ancestor(s)" is a well attested religious institution connected to the cult of the deceased kings.[419] There could have been more than one edifice carrying that name in the kingdom, but the one mentioned here is no doubt the one located in the town of Šamuḫa,[420] which perhaps functioned as the temporary residence of Šuppiluliuma's father.[421] The appearance of the Storm-god of the Ruin as one of its gods may indicate that Šamuḫa had suffered some destruction, perhaps during an attack from

[414] *JEOL* 28 (1983-84), 68 ff.; but cf. J. Freu, *LAMA* (*Centre de recherches comparatives sur les langues de la Mediterranée Ancienne, Université de Nice - Sophia Antipolis*), 11 (1990), 15-28.

[415] Unless the unnamed Storm-god in this prayer *is* Muwatalli's personal god. See Ch. X.

[416] "The Toponyms Tiwa and Tawa", in Th. P.J. van den Hout and J. de Roos (eds.), *Studio Historiae Ardens: Ancient Near Eastern Studies Presented to Philo H.J. Houwink ten Cate on the Occasion of his 65th Birthday* (Istanbul 1995), 271-274.

[417] So V. Haas, *Der Kult von Nerik*, 110, n. 2, relying on the singular form of SAL.LUGAL,which should be applied in his opinion to both goddesses. Later the synchretism is clearly stated in the well-known prayer of Puduḫepa; see V. Haas, *Gesch. der heth. Religion* (1994), 386, 425 (with previous refs.).

[418] KBo 9.98+KUB 40.46 i 7 (see below, and Ch. XI). Ḫebat must be the Queen of Tarḫuntašša to whom a Hittite queen, probably Puduḫepa, addressed a prayer in her dream (KUB 15. 1 ii 45 ff.; Otten, *StBoT* 15, 10, n. 3).

[419] J. Friedrich, *SV* II (1930), 88 n. 2, 168; J. Börker-Klähn, "Ahnengalerie und letzte Dienste derer von Ḫattuša", in H. Gasche, et al. (eds.), *Mesopotamian History and Environment: Hommage à Léon de Meyer* (Leuven 1994), 361 f. Compare also the gods of the grandfather, the father and the grandmother in ii 56 ff.

[420] Cf. the ritual for IŠTAR of Tamininga which is celebrated in Šamuḫa in the É *ABI ABI* (KUB 12. 5 i 1 f.; *RGTC* 6, 340 f.).

[421] G. del Monte, *RGTC* 6, 341; see also Ph. Houwink ten Cate, "The Hittite Storm God", *Natural Phenomena* (1992), 133, n. 17.

Azzi.[422] The fact that the author of the text listed the "Palace of the Ancestor(s)" in a separate entry, with separate deities, rather than including it within the paragraph relating to Šamuḫa, may perhaps indicate that this prestigious institution had some sort of autonomous status. The association of the Storm-god *piḫaššašši* and his consort with it must have carried considerable religious-political weight. Whether the connection was real or tailored to serve Muwatalli's plans is hard to know, but, as mentioned above, there is no evidence for the cult of the Storm-god *piḫaššašši* before Muwatalli's reign.

According to Ḫattušili's well-known account, Muwatalli took the gods of Arinna, the gods of Ḫatti/Ḫattuša, and the "Cedar gods" (DINGIR^{MEŠ} ^{GIŠ}ERIN-aš) down to the Lower Land (KUB 6. 29, 30-33). The "Cedar gods" must be the gods of Kizzuwatna and other southeastern lands,[423] and they could very well include the Storm-god *piḫaššašši* and his consort Ḫebat. The two appear as the patron gods of the Land of Tarḫuntašša in KBo 9. 98+KUB 40. 46 i 6-9, possibly a late prayer of Muwatalli (see Ch. XI).

When Urḫi-Tešub moved the capital back to Ḫattuša, he also restored the gods to their "homelands." Although none of the relevant texts (see *RGTC* 6, 468) specifies which of the gods were taken back to Ḫatti, I assume that the Storm-god *piḫaššašši* remained in his new abode. He appears as the patron god of Tarḫuntašša in the Kurunta and in the Ulmi-Tešub treaties.[424] Significantly enough, in neither treaty is the list of divine witnesses divided between the two contracting parties as is customary in vassal treaties. Rather, in both cases the list consists of one long entry concluding with "male gods, etc. .... of the Land of Ḫatti and of the Land of Tarḫuntašša" (BronzeTablet iv 4). The Storm-god *piḫaššašši* occupies here a "modest" place at the end of the list of Storm-gods.[425] His role as the main god of Tarḫuntašša is disclosed in another paragraph, which deals with exemption from *šaḫḫan luzzi* duties: .... *ANA* ^{d}U *piḫaššašši* ^{d}*Šarrumma* DUMU ^{d}IM *Ù ANA* DINGIR.MEŠ ^{URU} ^{d}U-*tašša ḫumandaš* ... (iii 67 f.). The editor of the text, H. Otten, commented that Šarruma, the son of the Storm-god, appears here in his capacity as Tudḫaliya's personal deity (*Bronzetafel*, p. 52). This may be so, but I would not exclude the possibility that Šarruma was also a god of Tarḫuntašša,[426] forming with his parents, the Storm-god and Ḫebat, a typical Hurrian triad, as found in Kummanni and other cult centers of Kizzuwatna.[427] A fragmentary religious text may support this inference:[428] A king worships six divine entities, the first of which is the Storm-god *piḫaššaššin* and the fourth *šarkun* AMAR[-*un*], "Prominent Calf", which may very well be an epithet for Šarruma (see Ch. XIV). Another deity in the pantheon of Tarḫuntašša was probably the Moon-god (KUB 56.13 rev. 23), and there may have been many more.

Once established, the cult of the Storm-god *piḫaššašši* was embraced not only in Tarḫuntašša, but in other parts of Anatolia as well. In the Bronze Tablet, Tudḫaliya exempts from taxes all the places belonging to the Storm-god *piḫaššašši* (and to two other deities) which are situated in other lands, including Ḫatti and Kizzuwatna (iii 47 ff.; *RGTC* 6/2, 44).

---

[422] According to the so-called "concentric invasion" into the Ḫatti lands (KBo 6. 28 obv. 11 f.) the enemy from Azzi attacked the Upper Lands and established his border at Šamuḫa.

[423] The "Cedar gods" are closely connected with the *šinapši*, a cult edifice often appearing in Kizzuwatnean rituals. See F. Gentili Pieri, "L'edificio 'šinapši' nei rituali Ittiti", *Atti Acc. Tosc.* 47 (1982), 21 ff.

[424] D. Hawkins, "What does the Hittite Storm-God Hold?", in D. J.W. Meijer (ed.), *Natural Phenomena*, Amsterdam 1992, 72 f.

[425] In the Bronze Tablet the Storm-god *piḫaššašši-* is written phonetically after ^{d}U NIR.GÁL (iii 86). KBo 4. 10 obv. 53 has an interesting ^{d}U ^{m}NIR.GÁL(sic), followed by ^{d}U *piḫaimmiš* and ^{d}U ḪI.ḪI-*aššiš*. The addition of ^{d}U *piḫaimmi-* here was probably due to the phonetic similarity, but it should not obscure the clear equation between ḪI.ḪI and *piḫaššašši-*. For ^{d}U *piḫaimmi-* see commentary to i 66 f.

[426] So also V. Haas, *Gesch. der heth. Religion* (1994), 326 n. 85.

[427] For the centers of the cult of Ḫebat and Šarrumma in Kizzuwatna see Laroche, *Syria* 40 (1963), 277-302; on the map showing the distribution of the cult of Šarruma in the imperial period (p. 297) one may now add an arrow leading to Tarḫuntašša in the southwest.

[428] KBo 22. 169, 1' [LUGAL-u]š-ká[n $^{G]IŠ⌈}$DAG-ti⌉ [kat-ta(?)] (2') [t]i-ia-zi nu VI ir-ḫa-⌈a⌉-i[z-zi] (3') ^{d}U pí-ḫa-aš-ša-aš-ši-in DINGIR^{MEŠ} [LÚ^{MEŠ}(?)] (4') [ḫ]u-u-ma-an-te-eš ḪUR.SAG$^{ḪI.A}$ ÍD[^{MEŠ}] (5') [ḫ]u-u-ma-an-te-eš šar-ku-un AMAR[-un] (6') [ ]x^{MEŠ} ḫu-u-ma-an-te-eš ^{d}Pí-iš-ti-x[ ] (7') [ir]-ḫa-a-iz-zi..

A list of *nakkušši*-offerings pledged by Urḫi-Tešub to various towns mentions the Storm-god *piḫaššašši* in the paragraph relating to Gaštama.[429] In another fragmentary list of deities the Storm-god *piḫaššašši* appears after the Mighty Goddess (DINGIR.MAḪ) and the Storm-god of the Palace (^{d}U É. GAL) and before the Storm-god of the Army (KBo 17. 79, 4'; Lebrun, *Šamuḫa*, 183). The 18th and the 19th days of the AN.TAḪ.ŠUM-festival (*CTH* 613) are entirely dedicated to the Storm-god *piḫaššašši*; he receives offerings together with the Sun-goddess of Arinna.[430] The two deities may be regarded as representative of their respective lands: Tarḫuntašša and Ḫatti.

In conclusion, the Storm-god *piḫaššašši* first appears in the reign of Muwatalli as the king's patron deity. Later he becomes the main god of the new capital, Tarḫuntašša. His geographical and theological origins remain obscure, but to judge by his consort Ḫebat and (probably) their son Šarruma, the top of the Tarḫuntaššan pantheon was at least modelled after, if not directly adopted from the Hurrian cult centers of Kizzuwatna and the Upper Land. The Storm-god *piḫaššašši* may himself be a hypostase of the Hurrian Storm-god Tešub, but his name was no doubt the Luwian Tarḫunta, from which derives the name of his newly built abode, the city of Tarḫuntašša. There is conclusive evidence connecting his epithet *piḫaššašši* to a Luwian designation for "lightning" (or "shining"), but this does not necessarily exclude the possible existence of a toponym *Piḫašša. As tentatively proposed by M. Forlanini (*Vicino Oriente* 7, 148 n. 91), Muwatalli may have converted a small sanctuary in a remote place in the Lower Land into his new capital and renamed it after his patron Storm-god. An obvious Near Eastern analogy would be Akhenaton's transfer of his capital to a remote place in Middle Egypt and its christening in honor of his patron deity.

---

[429] KUB 54. 70, 6' [*M*]*A-ME-TUM* ^{M}Ur-ḫi-^{d}U ^{URU}Ga-aš-ta-ma *ŠA* ^{d}U ^{URU}G[a-aš-ta-ma] (7') [^{d}Za-a]ḫ-pu-na-ia ^{d}UTU ^{URU}TÚL-na ^{d}IŠTAR ^{URU}Ša-mu-ḫa[ ] (8') [ ]x ⸢^{d}⸣U pí-ḫa-aš-ša-aš-ši *A-NA* DINGIR^{MEŠ}-ia [ ] (9') [na-ak-ku-uš-š]i-uš tar-na-an-zi 1 UDU na-a[k-ku-uš-ši-in] (10') [ ]x *A-NA* DINGIR^{MEŠ} [

[430] The two receive offerings together also in VAT 13016 (cited by V. Haas, *Gesch. der heth. Religion*, 326), but not necessarily as a divine couple.

Epilogue: From Ḫattuša to Tarḫuntašša

The question of the dating of *CTH* 381 has been tackled at several junctures in this monograph. In dealing with the text's redactional history (Ch. V), arguments were advanced to the effect that both main manuscripts were written during the reign of Muwatalli. The geographical-historical analysis of the Long List of cult centers (Ch. XII) points to evidence that the text was composed before the transfer of the capital to Tarḫuntašša. The main argument is the very fact that Tarḫuntašša itself does not appear in the list, whereas the River Ḫulaya, which in one way or another must be located within the territory of the kingdom of Tarḫuntašša, is listed here in the entry of the Lower Land. This conclusion is underlined by KBo 9.98+ , a similar but later list of cult centers, in which the gods of Tarḫuntašša appear as a distinctive unit in a prominent place (Ch. XI).

Even though *CTH* 381 is plausibly dated before the transfer of the capital to Tarḫuntašša, the text may still contain some clues anticipating this important event in Hittite history. In the geographical discussion (Ch. XII. 2), attention was drawn to a series of rare toponyms, some of which recur in KBo 9.98+ and in the Bronze Tablet (Ḫurniya, etc.). Several of these places were probably located in the central Anatolian plateau, bordering on the future kingdom of Tarḫuntašša. This cluster of south-central cult centers may perhaps reflect hightened interest on the part of the text's author in this poorly explored area of Hittite Anatolia. Needless to add, the Storm-god of Lightning (*piḫaššašši*), Muwatalli's personal god and the future patron god of Tarḫuntašša, already plays a prominent role in the prayer. At this stage, however, he and his consort Ḫebat are still associated with Šamuḫa and Tiwa (see Ch. XV).

The tantalizing subject of the transfer of the capital is beyond the scope of this monograph. I hope to return to it at some future date (preferably after the discovery of Tarḫuntašša...), but I would like to venture here a few preliminary thoughts.

Having focused on Muwatalli's age in general and on his religious texts in particular, I have gradually come to entertain serious doubts about the universally prevailing view which explains Muwatalli's move in terms of military strategy – the Kaška threat[431] and the desirability of greater proximity to the western Anatolian and Egyptian fronts.[432] True, the deep incursions of the Kaška hordes into Hittite territories did pose a serious threat to Ḫattuša, especially at a time when the bulk of the Hittite army was engaged in Syria. But the Kaška were a chronic problem, and none of the previous kings ever ventured a permanent dislocation of his capital, even in more critical situations (e.g., Arnuwanda and Ašmunikal). In his sound evaluation of the sources on the Kaška, E. von Schuler advised caution in dealing with this period (*Kaškäer*, 53). Practically all sources are attributed to Ḫattušili, who had a vested interest in overstating the Kaška danger and his own contribution to the defense of Ḫatti. As pointedly put by A. Goetze (*CAH*[3] II/2A, 128), "the so-called Kaskean War can hardly have been more than an annoying series of small-scale raids and counter-raids." The number of chariots engaged at any one time in the battles against the Kaška rarely exceeded a few dozen.[433] Would an emperor, who on the eve of the Battle of Qadesh mustered a formidable army of 37,000 infantry and 3,500 chariots,[434] abandon his capital in fear of a Kaška attack? Besides, if the main objective were to flee the Kaška and to get closer to the Egyptian front, why bother building a new city if one could more easily move one's forces to an already existing stronghold in Kizzuwatna or northern Syria? Unless, of course, the effort of building a new capital concurred with a

[431] E.g., A. Goetze, *CAH*[3] II/2A, 129; H. Otten, *Fischer Weltgeschichte* II (1966), 154; K. Bittel, *Hattuscha* (1983), 30.

[432] E.g., Otten, op.cit.; F. Cornelius, *Geschichte der Hethiter* (1973), 224 ; J. G. Macqueen, *The Hittites*[2] (1988), 55; O. R. Gurney, *The Hittites* (1990), 28. E. von Schuler , *Kaškäer* (1965), 55, adds to the strategic considerations Muwatalli's sympathy for Luwian-speaking regions.

[433] E. von Schuler, *Kaškäer*, 73 ff.

[434] For the Egyptian data on the size of the Hittite army, see W. Helck, *Die Beziehungen Ägyptens zu Vorderasien im 3. und 2. Jahrtausend v. Chr.*[2] (1971), 205 f.

"grand plan" inspired by other motivations. Incidentally, there is nothing in the texts[435] or in the archaeological record[436] to prove that Ḫattuša was overrun by the Kaška in the age of Muwatalli.[437]

Capital cities looking back at a long history, tradition, and sanctity are rarely abandoned for reasons of military strategy. Throughout the ages, and especially in antiquity, the transfer of a capital was usually associated with fundamental religious, ideological, or political motivations, a deliberate break with the past in order to start anew in a new location. Akhetaten (Tell el-Amarna) is the showpiece example,[438] but an ideological dimension can easily be discerned in other cases of transfer of a capital city.[439] I think that the move to Tarḫuntašša was no exception to the rule.

While many of Ḫattušili's statements require critical evaluation, the basic fact that he was appointed by his brother to rule the northern provinces, practically half of the kingdom, is beyond any doubt. Although this unprecedented decision eventually led to civil war and to the partition of the Hittite kingdom, it was no doubt a carefully premeditated move, part of a "grand plan" conceived by Muwatalli from the beginning of his reign. It was a conscious choice of a southern orientation, replacing the traditional northern (the Ḫatti Land) and northeastern (Šamuḫa) focus of the Hittite monarchy. That the transfer of the capital was intended to be permanent is shown by the fact that Muwatalli took with him the main gods and the *manes* of the royal family. What would cause a Hittite king to abandon the centuries-old hub of the Hittite state and religion and build a new capital? Perhaps one day autobiographical texts of Muwatalli will be discovered, but until then we can only speculate about his motivations.

Ḫatti in the age of Muwatalli was still recovering from the terrible calamity of the plague which decimated the population for several decades. Muršili's Plague Prayers provide a vivid picture of the incessant attempts to discover the causes of the gods' anger (Ch. VIII). It would have seemed to the Hittites that one of their gravest offenses was the violation of their treaty with Egypt, guaranteed by the Storm-god. Now another war against Egypt was imminent and the support of the Storm-god was indispensable.

The transgression against Egypt was not the only offense committed against the Storm-god. Perhaps even more severe were the sins admitted to in *CTH* 382 (Ch. XI). In this confession and penitence Muwatalli lists a series of cultic transgressions amounting to a general neglect of Kummanni/Kizzuwatna. The offended gods of the land, first and foremost the Storm-god, are implored to restore their benediction. In return Muwatalli takes a solemn vow to make amends for sins of the past, including his father's expropriation of "good things" from the gods of Kummanni.

In this state of mind of deep remorse for sins committed against the Storm-god over a long period of time, the ultimate way to appease the angry god would have been to leave behind the scene of the sinful past and to begin a new chapter of cooperation in a newly founded capital dedicated to the Storm-god. There are other, more trivial indications that Muwatalli kept his promise to the gods and meticulously restored former cults in southern Anatolia. Despite the scarcity of information relating to his reign, we do find Muwatalli's name associated in later sources with religious reforms, some of them in the south.[440] He

---

435 For possible Kaška attacks on Ḫattuša in earlier periods, see E. von Schuler, *Kaškäer*, 34.

436 K. Bittel, *Hattusha, the Capital of the Hittites* (1970), 88; *Hattuscha, Hauptstadt der Hethiter* (1983), 130.

437 As unequivocally stated, e.g., by R. Lebrun, *Hymnes et prières*, 32, n. 22; "Observations sur la prière hittite" (1980), 41: "...brutale invasion des Gasgas qui endommagea notamment Hattusa et obligea donc la famille royale à fuir en emportant l'essentiel de l'appareil cultuel."

438 See, e.g., C. Aldred, "The Horizon of the Aten", *Journal of Egyptian Archaeology* 62 (1976); D. . Redford, *Akhenaten, the Heretic King* (*Princeton* 1984), 139 ff. For the founding of Piramesse, the delta residence of 19th dynasty pharaohs, and the revival of the cult of Seth, see, e.g., E. P. Uphill, *JNES* 27 (1968), 291-316; *JNES* 28 (1969), 15-39; *The Temples of Per Ramesses* (Warminster 1984).

439 See, e.g., H. Tadmor, B. Landsberger & S. Parpola, "The Sin of Sargon and Sennacherib's Last Will", *State Archives of Assyria Bulletin* III/1 (1989), 3-51, (esp. p. 29), on the circumstances of Sennacherib's abandonment of Dur-Šarruken and the transfer of the capital to Niniveh.

440 See Ph. Houwink ten Cate, "The Hittite Storm God", *Natural Phenomena* (1992), 102, 139, n. 40.

augmented the offerings for the cult of the Storm-god of Ḫalab,[441] for the *ḫišuwaš* festival,[442] and for a festival celebrated in Utruna.[443] Muwatalli is also mentioned in a fragmentary text describing some military expedition to, or more probably passing through, the Land of Kummanni.[444]

Muwatalli's role in expanding the southern element in the state cult has been somewhat overshadowed by the fame of Puduḫepa, a native Kizzuwatnean generally considered to be the great promoter of Kizzuwatnean traditions. As a matter of fact, an overall view of the religious life in the era of Puduḫepa and Ḫattušili may show that the state cult focused primarily on IŠTAR/Šaušga of Šamuḫa and the Storm-god of Nerik and only to a much lesser extent on the great cult centers of Kizzuwatna. At any rate, it is time to reassess the religious developments in the late Hittite Empire, giving Muwatalli his due. His strong bond to Kizzuwatna is epitomized by his only known rock monument, the relief at Sirkeli on the River Ceyhan, north of Adana. Perhaps the new excavations at the site will throw light on the the nature of this monument[445] and on the poorly documented age of Muwatalli.

To conclude this brief and tentative epilogue, I would reassert that the transfer of the capital to Tarḫuntašša must be viewed in the larger context of Muwatalli's religious reforms. Strategic considerations may also have played some role, but on the whole I would concur with Ḫattušili's statement that Muwatalli moved his capital "at the command of his god" (*Ḫatt.* i 75 f.).

---

441 *CTH* 698: KBo 14.142 iii 31-34; KBo 26.183 iii 5-7. See V. Souček & J. Siegelová, *ArOr* 42 (1974), 45; G. del Monte, *RGTC* 6, 489.

442 *CTH* 628: KBo 20.106+KBo 34.181 v 4'-7', 10'-12'. See *CHD*, L-N, 363; V. Haas & I. Wegner, *OLZ* 89 (1994), 273.

443 *CTH* 525.7: KUB 42.100 i 17'-19', iii 32', iv 38'. See G. del Monte, *OrAnt* 17 (1978), 182, 186.

444 KBo 22.11. This fragment is quoted by Houwink ten Cate, *JEOL* 28 (1983-84), 68 f., as supplementary evidence in support of the hypothesis that Muwatalli transferred his capital in two stages, first to Kummanni and later to Tarḫuntašša. See H. Otten in *Fischer Weltgeschichte* 3 (1966), 154; *StBoT* 24, 15; K. Bittel, *Hattusha* (1970), 20 ff.; note, however, that in the German edition of Bittel's book the hypothesis was abandoned (*Hattuscha*, 1983, 29 f.).

445 A. Ünal, *Ḫattušili III.* (*TdH* 3), 1974, 221 and K. Bittel, *Hattuscha* (1983), 29, have tentatively suggested locating Tarḫuntašša at Sirkeli. This was categorically rejected by H. Otten, who would rather associate this site with the mortuary temple of Muwatalli. *Die 1986 in Boğazköy gefundene Bronzetafel* (Innsbruck 1989), 12, n. 5; 44 n. 78.

KUB 6.46 obv.

KUB 6.46 rev.

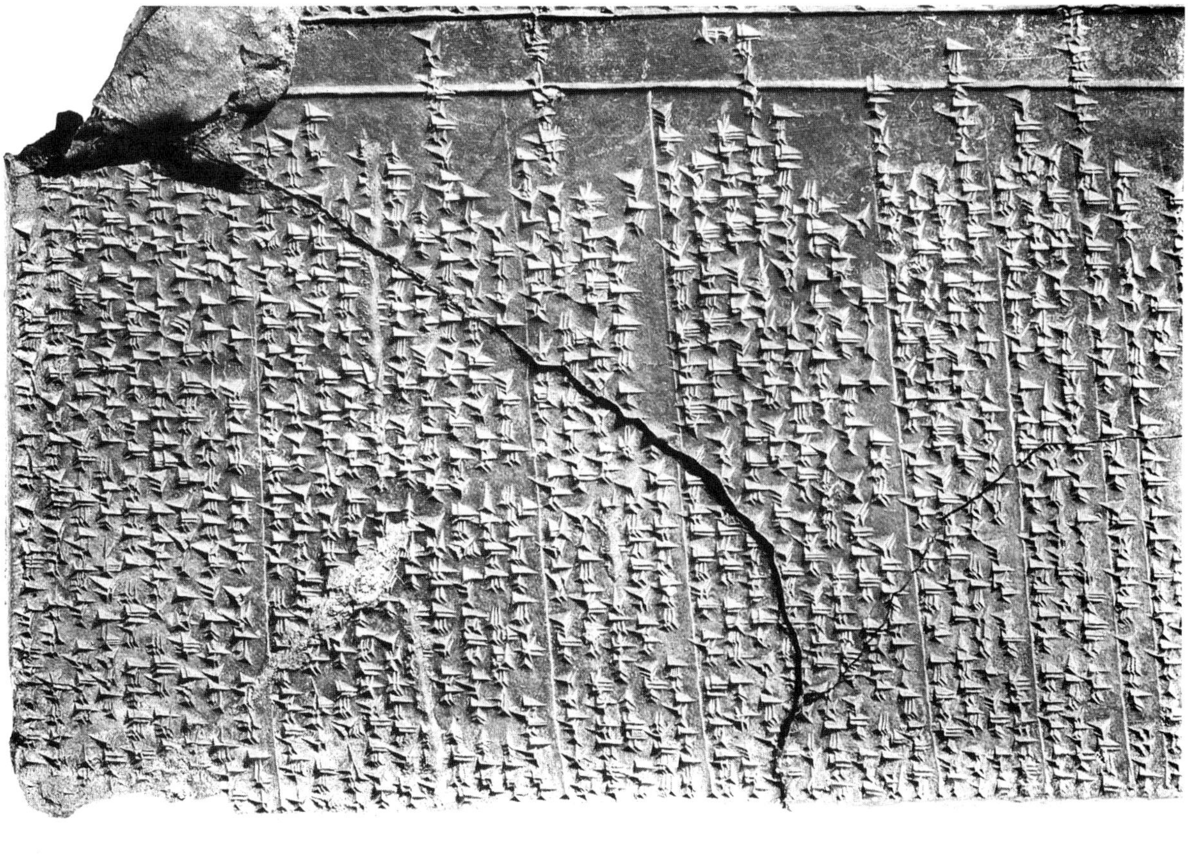

KUB 6.45 obv. I

PLATE IV

KUB 6.45 obv. II

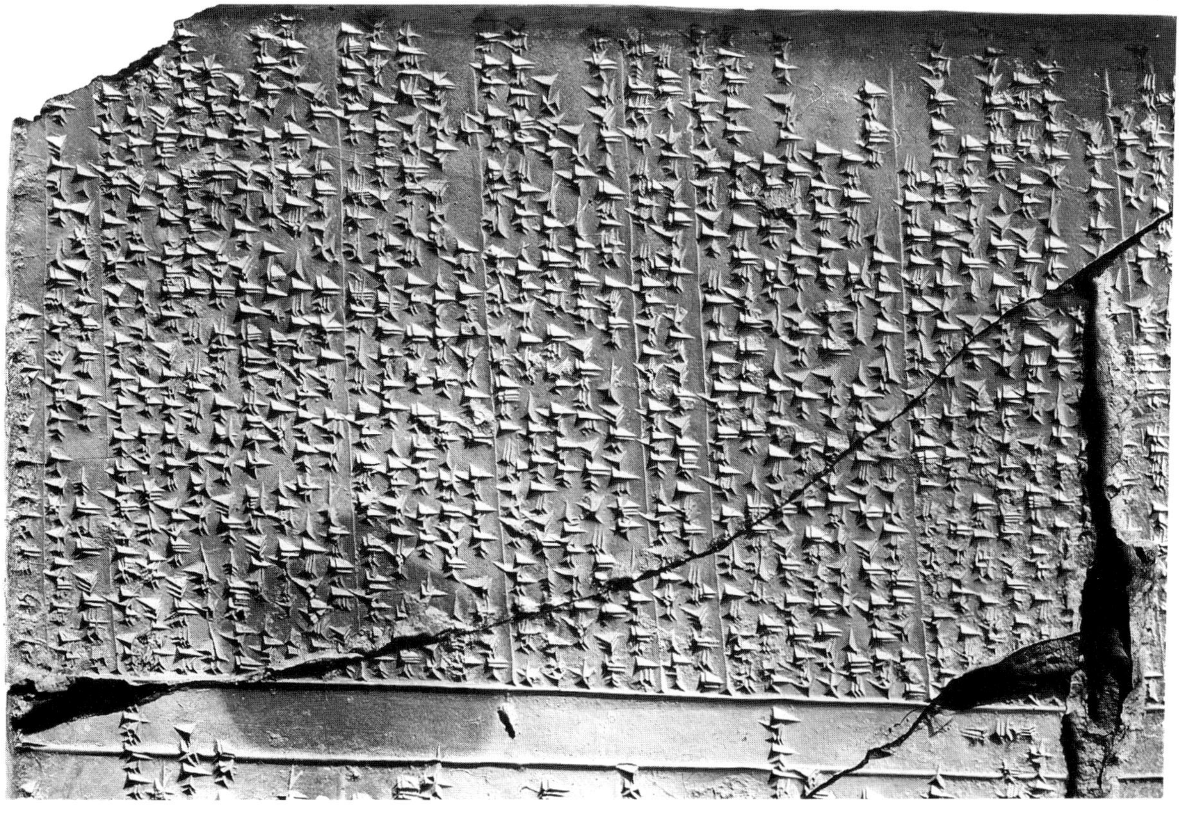

KUB 6.45 rev. III

PLATE VI

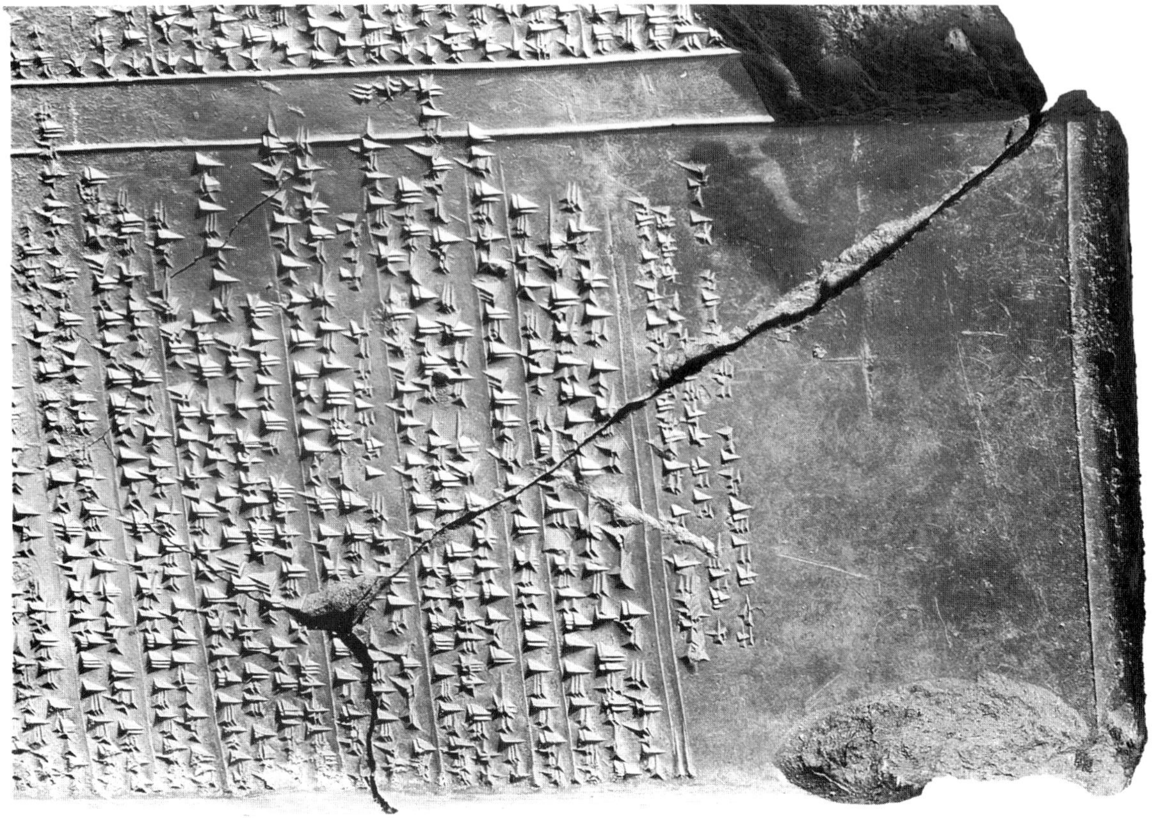

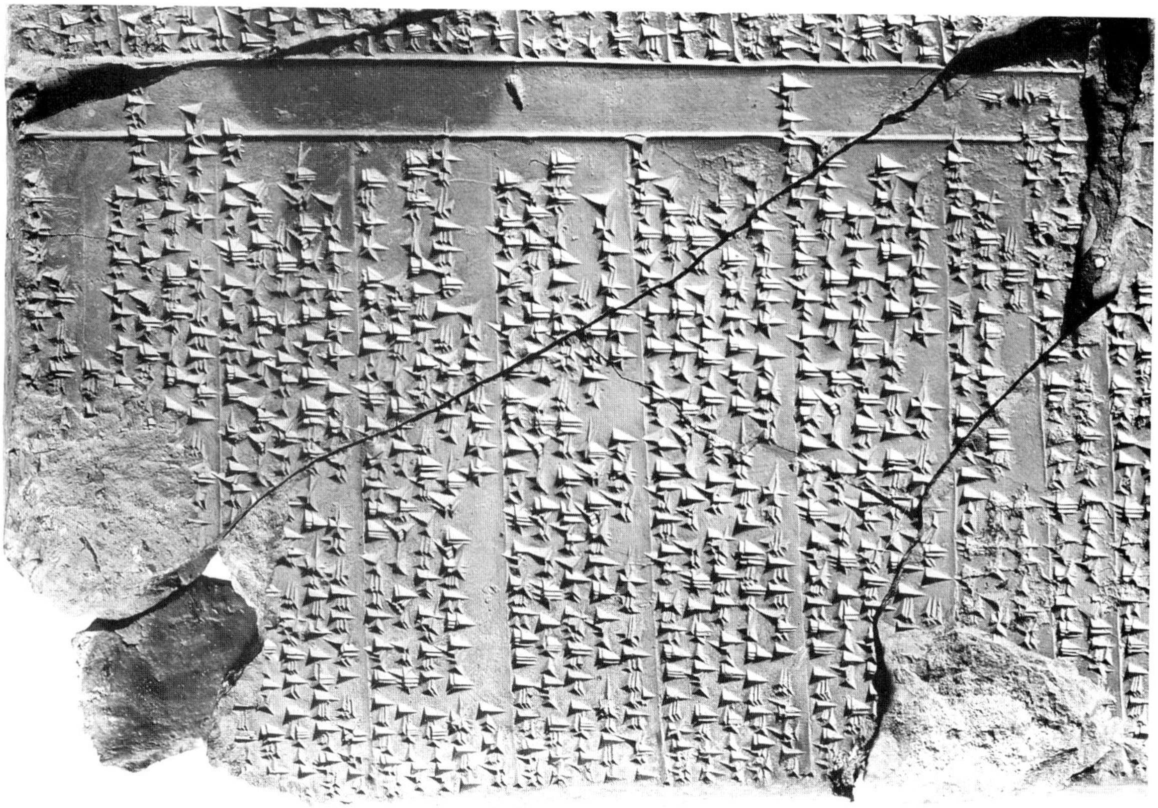

KUB 6.45 rev. IV

KUB 6.45 edge

KUB 6.46 edge

A.
1111/z +

C.
KUB 12.35

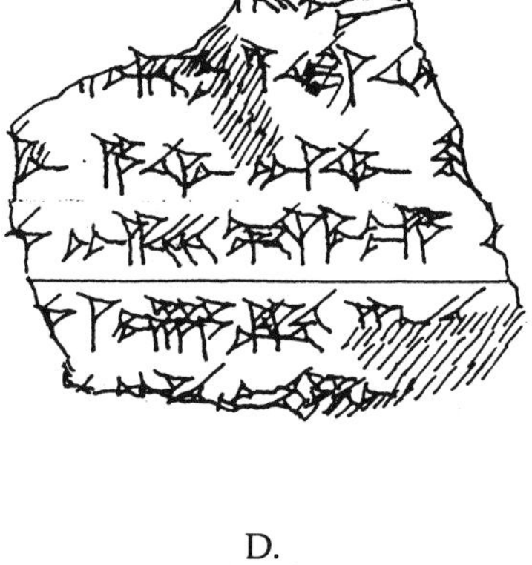

D.
1785/u

Muwatalli's Prayer is the first full philological edition of the longest and best preserved Hittite prayer (290 lines). The two main duplicates were already published as early as 1916, but collation of the originals in Berlin by the author has provided numerous corrections and new observations on the redactional history of the text. Comparison with other prayers of Muwatalli and with the prayers of earlier and later kings sheds new light on the development of royal prayers in Ḫatti and in the ancient Near East in general. An in-depth study of the list of deities in the prayer, arranged by their cult centers, provides new insights into Hittite theology and history. Not least, *Muwatalli's Prayer* offers a better understanding of the poorly documented age of Muwatalli II and the theological climate that led to the transfer of the Hittite capital from Ḫattuša to Tarḫuntašša.